Bernard Peter Atha

Variety
the Spice of Life

novum pro

This book is also
available as
e-book.

www.novum-publishing.co.uk

© 2019 novum publishing

ISBN 978-3-99064-325-9
Editing: Julie Hoyle, B.Ed (Hons)
Cover photo: Bernard Peter Atha
Cover design, layout & typesetting:
novum publishing
Internal illustrations:
Bernard Peter Atha

The images provided by the author
have been printed in the highest
possible quality.

www.novum-publishing.co.uk

Prologue

You are old Father William the young man cried
And pleasures with youth pass away
And yet you lament not the days that are gone
Now tell me the reason I pray.

(Robert Southey)

I have been greatly blessed by being given the opportunities to enter a number of different worlds such as the worlds of the stage, ballet, arts council, Paralympics, sport, the theatre, local and central government to mention just a few. I have been pressed by a number of individuals to record and reveal these various worlds. I started to do this when I was asked to relate the work of the development of sport for disabled people and in my search for this, was struck by the variety of life which I have been lucky to experience. As I too rapidly approach my ninetieth birthday I hope the reader shares some of the pleasures and sadnesses of a long and varied life and that future generations have a document which is a form of social history. I have recorded in some detail the appointment of artistic directors, major building schemes, the role of the local council leaders and certain sections so that those who are interested specifically get a fairly dispassionate flash shot picture of things as they were.

The way to success, disappointments and life's double entry system

I have been fortunate in that over the past five or six decades I have been associated with the success of a number of major ventures such as bringing the Northern Ballet Company to Leeds in a world class dance house, developing the new two-theatre Leeds Playhouse, creating the Yorkshire Dance Centre, the creation of the British Paralympic Association, the UK Sport Association for People with Learning Disabilities, Sport Aid, et al. To claim more than an involvement with these successes would be untrue and offensive as in each case the achievement was that of groups of determined, talented people. When being asked during a BBC interview, what is the secret of my "success" I answered jocularly but in all honesty: Decide what one wants to achieve, find someone who can make it happen, give that person his or her head and sit back and claim personal success.

The truth is that the so-called successes so generously attributed to me in many different fields are the success stories of a large number of men and women who have shared ambitions and have turned them into reality. I have felt it a great honour to have been associated with so many brilliant and honest men and women who have achieved so much. For instance: The Playhouse – William Weston; Northern Ballet – Mark Skipper; The UK Sports Association for People with Learning Difficulties – Liz Dendy and Tracey McCillen; The British Paralympic Association – Barry Schofield; three remarkable women who came up with the idea of the Yorkshire Dance Centre, to list just a few. They deserve our admiration, recognition and respect. For much of my life, 57 years as a Labour-elected representative and member of council in Leeds, I have been honoured to work with some outstanding public servants and volunteers. "Honour" in this case is not a fulsome hyperbole. Quite early on in my life I realised that if one was to achieve anything one had to have access to the source of power whether it be in local or central government or in the private or voluntary sectors. Thus I became a Leeds City Councillor, stood twice as a parliamentary candidate and was thrice generously recommended for the House of Lords by Denis Howell, Lord Dean and later by Lord Merlyn Rees. If you have the power or just enough influence, you have the chance to make a difference and that is what I believe we all are on this earth to do.

I was born in 1928, a year which someone wrote facetiously was otherwise an uneventful year, a year in which train drivers earned £ 3.50 a week in the old currency (240 pence to the pound), female cotton workers earned £ 1.25 a week, a pint of beer cost 2p and a postage stamp cost 1/2p. In that year in Leeds, 53 cases of smallpox were recorded, 351 of scarlet fever, 36 whooping cough, 21 measles, 634 diphtheria, 105 child deaths from diarrhoea and 485 cases of pneumonia. Doctors would normally charge two shillings and six pence before they would see a patient. For many families this was a sum they could not afford. Often doctors would not demand the two shillings and six pence. Local remedies were deployed, like taking a child with a whooping cough to a neighbouring gas work to breathe the ambient air. Specifics like antiphlogistine, brimstone and treacle, Indian brandy and Fennings' Fever Cure were common. The working class in cities lived in appalling slums and the number of pawnshops in an area was a barometer of local poverty. The greater the poverty the more pawnshops there were.

Had I been at birth a sentient creature I might have had second thoughts about entering this pestilential place and life. I was enormously fortunate in being born into a marvellous family living in the centre of Leeds, the third child of five born to father and mother of blessed memory, Horace Michael and Mary Elizabeth. We were an exceptionally happy and argumentative family, a family of great love and tolerance. The first home I remember, a stone's throw from the present Civic Hall, had four bedrooms, a bathroom, toilet, two living rooms (the front room only to be used on special occasions, visitors or musical evenings), front and back doors and a small garden at the front and a yard at the back. It was a house surrounded by slums, where middens were the norm as were homes with no hot water system, sharing a toilet with other families and homes often lit by gas lamps. Leeds had some of the worst slums in the UK. Poverty was stark.

I remember an incident which has stayed with me for my whole life. A lady who knew my mother called to ask if she could borrow a toilet roll as she was expecting some relatives to call and did not want them to have to use the normal toilet paper which was torn sheets of newspapers. It is a strange memory to have retained as I must have been no older than five at the time. I find it poignant as it shows someone trying to put a brave face on their adversity. Another memory also remains and that is of families being literally turned out of their homes into the street because they could not pay the rent and of learning what was meant by the term moonlight flit: leaving without paying the rent arears.

It was, however, an interesting place to live. We were poor in the sense that money was extremely tight but by comparison with those living in the neighbouring slums we were well off. Just a hundred yards or so from our house was a blacksmith's shop which fascinated me as a small child to see the forge burning so hot and bright and roaring when the blacksmith used the bellows. I was immensely impressed by his courage and ability to shoe the big dray horses. I always wondered why they did not kick him over the road instead of patiently letting him do his job. The horses seemed enormous to me and I never went near their rears expecting quite stupidly that they would kick me. The blacksmith was a jovial man and was always ready to give me a smile and let me look at what he was doing. Just opposite the forge was a factory making men's clothing. Little did I know then that many years later I would be of great assistance to the lovely Jewish family who owned the factory and wished to relocate to other premises. Just a bit further away was a large clothing factory called Hepworths and in a slightly different direction but close to home was a factory called Zanuk which was a medical/chemical factory with a pervading smell of ointment at a hundred metres. We used to say if someone led us blindfold from home to the city centre we could tell from the smells or noise where we were: fish and chip shop, Carlton pub, Zanuck (smell), Hepworths and Woodhouse Lane (tram cars sound).

We lived in and enjoyed 19 Carlton Mount, a large end of street house with full toilet and bathroom facilities which the surrounding homes did not have. My dad had got a local builder to dump a load of sand in our small front garden which became a playground for the local small children who would never have the chance to go to the sea side. Carlton Mount was different from the surrounding streets for they all were "through houses", the condition of some not so great but they were palaces compared to the back to back houses all around. Our home too had electric light in an area where gas lamps were the norm. The local poverty was a scandal. We moved from Carlton Mount and years later the area was cleared under a massive slum clearance programme. By one of those weird coincidences, decades later I was asked if I would agree to my name being given to a residential block to house students at the Leeds Polytechnic/Met University. I agreed most willingly and found that Atha House was built almost on the same spot as our old home. I found the brief ceremony quite affecting.

Blandford Gardens

The move to our new home was only a distance of a few hundred yards but in terms of environment it was a move from purgatory to heaven. Our new home was a well-built house, two attics, two bedrooms, one bathroom and two ground floor large rooms, a front room – preserved as a Front Room – and a living room with a quite large kitchenette attached plus a tiny back yard. Situated close to the Leeds University, the house still stands and is in an area which has been taken over by people presumably on decent salaries who wish to be within walking distance of the two universities, colleges, shops and offices. I never pass the end of the street today without glancing in the direction of 11 Blandford Gardens, our home for three decades. By one of those remarkable coincidences, three or more decades later I was chairman of the Social Service Committee and we were looking for a suitable home for young lads leaving care. I was asked to visit a house and to my overwhelming surprise it was 11 Blandford Gardens. The house was being decorated and the front room had been stripped to the plaster and there on the plaster were the pencilled names Paul, John, Bernard and Sheila, marking our individual heights. I was quite moved by this remarkable coincidence. It seems that my dad marked our heights on the plaster before applying the wallpaper at which he was quite adept. I cannot quite remember what my feelings were – very mixed I am sure. Opposite the end of our street was a long complex of Leeds City Council buildings: a council school, Blenheim for boys and another for girls, a school for the deaf and the dumb (sic) and another building to train the blind. The presence of Blenheim Boys Council School so close meant we could get there in a matter of seconds which meant we should always have been there on time but that was not always the case. It was an exceptional school in those days because it had a special relationship with the university which was five minutes' walk away. The school admitted on a regular basis men, I do not remember any females training to be teachers and this had the effect of making the school rather more academic than so many others. Why we were not exposed to the good ministrations of trainee women teachers I know not especially as we had two women teachers on the staff.

Miss Kelly

As a little boy I looked on one of them with the admiration I would show for some lady of the silver screen and the other appeared to be a strict tyrant and more associated in the film metaphor with a witch. She was the formidable Miss Kelly who did not need the ubiquitous stick, i.e. the cane, to maintain discipline and who became friendly with my mother not surprisingly as she had taught my brother Paul, then John and finally me. In many ways she was remarkable. She lived in Arthington, a tiny village on the opposite side of a wide valley. There was no direct route from there to Leeds, the roads being quite circuitous given the terrain except for the train which crossed the valley by a great viaduct. Miss Kelly lived in a lovely old cottage right at the end of the viaduct. Walking on the viaduct was illegal and prosecutions were not uncommon. Miss Kelly however, received permission to use the viaduct as a pathway so saving her considerable time and effort in those days when cars were a rarity and bus services extremely rare. She was never late for school and never left early unless we all did. As part of my mother's entente cordiale with this Madame Desfarge I was delegated to perform certain duties in support of the lady. One of the duties was to take her discharged accumulators to have them recharged and then later collect them after they had been charged. Accumulators were basically wet batteries which could be recharged over and over again and were a blessing to those who lived too far out to be connected for electricity or gas. They were glass and contained a liquid, an acid, the formula for which escapes me.

Baxter and I, Baxter being my closest friend then and in the future, formed a deep affection for this vinegary spinster hiding behind a reconstruction of one of Macbeth's witches and for at

least a decade and a half we would go over on our bikes, then motor bikes and then by motor car to see the old girl, cut her grass
and tidy her hedges. I never saw anyone visiting her nor did she
ever refer to relatives or friends.

We were often given a jar of her home-made jam or marmalade, the ultimate sign of her affection or appreciation. I often wondered was there some past affair which had turned out
badly and that caused her to live the solitary life, my imagination creating a picture of another Miss Faversham. Who knows?

One of her most enduring characteristics was her passion for
making jam or marmalade which was not like any marmalade I
had tasted. She had cupboards full of this delicacy, each jar standing upright in ranks order by year so one could see that some had
been made twelve years or more ago. Some of the early vintage
jams seemed to be rebelling by growing their own whiskers. As
during the war and for many years after food rationing, a jar of
jam would have been greatly appreciated but not if it was of the
older be-whiskered vintages.

Blenheim School

Miss Kelly was a character in the play and her leading man was the headteacher, a character which in a way reflected the school. Mr Percy Smith, the headteacher, was a small fellow, rather rotund and in retrospect a first class headteacher. Discipline in the school was strict, the use of the cane used as a matter of course by some. Smith was a dedicated educationalist and worked hard to get some students up to a level where they might win a Leeds City Scholarship to a Grammar School – the ultimate success. In its own way, it reflected the way in which some state schools worked all out in order to get one of their students into Oxford or Cambridge. These scholarships were few in number and the competition fierce. My eldest brother Paul was highly intelligent and was a natural student. I still have a copy of a letter Percy Smith wrote imploring the council to grant Paul a scholarship which he was in due course given. This was treated by the school as a great success. The family relations with the school were very warm. My mother had received a very lovely wedding gift of bone china cups, saucers and plates which only appeared from the cupboard on very rare and important occasions, one of which was when the school borrowed them when they were having important visitors to the school whom Mr Smith wanted to impress.

I have happy recollections of Blenheim School. The teachers were strict but fair. Some did not resort to physical punishment but others did. Many a child received a clout on the back of his head for some misdemeanour but this was accepted by the boys as a natural part of life. One of the teachers, Mr Dunn, God bless him, played the violin and he taught any boy wanting to learn the violin to play using instruments belonging to the school. Both my brothers learned the violin with him and progressed very quickly as they also received lessons from my mother who was a good violinist who before her marriage had earned money by playing at dances, weddings and other jollies. I had my first violin lesson with Mr Dunn and then war broke out – a case of post hoc rather than propter hoc.

I enjoyed Blenheim school and the rough and tumble with the other lads. There was bullying by some boys but this never happened to me as I had two big brothers and although not quite the mafia, were an unspoken threat analogous to and a lesser form of the current political reason for having nuclear weapons: a working deterrent. I am sure neither had any idea of nuclear or other deterrence and indeed in those years the nuclear threat to civilisation did not exist except in the minds of some remarkable individuals. The school had no playing fields or playing areas. There were two playgrounds, one on the roof and one encircling the building but they were not designed for ball games or any contact sport. For cricket we were walked fifteen minutes to Woodhouse Moor where we played on a cinder pitch, no green and pleasant land. The surface meant if a cricket ball being bowled or hit contacted the ground there was no way in which even a genius mathematician like Turing could have projected the angle, speed or direction of the ball. This made the game exciting but not designed to produce cricketers for Yorkshire.

The facts of life and health issues

A number of abiding memories of the school remain with me today. One was being taught the facts of life. Until then as a wee lad I had imagined children being created in heaven and sitting on a long bench waiting to be born. When a child was needed on earth the child at the end of the bench dropped off to land in the appropriate bed and arms of the mother and the others would shuffle up so the next one was ready to go when called. This quaint belief was of my own making sense of the phenomenon of birth which did not occupy my mind in any particular way. I was eight when the facts of life were told to me graphically in the playground by a slightly older but much better versed child than I. I can recall that moment and its precise location in the schoolyard. I dismissed this as dirty talk as my mother and father would not dream of doing that kind of thing. Quite unthinkable. However, my concept of newborn babies coming down from heaven was shaken. Another scene which stays in my mind was the daily morning procedure before class could start in the classroom. Certain boys identified by a doctor or nurse had to stand in class, proceed to a cupboard, take out a large jar of cod liver oil and a spoon, take a large spoonful of the cod liver oil, swallow it, lick the spoon clean and put it and the jar back in the cupboard and return to their seats. Class could then begin. By the next day the licked spoons had acquired a fine layer of fluff which was consumed by the lads who did not seem to be concerned as this was a daily habit Monday to Friday.

At this time in the 1930s very many children had bow legs, skin disorders, rickets, bronchial and other chest complaints, ringworm and disorders solely attributable to poor diet and poverty. The death rate was high from serious disease like scarlatina, scarlet fever, diphtheria, mumps, measles, tuberculosis, whooping cough, et al. All are recorded in the published annual reports of the Medical Doctor of Health. The labour council of that time had commenced a campaign to meet the medical needs of the poorest children. This included regular inspection by the "nit nurse" who regularly inspected the hair of all the schoolchildren for lice and nits. They also started a dental service for children and I remember with some horror my first drilling by a dentist who operated the drill by a pedal i.e. a treadle. The treadle driving the drill was similar to the one I was familiar with at home where my mother used a treadle-driven Singer sewing machine. The pain inflicted by the dentist's drill was in inverse proportion to the speed of the drill which in turn depended on the use of the treadle. Slow speed – maximum pain. High speed – just pain. There were two dentists in Great George Street, one good at the treadle and the other more reflective and possibly motor deprived and so poor with the treadle. A number of ruses were used to make sure you got the fast one and not the slow one. Some dentists could use the treadle very effectively.

Boots for the Bairns

In addition to the labour council's efforts to ameliorate the condition of the working class there were numbers of excellent initiatives by some of the haves to help the have nots, one of which sticks in the memory, namely the Boots for Bairns initiative. This was a genuinely altruistic organisation which provided boots, not shoes, for those in greatest need. It was a great service but had one big drawback. The wearing of such splendid boots immediately identified the boy or girl as being so poor they needed this help and so with the lack of any human feelings the kids with Boots for the Bairns often experienced catcalling and the occasional fight. This seemed so wrong to me at the time. I believed in solidarity, though I am sure I never knew that word when I was young. We should have been supporting the bairns with boots, not laughing or worse at them. Sadly I have seen similar attitudes in adults over the years.

Early years Convent School

My schooling had preceded Blenheim School for I was sent at the age of five to a convent school nearby which little Catholic boys could attend until they were seven. Then they had to leave. Both Paul, my eldest brother, and John who was 18 months younger than Paul, had had this experience and shown no adverse effects. It was, however, to prove to be of inestimable value for me as there I met another five-year-old boy who lived in a pub – the Fenton Hotel – which I imagined to be rich palace – and who became my life-long friend. Tony Baxter was diffident, very quiet and not good at the education game. He was regarded unfairly as being a "bit backward". He and I after being let out to go home would often go adventuring, i.e. exploring the immediate neighbourhood in a way no six or seven year would do today. We of course never got more than a couple of streets from our proper itinerary in our voyages of discovery and if Tony had to cross a main road to get to his home, the public house, there was always someone to see him or us across whether we liked it or not.

The nuns varied from the very kind and loving to the harshness of a company sergeant major. I most feared Sister Veronica who walked with a thick walking stick, which she would wave in remonstration or anger like Bluebeard rather than a member of a Holy Order. We learned, however, to read and write using a slate, chalk and a duster which was like a large dumpling and which every now and then caused us to go to the door of the classroom and bang the duster against the outside wall to clear it.

I must have found the two years satisfying as I have no bad recollections. Some fun ones remain. I can still see a nun sticking her head out of a window which was directly above the outside urinal where the boys went to pee. On this occasion three boys were contesting who could pee the highest. They were cheered on by other boys including me, and we were making a lot of noise. The nun's head appeared and she told us to be quiet and hurry up and do our business and get out. She reinforced her order by tipping out a bucketful of water. This interruption broke up the competition and caused strong argument as to who had been the winner. Another episode which I remember with some despair is when during a lunchtime break, a girl said to me something to the effect: "I will show you mine if you will show me yours". I had a little sister and had seen young babies being bathed and so I had a good idea of what I was to see but thought "You never know". She, on the other hand, had never seen a boy baby, hence her interest. Having seen "hers" I showed her "mine" and then came the comment I remember today: "It's not much". Such wisdom/acuity from a six-year-old totally innocent child.

Brothers and sister

My brother Paul was the oldest and academically gifted by comparison with John and then myself. Next came my sister, Sheila Mary Elizabeth and finally David, the youngest of us all. (My parents felt that naming us all after saints, we might become saintly. Not sure it worked!) Sheila was an **extremely** bonny child and later a very good-looking girl, then woman. She was, of course, my mother's pride and joy and we, the others, were very protective of her too. I remember when I was about six sitting on the sofa with Sheila at the other end. My mother asked me to eat some tomatoes because if I did Sheila would. I hated tomatoes but did as directed and pretended it was manna from heaven; an early indication of my acting career (if that is what I can call it). The result: I still hate tomatoes. She likes them a lot. The final addition to the family was David who being the youngest was deeply loved by all. He was a lovely little boy with a beautiful personality. Then tragedy intervened. He died. Pure distilled tragedy. He still remains in my daily prayers after eight decades. David became ill and the doctor was called. Later he called back and we were all told to go upstairs out of the way. We watched from the bedroom window of our home in Blandford Gardens the street below and saw the doctor hurry out to his car and rush back into the house. It was not long after that, that we were told David had gone to heaven. The tragedy affected us all deeply, my parents particularly so. I remember nothing of what happened then, as my mind involuntarily seems even today to expunge memories which are too tragic to replay mentally. This strange trait has persisted all my life and I find I cannot recall many of the tragic moments of the loss of such dearly loved ones at the end of their lives. A protective mental aberration or blessing – I am not sure which. By contrast, I remember other minimal things. For instance, I still remember as a small child the lovely smell of baking bread. My mother baked all our bread and to enter the living room on a cold winter's day when the bread was rising in their containers around the fire to encourage it to rise, remains with me today.

Paul went on to graduate at Leeds University in modern languages having already learned Russian in the Royal Air Force, achieving the rank of sergeant. He was a bit of a polymath and ultimately became headteacher of a school in Leeds. John was not seen as academic initially and his school progress was undistinguished, a euphemistic expression in his case. He was regularly in trouble and was rusticated for one week for being seen without his school cap and with his hand on a girl's shoulder while he was riding a bicycle by her side. He later graduated from Carnegie College, then the most distinguished PE college in the country, won a Fulbright Scholarship to go to the USA to do a Master's degree followed up by a Ph.D. and finishing his career as a lecturer at Loughborough University. Sheila was not in any sense academic. She loved reading, was interested in art and went to the College of Art in Leeds where Henry Moore and Barbara Hepworth had been students. Her real love, however, was dancing. She trained in a local ballet school, the Pamile School of Dance, to go on to make a career as a professional dancer appearing on one occasion as principal girl with an up-and-coming couple called Morecombe and Wise. As the years passed she made a good career in television, working inter alia in Coronation Street and directing some episodes.

The Modern School

I was a bit of an idiot at Leeds Modern School, which was a grammar school run like a public school with all its advantages and weaknesses. It was a very good school as evinced by the number of students who went to Oxford or Cambridge. Perhaps the best known of these supreme achievers was Alan Bennet who joined the school as I left. Again, the weirdness of life is evinced in that many years later as a member of Equity and a small-part actor on film and TV; I appeared in one of his TV films shot in Morecombe. I have kept the very kind letter I received from the director thanking me for playing my part so well. I cannot remember how big the part was – possibly just a few lines. It was only when I got into the sixth form that I learned the joy of study. I wish every child could discover this thrill which does not just occur in academic studies but in every aspect of life. When one sees the magnificent engineering in a jet engine, for instance, one wonders at the skill of those who physically produced it. In those days there was the School Certificate, equivalent roughly with GCSE or GCE and the Higher School Certificates, the equivalent roughly of A levels. I wanted to do French and History A levels and one subsidiary subject, German. As I had not done German before the school refused to allow me to join the German classes as I would slow the process down and I would be unlikely to meet the standard required by the examination. Subsidiary subjects did not require study of German literature but the German language exams were the same. My parents, keen to get me to do what I wanted suggested, I should take private lessons. A Jewish family, Steinitz, of escapees from Germany just after the war had started, were recommended. I met them and one of them agreed to prepare me for the examination. That old lady seemed to me to be old but was possibly in her late fifties. I had a one-hour lesson each week in her front room. As many young people do, I had scrawled on the front of my exercise book and I had drawn a swastika because I had found out that in a different culture, India, it represented healing. I turned up for my hour-long lesson. Miss Steinitz saw the swastika, immediately became physically sick and had to run out of the room. My lesson was abandoned. These three old ladies had lost all the members of their family in Germany. Not one was believed to be still living; aunts, uncles, cousins the lot. I felt quite awful that I had so distressed the family I had come to love. The damage was repaired the next week when I explained the reason the swastika was drawn on the book. I was definitely not a Nazi supporter. Her teaching was so good that the headmaster, Dr Geoff Morton, on the advice of Mr Fritschi, the German teacher, allowed me to join the German classes for the final term which produced the necessary result for me to go to university. I have always felt Miss Steinitz got me into university and not me.

The Nineteen thirties and Grandad

It is difficult for me to convey the essential quality and sense of the 1930s when I was a small boy. Leeds had one of the worst slum problems in the country and in the case of the worst slums they would equate to what one may find abroad in parts of India today. My grandfather used to take us boys for a walk after coming out of Sunday Mass. The itinerary always had some lesson to teach us or something interesting to see. I remember seeing a donkey, which was a rare sight (horses by comparison were everywhere), pulling a small cart behind it. My grandfather explained that it was carrying night soil to the leather works just a quarter of a mile away where the night soil was used in the tanning process. Leeds had a considerable number of tanneries at that time. The trip we pestered him to take us on was to East End Park where the so-called Paddy train pulled in carrying miners from the adjacent pit. They were covered in black coal dust – no pithead baths existed for them in those days and as they advanced in a crowd from the train to the road where they would go their own ways, they seemed to me to look like an invading army.

My grandfather had been a miner at one time, a quarryman at another and a bricklayer's mate before he retired. He was full of stories which I positively loved. He was keen to show us evidence of how unfair life was for so many. This, of course, was a time of deep depression. He took us on one of our pilgrimages though not a Sunday trip, to the Leeds market and a very fine market it was. Very grand and listed. He took us, however, to the very bottom of the open market to what was called the Tatters Market. There people would buy and sell clothes which looked more like rags, kitchen articles or anything that you could get a half penny or penny for. There was a pile of spectacles for the poor to try on and see if they could read as a result. The vision I have which will not go away was seeing what looked like an old man trying on false teeth. I was horrified and at the same time mesmerised. How could anyone think of putting in their mouth the false teeth of someone you knew nothing about. My grandfather pointed out that if you had no teeth, you found it difficult to eat anything which was not soft. I remember Jim Quinlan, my grandfather, with deep affection. He was a rough and tough little feisty Irish working man who loved his pint or two or three or more. Although quite small, about 5ft 7inches, he was very strong. My mother felt the disgrace of his very occasional street fights and inebriation but always welcomed him into our home where he lived for some time in our family and indeed died in Blandford Gardens at the age of 72 which was in those days, considered to be very old age. May he rest in peace.

An alien world

The world I knew in the 1930s was so different from now that it seems an alien world. There were few private cars on the road and so a car was a very significant indication of wealth. Horse-drawn vehicles were everywhere but were rapidly decreasing as the petrol-driven lorry began to increase. As boys we loved to hang on the back of the horse-drawn vehicles which often prompted a cry to the driver of "Whip behind", a shout which suggested he should deploy his whip towards the back of the cart where the miscreants were stealing a ride. Also in that period there were Leviathan vehicles driven by steam and belching thick black smoke from their fire grates. These vehicles were so heavy that they ran on wheels of steel with a rubber tyre which was not pneumatic, just an inch or so of a thick coating of solid rubber. The air was so polluted with soot that the day after my mother had washed the kitchen window sill, it was covered with a fine film of soot. A shirt collar in one day would carry a black mark from the pollution. When the city became fog bound in winter the fog turned into smog, that is fog containing smoke with its sad effects on chest complaints. The effects on the inhabitants were such that Leeds had its dedicated Chest Clinic. The atmosphere could be so corrupted that it was difficult to see more than a pace or two ahead. I remember years later driving my motorbike from Headingley to our home in Blandford Gardens in a very intense smog. Sitting on the bike gave me much better vision than someone driving in a car with a bonnet stretching ahead. On this occasion I drove slowly and was followed by a long trail of nose-to-tail vehicles including buses. When I got to where I needed to turn off to go to my home a hundred or hundred and fifty yards away, I turned off the main road, Woodhouse Lane, after giving the appropriate signal. I was horrified but vastly amused to see this very long caravan of cars and buses following me down Blenheim Walk, not realising they had left the main road. When I got to my street I stopped, walked back the few paces to the bus at the head of the queue which had stopped when I disappeared and offered the driver to walk him down to the road he should have been on, a matter of a couple of hundred yards. I had to laugh inwardly whilst acting the good Samaritan as I remembered reading that when the first cars appeared on the roads, a man with a red flag had to precede him and here I was doing something similar so many years later.

The Medical Officer of Health for the city collected statistics which were recorded annually in his report. This showed that annually 120 tons of solid particles fell on the city centre and 140 tons on a major engineering site, Kirkstall Forge, the great steam hammer the pounding of which could be heard at a distance of more than a mile away. It was often said that one reason Leeds, the third biggest city in the UK, was not bombed more heavily than it was in the war was because it is based in a series of small valleys and hills which contained a constant cover of pollution so aircraft could not see it as a city. We know the Germans were intent on bombing Kirkstall Forge, a very large industrial complex, because after the war photographs of Leeds and Kirkstall Forge were found in the Luftwaffe archives. They were taken by the Graf Zeppelin which made a tour of England ostensibly on a good will visit just before the war but in fact it was taking photographs which would be useful when war came. I remember the Zeppelin flying over Leeds. I remember with absolute clarity hearing the sound of its engines whilst reading a book. I would normally have rushed outside as on hearing a plane you wanted to see it as they were still something new and wonderful. I, however, continued reading and so missed the sight of this great gas bag which almost everyone else had seen. It flew very low over the city as the post-war photos showed.

A childhood in the working-class areas had its benefits. Opportunity for play or mischief abounded. For instance, it was possible to light the street gas lamps by a sturdy kick so many of the gas lamps in the area were lit during the day. An act of vandalism of sorts and subject to passer-by intervention followed by exit left at speed. If you were up to no good any adult would speak to you, chase you off if necessary. However, if you were lost or crying almost everyone would stop to help. The communities did exist on a street level, on a small area level and a wider level. People helped each other in a way which does not happen now. I remember a neighbour knocking on the back door and asking my mother if she could spare a cupful of sugar ...

Materfamilias

My mother was always being called out, often for some minor thing such as a child getting hurt or a call to my mother to go and help Mrs Baldwin (a midwife and layer-out with her own portable table for that purpose) "lay out" a neighbour who had died. The custom then as I understand it was that the women washed the body and then put the best dress or suit on the corpse to receive those coming to express their respects. In a society which was not homogenous the death rituals could be very different. The Jews had their own very impressive rituals, the English were pretty conservative in their grieving but the Irish working class had a much more rumbustious approach and turned the grieving into a beer-drinking session whilst the chat got louder and louder, pierced from time to time by someone singing one of the melancholic and lovely Irish songs. Those lovely songs were part of my childhood, pace my grandfather, who never lost an opportunity to declaim his Irish ancestry. When I was about nine or ten, if he called to see my mother I would escape to the Front Room and sing to a single-finger accompaniment on the piano, *Danny Boy*, or *Rose of Tralee*, or some other favourite from the Irish Song Book. I also from time to time "did" some of the more lachrymose music hall songs like the *Poor Blind Boy* which I sang loudly, the words of which I can still remember. "I am just a poor blind boy though my heart is full of joy, though I never saw the light, etc, etc." This concert nearly always produced a penny from my grandfather, though my older brother John suggested giving me a penny was just to shut me up.

Music

Our family was a musical family. We owned an upright Angelo piano. My father had joined the army as a boy entrant well before the war broke out in 1914. He was put into a music school as a boy soldier which proved to be a major contributor to his life. The Army Music School must have been good because my father was a professional musician before he married my mother, making a good living on the cruise liners like the Mauretania. In the afternoon he and two colleagues, one on the piano, one on the violin, and my father on the cello played in the first-class lounge and in the evening he played the drums and trumpet for dancing. My mother was a good violinist who had also played professionally for dances and other social occasions. I have no idea how my mother could have learned how to play it so well. We often had "soirees", though that would never be a term used, in the Front Room which was only used occasionally and on a Sunday. Dad, Mam and a pianist, Miss Driver, who also played professionally for the Pamile School of Dance, played trios, and my mother would sing an aria or two or a couple or so Irish songs. My mother had a fine operatic voice, good tone, wide and accurate range. In summer the windows were open and we often collected a small crowd who sat or stood outside our open windows to listen to the "concert". In those days not everyone had a wireless and almost all could never afford to pay to go to the Town Hall for its frequent concerts. They would occasionally call out to suggest a song for my mother to sing. My two brothers learned to play the violin quite well and their playing was good enough to appeal to the ear. I was forced to play the violin but never mastered it though several years later I found great pleasure in playing in one or two of the very simple amateur orchestras which abounded. I, of course, was immediately condemned to join the school orchestra when I could barely read the music and play it at the same time. It seemed to me that one could not do both at the same time. Particularly difficult it is to be in the third violins. If you are in the first violins you have the melody and so, if lost, easily identify where you are in the music. In third violins there is no such help. So three bars rest is a trap for any unware violinist leading to a whispered question to one's co-murderer of the piece: "Where are we?" The answer was often a shrug. We were both lost. Over the years I had no proper tuition but my mother from time to time showed me how to use the different positions on the violin and a love of classical music was enhanced.

I find it difficult to understand how a very basic working-class family could have been so well educated at home. I knew arias from operas which were so abstruse at that time they are only heard in London or the International Opera Houses today. My mother's repertoire was highly selective and contained arias from operas rarely if ever played except in major world opera houses.

I have not played the violin for decades, not since we moved from Blandford Gardens, a family-sized home to a tiny bungalow with no room to have anything but the essentials. I never learned to play the piano but I could read music. I have missed the piano the most as I loved to "do" the *Moonlight Sonata* first movement, both hands and any slow bits of Beethoven sonatas which I could finger out and hear in my mind – Schnabel. To anyone listening it would have been torture. To me Schnabel. I could only do the slow bits and had to give up the fight when the Beethoven sonatas moved from andante to presto or appassionato. When my mother died my father simply could not involve himself in music as this made the loss even more painful. It was some long time before he turned to the cello again. I loved to hear him playing Bach's unaccompanied cello variations. Looking back to my childhood in central Leeds I feel a massive sense of appreciation of times long past. As a little street Arab as we were sometimes called, we experienced a freedom not available to the modern day's boy of 10 or 11.

Air Raids

Particularly haunting is the memory of the air raids which Leeds suffered but on a miniscule scale compared with Sheffield, Liverpool or Hull. Our cellar had been strengthened by a large girder and a large hole made in the coal cellar wall between our house, 11, and next door, number 13. The bricks were then replaced without mortar so that if our house was hit and demolished we should be able to knock out the bricks and get into the neighbour's cellar. If necessary, we could move on to the next cellar by a similar hole made in the cellar wall. The air raid sirens went off quite frequently but we were never subjected to the horrors of an outright blitz. We quickly became able to distinguish between the sound of "their" aircraft and "our" aircraft. The sound of the Germans was quite distinctive as their engines were not tuned to match each other, i.e. synchronised, and so made a quite distinctive sound. If there was a German plane about, the ack-ack (anti-aircraft fire) would start which made such a noise only a bomb going off nearby might be heard. As the noise was so great we often felt we were in greater danger than we were. After a raid we young lads went searching for bomb fragments or ack-ack debris which we collected and swapped very much as we swapped (exchanged) cigarette cards. During the heaviest raid we experienced a string of four bombs. The first hit the City Museum, then the Town Hall and then the Infirmary, doing only superficial damage except for the museum which later had to be pulled down. The final bomb of that string hit a house which was part of a terrace in multi occupation. It housed the Rose Family, a very poor but lovely Jewish family, though only the old folk followed the formalised Jewish ritual to their limit. Sadly the bomb killed a close friend of mine, Clive Arnold

Rose, aged twelve. He was very bright and would have been a star pupil. He was also a very nice lad and a constant visitor to our house to ask the question, always in the same words as I remember: "Are you coming out?" My mother always mothered all my friends over their early years and was deeply affected over the years as tragedies overcome some of them. The loss of this lad had a deep effect on my mother. Clive's older brother, John, was the same age as my brother John. He was injured but survived and if I understand correctly, became a medical doctor. Who knows what poor dear Clive Arnold would have done? He was buried in a local churchyard, now part of the university and kept as a grassed area. Later, as we drew a line on a map showing the line of the bombs which killed him, we saw that if there had been another bomb in that same line we would have been close to its impact. I remember another event which reminds me of those early years. It was not unusual to be approached by another young boy but generally significantly bigger who said, "cock or hen". This was a challenge. If you said cock, you would have to fight him. If you said hen, then you acknowledged his superiority. On one of those occasions a lad challenged Clive who was a childhood pacifist and he refused to answer the question whereupon the bully challenged me. I, of course, said cock and looked to the best way to run before he could catch me. However, the good Lord intervened in the shape of a large lady carrying a large bag. She swung it and caught the boy saying: " Which are you lad, cock or hen?" The swinging bag was a common form of defence or attack in this kind of situation. It was a glorious bash with her bag. He departed. I felt relieved. Clive thanked the lady. Peace reigned. This kind of challenge was most evident at the time of the annual local elections which were held every November. Lads used to roll up a couple of newspapers and tie them onto a long piece of cord. They would then go out in a little gang and their challenge was Labour or Conservative or Liberal? If you said the right word you and your gang could go on your way. If, however, if you said Labour and the other side was Conservative or Liberal, a battle ensued, each side swinging their paper weapons which could hurt. Politics were taken very seriously as there was extreme poverty and unemployment and so politics were an everyday subject for argument. My parents were very active members of the Labour Party and we children were often coerced into delivering leaflets at election time. My parents were strong supporters of the forces standing against Franco when he started the Civil War in Spain. To its everlasting shame, the official Roman Catholic stand was for Franco as his opponents were deemed hostile to the Church, as indeed many were as they saw it as a pillar of support to the ruling class who were grinding down the poor. This led to letters to the papers which so incensed the Catholic priests in Leeds that they at one mass, denounced our family by name in the cathedral. This was quite unheard of and caused considerable public debate. I was present at the mass when this denunciation took place. I hated it and just wished my parents were like everybody else's parents and would not get involved but I remember hearing of the terrible fate suffered by Guernica without really understanding how awful it was. They were also involved in a matter which seems strange today.

Birth Control and
Leeds Weekly Citizen

The Church was against artificial methods of birth control and my parents, although recognising the strength of that argument, also knew that the lot of most poor women would be immeasurably improved if birth control was more general and they were the majority demanding a change. Mam and Dad had one weapon which they used effectively and that was the *Leeds Weekly Citizen*. This was as its name indicates, a weekly newspaper published by the Labour Party in Leeds. It was quite simply a political publication carrying the message of the Leeds Labour Party. It was run editorially by a small group of Labour activists and was published by a local printing firm. It lasted for decades, finally ceasing to publish as attitudes to politics changed. It was trenchant and carried news only of a nature which was political in its broadest sense. I later supported it in a number ways when I grew older and was extremely sad when it ceased publication.

As the war extended geographically, my father had a large map showing what was happening all over the European continent and the Soviet Union. I became familiar with names like Kharkov, Stalingrad, Moscow, Kiev, the Ruhr, et al which ensured that we children were aware of what was happening on the continent. I remember my parent's horror when they heard of the pact between Hitler and Stalin as they both were admirers of the Russian Revolution but not its purges. At that time I believe we must have accepted the Russian propaganda and I was well into the Sixth Form at school before I came to see the internal horrors of the Stalinist regime. I was horrified how Stalin eliminated his former friends and allies and created a police state which was as rigid and diabolical as that of Hitler.

On the outbreak of war my father, being far too old for the Services, joined the LDV, i.e. Local Defence Volunteers, later to be named the Home Guard. It is comical to remember that my father became a motorcycle despatch rider on his little Coventry Eagle two-stroke motorbike, which was so powerful that I often had to get off the pillion if we came to a very steep hill. I still have, at home in the garage, the little brown shoulder bag which was the only equipment the LDV originally had. Later on, the Home Guard received delivery of a proper new 350cc Royal Enfield, a genuine despatch rider bike as used in the regular army. I thought this was a miracle as, though I loved going on the back of the little 125cc two stroke, this new monster bike was the bike of my dreams.

Evacuation

My birthdate was 27th August, 1928 and a day or so after 27th August, 1939 the four children of the family were evacuated. I was lined up with my colleagues from Blenheim School, was given a gas mask in a small brown card board box, a bag with two tins of Nestles Condensed Milk and the clothes we were wearing and marched off to be taken by bus to a village called Sprotborough three miles out of Doncaster. We were assembled in a long line and followed two women who stopped at every house to ask "How many can you take?" We went literally from door to door. I and two others I knew well were taken up the small drive of a detached house still there today and the old lady said she would take three. Just like that. Difficult to believe nowadays. Mrs Nelson seemed ancient to me but was in her late fifties. She put up all three of us for a couple of weeks when her daughter who lived a few doors away agreed to take two of us which left me with Mr and Mrs Nelson. Mr Nelson was a road sweeper. He left every morning with an old-fashioned wooden wheelbarrow, a brush, shovel and shears. His job was to sweep the road and clear the ditches for a three mile stretch. It is strange that in this humble road sweeper I saw a man of utter gravitas. Their son, Fred, was a young man with a splendid physique. He was to become my mentor and friend. Looking back now to those anxious days, my parents must have felt they had been hit with an earthquake. Their four children had been taken away. They did not know where. They did not know who, if anyone, was looking after us and they must have been particularly worried because my sister Sheila was 18 months younger than I. It must have been harrowing for they did not hear any news of us for several days. My two brothers were sent to Scarborough, and my sister to Kirk Sandall, also not far from Doncaster. Doncaster was one of the biggest railway junctions in the country and an obvious target for the Luftwaffe.

To me, the evacuation was a marvellous adventure. I had had no experience of living in the country and this new world proved to have fascinations at every turn. The Nelsons had a large hen run at the bottom of their large garden. They had shown me the boxes in which the hens laid their eggs. On my third day in their home I volunteered to collect the eggs for that day. I went up to the hen run and with great care picked up all the eggs. When I returned to the house they were amazed at the number of eggs I had collected. A record. I felt pleased. Record holder. A moment's inspection a moment later revealed that of the dozen or so eggs, half were pot eggs left in the nests to encourage the hens to lay. I was never allowed to forget this gaffe by Fred, their son, who became my very best friend. To me, he was a god-like figure.

Fred

Fred taught me how to shoot a shotgun. The first was a lesson I shall always remember. He let me fire a 12 bore shotgun, warning me that it had a big kickback and I was to hold it very firmly in my shoulder. I did this, fired the gun and was driven back a good yard, recovering quickly enough not to go down. Great laughter all round at my expense which I quite enjoyed. He then let me have the use of a smaller bore gun for when we went out poaching which was, if I remember correctly, a 4.10. It certainly worked but without the kickback. One method of poaching was to get a large net and when it got dark stretch it out between us and drag it as quietly as possible in the dark over where birds had been seen to settle. This was quite effective if we could remember precisely where the birds had settled. Fred also taught me how to harness a horse and put it in the shafts of a cart, and to drive it. Once a week Fred drove a cart full of vegetables and flowers to the market in Doncaster just over three miles away. He drove out but let me drive back once we had got on the main road home. As I look back I merely held the reins, for the horse knew the way better than I and had no need of close attention. I am sure if Fred and I had dropped off to sleep we would have woken to find ourselves back at the stables. I still loved the feel of the reins and the sense of power which of course, was imagination. The horse was a lovely animal with a splendid temperament. It was horse of mixed parentage. It was equally able to serve pulling a cart, a small plough or as a horse for riding. Its name was Dobbin.

Fred was a super gift from God to me. He took me places which remain in the memory. Occasionally on an evening in the autumn or winter we would go to a very large farm in Lower

Sprotborough next to the River Don. This was a very big farm and the stable housed something in the order of 20 enormous farm horses. They each had a stall in the very large stables and the men, by the light of paraffin lamps, played darts, the dart board hanging on a nail on one of the wooden stall partitions. I was amazed as they threw darts at the board as I thought if they missed they would hit the rump of one of these enormous beasts. Of course they never did or were near to doing it. During the evening a strange ritual took place. The darts players went into each stall in order, releasing the horse which without being guided, made its way past the other stalls and exited into the yard where it would drink from a trough and then return without direction to its own allotted stall, each horse performing in exactly the same way. No overtaking. Almost to me a circus act. I confess, however, to being initially terrified of being trodden underfoot by these giant animals and so to everyone's amusement I took up a place of safety above the carnival of animals below. Fred also introduced me to home-made wine. He took me with him to a friend's home in a place called Warmsworth. It was an evening in summer and our host had a series of bottles of home-made wine for what I now would call a tasting. I thought it was for drinking and so having quaffed one tumbler full of this fruit juice I thought it would be good to explore further this lovely drink so I had another. This began to affect me and to every one's amusement I appeared quite drunk. I cannot remember anything much after their initial amusement except that on the long way home, on foot of course, Fred had to carry me some of the way on his back. This was the first time in a long life that I have been drunk and the only time I can remember being drunk in this condition. I had no idea the various fruit juices had been turned into wine. Fred used this occasion to show me the adverse side of drink, a lesson I have always remembered but not always followed.

Fred was in charge of a large nursery-cum-farm. He was very strong physically and a person to whom people would come to ask his advice on any number of country topics. He should have been conscripted like everyone else but as growing food in this country was vital to the war effort, he was excused military service so long as he was in charge of the nursery which was now turned over to the growing of food. The nursery was a large area housing a host of greenhouses and acres of arable land. It belonged to the Burley family as did the local grocers shop on the village street. The family consisted of some older sisters and two lads both older than I. They were a wild couple, obviously close to each other in brotherly love which did not, however, prevent them from having the most heated arguments which on one occasion, to my surprise and horror, they were picking up horse droppings to throw at one another. I could not understand how they could pick up horse droppings with their bare hands. I became very attached to the lads, Bob the younger and John the elder by a couple or so years. I thought they were two very highly-charged individuals with outstanding competences for lads of their age. I was immensely impressed by their apparent inborn ability to look after, ride and treat horses of which there were four, to handle shotguns without reeling back, to ride bare back whooping like the Red Indians of the cinema of those days. They seemed to have complete freedom of action. No parental influence was ever manifest. Being with them was an experience I shall not forget. A good example is the occasion when they decided on the spur of the moment to harness up Sugar, one of the four animals and go for a drive in the pony and trap. Sugar was a very attractive pony, almost big enough to be a horse with a splendid rather fiery temperament. Riding Sugar was always more exciting than riding any of the other three equines. We harnessed Sugar up and we drove off in the quite old but serviceable trap – a vehicle with just two wheels with a little door at the back to get in or out of the little vehicle. Sugar was always good for exercising her strength and trotted at a good speed until we were passing a field a few yards away when a very big horse put its head over the hedge and gave an enormous whinny at a high decibel level. I do not know what the noise meant but it set off Sugar at a gallop, a genuine runaway bolt. I did not understand this until I turned to the lads to say how splendidly exciting this turn of speed was. It was then I realised something was wrong. Both Bob and John were hauling back on the reins as hard as they could and swearing with a flair and an imagination to wonder at. This caused a change in my appreciation of the mad rush. Sugar literally got the bit between her teeth and was not responsive to the a straight pullback of the reins but a sawing of the reins seemed to work and in a short time we had come to a stop so the boys could pat Sugar and swear at her all at the same time. The lesson for me was that if a horse bolts you are in serious trouble, whether it is in harness or being ridden. The power in a pony like Sugar is pretty awesome and very awesome when you have a full-grown beast. After this, the bit was enhanced by a curb, that is a small chain which could cause a pain which would hopefully allow the bolting animal to be brought to a stop.

I was so blessed in being billeted with the Nelson family. Fred and Doris, his wife, became lifelong friends and every year until I was nearly forty I visited and stayed over with them. Fred and Doris are engraved on my heart. I attended Fred's funeral. I grieved deeply. It is a pity men are "not allowed" to cry. I have another memory which I am not sure is a faux or genuine memory. Fred was doing some work in the home of the vicar just opposite the Burley site. I, as a ten year old, was introduced to the wife of the incumbent vicar who was accompanied by a handsome fellow in RAF Uniform. If my memory is correct, I was introduced to and shook the hand of Douglas Bader. the famous fighter pilot.

Nemesis

There was one factor which proved to be important in my being evacuated. From September 1939 to June the next year, I and my fellow evacuees had virtually no formal education. For some time we only had to walk to a building on the outskirts of Doncaster once a week to ensure that a tally could be kept. We experienced very few classes for the whole of that period. I simply thought this was fine. I was enjoying this wonderful life in the country. Every day was an adventure, a new experience. For instance, I joined a group to help getting the harvest in, in this case a very large nine-acre field of ripening corn. The cutting was done by the men with scythes, and we the followers, women and children, followed picking up the corn to make sheaves which were then made into stooks, later to become stacks. Then came the magic moment when a huge steam machine came to thresh the corn. It was exciting and we were kept well away from this monster as there were so often fatal accidents caused by someone being caught by the very large belts driving the machinery. There came, however, the time of judgement. I sat the equivalent to the 11-plus exam in the Doncaster Grammar School. I am sure that my papers would be among the worst submitted that year. I did not appreciate at the time what a financial burden my failure to get a scholarship would put on my parents. Only now in reflection do I see how careless and self-centred I was as a child, but to compensate, how lucky I was as a child to have a marvellous family and Fred – a good example of my theory of the double entry system which governs all our lives.

Born a Catholic

I was born into a Roman Catholic family. My parents were very devout, great believers in prayer but frequently at odds with the Catholic hierarchy. For instance, they were strong critics of the Pope's relationships with the Nazis and Fascists and were at war with the church over the Pope's relationship with Franco. All four of the surviving children went to the St Ann's Higher Grade School which admitted children of five years but if they were boys they had to leave at the age of seven. My mother had lived in a desperately poor area called the Bank. It was Irish territory. The local church was St Patricks. By one of those strange coincidences which litter most of our lives, this lovely church, about to be demolished and its internal beauty lost for ever, was saved. I, acting as chairman of the adjacent Playhouse, bought it at a nominal price to act as a store for props and scenery. I had substantial discussions with the planners who had to agree to this change of use and got them to include a number of clauses which protected some of the most beautiful altars and internal walls. It has served the Playhouse well as a store and as a number of parking spaces which are like gold in that area of the city.

In modern society, practising Christians have declined in number and in a number of States. To those of us who have a religious belief, this is very depressing. I know from my own limited experience that when people are in extremis they so often call on the Lord for help, even though they are not practising any religion. For believers, there is great comfort to be a holder of the gift of faith. The Christian belief of life after death is denied by many and some distinguished philosophers and scientists spend much of their time trying to persuade believers to recognise their activities and beliefs as mumbo jumbo. I wonder why some are so keen to damage the faith of others. If they are right and there is no life after death, the believer will not know that this is the case and the nonbeliever will not be there to know he/she was right, namely there is no life after death. For the believers there is great comfort in their beliefs and this comfort would be lost if they lost their faith. I have since very early childhood been a practising member of the Catholic Church and have seen it change over the years. Sadly churchgoing has declined across most religious groups but when there is a calamity or great threat, church attendances jump. Even one of the most evil men the world has seen, Stalin, encouraged church-going in the war as he recognised the strength it gave to the church-going population. As a Catholic I am expected to go to church each Sunday and on a few other days in the year known as Holy Days. I suppose I have missed this mass possibly little more than a dozen or so times in my 80-plus years. Catholic churches are to be found very widely. I have attended a mass of eight people in Iceland, an outside mass of thousands on the beach of Les Sables-d'Olonne and a mass in the Church of the Holy Sepulchre in Jerusalem. When a student asked me why I went to church the answer, though simple, was not particularly edifying: because I believe my prayers will be heard in heaven but not necessarily answered. There is one major area where I feel my faith does not give me an answer. Why is there so much suffering in this world? Why did not God stop the massacre of Jews in Germany and Europe? Why did God allow the plague to wipe out whole populations? Why do little children who could never have done any harm to anyone be made to suffer so often? I had a similar conversation with an old friend who said I was just hedging my bets by believing, but that would not work. For if God is all powerful He would see through my efforts to be good as efforts to claim immunity on my deathbed. Religion is always a great topic to engage one's intelligence, gullibility, sense of ridicule and hope.

The Leeds Modern School

The Leeds Modern School originated more than a century ago in a school in the Centre of Leeds in a building which has served many purposes over the years. It was called the Mechanics Institute. In due course, the school moved to Lawnswood, only three miles away but leagues in terms of environment as the original site was surrounded by some of the worst slums in the country. The new school was a delight to see and it had its own swimming pool, extensive playing fields, first class laboratories and a fine main hall to accommodate all the pupils at once. Twinned in terms of locality but in no other sense was a girl's Grammar School. Both were quite independent and seemed barely to be on nodding terms. Very stupid but not seen as such in those days.

As I had failed to get a scholarship my parents had to pay an annual fee which today would sound modest in the extreme but for my parents the fee was a major problem, particularly as my elder brother John had also failed to win a scholarship and so was also being paid for. Ironically, the fact that I was a paid-for pupil and not a scholarship boy elevated me to the middle class school population which rather looked down on the scholarship boys, even though some of those boys could have come from much wealthier homes than mine. I enjoyed school but for four years I never took it seriously. I loved to act the fool as did a number of my friends. For instance, my friends made an "explosive" in the lab. This, when dried, exploded with a crack if hit or compressed. We, that is the three whiz-kids and me, would put the powder on a surface like a seat hinge so when someone put the seat down to sit upon it there would be a sharp crack. It was always fun to see a lad about to sit down at his desk, shoot back up when he heard the crack on the seat he had just vacated at speed.

I did come to enjoy playing in the school orchestra which, when I arrived as a pupil, played extremely well as so many in the orchestra were studying an instrument. I remember being dazzled by one boy who played Monti's *Czardas* quite brilliantly in a school show and another being quite brilliant on a clarinet.

I did, however, enjoy taking part in the plays but as we were an all-boys school someone had to play the female parts and that fell to be my lot on more than one occasion, including my playing Bianca in a full scale production of the *Taming of the Shrew*. I did not like the play as I was more on the side of the shrew than on anyone else, a subliminal effect I imagine of my upbringing where equality between the sexes was taken for granted. I also disliked the antisemitism in the *Merchant of Venice*. My school reports said I was bright but not trying and too keen to act the fool "which he does splendidly". It was not until I reached the fifth form that I became a serious student getting enough Credit Results in the School Certificate Examinations, the equivalent of the modern O levels, to matriculate, giving me access to the Sixth Form, my parents still paying the fee. Becoming a sixth former changed one's life immediately. First you were treated as an adult by the teachers. You had a timetable which left one with many free periods. You could use this time in the school as you wished. You had a Prefects' Room in which you could lounge if you were a prefect which I became in my first year – Junior Prefect first and Senior Prefect when I got into the second year. The middle class and upper class simply love to have a hierarchy into which one can slot individuals. I was a "fee payer" and so superior to the scholarship boys, a contrast frequently noted by the boys.

I look back on my years at the Modern School with great pleasure and deep nostalgia. I owe so much to my parents for making the sacrifices which gave this excellent start in life and gave me friends which have lasted a life time. I also owe so much to those teachers who injected me with a love of language, and languages, of literature, of logical thought and so much more. The school building was pulled down and a modern school built under that most pernicious system called the PFI. The school was one of the first PFI schools to be built and opened. It was a disaster as in summer it was too hot for study and in winter it was too cold.

I know now that if the old school had remained I and countless hundreds of others would have returned just to get the flavour once again of those heady boyhood years. I get a lump in my throat if I hear the song "Forty Years on when afar and asunder parted are those who are singing today", etc. I regret the decision to pull down the old school as it creates a gap in our local social history and for old boys of the school to support and develop something which was more than a hundred years old. *The Owlet*, the school magazine in the period I was a student, records the number of former pupils who gave up their lives during the war. It reminds me too of the lads who were my friends when I was there, people like Reg Parks, a lad who went on to win world fame as a body builder, became Mr Universe, and who made one or two films of doubtful artistic merit in South Africa co-starring in one with Marilyn Monroe, or Len Browning who played football for Leeds United and cricket for Yorkshire or for the lasting and deep friendship between myself and Richardson and Hartley, a friendship which lasted all our lives.

University Germany graduation holiday jobs morty

I was successful in obtaining a place in the Law Faculty of the Leeds University. My parents paid a very modest fee, £ 15, to the Leeds University; modest, but it would have been a significant part of my father's weekly wage. I was very impressed by the student intake, nearly all the men being just released from the armed forces, quite different from the callow primarily middle-class students of before the war. These were men and the occasional woman who had been in the war for a long time the rule being, first in first out. As a very innocent teenager I looked on these characters with great respect. Never once in their company did I hear a line shoot (a term current then for boasting) without it being greeted with laughter and jeers or told as a joke. I was a pure innocent in this company but found the experience exciting. For example, I made the acquaintance of a singular man who became a lifelong friend – Jan Palka.

In June 1940 Mr Zymunt Palka and his son Jan were deported by the Russian Secret Police from their home in East Poland to undertake forced labour in Siberia. Such was the severity of this work that Mr Zymunt died but Jan continued to live and plan his escape. In 1941 he escaped to the Middle East where he joined the Polish Forces in the British Army in which he served until the war was over and he was demobbed. I got to know him through the university boxing club which he joined at the same time as I joined and we spent many hours over the years sparring. As our friendship ripened I learned a little of his history and we became good friends, a relationship which endured until his death. He enlisted me to chair a committee which organised student visits to the continent in the hope that the greater the contact the greater would be understanding. Having seen the horrors of war he was determined to do something which would prevent in the future the horror he had known. This organisation operated for many years; a testament to Jan's philosophy and energy.

I lived only a hundred or so yards from the university and could see the clock on the tower from my attic bedroom. This propinquity was important as I could not afford to buy text books and had to rely on the library books, most of which were classed as reference and could not be taken out on loan. I have only bought two law books in my life having this resource so near and my money so limited. The university had a splendid resource, the Brotherton Library. named after a benefactor and then only recently completed. The Law Department was based in the basement of the library as was the Law library. It became my home for nearly four lovely years as I became engrossed in the study of the law. I became fond of this dungeon-like area and found it had a unique smell, not unpleasant, which I shall always associate with "our department". I had never been a good student but now I changed, happy to spend hours looking up references, reading the law reports, feeling rising anger at much of the law which needed changing. One particularly dismayed and angered me. It was the Doctrine of Common Employment. This was a Victorian-style rule that if a person was injured at work by the actions of another fellow employee in the same firm or company, he or she had no claim against the employer, merely a claim against the workman which of course had no value as he would have no wealth. We only had a modest series of lectures some of which were very good and some not so good. One lecturer, Mr Haggan, an expert in land law, lectured by walking across the front of the lecture theatre and then back again. He spoke in a conversational way, no projection, so if you were not careful you could only record in note form half of what he said because the other half was said too far away to be heard. We found a solution. There was a Jewish lad who was almost blind. He recorded his notes on a braille machine which could be programmed to change the braille into modern English. He was quite a sport and as he sat in the middle of the front bench he caught almost

all of what Mr Haggen was saying. He then gave to his immediate friends, me included, the lecture in perfect English. I was
so impressed by the young determined fellow who had a serious
defect but who was always ready for a joke or to assist some student who did not quite understand the meaning of a fee simple
absolute in possession or a restrictive covenant. He was also very
good in helping us with Roman Law which he seemed to absorb
rather than as most us did – the reverse.

I was fascinated by the criminal law and regularly visited the
assizes which were held in Court One in the Town Hall. A special bench was reserved for students which gave us an uninter-
rupted vision of the whole court room. Murder cases fascinated
me as the ultimate penalty, death by hanging, was still automatic on a jury finding of guilty. Other punishments available to
the court were birching and flogging with the cat o' nine tails.
When a criminal was flogged a doctor attended to see the flogging did not lead to death. It seems medieval to us now that that
kind of punishment existed and was administered. On three occasions I witnessed the passing of a death sentence. A clerk would
place a black piece of material on the judge's head and he would
then pronounce the terrible words "be hanged by the neck until dead ... be buried in unhallowed ground". I found this profoundly disturbing as I looked at the condemned man knowing
that within three weeks he would be killed. I have watched innumerable dramatic and frightening films and plays. None comes
close to creating the feeling of dread when the death sentence is
awarded. Thank God the punishment was abolished for murder
in 1965 as an experiment and later confirmed in 1969. The last
execution was in 1964. Subsequent research has produced evidence which shows that a number of executions took place of men
innocent of the crime charged. Armley Jail in Leeds opened in
1847, is a forbidding structure with an awful record. Immediately
prior to that date the last public hanging in Leeds took place at a
site called Gaol Field attracting an estimated crowd of 100,000.
It was in fact a double hanging on a scaffold deliberately built
high to ensure a good view for the crowd. Hangings in the jail

itself did not always go well if that is not an oxymoron. In 1887 an individual claimed the definitely unhappy title as a man who was hanged twice. This name was accorded because the first attempt to hang the man failed when the rope broke. He had to wait at least ten minutes before another rope was found. That did not work well and it took at least five minutes before he could be pronounced dead after the second drop.

Rag Week

Each year the university students held a rag week and during this week they would put on a show. Ambitions grew and the Grand Theatre was chosen as the venue for a major production. The two people organising it were well known to me. The man, a talented but diffident man who produced the rag week and Noni Brown, a principal of the Pamile School of Dance who was responsible for a couple of big production numbers. Eager to show an academic background, the students prepared an opening chorus for all to sing:

Nos studentes salutamus qui venistis hodie
In hoc cantu nuntiamus quid potestis facere
Cum spectaculum vidistis quod multum amatis
multum argentum gratis etc

The shows were excellent, showing a wide range of talent. A close friend of mine, for instance, Pam Constable, played a brilliant piece on a well-tuned grand piano. It was top class playing and well received by the full house twice nightly. At the other end of the aesthetic spectrum was an excerpt from Swan Lake. Here, four very large and hairy rugby players came on to do the ever popular dance of the our baby swans – cygnets. They were billed as ducklings. It was a hilarious item. Pam Hudson, my ballet mistress, had taught them the actual steps and made them repeat them over and over again so that on the night they brought the house down, dressed in ballet tutus as in the true ballet by making every entrechat count or the nearest thing to it. It was extremely funny as the men were trying so hard to do it properly. As one said to me: "It's harder than rugby training". Nightly, they had to do an encore performance. Another young man by the name of Abelson did a couple of songs which were extremely well received. I liked him and his flamboyant attitude especially on stage. He later changed his name to Frankie Vaughan and became a world recognised performer and something of a film star playing opposite in one film Marilyn Monroe. I still have a letter from him in Hollywood as he asked me to look in on his parents to see they were as well as they pretended to him.

The rather staid *Yorkshire Post* Revue dated June 20 1950 under the headline "Leeds Rag Revue better than ever" kindly referred to my efforts: "Bernard Atha, a 21-year-old law student shows a wealth of versatility, miming in a satire of a Victorian photographic group and dancing the male lead in the ballet Kismet". I was featured in two major dance epics, Kismet and Slave Ship, sort of dance dramas. The shows were tremendous fun and were sold out every performance.

I enjoyed a great privilege when I was at university. Marie Rambert, an outstanding figure in the dance world brought her tiny company to Leeds, performing in the large hall in the Students' Union. As a student I asked her about a career as a dancer and she invited me to show the level at which I could perform. The next day I turned up in tights and had a half an hour lesson at the conclusion of which she gave me some good advice. She said that it was possible that young males could avoid national service if they joined her company. She could offer me a student's role during which time my ability would be greatly advanced. However, she suggested quite strongly that to stay at university was her advice, though if I decided against that the offer was open. I thanked her and she let me join in some of the classes she held for the company. Marie Rambert was a towering figure in the world of dance and she has left a legacy for the benefit of today.

Berlin British Sector

In my second year at Leeds I was approached by a member of a drama group to see if I would be interested in joining him and his colleagues in a dramatic society production. They had seen me dance ballet style and thought I could be useful to them as they prepared to take two plays to Germany. I was very interested and I arranged to meet them in a room in a major hall of residence. I arrived as agreed and found four or five naked men enjoying, one presumes, what they were doing. I evinced no surprise so I could show my worldly-wise attitude to such activities although I did refuse an offer to take my clothes off and join in. I wondered what kind of theatre group this was. In due course, we were all introduced and I was told that the plan was to take a play to Germany. The play would be Marlowe's *Dr Faustus*, done in English. Would I be interested? I most certainly was. At that time Germany was just beginning to creep out of the terrible cataclysm which had struck that country at the end of the war. It was divided into zones; French, American, British and Russian. To enter any of the zones, one had to hold a special visa provided sparingly by the specific zone one hoped to visit. Such visits were hard to get as the military did not want civilians from all over the planet coming to see for themselves. Food for the Germans was strictly rationed and initially hardly enough to maintain good health; the penalty for being on the losing side.

I provisionally said yes which would be a commitment when I was aware of details such as cost, dates, etc. I did, however, show great enthusiasm for the project. The group was made up of a number of males, all seemingly homosexual and four females who appeared to be not homosexual. The homosexual men called themselves queers as a sort of two-finger gesture to the world that we are what we are and we do not mind who knows it. They even did a cabaret act based on a song popular at the time from a film in which two famous Hollywood stars sang a song: "We are a couple of swells, we stop in the best hotels" etc. They came on singing, "We're a couple of queers" and continued in a very comical and scabrous take on the song. I grew to like these men deeply. They were constantly ribbing one another. They saw me as being quite droll. For instance they asked me if I thought the king was "queer". I answered in good faith, unaware of the special meaning of the word queer that I did not think so but he might be a haemophiliac given past history. For some reason they thought this was very funny.

Their leader was a very talented individual, an accomplished pianist, with an extensive knowledge of English Literature and stage productions. Another was a young man with a beautiful speaking voice. It was one of the most mellifluous I have known. He was extremely bright academically but a sad case for a few years later he committed suicide by hanging. I have no doubt that the decision to end his life was the result of being a homosexual in a world where its practice was illegal. The law books of the day entitled the homosexual act as the "abominable crime of buggery." For some reason the police pursued homosexuals, often with an incredible intensity, for instance, erecting false roofs so they could watch and wait for punters entering the public lavatory in order to achieve a conviction.

We embarked on the continent and travelled to Gottingen, our first port of call, in a train which was just for the occupying force. I was fascinated by the large number of drinks in the bar which I had read about but never encountered. I decided that if I could I would try each liqueur to see what it was like. They were quite exceptionally cheap – another benefit of winning the war. We stopped at a major station in the Ruhr, Essen if I remember correctly. All around us was devastation; rebuilding had yet to commence in earnest though all the roads were cleared and water and power widely reconnected.

We were stationary for nearly half an hour in the station. It was lunchtime and we were sitting in the dining car eating a splendid meal whilst the large crowd on the platform waiting for their train watched us with envy as we consumed every forkful of our meal. I am sure there was a little hatred as though we were showing off our victorious position. I felt genuinely uncomfortable as we were gorging and they nearly starving. Their rations were very low as indeed they were in England. I was appalled by the devastation as we passed through the great industrial area, the Ruhr. The blitzes in London and elsewhere had been traumatic but they were nothing compared with what we saw mile after mile after mile. One wonders how anybody managed to survive whilst being bombed so heavily. We were made extremely welcome, billeted in a very nice but unpretentious hotel in Gottingen. We performed our play and stayed to discuss the play with very large numbers of youthful students who were keen to practise their English. The fact that I had studied the German language at school only two years earlier meant that from time to time I was called in to interpret. I hope I got the translations correct but I have my doubts.

Our itinerary included Kiel which was a regular strategic target for our aircraft and consequently was one of the most bombed cities in Germany. After the show we had a long discussion with the students who made up our audience. One very nice looking girl/woman got on particularly well with me and when the evening was over I asked if I could walk her home which she said was not far away. We walked for perhaps 20 minutes. There was a full moon and all I could see was total devastation. There was hardly one building which had a useable second storey. I saw no house which had not been devastated. We arrived in a street where there was not a building above one storey standing and most if not all looked non-habitable. The girl invited me into her house which turned out to be cellars converted into living space. No electricity but oil lamps. Her mother and two young people, my friend's sisters, made me most welcome. I felt moved that my coming down to meet them meant so much to them. I could not have been more warmly welcomed. I had a cup of tea with them although it was not tea but some other drink as they had no tea until the next week. I stayed talking to them for some time, finally bid them adieu, oder auf wiedersehn, and walked back to the hotel, or that was my intention. Sadly, in walking to her home, I had been guided by my new friend and so had not given much thought to the route we were following. The result of this stupidity meant I was walking for well over an hour trying to find the hotel. I did not find it. Two army types who were patrolling the streets in a jeep like policemen picked me up on suspicion, took me back to the hotel where my identity was confirmed and I finally got into bed. Warm clean sheets, electric light, adjacent toilet and the certainty of a healthy breakfast compared with where I had seen.

Our permit to enter the British zone was for a period of three weeks and it was with regret we left Germany to return home by boat. I love foreign travel and have pursued this interest over the decades in Russia, South America, North America, Asia, et al, but few of these journeys were as affecting as this wonderful opportunity I had been granted.

As I had missed my graduation ceremony I was "graduated" at a smaller ceremony largely for medical students. When I was called I walked the few yards to the stage steps at the top of which stood the Vice Chancellor. I tripped on the top step and more or less fell into the arms of the Vice Chancellor. For this I got a small round of ironic applause as I picked up my mortar board and put it on, not quite correctly. The tassel has to be over the left eye and not the right or vice versa. After that there were no further embarrassments. I was sorry I had not graduated with my fellow law students as I had established strong relations with some who included two Palestinian boys with whom I kept in contact by letter for some time. Later I learned one was working in Libya as being a Palestinian Arab, work in Israel was difficult or nigh impossible for them.

I had and have great sympathy for the Arabs which did not exclude my belief that the Jews needed and deserved a homeland

and that could only be in Palestine. The Jews had had to fight for this right and there was a number of well-named terrorist groups which carried out any number of murderous attacks on the British. It is so sad that the land where Jesus and the apostles lived, where the Jews had lived for centuries, and how the Arabs could make a similar claim, was a corner of the Earth to be fought over rather than negotiating a system where each is liberated.

My life at Leeds University was extended as I had to prepare for my Bar Exams and could not afford to go to London where students were prepared specifically for the Bar Exams. I had to face the exams without that assistance and this was done by my spending another year in the bowels of the Brotherton Library which I look back on with great pleasure. Thankfully I passed the Bar Examinations held of course in London, without a problem but with a deep sense of relief. Immediately afterwards I received my calling up papers.

Holiday jobs

Over the years, during the university holidays which were extensive, I did a number of jobs to raise some money. One was with a building firm in Headingly opposite a lovely old cinema still operating, The firm did all kinds of jobs. I especially liked the roof jobs as it was exciting to be on a roof to point a chimney, or replace worn slates. I am sure there was a sense of bravado. Look at me here on the roof. The men were very supportive and let me have a go on a number of jobs. I worked for this firm during three of four August breaks and it was there I heard for the first time the words "Go and get your cards". This was said when a man was being sacked on the spot. The card referred to was a card which every worker had and on which stamps were stuck to record the person's work record. Summary sacking was the norm. Quite brutal. I only saw this once and the man sacked deserved to be sacked as he had done a job in a way which could have injured him and his workmates. There was no appeal against summary sacking for any reason or none. The men were very kind to me and taught me many simple jobs like cutting a slate with a large trowel or making the hole in the slate through which the nail would go to secure it. I enjoyed it immensely and had a lot of laughs. On one occasion we were moving the scaffolding from a job. Some of the scaffold poles were made of very heavy duty iron and were heavy enough for carrying just two on the shoulder. Other poles were made of aluminium and so one could carry a few at a time. We had to pass through a small group waiting for the tram. My two colleagues each picked up two iron poles and I picked up four aluminium poles and followed. A woman in the small group said to her neighbour, "He be strong that lad." The men I worked with and for whom I became very friendly and treated me as something of an oddity. On my last session with them I had to say I would not be working with them anymore as I was going to be called up. As a gesture they allowed me to put a large chimney pot on a house and from time to time I do as they said I would. "Every time you pass it you can say to yourself" "I did that". The chimney is still there. My final session with the hard physical world was with a major firm, Spooners, who were building an estate in Moortown, a few miles from the city centre. This was not nearly as interesting as my previous jobs but it was better paid. It involved for me filling a space with small rocks and then concreting it to form a base for the house. As the structure developed we laid a concrete floor in the second storey. That was that. Hard physically and essentially boring.

I got work as a cleaner at the Leeds General Infirmary. I was part of a three-man team. One, our leader, had a scrubbing machine. He was the boss. The second in the hierarchy was a man with a large mop and the third, in this case, me with another mop. We were to do just the corridors which were endless. We started at 6 am and worked until midday. Our boss had been involved in a serious fracas, injuring his throat and could barely speak at all – quite unintelligible. The second in command was a "displaced person" and could speak no English. The third man – me, was working in all parts. It was extremely boring work though for some innate reason I was fully committed to doing the very best job we could. One morning when on the main corridor, a man went up to the boss and asked for directions to ward nine. The boss, unable to speak just grunted and pointed back to second in command. He, however, spoke no English and pointed to me. I decided to be silly and when he asked me for directions to ward nine, I pretended not to understand and pointed back to the boss. The man shrugged his shoulders and expressed his frustration in language which it would be inappropriate to record in its stark vocabulary. About nine o'clock we had a break in a quiet spot close to the mortuary and I soon came to know the person in charge quite well. The name I knew him by was strangely Morty. He regularly invited me into the mortuary with a phrase he used so often. "There's something interesting you should see." For some reason I was unaffected by the corpses he was working on. This surprises me as I thought I would have been greatly affected. He showed me how to cut the skull, take out the brain and pull the scalp back and sew it in place to be ready for burial. On one occasion, he showed me a large fat man whose back he had opened up to reveal what Morty told me was an advanced cancer. All kinds of body parts were taken and then sent to the lab for investigation. He treated me as if I were a medical student. Look at this liver, this kidney or this heart compared with this healthy one. It was all so very fascinating to have what in effect was a medical lecture which medical students would have as part of their studies. The word gruesome fits exactly what I saw but I did not feel this in any way, such was the fascination of having the working of the body explained to me so objectively. If one is interested in how things work, which I am, I found his showing me the reason a heart had failed to be fascinating as was his explanation of the brains which he had abstracted and how they were different for different reasons and how important it was to leave the cadaver looking at its best even though the skull had been trepanned and then replaced. He prided himself that when the body was laid out for the funeral it would not be possible to see that the skull had been trepanned. I also respected his constant preoccupation to see that the body was perfectly prepared for release to the undertakers so as to prevent any awful concern from relatives who might see the deceased. This, he once said, was the most important thing he had to do. I had many such visits and explanations and kept in touch with him sporadically for some time. Some years later I returned to see if he was still working there. Sadly he was not.

I followed a family tradition by handing in any wages I received to my mother – a real pleasure.

Parliamentary Ambitions
Penrith and the Border

My father and mother were both strong characters and both very committed to the Labour Party in which they were both very active. Some of my earliest memories as a child were delivering leaflets with my dad for the Labour Party. Years later after leaving the RAF and enjoying a short period on the variety stage, I took up teaching as a useful way of earning a living while I was living at home because of the ill health of my parents before going back to the stage if that was how my career might take me. I very quickly was involved in local politics and was persuaded to register my name to be listed on a panel of individuals looking to fight a parliamentary seat. I was invited to attend a selection panel in Carlisle and was selected as the prospective candidate for Penrith and the Border. This was a primarily agricultural area with isolated areas of old-fashioned occupations like mining and chemicals. I treated the selection as committing me to working the constituency as if we could win it at the election. The realty was that this constituency was true blue throughout and any change was seen as virtually impossible. The sitting MP was a chap called Willie Whitelaw, a true blue of the old Tory Party and later to become one of Mrs Thatcher's strongest supporters in a very right wing government. He gained countrywide recognition when, as Hansard records, she referred to Willie Whitelaw as "my own little Willie". He was her staunchest supporter and showed his loyalty to her throughout his and her political life. I met him once or twice and found him very friendly, perhaps just a little condescending about the forthcoming election result. We met by chance in a pub and he invited me to a drink. During the ten or so minutes we were chatting he said with a certain pleasure: "We do not count the votes for Conservatives here, we weigh them."

Almost every second week I would drive up to Penrith where the Penrith and the Border Labour Party had its HQ, stay overnight and return to Leeds on the Sunday morning. This was a very big commitment suitable for a winnable seat but too demanding for a hopeless seat. The Constituency Party had an excellent paid agent, a wee Scottish fellow called Bill Cowan. He was a typical Labour organiser of that epoch. They are now sadly an extinct breed. He had had only the minimalist form of education of the time, but he had benefited from educational training from the Workers Education Association. He was very committed, a splendid organiser and highly intelligent. I respected and liked him enormously and envied his ability to persuade and cajole individuals to undertake responsibilities.

I could not afford to stay overnight in a hotel and the Constituency Party could not afford it either and so I was quartered in the large home of a leading Socialist guru who commanded enormous respect by party members. I liked him because of his outstanding intellect and opinions and we had many fierce and friendly discussions at his home. There was one awful drawback to this arrangement. My host did not appear to believe in washing. His clothes looked as if they had never been washed and his personal hygiene left much to be desired. He was in fact very dirty. I was reluctant to sleep at his home as the bedding was suspect in my mind. However, a good fairy came to my rescue. A very congenial woman who seemed attached to the agent Cowan (where he went she went), insisted that new sheets should be bought and used solely by me in my allotted bed. She would ensure they were laundered and retained for my sole use. I capitulated and stayed regularly over Saturdays until after the election. I enjoyed the kindness of this lady over the whole period I was involved.

I was fortunate that I knew Gaitskell and Healey, who each very kindly came to speak for me in a constituency which was regarded as hopeless. I addressed supporters in all the major towns in the constituency but knew I was speaking to the already converted.

My agent's plan was to get every village and town to elect a Labour Beauty Queen, as these generally attracted the press photographers. During the run up to election week I would tour the area of each of the twelve queens in my car with a PA system, the queen directing me to follow the itinerary drawn up by the agent. The election week turned out to be sunny and so I enjoyed fine weather, a pretty young person as a guide and practising my broadcasting talents. Every time we stopped I became aware of a remarkable fact. Humans tend to behave similarly to others when in the same circumstances. I found that as soon as I spoke over the loud speakers two phenomena ensued. Every person in his or her garden or hanging out the washing immediately disappeared as though terrified some awful consequence or worse might be wreaked on the listener. The other strange manifestation was that as humans disappeared into cover, every hen, cow or sheep or goat which roamed freely, were attracted to the sound. I found it strangely comical that I appeared to be speaking to a mixed audience of cat, hen, goat, sheep and the odd bird which alighted to increase the numbers in my audience. This form of electioneering may not have produced a victory but it did attract extensive publicity as there were a number of local newspapers serving the area who always report community beauty contests and queens as they know it helps sales.

There is one experience I shall never forget. On the hills of the constituency a major development was taking place. On a fell by ironic chance called Moscow on the Maps, the government of the day was building a site for the development of rockets. We were building our own Rocket Centre. The very large site was surrounded by a continuous alarmed fence. Entry was by one gate only and only one gate. I was welcomed by a small group of men, all working men by appearance. I explained that I wanted to get all workers to register to vote and then vote for me. My hosts were more than happy to oblige. Some of this small group were very Irish and I subtly let them know of my love of Ireland and its singers and poets. I said there would be a polling station for the people on the site and I hoped everyone would use this special facility. The leader of this welcoming group, as Irish as County Cork, put his arm on my shoulder and said that they believed in voting a little and often. You can rely on us. I remember those words when it turned out that a large number of individuals had either died or left since the register was drawn up but nevertheless had voted a little and often. An inquiry took place but I believe that the matter was not pursued given that it could not have had any effect on the final result which was a landslide victory for Whitelaw, who polled very much more than me, Labour and the Liberal combined.

Visiting this development was a singular bit of good luck. Entry was not normally permitted on security grounds. The committee I had met ran the organisation to a large extent. It was like an independent colony on a bleak fell in northern England. The site was never completed after millions of expenditure and with it died, I believe, Britain's place in the rocket world.

There was another lesson I learned. I was familiar with the word truckle in literature but thought it had disappeared in real life. Truckle can be said to mean "behave obsequiously". In those days if one wore a hat, one would raise it to a friend or to a much older person or to any lady as a courteous gesture. This was standard behaviour across the class divides. Working men, however, especially in the countryside, might pull their forelock if they had no cap to lift. I saw working men tugging their forelocks while holding their caps which they had taken off in deference. I also saw in the late forties men being told to remove their caps "when talking to me". In Leeds I saw very little evidence of truckling. Other gestures, however, were common such as the V for Victory sign which in due course of time represented the phrase "Get Stuffed" or something of that sort.

Another memory abides. A distinguished local woman, an aristocratic Lady Mary, if I correctly remember, was a supporter of sorts. Knowing that I liked riding she took me on a ride round the local villages, knowing that being seen with her was likely to impress. At one point we came to the top of a small hill and looked down on a hamlet of stone houses. I said: "Shall we go down?" She said: "No point – they are only interested in one thing and that is incest." We did not go down. I really liked her aristocratic attitude to life and her attitude to politics. Additionally, in a life which has been much spent on electioneering, this is the only time I had the opportunity to do it on horseback.

My next foray was in a constituency nearer home. Pudsey is now part of greater Leeds and was represented by a chap who had been on the Leeds City Council. On the ballot paper his description was yarn spinner. A teacher colleague lived in the constituency and on learning of my becoming, the candidate offered to show me round the constituency. I thanked him but found that this offer really meant he was showing me all the pubs which seemed countless. He had an old car made in the area, a Jowett, which had to be started by using a starting handle but only after he had made a few micro adjustments inside the car. He was of slight build but he had an amazing tolerance to beer. Our journeys of discovery were always very pleasant but I fear did not in any way improve my chances of a win. I did like him.

The Labour Party ran a well planned and executed campaign but my yarn spinner won the day yet again. I spent countless hours on the doorstep canvassing from the date I was selected to the day of the poll. I was always part of a band of individuals whose devotion to getting me elected was equal to mine. It made me feel humble as it does every year when I see Labour Party members working in their ward or constituency even when the seat can be regarded as non-winnable. Politics in Leeds, in my long experience, always has been contentious. For instance, ultra left wing individuals, often called Trots or Trotskyites, organised to take over the Leeds Labour Party. They knew they could never win an election as an ultra left wing group so they decided to achieve their objectives by subterfuge. A number would join a local Labour ward Party to gain enough votes to have one of their group elected as candidate. For a few years this was a really serious problem and in my ward, Kirkstall, this was an internal battle which involved much time and effort better spent elsewhere. Again I am moved by the courage and conviction of my colleagues in preventing this political takeover. Times then were very different. In Leeds once a month, a meeting called the City Party, took place in the Trade Union premises. As many as more than a hundred individuals regularly attended in highly contentious debate. Often it was for many, standing room only. The leader of one group, seen as far left, was led by a very forceful young man called John Trickett. George Mudie, the leader of the Labour Party, decided to deal with him by inviting him into the establishment. He later became a councillor and then, after some years later, the leader of the council when Mudie was elected an MP as he himself was later, winning one of the safest Labour seats in the country, Hemsworth. I got to know him well and found him highly effective and open to suggestions. He, in fact, followed Mudie in making Leeds into a "major modern" city in the arts and sport. For instance, when I wanted to bring Northern Ballet into Leeds, he did not hesitate to make it possible just as Mudie had made the Playhouse possible, although working with Mudie was much harder than "working" with Trickett.

My greatest opportunity to be an MP arose when a vacancy occurred in the Central Leeds constituency, a safe Labour seat. I had been chairman and secretary for many years and was well liked and respected by the Party members. My major threat came from a small undistinguished man whom I liked and respected. He worked as a clerk in the railway station, was intelligent and a very decent human being. He had one big advantage over me. He was a sponsored candidate That is, his trade unions offered him substantial financial support; he would attract a substantial sum every year from his union. £ 300 per annum in those days was a very strong inducement to the usual impoverished members. He won by a substantial margin, the financial inducement working even on some of those who were my original supporters. I felt let down but that feeling did not last too long as what cannot be undone should be accepted. I did, however, continue as an officer of the constituency and was very sad that my opponent quite rapidly gained the reputation of a "soak", that is an alcoholic. I was extremely sad to see this very decent human being losing his way and finding another by drink. He had lots of support as people tried to hide his obsession with drink. It was a minor tragedy but for him and his family it was a major tragedy. Winning the selection and then the election must have seemed incredibly exciting to this very decent intelligent railway clerk, but a cruel fate decreed otherwise. A real tragedy. At this stage I jettisoned my hopes of becoming an MP and making a real change for those I represented. I could not face the so-called "Beauty Tests" by trying to get a safe seat. I was flattered by a number of recommendations of a peerage for me but each time my sponsors were told that places were few and there was long queue of MPs who had lost their seats and expected to go to the Lords. I regret this as if you want people to listen to you and hopefully be persuaded, a title like Lord of the Realm would be very helpful. Among those who formally proposed me to the Labour Party for a seat in the Lords included Lord Dean, Alice Bacon and Lord Rees. Knowing how few seats available there were and how many former Labour MPs there were hoping for the Lords, I did not think I would ever have the chance. I did appreciate the kindness of my proposers.

I have over the years visited very many times the Houses of Parliament for meetings. I always get a genuine thrill in entering the Great Hall, still remaining since Norman times, where Charles I was tried and sentenced to death, where the old courts were held, courts like the Court of Common Pleas and suffragettes vented their fury. Walking through the Great Hall is like walking through centuries of history. Sadly much of the very ancient parts of the Parliament buildings have been lost but the aura of the old seems to create a similar aura surrounding the new.

Local Government
Holbeck Elected Council

One hundred and fifty years ago Leeds was notorious for being a "pestilential place" being riddled by cholera, the plague and typhus just to mention a few of its ill health problems. Life expectancy was short. A succession of charters over the centuries ultimately provided Leeds with a form of local government which finally brought to the city town gas, electricity, trams, buses, clean potable water ranked the finest in the country, modern sanitation by building a massive sewerage system still serving the city as it has done over the decades and providing more than two thirds of the beds when the National Health Service was created. However, a report of 1957 listed 45,000 designated slums – houses with no lavatory, bathroom, or hot water system with the majority being back to back homes. This was a period when slum landlords became rich at the expense of the poorest in society. The Labour council undertook massive slum clearance which was labelled in the local tory press as Red Ruin. In 1952 I had been elected to sit on the Education Committee as one of its three lay members, i.e. not elected councillors and this provided me with a very necessary political education. After two unsuccessful attempts to be elected to the council in so-called hopeless wards i.e. wards I was not expected to win, I was chosen to fight the City Ward which included Holbeck and parts of Hunslet. This was a very deprived area ironically because it was the heart of the industrial revolution in the century earlier and depended heavily on heavy industry which was disappearing. Poverty, stark poverty, affected many of the residents most of whom lived in houses which were condemned as slums. Streets and streets of back to back houses with no hot water system, no bathroom or bath and no toilet facilities, such facilities being provided in small blocks in each street containing two and sometimes three lavatories which were shared by designated households. One has to wonder how people coped at night in mid-winter when they had to use the toilets down the street. Chamber pots were essential. The chamber pot became known as a "guzunder", that is something which goes under the bed. I visited many families on a monthly basis to collect six pence per month as a membership fee of the Labour Party which was at that time 6d per month. We had quite a large number of members and my monthly visit ensured that they never felt isolated and I was reminded every month of the terrible conditions in which my fellow men, women and children had to exist. One experience remains with me and still makes me smile.

I was sitting in the downstairs room of a home which was built on an embankment which carried the main train line out of Leeds to the south. Cup of tea in hand I heard a rumble and then a shaking which caused the tea in my cup to overflow. I thought a bomb left undiscovered from the last war must have gone off but was reassured by the man and his wife that it was just the London train leaving the station. They laughed at my surprise and when I said how terrible it was for them to live in such a house where every heavy train was felt; the man said it had its advantage if you were making love to your wife. I was too innocent to understand his levity.

I represented this ward for twelve years, most of which was spent on slum clearance and a frustrated desire to replace old houses with new in the same area in order to preserve the strong local bonds which existed in the community. We ultimately succeeded in this ambition by what became known as "teeming and lading". Quite what the etymology of that phrase is, I know no more than its shipping use but in this case it meant clearing an area, building on it and moving into these new houses those who had been moved out to allow this to happen. This retains social cohesion which is very important for a healthy community. I had been arguing for this over the years and was defeated by experts who said it could not be done. I enlisted the aid of the most senior member of the council, a most revered Alderman Hemingway, a person of great gravitas. He wanted to do the same in some of the areas he had been connected with. His political clout enabled the "experiment" to be undertaken.

It proved to be successful and proved to be very popular with people who saw their hopes of a new home in the locality they called home realised.

Ironically half a century later the positions were reversed. My two ward colleagues and I were savagely attacked by fellow Labour councillors as we opposed the clearance of several hundred back to back homes in our ward. I always find it disturbing to be on the opposite side of an argument to colleagues I respect and admire but regret they often act on the basis of some dogma such as back to backs should always be demolished on principle, rather than exercising their intelligence in an objective appraisal of the individual situation. The Labour Party over decades has earned a high reputation for clearing slums or areas of poor housing. In this case my colleagues in the Housing Committee had decided on the demolition of some hundred or so back to back houses close to the city centre. These homes were well built. Most had been converted to accommodate a bathroom with bath and lavatory and were very popular for a number of reasons. By definition, all homes except those at the end of the street had a contiguous home on both sides and on the rear. This meant that in winter they were quite cosy, each home helping to heat the others. Many old folk liked them because the only door to the house entered onto the street giving them a feeling of security. Others liked them for those reasons and because the houses were relatively cheap to rent or buy. They remain today fully occupied and just as popular as they were when my two fellow members of council and I organised decades ago a successful campaign to save these homes. Sadly, it was in this area of Leeds that many years later a small group of terrorists prepared their terrible campaign which led to the London bombings. TV cameras appeared everywhere tragically for the wrong reasons.

It is a fascinating multi-racial area which contains: the largest Mosque in Leeds (formerly a new major Roman Catholic Church), the local Catholic church five minutes walk from the mosque and even less to the Hindu Temple. My ward colleagues and I were honoured by the Hindus by being asked to participate in a ceremony to mark the start of the building of a new temple to replace the old school they had been using for worship. This was a very cheerful, warm and friendly occasion and we genuinely felt honoured to be asked to play a considerable role in the formalised process. That good relationship remains intact today.

I have always felt that I was extremely lucky to be selected for City Ward, the most varied in the city. It stretched from a street in Hunslet, encompassed all Holbeck, extended to the centre of the city and then on out to the fringe of Woodhouse. It contained the poorest areas in Holbeck and Hunslet as well as the vibrant city centre which surprisingly had a considerable number of voters. They were mainly working men and women living in pubs, or businesses where they were caretakers. Others by distinction were affluent and chose to remain in the centre where their very fine homes can still be seen being preserved as much by chance as anything else. Now this central area of the city contains thousands of flats which only the relatively affluent can afford.

After each election one has to put in a declaration which gives details of income and expenditure. One had to ensure that one did not exceed the permitted limit by even a penny. Our elections in those early days of 1957 cost between £28 and £34. Today one could not get enough leaflets for one delivery for that sum.

Election expenses have always been closely scrutinised as the result of which a person I much admired was forced out of politics. His election expenses were properly evidenced and well within the limits. His election return had to be signed by the election agent, the person responsible for keeping expenses within the law. On the last day for the return, my friend was told the election return had not been submitted and he thought this might mean he would lose the seat he had just won. Foolishly but understandably, he signed the return with the name of the agent who had gone on holiday and presented them before the final day expired. Within a day or so his "forgery" was discovered. He was prosecuted under the law relating to elections and felt forced to resign from the council to which he had just been elected. A great deal of political poison was thrown at the very decent, very competent and caring individual and a valuable caring councillor was destroyed politically and I am sure mentally. In my view he had done no wrong morally. He had been wrong to forge another's name but the expenses were in apple pie order and well within the limits proscribed.

Looking at these old and tattered papers today which relate back several decades, I have the greatest difficulty in throwing them away. They have a seriously strong effect on my psyche. It is as though saving these old bits of paper which bring back so many memories keeps alive those memories of men and women now long gone. A form of immortality. Silly. Unreasonable. But real. The sentimental words of Moore poetically make the point: "I feel like one who walks alone some Banquet Hall deserted, whose lights have fled whose garlands dead and all but he departed". I have the same pangs on destroying old photos. One I will always retain. It shows me arm in arm with a beautiful young women in a wedding dress apparently coming out of church after being married. Actually, it was taken when we were entering the church, I acting in place of the missing father and my duty was to "give away the bride" in his absence. We turned at the entrance to the church at the request of the photographer. The young bride was Rita, a beautiful girl who became a lifelong friend and who was an inspirational worker for the Labour Party. Her mother was a splendid woman, reminding me of the actress Anna Magnani. This looks like a genuine wedding day photograph which I rather mischievously left on a shelf in my study in Huddersfield Technical College. It caused great interest which I affected not to notice. The staff, mainly female, thought I had married secretly and this was the photograph of the event. In the end I had to come clean as I learned that some of the ladies were proposing a collection to give me a wedding present.

I thought it fun until that moment when I had to disabuse these friendly members of staff.

In Holbeck there was a bathhouse-cum-washhouse, a council owned and operated building which offered a hot bath for a small payment of one penny (240 pence in the pound) and a splendid washhouse for laundering of clothes. The washhouse, when busy, resembled one of Breuguel's paintings. Women brought large baskets of dirty clothing, put it into the steaming hot washing machines, rinsed in scalding hot water and then dried in enormous drying machines. In addition to its proper function the building became a place where women could meet socially in what was a very male dominated society. The council decided to close it which meant that these facilities would be lost in an area of dense back to back properties with no bathroom or washing facilities. My two council ward colleagues and I started a campaign to retain the baths. Rita's mother was splendid in leading a mass march on the council, on organising petitions and raising public awareness which is so often lacking in domestic matters. We were successful and the washhouse remained operational for many years, only closing when the homes in the area had their own bath-rooms and washing facilities common now in every home. Driving through that area today as I frequently do as a short cut, the memories are still vivid and just a bit nostalgic and sad for some reason. I also think of the unique occasion when the Riot Act was actually read. A very large crowd of football fans had congregated near to the site of the old washhouse in Holbeck. They were rioting in a way which in those days was considered a real danger to the public order. The Lord Mayor was asked to read the Riot Act, an old instrument to deal with rioting crowd, very rarely used in the 20th century but it gave the authorities legal powers to apply military forces to disperse the crowds and additional powers of arrest which they did not have otherwise. A hundred years earlier it had been read in almost the same place in order to attack the mass protest of the working class against impossible levels of poverty. In this case it was an invasion of football followers fighting Leeds United supporters. The situation was dealt with without the calling up of army resources.

My life and that of the city council of Leeds have been closely related. I have had the enormous good fortune to have been chairman of most of the major committees such as the Education Committee, the Leisure Services Committee, one of the biggest in the country, Social Services and Watch, i.e. Police Committee. When I was first elected, one could claim loss of income if the employer deducted a sum from the wage of the councillor equivalent to the time missed. This system has its advantages as it does not attract anyone who is not genuinely interested in civic matters. In due course, claiming expenses became easier and the legislation to pay councillors was passed. This may seem reasonable. I think it got out of hand and it was attracting people whose main interest was joining this bandwagon. How big was this bonanza? All received a quite modest and reasonable sum. The big money was payment to chairs of committee. For example, in 2004–2009 the then Tory leader of the council received £ 242,599. His deputy, a Liberal, received £ 113,748. The Tory leader of the council in order to get a majority in the council, needed the support of a small number of councillors from Morley, a small town part of Leeds. He offered an award to a former Labour councillor, now a Morley Independent, an annual payment totalling £ 108,353 in five years. If you accept the money you lose your independence. It is also legal to receive quite independently of and additional to grants from the City Council, other allowances for being on other committees like the Police, or Transport or Fire Brigade Committees. These sums were reviewed annually and as they were so attractive financially, they became a method of persuasion at its most kind expression. In the fifty plus years of my life on the council I have seen the development of a culture which I regret, but can well understand how people with low income can welcome this additional money. It does however in some cases raise the question: Why did you decide to become a councillor? To what extent is the allocation of jobs by the leader, seen as a form of legal bribery, unfair influence? You scratch my back and I will scratch yours. To some who are well placed in jobs which pay well the additional sums are welcome but not decisive in determining his or her life whereas for councillors who have just a week's wage to support them and their families, the payment carried by some committees are most welcome. Many decades ago I decided I would not accept a basic allowance then being introduced as I felt strongly the danger that this could destroy the independence of the receivers. The Labour Chief Whip, Billy Merritt, was a male nurse by profession and was in my view a splendid representative of a good honest party and a close political friend. He berated me saying that my gesture was sufficient to affect those who really needed some support. He suggested that if I wanted to be holy I could accept the basic allowance and then give it away. This advice I decided to follow as with the development of Gift Aid one can vastly increase the value of the gift. I greatly respected Cllr Merritt, a decades-long political relationship. He became ill and despite all efforts his decline continued until one prayed for his soul and not his survival as death was becoming the inevitable and hopeful conclusion to end his suffering. I incline to the view that being an active person in what we now call the Gay Community, he died of AIDS which at that time had not been "discovered". However that may be: may he rest in peace.

Lose one gain another

My happy days as a councillor for that area came to an abrupt and ignominious end. At the local elections in Leeds in 1969 all the 99 seats were being fought in an "all out election". Labour was nearly wiped out returning just nine Labour members in a council of 99 seats. It seemed incredible to all local politicians and led to some strange results. A very nice young man I knew who was in the Young Conservatives had been asked to stand as a candidate in Hunslet, a "safe Labour seat" and he had agreed to help out as the Tories were pushed to find enough candidates in the all-out elections. He was elected to his complete surprise and horror as he had already made arrangements to leave the country and live in South Africa. My advice to him when he came to see me, the candidate he had defeated, was to attend the first council meeting and then put in his formal resignation and then leave the country. This he did and later sent me a card from Cape Town of good wishes. In the succeeding years, Labour regained its overall majority but that took some years. He was not the only one to have been shocked by their success and a number of new Conservative councillors resigned or did not bother to attend meetings, yet we still with some truth claim we are the home of democratic rights and organisations.

I returned to the council the following year, this time to represent Kirkstall Ward. This is a predominantly working class area with a very substantial middle class element in some of the old Victorian houses adjoining a most beautiful monastery, Kirkstall Abbey. It has also been colonised by students who have injected new life in some areas, often to the annoyance and despair of residents. Landlords were making fortunes by buying two or three bedroom houses and converting them into flats for students. It took a long time before there was any real control on basic specifications and there have been some tragedies caused by defective premises.

In medieval days the Kirkstall Abbey was very extensive in its land holding and at its centre still stands the beautiful Abbey celebrated by a number of Turner paintings and desecrated by the avaricious Henry VIII. It has been well preserved in the last decades since it was given so generously to the city by a wealthy magnate. The city in the form of the council of many different political persuasions has, thank God, preserved it well. For four years or so it was in my councillor's brief which gave me the a major problem when new lead roofing was stolen. We replaced it by a different metal so that thieves would not take the second roof off to sell as valuable lead. We attached a message to this effect. It is not so many generations between this despoiling of the Abbey and Henry. There is now a delightful museum housed in the Priest's House, very worth a visit. My relationship with this ancient monument illustrates why I have given so much of my time and effort to local politics and why I had hopes of becoming an MP. By being a councillor I had power to make a difference, If that meant pulling down the slums, supporting the arts, developing its tourist trade improving the social services so be it. If being on the council is at a considerable cost of time and effort, the return can be enormous in human terms and satisfaction. For instance, one old Labour councillor, a totally unlettered man, made his aim to get the working class reading as the first steps to understanding political issues which would then lead to political change. Leeds owes its libraries, greater in number than those of Liverpool and Manchester combined, to this working man who became a councillor. I remember too, a woman whose interest was green spaces for the poor to enjoy some fresh air and relaxation in sylvan surroundings. Leeds owes the existence of its very fine and extremely extensive green spaces and public parks to this forgotten woman. Another firebrand of a woman, who owned and managed a very successful construction company, became chairman (sic) of the Works department and made it a very valuable asset despite strong Tory opposition who opposed council enterprises as it excluded the private sector. In my early years on the council there was a number of outstanding women chairmen who were highly influential on the council's policy.

The Revd Father Jenkinson, a member of the Labour Party in the early thirties, set out to clear the slums in a campaign he led. He was vilified and attacked and ridiculed to no effect. His work was christened in the press as Red Ruin. He was a councillor for only a few years but in that time he led slum clearance with a messianic zeal and encountered violent opposition from the Tories in council who repeatedly used the abusive phrase of Red Ruin. God bless Revd Jenkinson. Individuals can make a difference as the lives of people like Gandhi and Mandela show but with those outstanding exceptions, real progress across a wide spectrum can only be achieved by large organisations such as local authorities. If one feels like making a difference then membership of some pressure group is more likely to achieve success than any individual's effort. That is why I joined the Labour Party as soon as I was old enough and later became a local councillor, eager to do good as I saw it. Over the years I have received a regular succession of hostile letters most often to do with specific decisions or actions, e.g. advocating the demolition of a slum area or the retention and improvement of them. These I try to answer as honestly and fully as I can. Others fall into the category of hate mail of which the following dated 11.08.11 is a fairly typical example, reported as written.

Hostile letter

Dear Councillor Atha,

*So you are 83 and choose to blow your trumpet publicly via
an interview with Rod McPhee published in the Yorkshire
Evening Post. Well busy Bernard here are a few home truths
or if you like a realistic reality check: called to the bar but no
serious career in the law-Why? dabbled with ballet and acting but never achieved much in either, a Catholic but not
a priest, no desire to have children-most unusual, you say
Catholics believe pride is a sin and you don't seem to think
you are a proud egocentric narcissistic individual who puffs
out his chest bragging to be Lord Mayor having met Nelson
Mandela and had many "lady" friends! The bottom line is
you are a two bit Councillor and patron of local arts groups.
Most people now regard Councillors as lower than pond life –
the sludge that stinks at the bottom of the pond, grabbing public money. This comes from someone who knows many people (Irish Background) who have known you and yours. Get
real Berni, Yours very sincerely, M Smith PTO. A couple
of postscripts: Even as a local politician you could never get
any further i.e. become a MP did you? If you are a practising Catholic don't you think a confession around ego, boasting etc would be appropriate? You havnt really reached the
pinnacle in any of your diverse activities, have you? Always
a self adoring big fish in a small local pond. Anyway despite
these home truths, may your god bless you as David Allen
would have said.*

Signed Mr Smith

I never knew what triggered this literary masterpiece but it is always salutary to receive such missives which are presumably designed to hurt which they singularly fail to do. I have from time been involved in plans or developments which arouse strong opposition. If there is a name and address to a hate letter I often take pleasure in thanking the writer of such a letter, totally misconstruing his or her message and treating them as complimentary and happily received with thanks. Petty really and a failing the anonymous Mr Smith should have included in his description of me.

Life as a councillor can involve unusual situations. One December afternoon I was returning to my car after visiting an old couple who needed some help with a neighbour when I saw a group of adolescent girls, most in school uniform, on a grassed area. One girl wearing a white shirt or jumper was attacking another girl in school uniform and was clearly trying to put her on the ground. Recognising what I thought was blatant bullying, I immediately turned towards the girls, shouting, "Stop that." The girl in the white top broke away from the object of her attack momentarily and then returned to her victim and delivered a very strong and effective right cross to the face of the smaller girl. The hurt girl went down crying and shouting leave me alone but the girl in the white top continued the attack by falling on her and pulling her hair. I separated them and stood between the two girls to stop further attack. The girl in the white top, however, continued her attack from which I protected the victim. A group of other girls then ran towards me shouting for me to leave the girl in the white top alone and for a moment I thought they were going to attack me. This was prevented by the appearance of a strong looking chap who had stopped when he saw the bullying take place and came to join me in intervening. He told the girls to push off in a very persuasive if positive manner which had the appropriate effect on the aggressive girls. He clearly looked to them a more serious opponent than I. A few seconds later the group of girls ran off, obviously impressed by this gentleman's intervention and the realisation the police were coming. I offered the girl who was the victim of the gross bullying a lift home with two of her girlfriends who were comforting her as I thought her attacker might ambush her on the way home. They accepted my offer but before I could take them off, the police arrived spectacularly in numbers and took over. I was told I need not give the girls a lift as a relative was coming by car to pick them up.

I gave my name to a woman PC and commended the police for arriving with such incredible speed. The whole event from my shouting at the girl to stop to the disappearance of the group of girls must have occupied less than five or six minutes. I believe too, that the intervention of the man from the van was instrumental in preventing a more serious situation. If the girls had attacked me I am not sure how I would or could have responded physically. I find it difficult to envision my using the same offensive measures as I would have used had they been lads and not lasses. I thanked him.

From Vision to Reality Quarry Hill – Major Arts Centre

In 1995 as part of the discussion of future use of Quarry Hill, I had outlined to a journal called the *Arts and Management Weekly* my vision for the cleared Quarry Hill site, an article which the *Evening Post* and the *Yorkshire Post* followed up. It was to create a unique centre for all the major arts bodies in Leeds and as many of the smaller ones which could move to the site. The aim was to create a unique arts centre on which would stand the Leeds Playhouse, the third largest producing theatre in the country, Northern Ballet, one of the four national ballet companies, the Yorkshire Dance Centre, one of the biggest dance centres in the country, Phoenix Dance which was gaining an international reputation, and significant bodies like Red Ladder and East Street Arts. I had hoped that the site would accommodate Opera North but my suggestion was rejected on the sound grounds that Opera North wished to be part of the Grand Theatre as its home. Ever suspicious however, of such ambitions and generous ideas I got the council to adopt formally the policy that the Grand would be the theatre home of both national companies, Northern Ballet and Opera North to prevent Opera North becoming too powerful in the control of the Grand Theatre. This is crucially important to Northern Ballet for if it can put on a suitable show for Christmas this can do excellent business which helps to meet the deficits and costs.

I am reported as saying: "The site will be unique in that it contains in a very small area of the very large 200 plus square miles of the city, great artistic companies which will have endless opportunities for collaboration and mutual support. Leeds is the only city in the UK outside the capital cities which has its own Opera Company, Ballet Company, the largest Music School in the country, the home of the Leeds International Piano competition, one of the three most recognised piano competitions in the world, Phoenix Dance, the Yorkshire Dance Centre, Red Ladder Theatre Company, The Northern School of Contemporary Dance and a number of small groups. I was particularly concerned to ensure that there would be a binding agreement with Northern Ballet to establish a high quality dance education programme, a ballet school, so children in the north can have the expert ballet tuition which they could otherwise not afford. Such a decision is a fundamental part of the NBT."

The report dated 1995 in the *Arts and Management Weekly* magazine raised a lot of interest and reaction. *The Evening Post* carried a lot of persuasive weight and it came down strongly in favour of my vision for the desolated wasteland. "It has taken too long" was one of its headlines. This high hope of mine just 16 years later became a complete reality. It was now the home of The Playhouse, Red Ladder, Regional Dance Centre, Northern Ballet, Phoenix Dance, The Dance Centre, the Leeds College of Music, The Wardrobe and East Street Arts, one of the developments I most admire, situated just across the road. The uniqueness of the site of so many arts bodies has been enhanced by the BBC transferring its Yorkshire HQ from Broadcasting House near the university to a purpose built HQ on the site and a Leeds entrepreneur establishing a major jazz centre called the Wardrobe which is part of the Playhouse property. My feelings in retrospect are a combination of my view that if you think small you will end up small. If you dream big you have at least a chance of achieving high artistic and social goals. To succeed, however, you do have to have individuals or visionaries who are going to make things happen and the Quarry Hill site, with its current riches, is a tribute to all those who made it all happen and whose identities are or will be lost in the mists of time.

Leeds has of course got a major library service, national collections of paintings and sculpture in its Art Gallery and the world recognised Henry Moore Centre, a vibrant amateur theatre culture, a new Civic Theatre, an outstanding annual programme of classical music, the Leeds International Piano Competition, a number of nationally recognised museums including the National Armouries Museum, etc., etc. Box office receipts indicate that approximately half of the users of these facilities are from outside the Leeds Local Authority which is exactly as it should be. Centres like Leeds provide the only hope of certain artistic experiences this side of the Pennines.

I also had another dream and that was that Leeds should become a centre of excellence in the field of sport. This has only been partly achieved as what I was hoping for was a centre like the one in Sheffield which has produced so many medallists. Sheffield only got its splendid facilities after much discussion and great effort. It deserves what it has got and our envy in Leeds is a reflection of the high standards in Sheffield and long may it remain so.

Outside lecturing
Sport Dror Howell

In the 60s and 70s I spent a good deal of time speaking or, in some cases, lecturing which was always welcome as the lecturing fees, although modest, were indeed warmly welcomed by myself. The meetings more often than not provided no fee but travel expenses were often part of the process. For instance, on 9th October 1967, I chaired and spoke at a meeting of representatives from neighbouring local authorities, the Regional Sport Council, the CBI, Ministry of Housing and Local Government and the Dept. of Education and Science et al in the County Hall in Wakefield. This was not a fee occasion nor an expenses occasion either which was rather hard on me as I had travelled up from London only to return for a meeting on the morrow in London. That was of no concern. My arrangements with the Middlesex Polytechnic, now a university, however, were even more a pleasure because I received a fee as well as expenses. By current standards the fees involved were poor to derisory. I did not see them in this way and was pleased to receive what was in fact a recognised modest fee. I was a regular visitor to the polytechnic as the courses the department put on were very carefully constructed so as to be seen as opportunities to learn and understand how local government organisations and charitable bodies work, their legal constraints, political attitudes, financing, et al.

Sociologists as a group are highly imaginative in their view of what works and what does not. Politicians match them in imagination.

Professor Yehezkel Dror of Jerusalem University introduced a new way of looking at what we do and he called it Policy Analysis. Even his simplified view of this new discovery is arcane, prolix, abstruse and convoluted and each adjective an understatement. There was endless discussion between academics and I was amused to receive an invitation to a seminar called "Rescuing Policy Analysis From PPBS". I declined the invitation. PPBS is the acronym for the process which stresses the need for strong links between planning and development and its budgeting system. (Planning, Progress, Budgeting System).

Thank God that in the industrial Revolution men and sadly few women made big decisions and undertook great developments like building railways, developing steam engines, erecting great bridges creating sewerage systems which have lasted a century and a half, etc., etc. I was frequently asked to discuss issues from a local government perspective and spoke at a host of meetings in the period 1974 to 1977 and had the pleasure of being asked to contribute a chapter in a book on the role of local authorities in the development of sport being prepared by Liverpool University.

I personally had been calling for the better use of facilities owned by councils. In Leeds, for instance, there were approximately 300 schools many of which had excellent facilities for sport which were largely being unused, the school being closed after school and during the many school holidays. Socially it is interesting to note that the obvious step of allowing the public controlled use of the sports facilities would be most beneficial both in terms of health and social interaction met with very strong opposition. At the meeting I chaired in Wakefield in 1967 organised by a splendid chap, Frank Templeman (the chief of the Regional Central Council of Physical Recreation), the representatives of a number of local authorities, Ministry of Housing and Local Government, the CBI, and the Department of Education and Science. The meeting was very positive even from those who might have been hostile. Today there is wide use of schools which properly are recognised as public assets and their use for sport and other social purposes.

Scope of local authority activities

I am sure very few realise the enormous portfolio of assets and initiatives a major city like Leeds possesses. For instance, when I was chairman of the Parks and Countryside Department, I and my colleagues were responsible for the management of 3,117 hectares of land, 440 sports pitches, 156 nature reserves, 3,500 allotments, 773 km of public rights of way, 185 playgrounds, 4 million trees and 25 cemeteries and crematoria.

The Sport division consisted of: 24 sports centres and pools, The International Pool, South Leeds Stadium and Tennis Centre, five golf courses, Yeadon Tarn Sailing Centre, Yorkshire Cricket School, Carnegie Gymnastics Centre and Becket Park Athletics Centre.

The Libraries Division: 57 local libraries, one big central library, seven mobile libraries and library provision for the four prisons in Leeds.

Museums and Galleries: City Art Gallery, Temple Newsam House, Lotherton Hall, Abbey House Museum, Kirkstall Abbey, The Industrial Museum and Thwaite Mills Watermill.

The Arts promotion and Tourism Unit was a major grant giver to bodies like Opera North, events like Party in the Park and Ballet in the Park both of which attracted over 40,000 individuals, Classical Fantasia which attracted over 10,000 individuals (full capacity), the International Film Festival and the very successful Tourism Unit which surprisingly made Leeds a "go to city" for weekend breaks.

This litany is just an indication of the cultural importance of the City Council as I could go on to enumerate other units such as the very successful +Music Department, the Events Team, the Hyde Park Cinema, the Grand Theatre, Opera North, the Playhouse, Yorkshire Dance, et al. In 1999/2000 the gross expenditure amounted to £ 64.399 m and the gross revenue £ 29.824 m.

Opera and Party in the Park

When I became chairman of the whole Leisure Empire, I was keen to encourage as far as it was possible the arts, high or low whatever the distinction is. I knew how much the "arts" had contributed to my life and wanted to ensure that it could do the same for all the citizens of Leeds. As a lover of opera I was determined to open this art form to a wider audience in Leeds. With the full cooperation of Opera North, the department staff organised Opera in the Park, the Park being the historical Temple Newsam House. This was a major event. A large structure was built to house the orchestra and the soloists to be taken down immediately after the event and an evening of opera was initiated. It was a resounding success. It attracted more than 40,000 individuals of all classes, backgrounds and ages. Even those who normally grumble at the waste of public money were silent. After a couple of these annual opera feasts I talked to the staff who manage so brilliantly these major events. I pointed out that it cost an absolute fortune to provide toilet facilities for these big events not to mention lighting and sound and that I wondered if they could be used on a consecutive evening. It was not possible to duplicate the opera programme which in any case I did not think would produce double the numbers. The staff as always came up with a solution – a pop concert for the young folk. It was to follow the Saturday night event by a Sunday afternoon event but this time aiming to attract the teenage folk to a pop programme tailored for them. Following their advice, I agreed to try it as an experiment and it was successful beyond our wildest expectations. As all the facilities were there, the unit costs were dramatically reduced and the Party in the Park became an annual feature. Most sadly these very successful ventures came to an end in 2014 when the most savage cuts in the council's budget were imposed by the Conservative government.

Warnings ignored

In 2000 I joined a committee set up by the Labour leader of the council to recommend where cuts could be made to the council's budgets given the savage cuts to central government grants.

I wrote to the leader of the council in 2009 warning him that the decision by the councillor then responsible for these events to continue with them despite the cuts and that he was going to charge for entry to the outdoor opera which would be a drastically expensive failure. My warning was totally ignored by the leader and the result was that about 4,000 people paid compared with the 40,000 who previously had attended for nothing. My prediction of an enormous loss sadly was correct. To my amazement the following year he adopted the same scheme and the loss was repeated against my protests. Thank goodness in the third year the event was pulled, a great sadness to me as I simply delighted in walking round the site when the opera was on and to see a tremendously rich variety of people, rich, poor black, white, male, female, young and old all sharing the same wonderful operatic experience. The local paper, the Evening Post, took a photo of one recumbent ageing fellow with a beer bottle in his hand and a string in his other hand attached to his dog. I thought it splendid in catching the variety in our audience. I wished I had kept the photo. Another similar event took the same course. Years before I had succumbed to a proposition by the splendid staff of the events section. They suggested a jazz festival in the grounds of Kirkstall Abbey, the very well preserved Cistercian abbey dating from the 12th century and set in a quite delightful city park only two and half miles from the city centre. I decided that this was a good venue but for a classical music concert. As chairman of the Northern Ballet Company I had to declare on numerous occasions the connection as I wanted to use the orchestra of Northern Ballet for this event. This was a very talented group of instrumentalists which toured as the orchestra of Northern Ballet. Giving a concert like this would help them as musicians and also assist with meeting the cost of the orchestra. This decision produced strong objections from Opera North who quite understandably thought that this gig should be their gig. We called the event Kirkstall Fantasia. It was free but by ticket only and was a resounding success, more than 10,000 people filling the space completely. Again I was delighted at the mix of people by age, colour, gender, et al. Sadly, Kirkstall Fantasia has also fallen to the axe of central government cuts.

Ballet in the Park, Grand Theatre, City Varieties

I experimented in Temple Newsam with Ballet in the Park, hoping that by using the technique of Opera in the Park to attract new opera goers we might bring ballet into the hearts of those who had never experienced it. The staff as usual designed and then built an enormous tent housing several thousand people, the orchestra and the stage which had to meet very severe standards as I did not wish any of the dancers to be injured because the floor was not right. The Ballet in the Park was a complete sell out. It was greeted fantastically by the audience, many of whom would have had poor sight lines. It did not seem to matter. Many hundreds could not get in because they had no tickets so they just sat down outside the enormous tent and listened to the music. I was delighted and decided to make this a part of our regular provision. However I was reluctantly forced to come to terms that we could not afford to continue given the unit costs and the stricture on our accounts. Thus Ballet in the Park was a genuine artistic success defeated by central government cuts.

Within months of the Tory victory in the elections it became quite clear that local government was to be subjected to cuts of a proportion previously never experienced. I had been chairman of the Grand Theatre Board supported by a Tory Councillor, Ronnie Feldman, for whom I had great respect. He had good experience in the private sector and was invaluable in looking at the Grand Theatre and its related City of Varieties as businesses. I felt sure that some of the board members had not read the papers which required some concentration and knowledge. For some years Ronnie and I ran the two theatres profitably. An independent assessment established by the council showed that for more than ten consecutive years we had produced a surplus

94

on the Grand Theatre for every year of that period and that the deficit on the City Varieties had declined every year in both actual and real terms requiring thereby a reduced subsidy in both money and real terms. I still have a copy of the letter. I sent to Councillor Mudie, leader of the council who had written to ask if I thought we should buy the City Varieties, one of the very few remaining theatres of this kind in the country. I replied: "Yes, but it will always make a loss. It will however save a unique old theatre, just one of three remaining in the country." They were part of our cultural heritage. Charlie Chaplin had appeared on the stage as had many of the most famous old stars of the Music Hall. The theatre became known to the whole world by Barney Colehan of the BBC broadcasting old music hall shows with the audience dressed in period dress. It was a series that ran for 15 years and even decades later as up to the present day recordings of the shows are being broadcast.

When the Conservatives won the council elections I was not appointed to the board. Ronnie Feldman, a Tory, took over and immediately demonstrated the kind of action required. The Lounge, an historical cinema in Headingly had recently been recarpeted and new seating installed. Soon after the owners decided to sell it off to become a night club in the heart of student land. Ronnie, like the good businessman he was, went over to the Lounge, did a deal on the spot, buying enough brand new seats and brand new carpeting to fit out the Hyde Park at a price which could not have been more competitive. It was brilliant but largely unrecognised by his own clan. What a stupidity. I kept in touch by looking at their annual reports which had to give full details of the finances of the Grand, City Varieties and Hyde Park Picture House. In 2011 I wrote to the leader of the council, Cllr Wakefield, a letter of which I still have the copy, warning him that the Grand Theatre Board was going to accrue significant losses. I suggested the deficit looked like something in the region of £ 300,000.

In discussions with him I always argued that appointments should be made on ability not as some pleasant task or gift. The role carried responsibility. It was not a "perk". He did not respond. There was no change.

A year later I warned him of a possible deficit on the balance sheet of £ 600.000. Again no action was taken. On the third year I said the deficit could be about £ 900,000. I had not seen the detailed accounts nor had been privately briefed. What I did know from the published accounts accessed electronically the management had been increased sadly by some who had no experience in this field and who got rid of the manager of the City Varieties.

Again the leader did not deign to respond. I told him that if he wanted to get the Grand Theatre City Varieties and Hyde Park Cinema back to a sensible commercial level he should get people who know the business on the board and get rid of personnel whom we did not need in my or Feldman's time. Ronnie and I had a simple structure. Each manager of the three theatres was responsible directly to the board. In the new scheme these managers had to report to another manager who ironically had no experience of running a theatre, much less three. Board members were appointed, not because of their suitability but as a "goodie" or pleasant reward.

I find this so sad. The theatres are businesses and should be run on business lines. There are those on the council who have that ability. Some of the new councillors are bright women who could rapidly inject a business approach and standard of performance. The right to sit on a board like that of the Grand should not be treated as a bribe or to reward close friends or allies. I also regret that a close friend, the then leader of the council, did not respond to my warnings or proposals. There have been any number of other commercial firms willing to advise on the leisure provisions. These very well respected companies have the advantage of auditing a whole variety of companies and systems and so can bring a wealth of knowledge to their reports. However, having seen more than one of them I recognise that each more or less states the obvious or most accepted views. For instance, the very well respected firm of Robson Rhodes made a pitch "to undertake a high level review of management arrangements within the Leisure Department" which at that time had a nett expenditure of £ 29,719,000. The bidding document states how important it is to have "timely management information, how its plans fit in with those of the city council, effective protocols for decision making and management structure and operational requirements". A more serious over looker was the district audit. This was a very rigorous audit of council's aims, objectives and actions. The report consisted of a number of items such as key issues, financial health, legislative changes, management arrangements, value for money, etc. District audit was a very healthy annual experience, just a little bit fearsome, a reflection of the medieval General Eyre. They queried very properly my use of the Orchestra of Northern Ballet for the Kirkstall Event, given my connection with NBT. I explained that I wanted to use the Orchestra of Northern Ballet for this event for a variety of reasons. This was a very talented group of instrumentalists which toured as the Orchestra of Northern Ballet. Giving a concert like this would help them as musicians and also assist with meeting the cost of the orchestra. The district audit, to my relief, accepted and endorsed my decision.

New ideas

National politicians should not be allowed to travel abroad without a minder. Clearly more than one or two politicians, both Conservative and Labour, visited the USA and came back certain that the future lay in police commissioners and elected mayors. At all costs we must keep them away from Disneyland or who knows what barmy ideas might result. Vote for Donald Duck? Nonsense, you might say but one local authority elected a mayor who stood as, and was elected as, a monkey.

I find the idea of an elected mayor in a city like Leeds abhorrent. I have a passionate belief in the democratic system irrespective of its obvious disadvantages. The protagonists of the elected mayor base their belief on the wonder man concept. I do not think a wonder woman was in their thoughts though wonder woman sounds rather more attractive than wonder man. I do not subscribe to the fuhrer concept of government. To put all the powers of a large local authority into the hands of one person over more than three quarters of a million people in Leeds, seems so undemocratic that I was amazed some local authorities voted for elected mayors. Some who did appoint a mayor came to regret it as commissioners were sent in to run their authority because of the failings of an elected mayor and one authority did in fact elect that "monkey".

I was appalled at the thought of an elected mayor for Leeds and so I emailed all my Labour colleagues inviting them to a meeting to organise a NO campaign. Only seven people including two non-councillors turned up. We were very disappointed that more than sixty of our colleagues were not prepared to join in. I was delighted that Cllr Illingworth was one of the few to join our group and in effect run the campaign with or without our comrades' assistance. We decided to print 250,000 leaflets at a cost of £ 3500. We had originally hoped that the unions would contribute, some of them indicating that this was the case. The time came to pay for the printing and the promised help was not there. John Illingworth, an inexhaustible ward councillor colleague, and I decided to foot the bill. From this inauspicious beginning of just a handful of councillors we were delighted when some colleagues agreed to deliver the leaflets in their wards and the unions which had not helped with the finance at this stage, more than made up for this by delivering leaflets to all their members.

The ballot paper presented to voters was very tricky by deliberate design to achieve a yes result. It read: How would you like Leeds to be run?

> Option 1 By a leader who is an elected councillor chosen by the vote of the other elected councillors. This is how the council is run now.

> Option 2 Would you like to have the city run by a mayor who is elected by voters. This would be a change from how the council is run now.

All political parties on the council said they were opposed to the elected mayor system but only the Labour councillors actually participated in the campaign. The small group of labour activists led by Cllr Illingworth whose energy and enthusiasm were infectious, organised the campaign and ran it most effectively. We were heartened as the campaign developed its own momentum and volunteers appeared to help and deliver. Public meetings were held and TV finally showed up and broadcast a very lively debate. The final result showed that for every vote for the elected mayor, there were two votes against. The campaign was a great success, made even more sweet when John Illingworth and I, to our surprise and pleasure, received the £ 3,500 sum we had paid for the printing.

The leader of council, no matter how powerful, supported by genuine supporters, sycophants and those trying to ingratiate themselves, knows that in the end, the Party group can change the leadership in a trice. In Leeds we have seen the leadership of the Lib Dems change three times in quick succession.

What annoyed me considerably was the injunction from the Labour Party apparatchiks at HQ in London that "No Labour resources – either in cash or in kind, and including the national membership system and the national electoral database – may be used to campaign in any of these referendums". The advice went further by saying "Vote No in the referendum" should be avoided. Whose Party is this? I felt like responding. What do you know about politics if your experience has been just university and work experience with an MP?

It was a pleasure to ignore these instructions and remind them that we do not live in a 1984 Orwellian-controlled society. Our leaflet which won much acclaim for its effect, was the result of much suggestion, ingestion and finally, digestion by a former Labour MP Paul Truswell, I who in an earlier existence had been a reporter on the *Yorkshire Evening Post*. I see this victory as being of great importance in preserving an active democracy in Leeds. The elected mayor system will destroy local government as we know it as a pretty democratic system. Who is going to work hard to be a candidate of any Party if his or her role is to carry no power or responsibility? Who will be able to stand up to an elected mayor who can deploy all the powers of the council or answer the floods of constituent's complaints? How can people like Blair, Miliband and Cameron be so blind as to believe that the elected mayor is democratic? How had they the nerve to thrust it upon Labour councillors all over the country.

Leeds in my lifetime has cleared more than 50,000 slums, built its own reservoirs, sewerage system, and provided the best drinking water in the country, had its own police force which when it was wound up, was one of the best forces in the country, had a public transport system hundreds of times better than the current private system, brought to Leeds its own distinguished Opera Company, Opera North, Northern Ballet Company (NBT tours to more venues than the other three big companies do in total), the Playhouse, the third biggest producing theatre in the country, a major contemporary dance company, Phoenix Dance, a major National School of Contemporary Dance, a Ballet Academy and the biggest College of Music in the country to mention just a few items. I could have further mentioned the Royal Armouries coming to Leeds, the East Street Arts complex, a renovated Grand Theatre and City Varieties, one of the largest RDA establishments in the country or the new highly successful Arena and one of the three major world piano competitions and the world recognised Henry Moore Centre.

The list of these achievements by committee is endless. Committees were successful because they scrutinised decisions before they were made and each councillor over the years could become expert in some of the disciplines necessary to run big concerns like a city. They were accountable as every year at election time, one third retired by rotation and had to fight for re-election.

The matter of elected mayors in my view was outside Party politics. In my time on the council I have admired some of the Tory Leaders, people like Frank Marshall and Irwin Bellow, both later given a peerage. I admired too, a rank and file Liberal councillor, Councillor Baker, now forgotten, a woman who all the Parties feared for her trenchant support of issues she thought should be discussed and decisions changed.

My hope was that if Labour won the election they would abolish the position of crime commissioners which have proved to be so very costly, money which annually would have paid for several active police men and women.

The word democracy is of Greek origin. The Greeks also had a word which appeared to be an antonym, namely tyranny. We should cherish the former and oppose the latter. Tyranny may be something of a harsh word in discussion of UK laws and their administration.

Falls from Grace

I have been heavily involved in local government for many decades and feel genuinely honoured to have known so many good men and women, councillors and aldermen who have devoted their lives to serve others. It is local government which affects the everyday lives of the population of this country. In my view, the vast majority of members of local councils irrespective of Party affiliation, act honestly and in accordance with what seems to them to be right in any set of circumstances. In any year a council, like the Leeds City Council, will have made in one way or another hundreds of thousands of decisions, both large and small, all of which will have affected directly the lives of some if not all the electorate. From time to time for one reason or another the council makes mistakes or behaves illegally. These are exceptionally few when compared with the total number of decisions and actions properly and honestly made by the council. That is no reason for accepting them. The press, for all its failings, is the best weapon by far in revealing the wrongs and injustices and obtaining a degree of honesty in local and central government. The *Evening Post*, dated 15th January, tells a tale of much ado about something which some may see as trivial. The *Evening Post* was once part of a newspaper group called the Yorkshire Conservative Newspapers or some such. It has since ceased to be so owned in name though some critics still say they see the bias. A gun club called the Association of Leeds and District Rifle and Revolver Club had used, with permission, a site in Knostrop, a fairly remote site in South Leeds as a gun club for 27 years during which time there had been a use unblemished in any way. The club asked for permission to make some improvements as, though the site was called the Bisley of the North, it did not meet the new requirements for international competition.

The council officials told the club they would have to vacate the site within the month as it was needed "for special industry". The club contacted me and I investigated the circumstances and found that the council officers were about to lease the site to a private gun dealer and the club, if it wanted to use the site, would have to deal with him. I made a statement to the *Evening Post*, which operating as good journalism should, checked the facts and then published an outline of what they had found. The leader of the council, a Tory whom I have known and respected for decades despite being in the opposing political parties, publicly ordered an immediate stop to all negotiations until the matter had been properly and openly investigated.

This case exemplifies two local government principles. One is: if the council decides to do something the population might not like or which may be a little close to the edge in terms of legality, the public statement is always made by officers who are never named. However, when there has to be a statement showing something good like a change of policy or a stop to proceedings until proper discussions have taken place, the statement is always made by a member of the council. Officers take the blame if any. Councillors take the credit if any.

A more serious fall from grace as I see it, involves duplicity on the part of councillors of the three main Parties. Three miles from the city centre is a glorious swath of green land used by amateur football teams, as a place for resort when the sun shines, a site for local celebrations or parties and a large number of pedestrians who like to walk over this area. At the entrance to the vast area of green open space is a school building. It originally was built as a secondary school and in course of time became a school for Asian girls. Subsequently, the pupils were moved and the school left empty. A very detailed report was produced which stated that the building was sound but it needed substantial work done on the electrics and other facilities if it became a school again. There would be very great costs to meet a school's specification. The former school building rapidly became a major arts and community centre. It was heavily used by a number of orchestras including that of the Opera North, a number of choirs from the surrounding area, a number of charities mainly supporting people with learning or physical disabilities and a venue used by a number of local residents associations. It was used heavily six days in the week and less heavily on a Sunday. It had two very large gymnasia with the necessary showers and changing facilities. It was the building with the biggest foot fall of any public building in Leeds. It was the place I chose to house the Northern Ballet until we built a purpose-built Home. The company remained there for more than a decade and to ensure the correct heating was available for the dancers, much electrical work was done. The Conservatives won the local election and decided that the centre should close and the land given over for housing. To further this aim, their official documents stated that 150 homes would be possible. As Labour councillors for that area, my colleagues and I led a very successful campaign to save the school and the surrounding land. I received a letter from the Labour leader of the City Council who had been the leader of the council before the local elections. In his letter he expressed his support for the campaign to retain the site for its present purposes. The Conservatives secretly got a QCs legal opinion that the restrictive covenants which would have stopped the proposed developments would most probably be unenforceable. The land on which the school was situated had been bought at a nominal figure on the basis that the land would be used solely for educational purposes. The Tories whilst they were in power wanted to get a substantial sum if they could sell the land for housing.

When Northern Ballet had built a new Dance House they moved out. The fight to retain the building for its social purposes was on. There were a number of large public meetings and much heat but little light generated.

What really affected me was that the Labour Party had gained control of the city and I looked forward to the issue being settled once and for all. Sadly, that was not to be the case. The council started to run down the centre on the grounds that it was not economic to keep it there for its current uses. I and my colleague,

Illingworth, ran a major campaign to save the school building which was so heavily used. Many Labour colleagues had joined us to prevent the Tories from closing the building down but now they were being accused of double dealings as they had to support the Labour decision to close it to save money. I hate double dealing. I continued to fight to save the centre as I knew just how much it contributed to the lives of so many people including a very substantial number of people with learning disabilities. It was by far the most active and well-used arts centre in the city and possibly the UK. I was challenged by the senior members of the Labour administration who pointed out how much it would cost to refurbish the building. I was supported by a host of the users and the two local community organisations which served the area. I became worried as I saw attitudes hardening so that the matter became a contest between myself as the leader of the fight to retain the centre and my senior Labour colleague who was keen to win the battle to close it. I certainly felt I had the better moral, legal and social arguments and above them the simple common sense of retaining this very successful venture. I was beaten by a subterfuge which I had always recognised as a possibility. One Saturday morning, council officials entered the centre in numbers and told everyone to get out as the place was extremely dangerous. Naturally the centre was evacuated and all the instruments and property of the organisations were left inside. The dispossessed were told that the danger to people inside the building was immediate and so dangerous they could not be allowed to go in and collect items which they needed. The lie to this was shown the next day, a Sunday, when thirty or more people arrived for a day's religious and ethnic convention in accordance with their formal booking. They were admitted and stayed for a full day and I understand part of the next.

I, like everyone else, smelled a rat. We had no proof of duplicity until a former user of the centre came forward a few days later with a sworn document that a named council official had boasted to her that he was the one who had closed the centre, by going to his superior and the Labour member responsible for council buildings claiming that there was immediate danger and that he had produced a document which showed how his decision to recommend immediate closure was essential. I later demanded to see this document. It showed no danger greater than the one which in theory had been present for the last decade. There was nothing new to precipitate closure. It was a ploy to avoid the long arguments had the council decided to announce the closure of the building. It was a fait accompli. The lady who revealed all this said she would swear on oath the truth of her allegations and produce witnesses present when the official made his boast. She also promised to keep her oath hidden to ensure it could be produced at the inquiry which she believed would happen. It never did.

The many users had to find alternative bases and had to wait until they were allowed to enter the centre to collect their equipment, despite the alleged immediate danger. For instance, a lovely group of ladies produced a "newspaper for the blind". They did this voluntarily and had used the centre as their base. It took me some time to find another base for them. Other users were not so lucky and there was an outcry of anger and dismay when a council spokesman averred that each and every one of the disturbed groups had been satisfactorily housed elsewhere. This was a lie. Some had been properly housed. The majority either did not receive any alternative space at all or were given quite unsuitable alternatives. I believed this to be an action which showed a large measure of dishonesty. There was no support from my colleagues who, when the Tories were in charge, publicly opposed their plans to close the centre. The alleged dangers were not dangers at all. They were not new and took no account of the major rewiring which had been effected by NBT at its considerable cost. The estimated cost of making good the defects outlined in a report produced many years earlier had been based on the standard needed for a school. These costs were high and would be unsupportable. The centre did not need that level of change. The main hall, the second biggest in Leeds, had been rewired and passed inspection for public use. It was in excellent condition and was used regularly by the Orchestra of Opera North and a large number of other orchestras and choirs every night of the week. The many offices were in good condition and met fire requirements. The reason for this calamitous decision to forcibly close the school building was because the Tories had secretly obtained the legal opinion that the restrictive covenant was possibly unenforceable and they had even published a notice asking for bids from the private sector for nearly two hundred houses on the site. The leader of the Tories denied this until I was able to produce the documents showing this offer. The Labour council, of which I am proud to have been a member, wasted no time in pulling down the building at very considerable expense. The councillor responsible for this stupidity and dishonesty should have been forced to admit the dishonesty of the closure. Scrutiny is supposed to provide the mechanism by which high standards can be enforced. In this kind of case, scrutiny in Leeds is a farce.

Like many or most I hate unfair treatment of those unable to prevent it. For thirteen years I had chaired the Board of the Grand Theatre, which was responsible for the management of the Grand, the Hyde Park Cinema and later the City Varieties. We were fortunate to find a man, Peter Sandeman, capable of running the Varieties theatre and of making great savings by setting up a friend's body of volunteers who staffed the theatre voluntarily, so saving a lot of money. The Unions, which quite reasonably oppose such volunteers taking away the jobs of paid staff, realised that this was something we needed to do to save the theatre. The Grand, the City Varieties and the Hyde Park Cinema were run as separate organisations. In Peter we had a splendid manager who, year on year, decreased the subsidy needed to run the Varieties in both actual and money terms. He was highly efficient and an excellent link with the public. I know of no one who worked harder and with less support than Peter, who used his connections to undertake maintenance of the theatre. For years he acted as manager and I consider him one of the most effective, reasonable and likeable public servants I have known. He genuinely devoted himself to the theatre, working regularly excessive hours. He was an excellent manager and we had few problems at board meetings because of his skill and application.

When the Tory Lib Dem coalition ousted Labour, I was ousted too. The coalition put on the board running the Grand, Varieties and Hyde Park Cinema, a group of individuals, the members of which had no experience in running such venues. They even excluded a Tory councillor who had been a very competent member of the board and who had been and would have been an excellent chairman. The results of these changes led to the board ending up with a cumulative debt of nearly one million pounds after three years. They also appointed three new officers to run the three venues and in so doing decided not to reappoint Peter. I consider this one of the worst and most unjustified actions. I felt the injustice even more when, after the restoration of the Varieties was completed, the Queen made a visit to Leeds, including a visit to the refurbished theatre. It made me feel physically sick to see the Queen being introduced to the people who were running the affairs of the theatre so badly and the one man who should have been introduced to the Queen was not to be seen. He is probably the person most responsible for the continued existence of the City Varieties, who had been instrumental and fully involved in its restoration of this beautiful theatre and who was treated abominably by those who should never have been given the task of running the three venues. Ironically, the council officer who was appointed as the senior officer to the board was an individual who many years previously had fallen from grace for some reason I do not remember, and who was facing redundancy. I rescued him by giving him a post in Leisure Services where he was invaluable. Pity he did not remember those days when he got rid of Peter Sandeman, or perhaps he did try and was overruled. I hate injustice and I hate it even more when I or others are unable to remedy that injustice. My anger remains unabated but ironically Peter shows no evidence of hurt or desire for revenge. A nobility I do not possess.

Water safety

A youth drowned in Roundhay Park lake in Leeds causing an immediate but unreasonable concern about water safety. Some members of the public advocated railings round the Roundhay Park lakes and also the rivers where, from time to time, tragedies emerge. This hysteria was fed by officers advising that if safety fencing was not put up in the Otley Park through which the river flows, they could be found guilty of manslaughter if someone drowned. I was very familiar with this area and the river as for many years when a boy, my friends and I cycled over in the summer months to swim in the river in Otley. Instead of laughing off such fear, the Conservative councillors then in charge agreed to a substantial length of fencing being installed alongside the river banks in the Wharfe Meadows Park. There was very substantial opposition to this desecration of the beauty of the park and a local cause celebre emerged – save Wharfe Meadows.

Inevitably, political bodies assembled like flies on a dead rabbit to extract maximum benefit from the dispute. The Lib Dem MP suddenly appeared from the dim recesses of parliament and declared himself the protector of all that was good in Otley, especially the pubs of which there are many – very delightful hostelries – and of course, the park. The Conservatives attacked the Lib Dems for being unwilling to face the reality that real danger existed to the innocent public and the Labour echelons enjoyed much satisfaction at the incomprehensible decisions of the Conservative Group which had replaced Labour as the major Party and was then controlling the council.

There was some understandable reason for the Tory view because they had received legal advice based on a recent case in the Court of Appeal and a substantial letter from ROSPA – an organisation which tries to prevent accidents. They had, per incuriam, not realised that the Court of Appeal decision had been reviewed by the Lords and as a result, the law was quite different. The judges in this Supreme Court gave their decisions which are a pleasure to read, which is rarely the case in such judgements. They are a model of the most senior judges exercising simple common sense which removed any imperative to set up the disputed fencing.

The veritable storm in a teacup did produce one major and most serious incident. The lawyer of the council dealing with this case denied that counsel's opinion had ever been sought by the Tories and no such opinion had been received. He was pursued on this and the evening before the Scrutiny Committee he suddenly remembered that he had written to a QC for an opinion and that an opinion had been received. In fact, two such opinions had been sought and two received. It was clear he had lied and he later admitted that he had lied right up to the moment he would have been found to be lying. Yet to those who knew the lawyer in question, he was an honest and decent individual and one on whom one would have relied. What explanation could there be? The only one I can conceive of, and no one has suggested any other explanation, is that he was extremely worried given the terrier-like behaviour of his political masters who he knew would not want the existence and content of the opinions to be known as they would show them as councillors to be silly. I am sure it was the fear for his job which forced him to lie. Rather than feeling like treating this dishonesty as a crime deserving the death sentence, I felt genuinely sorry for a decent individual operating under unfair pressure. In an e mail dated 05.07.05, he says: "I did say to Cllr Hanley that I could not recall off the top of my head whether I had arranged counsel's attendance at the conference with leading members and senior officers informally or on the telephone and verbally instructed him on what advice was needed or by way of written instructions as these were unusual circumstances." I regret that any officer should be put under such extreme pressure, direct or indirect to prevaricate, or obfuscate or otherwise act unprofessionally. Of course it is easy to say he should have resisted the pressure. It is more difficult if you are the object of such pressure. Every councillor should use every effort to see advice and professional opinion is treated as they would like their information or experience treated.

The council's senior officer is recorded as verifying the story as I have told it. The whole sorry story may seem to be a storm in a tea cup but that is to ignore the lesson it teaches, namely the danger councils encounter when the objectivity of the officer cadre is corrupted by political influence or worse, silent unsaid threats.

Commonwealth Games

Leeds made a bid for the Commonwealth Games. Leeds had a good case as the home of Yorkshire County Cricket and Headingley, a world famous ground for Test Matches known throughout the Commonwealth countries, Leeds United, which was then an extremely well-known club throughout the football world, one of the two 50 metre pools with full diving platforms in the UK at that time, a major TV company, Yorkshire Television which made a splendid programme in support of the Leeds bid, a BBC centre in the city, two rugby teams, union and league, Carnegie College which trained a vast number of individuals all over the world who had become major sport officials in many countries, and the third largest city in the UK after London and Birmingham. It also had a number of theatres, was building a reputation as a city to which people came for entertainment of all kinds —opera, ballet and pop. In the end, the decision was to be either Leeds or Edmonton.

We had costed the scheme, had plans ready to put into effect in a way that would exceed the standards previously experienced and were determined to give Leeds a world-wide reputation. We produced a certified copy of the relevant costs of travel to Leeds compared with Edmonton. We were convinced that we would achieve the explicit aims of the Games, namely the fostering of bonds of friendship between our several countries, nearly all of which had citizens in Leeds. Moreover, Canada was to stage the Olympic Games in Montreal in 1976. Thus, if Edmonton was selected, the two major sporting events in the world would be in the same country – Canada.

Leeds sent out two small groups of individuals, one to the Caribbean countries and one to Africa. I was appointed to visit all Commonwealth African countries accompanied by the Town Clerk, Mr Ken Potts, who now would be called Chief Executive. This proved to be an exhausting but exciting experience.

The itinerary was departing 23rd June 1972 for Valetta, Kampala, Nairobi, Dar es Salaam, Lusaka, Blantyre, Johannesburg, Swaziland, Lesotho, Lagos, Accra, Freetown, Bathurst, Las Palmas, Gibraltar and return to the UK on 14th July.

Wherever we went we were treated very warmly and I remember with satisfaction but surprise how many of those I met at our presentations had been trained at Carnegie College here in Leeds. One experience I remember very clearly occurred in Kampala, Uganda which had earned the unofficial title of Pearl of Africa because of its climate and growth – a wonderful place to live. I presume this title had been given by white colonists who enjoyed the pleasures of the climate and the locals who served them in the proper colonial manner. Outside the cities it was Africa as it had been for centuries – people living in small villages in the bush in huts with hard soil floors, thatched roofs and living a simple life as had their predecessors. One early evening on the first day of our two day stop Ken Potts and I were in the hotel swimming pool. There was in the pool a number of black Africans. Quite suddenly there appeared a handful of soldiers with guns and a large, very impressive looking black man in charge. The soldiers told everyone to get out of the pool. The very imposing black man, however, told Potts and myself to stay. It came more as an order rather than an invitation. We stayed. Later he engaged us briefly in conversation discussing our mission in a very intelligent manner. Later than evening I learned that he was called Colonel Amin. He later, of course, became the dictator of Uganda and turned the Pearl of Africa into a country which saw some of the world's most hideous and cruel atrocities. Some years later visiting Uganda on behalf of the Save the Children's Fund, I saw the evidence of these atrocities – villages with very few men and each with its own pile of human bones.

Kinshasa

We had a disturbing experience when our flight stopped at Kinshasa in the Congo. This was just a routine stop for the airline. We, however, were taken from the plane by an armed group and marched to an office where we were interrogated about our journey and the reasons for it. The long interview/interrogation during which we were kept standing, bristled with animosity but we were finally released and allowed to return to the plane where our luggage was removed from the plane and inspected very thoroughly and very roughly. The Congo is and was a sad and dangerous place, the result of a barbaric colonial history.

Another memorable event was crossing the Drakensberg Mountains to visit two tiny members of the Commonwealth: Lesotho and Swaziland. The plane was a little four seater and the first pusher plane I had flown in. This is a plane with the propeller at the rear to push an aeroplane forward rather than the conventional prop at the front of the aircraft to pull the craft forward. It does have the advantage of giving excellent forward vision which on this visit was spectacular. In these two tiny kingdoms we were treated "right royally". It was ironic that these two tiny specs on the globe, living in what we might in our hubris call backward, had the same vote as any other Commonwealth country which I totally applaud.

We gave the same presentation to these as we gave to all the Commonwealth countries though we had to improvise to show the film. The film was a splendid promotional film, most expertly produced to sell Leeds as the place to hold the Commonwealth Games. It had been produced by Yorkshire Television, gratis, partly I suppose because it would benefit commercially if the Games were in Leeds, but also because I and some of my colleagues had made good personal relationships with the senior executives who were keen for the right reasons to support the bid. YTV was a genuine Yorkshire company deeply embedded in the area. I am sad that it no longer exists as such.

I have tried to find a copy of the film which we took round Africa but without success. It would have been an invaluable "document" for the archives and for a new generation to watch. The presentation followed a set course. First words of thanks for the invitation to make our bid to them, a showing of the film which always, without exception, was most warmly received, followed by a short presentation from me and Ken Potts and then questions and answers for so long as the invited audience required. I remember Ken saying to me that the responses had been so warm that it looked most positive. I felt less certain knowing that the winner in the race would in the end be determined by what each delegation saw as its best return and in some cases personal benefit. Sad to be so cynical at such a young age.

The pilgrimage provided me with yet another marvellous experience. On arriving at the airport, Freetown, we were told that the flight was overbooked and we would have to take another plane in two days' time. This was crisis time. I managed to speak to the pilot of the plane on which we had our confirmed flight's booking, explained what we were doing, that at our next stop there would be a reception committee waiting and an assembled group of ministers, sport directors, et al. Not turning up on time was not possible to conceive. I felt like Clarence Darrow pleading for the life of a prisoner. Whatever clicked he said I could fly in the "cockpit" so long as I remained strapped in on the third seat but I could not bring anything heavy with me as luggage, such as our electrical equipment and heavy luggage, as the aircraft was nearing its maximum payload. Thus I achieved an ambition I thought would be impossible, namely flying in the cockpit of a commercial airliner. I said goodbye or rather more hopefully, au revoir, to Potts and left him to his own devices. The flight was a joy, seeing how things in a modern jet worked and seeing the calm and understated conversation between the pilot and his co-pilot. They were interested in what I was doing and I was interested in what they were doing. In those days pilots flew the planes a lot more than they apparently do nowadays when so much is undertaken by computers and programmes. I was fascinated by the approach and landing which is the most dangerous part of any flight, not that I had the remotest worry or had any cause to worry. Landing this quite enormous machine so smoothly looked so easy and done almost as a matter of course. Such self-confidence can only come from intense training and experience.

The kindness of the pilot, which is something I am sure could not happen today, enabled me to make my meeting on time, explain in detail the travails of travel and the absence of our film, etc., to gain their sympathy and made a decent pitch though I had no film and no audio or tapes and leaflets. The event was a success as I believe those who attended in such numbers felt I had been dogged by bad luck in their territory. They were very sympathetic and surprised by the way I had wangled the flight.

Gibraltar

There is one other memory which recurs from time to time. Ken Potts and I had a few hours to spare in Gibraltar. The hotel we were staying in had a large pool which attracted in the almost perpetual sun, a large crowd of sunbathers. My luggage had been lost so I had no swimming shorts. Ken Potts let me borrow his. I am fairly skinny and he was certainly rotund but his shorts seemed to accommodate this difference. I dived in and immediately lost my shorts, leaving me as I had heard it said "bollock naked." It was a moment before I could turn and retrieve them during which couple of seconds a hound shot into the water and paddled at speed to the other end of the pool with my/ Ken's shorts. This little vignette attracted the rapt attention of the sun worshippers, most of whom seemed to be British and were amused to hear the loudspeaker's message that there was a naked man swimming in the pool. The dog was adept at evasion but could not get out of the pool. I finally caught it and donned the shorts with some relief to a minor cheer from the sizeable audience which had come to see a naked man in pursuit of a dog with his shorts as part of their entertainment. Up to that moment I thought blushing was reserved for the face.

Sadly our efforts failed and Edmonton won by a large majority of the votes. I thought, quite objectively, that our case was by far the best. Had I not thought that I would not have felt so dispirited. I was frankly appalled at some of the things I saw and heard. Edmonton met every request from the delegates, some of a very dubious nature. We simply had not come with the resources to match their massive generosity nor I feel would we have wished to. I am not sure even if those countries with a strong UK connection voted for Leeds.

Many international sports officials will say that whether it is Olympics, Commonwealth Games, motor racing, tennis, et al, generous hospitality and promises to delegates is the norm. Not bribery but strong inducements. My experience since then as a member of parties looking at and evaluating international events and their venues tells me that is the case but feel with a sense of national righteousness that London secured the Olympic and Paralympic Games in a manner that can only be classed as honourable and effective.

Cases

As a councillor for an inner city area one gets a host of cases. People ring up, write or call on you with their problems, some of which are trivial and some which are life threatening. The majority are housing cases, that is people wanting to get a council house, or have it repaired, or deal with noise of their neighbours, payment of rent, et al. These are relatively easy to deal with but others are very different and time and energy consuming.

These others occur less frequently but are far more serious. For example, In 2002 I had to deal with a young asylum seeker case. The issue was: at the age of 16 should he still go into a care home or a foster home or should he be treated like an adult and get help in say, supported lodgings. If he or she is mentally handicapped (sic) the Social Services Department would meet this need which could mean a very expensive placing in a specialist foster home. In 2002 there was a problem re asylum seekers and a very creditable modus operandi was established by the efforts of many, including we councillors. In this case, the lad of 16 was found a place to live and received much support from Social Services. This was expensive and had to be met from the whole budget which meant others did not get the required level of help or in some cases none at all.

Also in 2002 I received a call from a man who required some help. He was a man who was continuously ill, had difficulty in walking but who retained a good spirit which I greatly admired. He complained of an inconsistency of service, lack of communication, no regular home care assistant and insufficient contact details. He was a super chap and deserved all the help to which he was entitled. I was pleased to help him but it did take me several visits to his home which is time consuming. Another kind of situation is exemplified by a case I dealt with in 2004. A girl had attended a special school for people with learning disabilities. On reaching her 19th birthday she was no longer able to stay in the school. Her major problem was what is euphemistically called challenging behaviour, a term covering very often violent and fierce behaviour of some poor soul who is not responsible for his or her outbursts. A placement was found which could accommodate her needs. The problem was there was an annual cost of £ 192,000. One of our budget problems was the expenditure of millions of pounds a year in such placements. Hitler had a solution to this kind of problem, euthanasia, which solves the financial problem, but please God it will never be introduced here.

In 2001 I was an "old friend" to a woman who had served for many years in the army and brought with it the mores of that experience. She had a robust vivacity, irreverence and fine sense of humour although it could be described as coarse if one was so minded. I liked and respected her and in her final months when she was so ill, I visited her regularly to cheer her up and to engage in some banter which she loved. I became suspicious that her relatives were stealing from her, not merely little artefacts but money she had secreted for safety. I told the Social Services which knew her well and whose assistants visited her twice a day, seven days per week, since her decline and also informed the police. Special arrangements were made for the collection of her pensions which prevented this happening. The old girl died. I was so sorry but so relieved. I do wish we had been able to convict the thieves.

In another case in which I was involved, a 92-year-old man was detained under Section 3 of the Mental Health Act in the High Royds Hospital which some of the less cultured community called "The Loony Bin". His family approached me for help and I was able to set in motion the procedure which allowed him to go into a special residential home which was adapted for this purpose. He served out the rest of his life in calm and serenity. How I admire those who deal with these patients who demand an infinite patience and a deeply caring nature.

In another case a parent taking the fostered child to the public swimming pool had to pay the normal adult charge. I was approached to ask for help and was able to get the appropriate changes made. Simple solution to a minor problem which to the individual concerned is important.

It is impossible to ignore letters like the one I received in 2001 when I was Lord Mayor of Leeds. It was handwritten in a large hand, four or five words per line.

"Dear Sir, Lord Mayor, Madam,

I am writing to you to complain how the authorities are unfairly treating me. I suffer from a bipolar life-long condition which makes me very ill. My mother is from Malta. I belong somewhere in the Med. I am getting terrorised where I live bullied. I have lived in Cxxxxxxxx all my life. Please can you do your best to help and get me out of this horrible dirty unpleasant hospital and environment. I do a lot of singing and dancing in the Majestic in Leeds I have already informed Sir Jimmy Salvile (sic). This letter has been written in desperation you are my only last hope."

I could do no more than check for any irregularities in his treatment but there were none. Often visiting people in such circumstances can be harmful for I found that by merely visiting prisoners, patients, sectioned individuals or detainees, I raised in them hopes of help when it was irrational to have that hope.

Menston Mental Hospital

For some time I was chairman of the Governors of Menston, a very large hospital for the mentally ill. As such I had to hear any appeal by a resident wishing to gain release. I heard these requests from time to time and one I remember with particular sadness. A young woman was being detained against her will. By a strange coincidence I knew the woman by sight and suggested that someone else should hear her appeal. She insisted I should do it as the rules laid down. She put her own case before me and I felt a deep sadness that this lovely young woman was detained against her will. I gave her as much time as she required to make her case and told her we would make a decision when we had discussed her case in camera. My two colleagues and I discussed what we had heard and reviewed the medical opinion which had been given during the hearing. She was a librarian by profession, was very coherent so one could assume her mental illness had disappeared. However, the medical view was that she should be retained at least for three days to see if she had been restored to a natural balance. I then had to reconvene our hearing and tell the woman we had agreed to re-view her case in the next three days and until then we hoped she would make a full recovery. She was distraught and I felt much the same. She was released two days later.

A typical Social Services case: I was contacted by Mr HXXX, someone I had known for a long time and had come to respect him greatly because of his determination to make life better for those with a mental handicap as the term then was. I wrote to Mr Brosnan of the Adaptations Agency: "HXXX, as you know, is now a very old man. He has a very old and infirm wife who needs extensive care and an adult daughter who is severely mentally handicapped, who visits and stays for periods of time with

122

her parents. Mr HXXX has made a will leaving the very substantial house in North Park Road to the council, for use by Social Services to house people with a mental handicap. He paid a figure just under £ 6,000 to have adaptations done so that he, his wife and daughter could have a shower room. He tells me he never saw a detailed specification for the work proposed for this figure. I would be grateful if you could send me a copy of the specification in question. Mr HXXX also tells me that there had been a retention figure which I assume to have been 10%, the disposition of which has not been explained. His experience with the contractors was very unsatisfactory and indeed you offered in your letter of 4th January your sincere apology for the inconvenience and poor standard of customer care given to you by the contractor. Mr HXXX's continuing concerns are a detailed matter of decoration and a much more serious comment on the outstanding issues, particularly in reference to the electrical installation. I realise these matters are for the contractors to deal with but as I understand it, the agency "project managed" this work. Irrespective of such issues, I feel it the council's obligation to look after people with special needs who are not capable of pursuing remedies on their own, particularly when they have paid a substantial sum to have a good job done." I am happy to say that after I used extreme pressure, the work was done to complete the alterations to the house which many years later was given to the council.

These are a representative example of some of the cases involving just one area of concern. The most common matters are housing and repairs. Thereafter would come issues relating to sport and recreation and street cleaning including bins. Noisy neighbours can be a real problem, especially in areas colonised by students and avaricious landlords. The number of letters and phone calls vary from ward to ward. Councillors in the so-called poorer areas of Leeds will receive many times the number of their colleagues in the greener parts of Leeds and the councillors for the very wealthy areas receive few if any, other than concerns about the environment and planning matters.

One of life's great privileges as a member of council is to be in a position to affect or effect change or support new initiatives. In 1998 I received a letter from Professor Holdcroft of Leeds University canvassing my support for a proposal to establish a new Textile Museum. Leeds has for very many years been a centre of the textile industry and the university's department was recognised internationally by those in the textile world. The proposal was to use the chapel on the former Grammar School site adjoining the university campus.

In January 1999 in a meeting with Professor Holdcroft, Dr Hann and Keith Burnley, who was a former colleague on the council, I promised to support their application for a lottery grant, to include the proposal in the City's Arts strategy and in the museum trail and that I would send a letter of support to Dr Hann. I also made a strong case for a lottery grant for £ 600,000 which I was told was very important to the final success of their application. In a relatively short time the Museum of Textiles was open. I personally find it very difficult to generate any enthusiasm for textiles but that is irrelevant as each one of us has different likes and dislikes. I was, however, enormously impressed by the museum when it opened and I found myself absorbed in the information relating to the objects on display. I attend the exhibitions when they occur. I always have been very generously treated by the academics who run the museum, a bonhomie enhanced so often with a glass of wine. I am happy to have played a part in its establishment even though such support was of a minimalist kind.

Another example of the ability to assist came from a splendid gentleman called Liddle. He had developed an outstanding collection of articles relating to the First Word War. I visited his museum which covered almost one floor of a building in the city centre and I was strangely moved when I was allowed to handle one of the gauntlets and goggles worn by a First World War Ace: Albert Ball, VC. When I was a child and when my fellow playmates and I were not killing Zulus or Red Indians we were buzzing around, arms outstretched like wings, shooting down German air planes and I claimed to be Albert Ball, VC. Others bagged i.e. adopted the names of other First World War aces like Mannock and McCudden. They quite outranked Biggles. The great contribution museums make is that sense of wonder or disbelief which artefacts arouse. I became a strong supporter of Peter Liddle, a well-respected academic and did my best to find him help, support and premises. I was later delighted to learn that his collections had been housed in the Brotherton Collection in Leeds University, a distinguished collection on whose board I had served for a number of years.

Thackray Museum

On the site of the current St James Hospital which is now internationally known as a major Centre of Excellence was a workhouse for the poor established in 1861. The last pauper was admitted in 1941. Soon thereafter it became a hospital building and served as such until it became clear it was not suitable as a hospital. The building was listed and so could not be pulled down. I was contacted by the grandson of a man who had started in Leeds a small business as a chemist shop. The business thrived and the Thackrays became a major supplier of medicines, medical instruments and later, devices like artificial joints. Paul, the grandson, contacted me to see if I would support his developing a museum on the site. I was keen to help but was not able to conjure up a large scale grant to start the process. I was able, however, to support his ambitions and to assist in the first small step in getting permission for the building to be used for a small exhibition. He and I knew if we got something started the possibility of creating a major museum was possible. This required money and this was something Paul could supply. We finally received permission to set up a museum which was at first, pretty tenuous but increased over the years until it became what it is now − a magical showcase. The development of medicine is shown with absolute veracity, sores and all, and is told alongside the development of this quite fine building as a museum of the social conditions in which the medical profession operated over the years. It is a splendid exhibition of medical progress alongside the social history of the poor. This very clever development makes the museum a splendid place to take children and young adults. It has also a strong emotional effect on adults as they mentally contrast then with now. I am delighted I was able to assist in the creation of an outstanding museum and feel we all owe a great vote of thanks to the Thackrays, past and present. I also smile inwardly when I contrast some of my council and other friends' original opposition or dismissal of the museum concept as unrealistic and how quickly they wish now to be associated with its success.

Wheelhouse dogs' home

Another case gave me great pleasure. I received a letter dated January 2004 from a woman I did not know who asked me to intervene to help a man who wished to set up a sanctuary for stray dogs in East Ardsley, a southern suburb of the city.

She assured me that the planning department was not acting fairly in this case and was biased against Brian Wheelhouse and his application. He had become well known in the Leeds area as he captured and cured a stray dog which for several weeks had established its den under a large pine tree in the courtyard of the Civic Hall. The dog's den in this august place captured the public's imagination and soon numbers of people took it food and so I imagine it became the best fed animal in the city. It was given the nickname Civic, was very shy and would not allow a human near it. Mr Wheelhouse, an expert with dogs, was called in and he captured the dog and within a few weeks the dog responded favourably to humans as well as other dogs. It is a happy ending story which the press, public and TV loved.

Mr Wheelhouse was attempting to build a sanctuary for stray dogs and his principles were clear. He would not permit killing any dog unless its health so demanded. Dogs were to be restored to physical and mental health. His attempts to get planning permission for his sanctuary were unsuccessful. A letter informing him of his failed application, dated 7th August 2002, said the application was for a development in the green belt and contrary to policies N33 and GB1 contained in the Leeds Unitary Development Plan and Government Guidance contained in PPGZ "green belts". Harm would be caused to the character of and openness of the green belt and to the purposes of including the land in it. The green belt in this location seeks to safeguard the countryside from encroachment. There were no special circumstances to justify making an exception to the general presumption against inappropriate development in the green belt. The letter continued, quoting further authorities to the extent that I felt I would come across a reference to the Treaty of Versailles.

The planning department's hostility to the man is revealed to some extent by the documents I have in my possession. For instance, in a heading "Unauthorised change of use at Green Acre Farm", the planners advised that he must cease to use the farm as a refuge, remove eight metal mesh kennels from the site and remove eight vehicles from the wooden barn. Another letter dated 13th October 2004, reported complaints about noise from the centre and stating that legal proceedings would follow with a penalty fine of £ 20,000 on conviction. In all, he received four such communications from the planning department which smacked to me of gross prejudice. I decided to call on Wheelhouse and found him to be a most impressive, quiet and determined individual. He had sold his business of buying and selling cars and had sold his house and put all his resources into buying this house and a couple or so adjacent fields to create a dog sanctuary. I received a letter from a lady who had attended a planning subcommittee meeting on 6th January 2005 in which she reported that one councillor said he would take no part in the proceedings as he knew Wheelhouse and had had a serious dispute with him but did not leave the meeting. The three minutes allowed to Wheelhouse to speak was taken up by questions by hostile councillors. The councillor who said he would take no part in the decision voted.

I visited the site on 30th December 2004, walked to the homes of the objectors and found it impossible to hear any sound of dog barking which was a major complaint by those hostile to Wheelhouse. I could hear very clearly the noise from the close adjacent motorway. The more I learned, the more angry I became at the planning department's staff involved. Wheelhouse had been told he needed planning permission to repair a barn which had been damaged by fire. This was not so. I wrote to a senior member of the planning department and referred to the committee's previous decision to reject Wheelhouses' previous application on grounds that the site was within the green belt and permission would "cause harm to the character of the green belt, the aim in this location being to safeguard the countryside from encroachment." I said that I had just visited the site where open cast mining was taking place, a road was being built to enable a hundred house development to take place and noise from the motorway was irreconcilable with a quiet countryside. I have always had a great respect for the planning department. The obviously dishonest reasoning for opposing Wheelhouse was foreign to the planning department I had so respected. I became resolutely determined to see Wheelhouse successful. There was only a handful of houses in the lane serving the sanctuary and I believe that for some reason the occupants had an animus against Wheelhouse. Their grounds for opposing the application were frankly nonsense. I had not expected the support I got once my interest in helping Wheelhouse was known. I received pile after pile of letters supporting my fight for justice as someone in the *Evening Post* called it. A petition was started called Save Whitehall Rescue and it received more than 450 signatures. At least another 75 or 80 letters were sent to the planning department or to me. In the end, planning permission was given, the objections shown to be spurious and the centre is now a large and effective organisation still powered by the remarkable Wheelhouse. He stuck to his guns, met the local hostility with calm acceptance and produced a centre that every dog lover would support. One oddity I remember. Whenever I visited I never saw one dog attack another in a group of 25 or more running free in the compound together. I have not been in touch with him since I left the council but I did receive each Christmas a gift which was a bottle of whisky. I enjoyed the consumption of the present but enjoyed more remembering being able to assist a man of outstanding character and resilience. I wish it were possible to clone Wheelhouse to espouse campaigns to assist the elderly, the infirm, a sensible housing policy, or public transport. He shows that members of the electorate can make a difference and can overcome seemingly impossible barriers. His current mission is to help only those dogs which face death unless he acts. Thank God for people of his ilk.

Medieval Conference

Very similarly I helped in a very modest way what was and is reputedly the biggest meeting in Europe of its kind, namely the Meeting of Medieval History in Leeds. I was approached many years ago to help a young man whom I found most impressive. He and his team organised annually a conference on medieval matters here in Leeds. It was good for Leeds by attracting folk into the city which is part of our economic programme. Over the years the meeting has grown to its now enormous size. The City Council should have embraced this phenomenon but seemed ignorant of its importance or existence. I suggested that an annual welcome by the Lord Mayor should be afforded the delegates who would enjoy seeing the inside of the Civic Hall. The meeting attracted foreign visitors in their hundreds making it the biggest in the country after the political parties' annual conferences. Of particular interest to the visitors was Kirkstall Abbey and its surrounding medieval farms and outposts. I was able to involve the city for a time but I have had no contact with the organisers since I left the council.

Another example of the ways in which a councillor can be of help is the Centre for Indian Music and Dance in Leeds. Leeds has a large Indian population and I fully supported this concept. A business development plan was produced in January 1997 and a grant of £ 6500 was promised from Leeds City Council. This was a figure which would be the basis or trigger for a host of other grants. Later, after the council had information re our annual government grants and their slashing cuts, the chief officer of Cultural Services reduced this grant to a mere £ 1000. This led to a rather tart letter from David Hoult, principal of the Leeds College of Music. He was someone I liked and respected. He pointed out that this reduction could cause Leeds to lose £ 100,000 of grants and end our chance of establishing the proposed centre. A number of letters were exchanged with some urgency as I was due to fly off to Japan for a meeting and so time was of the essence. I decided to readjust our Leisure Services budgets across the board which enabled me to instruct that a grant of £ 7500 be made which would ensure a number of other grants would be possible. David Hoult wrote me a warm letter of thanks. I also made available an office in the Dance Centre of which I was chairman and which is immediately opposite the college. Concerns disappeared and all was sweetness and light.

These are just examples of the capacity of any of my colleagues on the council to assist desirable developments. I have the greatest respect for my past and present fellow Labour councillors who have contributed enormously to making Leeds the biggest city in the country after London and Birmingham. If, however, we go wrong, we should have one aim and that is to correct mistakes and unfair treatment.

Concert Hall

In 1999 a number of very well connected individuals who had a passion for classical music and an equal commitment to reinforce the Leeds role as a centre of the arts in the UK, formed an association to build Leeds a new and top class concert hall. In 2000 the group changed itself into a charitable company called the Leeds International Music Centre Trust. The supporters were large in number and contained handfuls of distinguished figures like Melvyn Bragg, Simon Rattle, Colin Davis, Carl Davies, the Vice Chancellors of the two Universities, John Dankworth, Dame Cleo Lane, the managers of all the major orchestras in the UK, the artistic directors of bodies like Opera North and Northern Ballet and eight of the prize winners of the Leeds Piano Competition, names like Radu Lupu, Mitsuko Uchida, Andras Schiff, Karl Jenkins and Arnold Ziff, an altruistic business man.

Arnold, for whom I had the greatest respect and affection, was a self-made millionaire who in partnership with his doughty Scots wife, are the most generous patrons of the arts Leeds has known. He was a passionate advocate of this scheme and offered the city, through me, a very valuable site close to the City Railway Station for the new concert hall. The site was very valuable and ideal in many ways for a new hall and a most generous offer.

Initially I was the only real opponent of this scheme. If developed it would have put an end to the major use of the Leeds Town Hall. The argument was that the Town Hall could not rival the new concert halls which had sprung up in the UK and the Town Hall acoustics were bad but, as I pointed out when in public debate, acoustics are a matter of taste, although I had to concede that the reverberation time in the Town Hall was singularly long. This is according to some authoritative individuals a real advantage; for others, it was a serious disadvantage. I was having a coffee in the Town Hall with Vladimir Askenazy, who had been playing in Leeds, and he said he loved the acoustics of the Hall – very Russian and he, of course, as one of the world's greatest pianists and later conductors, carried some weight.

At that time the current standard of excellence was taken as that of the Birmingham Symphony Hall but that is also a matter of taste. The New Glasgow Royal Concert Hall completed in 1990, was heavily criticised by some and many changes were made as a result. Bridgewater Hall in Manchester also went through various acoustic checks. I was told, according to the experts, that a hall accommodating 2,500 people was the most one could accommodate to achieve the best acoustics. My opposition to the proposed new hall was based on a number of reasons. The first reason was money. If some multi-millionaire had come along and agreed to meet the cost of the new hall and subsidise its running costs for say a period of 20 years, I would have been delighted. This was of course a totally impossible prospect although a Bill Gates would not notice this cost. The Birmingham Symphony Hall cost approximately £ 30 m as part of a major development which attracted £ 53 m from Europe and £ 120 m from Birmingham City Council. The Belfast Waterfront Hall cost £ 32 m and was operating at an annual cost/loss of £ 1.5 M. All the major centres in the UK are running at a cost which is a term I prefer to loss. I felt that if the city decided to adopt the proposal to build and run a new concert hall, lots of other more worthy causes could be lost. Simply a matter of priorities. I was also conscious of how well our concerts in the Town Hall were doing. Year after year our concert programme won the country's annual award for the most successful programme. We won it so often I decided we would not re-enter the competition to give others a chance. I also pointed out to those who were calling me in the politest possible way a Luddite that our programme for the 1999–2000 season Included the Russian State Philharmonic, The Leipzig Gewand House Orchestra, the Hungarian National Philharmonic,

The BBC Philharmonic, The Orchestra of the Enlightenment, The Swedish Radio Symphony Orchestra, The Netherlands Symphony Orchestra, The Toronto Symphony Orchestra, The London Mozart Players, Moscow Philharmonic, CBSO, et al. Soloists and conductors inter alia included James Galway, Yuri Simonov, Yevgany Svetlanov, Lesley Garrett, Carlo Rizzi, Sir Charles Mackerras, Kent Nagano, Alfred Brendel, et al.

In life one has to entertain reality. In one's dreams one can indulge in one's wildest artistic extravagances. The paradox lies in the fact that one will never make progress if one does not have those dreams, ideas and ambitions.

In due course those splendid folk who had established the very impressive case for the new concert hall for Leeds recognised the battle would not be won. A very honourable defeat.

The Leeds Town Hall has had some acoustic treatment in a most sympathetic way which does not impair its magnificent interior and it does serve many other purposes which have included world championship boxing, wrestling and major exhibitions. Sadly it has ceased to provide a venue for ballroom dancing which once was a major contributor to its varied use but is a superb venue for the two great choirs in Leeds.

An example of
the Labour Group at its worst

I have the greatest respect for my past and present fellow Labour councillors who have contributed enormously to making Leeds the biggest city in the country after London and Birmingham. If, however, we go wrong, we should have one aim and that is to correct mistakes and unfair treatment. John Illingworth, a Leeds councillor for more than two decades representing Kirkstall Ward, had the Labour Whip withdrawn for a period of three months. I was absolutely certain that this decision was wrong and should have been rectified. I speak as one who has been a Labour Party member continuously since 1946 except for a two-year break in the RAF when it was not permissible for an officer to be a member of a political Party (unless of course it was Conservative) and have held the most senior positions on the council including the chairmanship of committees like Education, Social Services, Cultural Services, Police, et al, in a 57-year membership of the Leeds City Council which I gave up in 2014.

If the Labour Party stands for anything it is honesty and probity. Illingworth did nothing wrong. His suspension by a full Labour Group meeting was decided by a process which breaks all the proper processes of natural justice. His appeal, which was rejected, was a farce in terms of justice. Illingworth had the support of Kirkstall Labour Party and the ward and constituency in which he resides. This is a constituency which we should have won given the poor rating the Lib Dems possessed at that time. This dissention, along with the incomprehensible decision to introduce trolley buses to the city, however, was a conclusive and fatal element in seeing a Lib Dem win the seat again. There was widespread cross-party opposition to a planning application, 13/00868/OT, to build on the last remaining playing field that could serve a deprived area of inner city Leeds. The issues were debated at area committee meetings, the Executive Board and the Health Scrutiny Board in May and there was common cause in opposing the proposals but the main concern was whether, on appeal, given the government's policy of appointing inspectors of a particular hue, the decision could be reversed. Notwithstanding this concern, the Plans South & West Panel voted to refuse the application. Secretly Cllr Gruen, an Executive Board member, invited the councillors from the area affected to a confidential cross-party meeting with the chairman of Planning, plus planning, asset management and legal officers. Ward members reluctantly agreed to a deal to accept the profits from the demolition of a property to fund new urban green space elsewhere and in return withdraw their objections to the planning application. This meeting was kept secret and consequently some councillors continued publicly to oppose the Victoria Road planning application in line with agreed policy. On 26 March 2014 a Planning Officers' report was published recommending members to ignore public health objections and accept the application. Being unaware of the confidential meetings, Illingworth, as chair of the Health Scrutiny Board, publicly challenged the report, and suggested it be referred to the Health and Wellbeing Board or the Health Scrutiny Board for possible revision. No criticisms of Labour members were made. Comments on planning applications are public documents; they cannot in theory be made in secret and Scrutiny and Plans Panel business cannot be whipped in theory at least.

The then Chief Whip failed in his duty to ensure that Labour councillors knew of any agreements, confidential or otherwise, between Planning Officers and the local Labour and Lib Dem councillors. He has since been replaced. Illingworth continued to promote the existing policy, which had been debated and endorsed by the Executive Board, Health Scrutiny Board, Plans Panel and by the Inner North West Area Committee and its Planning Group. A special group meeting was convened and Illingworth was charged though with what it is difficult to state as there were initially three versions of the charge and so far as I can ascertain, no formal written charges were provided to Illingworth at the meeting. There are now four different iterations of the "charge". In effect, the meeting was called to approve the recommendation of the Advisory Committee to suspend him. This was not a fair trial. It resulted in a quarter page article in the *Evening Post*, a paper with a wide readership, headed "Heart Surgery Hero Suspended over e mail row." Illingworth had taken on the National NHS management in London and won a judicial review to enable child paediatric surgery to continue in Leeds. I understand that at the group meeting, which I could no longer attend, there was a proposal to suspend him and suggested amendments to the advisory recommendation were proposed but were defeated and the advisory proposal was agreed by a majority in a ballot which was as bizarre as I have known.

This was not a "fair trial". It is Kafkaesque and is not consistent with the Party's ethics or rules. The decision was made by a small group of individuals in the Advisory Committee, sure in the knowledge that no one can remember when the group overturned an advisory decision, whether it was about the closure of old people's homes, sport centres, community centres, et al. An appeal was agreed. It took place and to my best knowledge the following statements are true: Illingworth was not told in advance what the charges were against him and for which he had been punished. The then new Chief Whip produced a fourth version of the charges despite the fact that this was an appeal relating to the decision of the original hearing, not a new trial. The new Whip produced, without warning, two witnesses, Gruen and Mckenna. Illingworth was not informed of this in advance nor of his right to call witnesses. It transpired that the regional officer had not sent all the documents to Illingworth and so a brief adjournment was called, a very serious fault on the regional officer's part and to the great disadvantage of Illingworth.

Any lawyer would say this appeal process was fundamentally flawed as was the first meeting at which the group decided on the withdrawal of the Whip. I am appalled at this show trial when the rules of the Party are ignored and personal vendettas are pursued by these means. I am appalled that we were using our energy and time in pursuing personal vendettas in a manner which is a disgrace to the Party when we should be doing all we can to win a seat from the Lib Dems. Sad to say the faith in some of the councillors has been shattered and a sense of ill will was poisoning the atmosphere when we should be fighting not ourselves but the Tories and Lib Dems. Illingworth, an exceptional individual, modest, high principled and highly intelligent seems incapable of holding a grudge. If I were he, I should be looking for blood for this dishonourable behaviour. He bears no such feelings. I find it ironic that I see myself as a Catholic and as such believe in forgiveness but would be seeking redress and apology if not blood on the carpet. Illingworth, an agnostic or atheist I am not sure, has an unlimited capacity to forgive or at least not stick pins in a figure in his cupboard.

Greyhound Stadium

As a councillor I received a number of out of the ordinary experiences. I had never been slightly interested in greyhound racing and was surprised to be asked to attend an evening at the dogs. I agreed and was asked to take up a big issue for those interested in this "sport". The greyhound track in Leeds was under threat. I was told that Ladbrokes were buying up greyhound race tracks, closing them down and selling the sites off for development at an enormous profit. I was told that they had already acquired six tracks for £ 1.3 million pounds. My one visit to a track event did not light my interest in the sport at all. I, however, have always felt that people have different interests and deserve to have the opportunity to enjoy their form of entertainment. I was told a number of stories defamatory of Ladbrokes which I am not able to repeat as I had not the time or inclination to do the research to support these allegations. However, as a public representative, I was concerned to help those who wished to keep an activity going in Leeds, to some just as important as seeing Northern Ballet coming to Leeds was to others. I called a meeting to be held in the Civic Hall. I expected at most 40 to 50 people but was astounded by the numbers who turned up and it was standing room only for the vast crowd who attended. The track was situated in a poor area of Leeds not far from the Leeds United ground. There had never been any problems with the track over many years, a fact confirmed to me by the police. I have always seen sport facilities as not merely places for participation but something which has a social purpose, a place of resort where people of all classes can mix and be involved in the sport of their choice. The Greyhound Stadium met this criterion. The social mix was very mixed and people of all kinds of standing and of both sexes enjoyed their sport together. A proposal was mooted to develop the site of the Greyhound Stadium to include a first class football pitch, indoor archery and indoor cricket and adequate spectator accommodation for gymnastics, basketball, and other indoor sports. It made great sense to site these facilities in Holbeck which was until very recently a very deprived area and lacking all such facilities.

In a press release of February 1982, I said I was preparing a blacklist of greyhound stadia which have apparently been run down deliberately prior to asset-stripping, that I had received a petition with 700 signatures asking for the retention of greyhound racing in Leeds and that I was opposing the application for planning permission by Ladbrokes for industrial and warehouse development. There was much local support for this objection which I was pleased to see assisted the planning authority, Leeds City Council to reject the application. I received a large number of letters, and some anonymous letters. One was hand-written, several pages long, by an employee of Ladbrokes revealing their interest in capital gains by selling off tracks and the eventual control of what was called the BAGS service to betting shops throughout the country which would bring in considerable revenue. The letter pointed out that racing took place in all weathers and was held on almost all days of the week somewhere and so those working in betting shops could be employed without breaks. It went on saying "If Ladbrokes gained control of the BAGS service they could bypass Extel, and arrange their own service to betting shops. The private operator would then be forced to pay fees to Ladbrokes who could, by pricing them too high, force some shops to close down, leaving Ladbrokes in a position where competition was destroyed." Ladbrokes appeared to be the "villain" in these matters but I could see no sign of illegality, just a clever use of the law to gain extra profits. Sadly, in this world of economics and law, there is no David to take on Goliath though the council did its best within the law. The chief officer wrote in April 1982 to Ladbrokes Stadia Limited to which he received a reply stating that "the Stadium was closed on 19th March for reasons explained to the Planning Department when we made application to them for change of use and the company cannot now reconsider its decision in this matter. Incidentally, damage caused by vandals during the past fortnight has now made it impossible to reopen the stadium. I understand that the Totaliser indicator board was set on fire and destroyed". Thus the saga ended. I did my best to ensure that the site did not get the planning permission that it requested and persuaded the planning committee that the land should retain its present planning permission, namely public use for recreation. Decades later that permission was changed to enable a new Police HQ to be situated on the site. Life has its ironies. I was warned by more than one person during the period of my involvement that I should look after my own safety as big money was involved and there were many examples of physical force being imposed. I discounted this fear, believing there could be no such danger to my person and I regret that so much time and energy had been spent with so little to show for it. Companies like Ladbrokes have one aim and that is to get the best profits possible. I and my colleagues do not oppose them on that ground. We merely work to get the best service, amenities and environment for our residents. Big business can call on vast resources in terms of lawyers, accountants, brokers, enabling them to overcome domestic opposition. They have one aim – profit. We have one aim – service to those who elect us. At times it really is a Goliath versus David situation.

The Bedroom Tax/A DISGRACE

The Tory Government decided that if a person is living in a house or flat with two bedrooms where one would meet the needs of the person or couple, the rent would be increased significantly in an effort to move them to a house or flat with one bedroom sufficient for their needs. The council estimated it must provide 1,158 more council homes per year to house tenants that are deemed to have more bedrooms than they need. The current rate of construction will have very little effect, if at all, on the 30,000 on the Leeds housing waiting list.

The decision was made by a hard right group of Conservative politicians determined to save billions of pounds by the so-called welfare reforms. The result of this policy was to cause: an infinite amount of worry and unhappiness; a boost for avaricious landlords (47% of privately let households do not meet the efficiency standards) and chaos to thousands of people who are also affected by other consequences of the raft of changes being introduced.

In Leeds we attempted to get round this appalling decision by regrading the second room in many of its flats as a storeroom and not a bedroom. These rooms can, of course, be used as a bedroom as can almost any space, but the majority are so small they can equally be regarded as storerooms. Some of the most hard hit are people with a disability who use the second room as the store room for their equipment. This move may help a number of people who need this help but it can only help relatively few. A not untypical case I dealt with was of a man in advancing years who had slept in the small second bedroom as he remained to look after his aged father and mother, now a widow, for many years. He had lived in this constrained environment for many years. His mother died and he was faced with having to find another home after decades in his current flat. I wonder just how many bedrooms the home of the Prime Minister has or the other members of the Tory Government. It is to their credit that some Conservatives have stated their objections but these have not been heard. It took three years, a number of court cases, a judgement in the Supreme Court and campaigning notably in the *Mirror* for some concessions to be made. Exempt will be a room for a disabled child's care and a room for couples who cannot share a bedroom due to a physical disability.

I find it remarkable that the Supreme Court is now a strong force for justice. Before it became the Supreme Court it was known as the House of Lords and at times seemed to be the protector of out-of-date rights. It was in the eyes of many a strong and reliable defender of the status quo. Somerset Maugham, a prolific author of some splendid books, suggested that each judge in the House of Lords sitting as a court should have on the bench next to him a toilet roll to remind him he was human. His brother was a distinguished judge in the House of Lords. Since it changed its name it has become a very independent defender of human rights as exemplified by its judgment which said certain aspects of the "bedroom tax" were illegal.

Elected Lord Mayor

I was elected Lord Mayor of Leeds in 2000. It had never been my ambition to be Lord Mayor and had declined previously offers to nominate me. As the millennium was approaching I was persuaded to let my name go forward because it was directly pointed out to me that if I did not stand there was the likelihood of another being appointed which could be a disaster. This was hardly a vote of confidence but I appreciated the argument and was elected Lord Mayor, a position in which I had never been interested. The role is formal only. No power, just some influence. I was wrong. I enjoyed the year tremendously and was reminded almost daily of the kindness and consideration of so many from all strata of society. The Lord Mayor gets a substantial allowance to meet expenses and donations to good causes. I had great pleasure in returning nearly half of my allowance as a gesture indicating that we were not in it for the money. I was wrong in retrospect for I really should have given it to needy charities. Mea culpa. Looking back I do not know if I did this for the reason I have just given or was doing it to make a point about how good I am. It is sometimes a problem to analyse one's reasons for an act.

Claire Frisby of the BBC and Christa Ackroyd of *Calendar* were two extremely competent television presenters. They were most attractive young women and both agreed willingly to act as Lady Mayoresses from time to time. They were excellent exemplars for young girls and their older sisters of the saying: the door will open if you try it. Christa, in her new capacity, visited with me the *Ark Royal* which was being fitted out in the North. We were treated right royally by the captain as Leeds had had a long association with the ship since war days and every Lord Mayor was invited to visit the ship if it was in Home Waters. At that time there were few female officers on board and Christa disappeared into the officer's mess and I did not see much of her until we were due to return to Leeds.

Two more stars from the artistic firmament were kind enough to assist me. Jude Kelly, artistic director of the Playhouse and one of the most energetic and creative women I have known and another woman from a very modest background, Kay Mellor, showed how, with talent and perseverance, there is no limit to what you can achieve. Jude ultimately left the Playhouse to take up one of the most prestigious roles in the artistic life of London and Kay, an equally loveable person, has made herself a splendidly successful career as writer, actress, director and general entrepreneur. She achieved this despite the hardest possible start in life.

Leeds holds a West Indian Carnival which rivals its more famous sister event in London. It is organised by the black community and a principal mover and shaker in the rather male dominated West Indian Community was a lady of distinction, Susan Pitter, who became the first black Lady Mayoress in the history of Leeds. Many years later she was to join me on the steps of the Civic Hall to welcome none other than Nelson Mandela, who was surprised but impressed by that fact. Over the year I was happy to call on Sue Reddington, who has produced a miracle in the city. Just one mile from the centre of Leeds there is hidden away but heavily visited city farm. It is so successful that the Prince of Wales has visited as have innumerable individuals concerned about conservation. I called on a breast cancer nurse, Belinda, to join me as Lady Mayoress on a number of appropriate occasions. Liz Dawn and I had raised money to completely refurbish the breast cancer unit in St James Hospital in Leeds and Belinda was the very effective nurse in charge of the centre. Pat Oddy was "just" a woman who lived on the oldest corporation housing estate in the city. Her work in the community was incredible in its content and success. She joined me on a few occasions, a perfect example of how anyone can, if determined, make a difference. One of the most memorable of these characters was a lady who had just turned 100. She was as bright as a button to use a local simile. I took her along as my Lady Mayoress to a major meeting of Age Concern in the crowded Banqueting Hall in the Civic Hall. She spoke at some length without notes and with complete clarity. One thing she said I shall always remember: "I shall know I am getting old when I cannot put my knickers on when standing up". I shall always remember this daily as I do the same thing but with trousers, in the hope to end up as fit and savvy as this old lady. Even more remarkable was a delightful young lady, Heather Clark. She was a Thalidomide baby and had been most severely physically disabled since birth. Her spirit and intelligence enabled her to overcome this seemingly impossible range of disability, creating a career for herself, driving her own specially adapted vehicle and becoming heavily involved in riding for the disabled. I invited her as Lady Mayoress to welcome Princess Anne on her visit to the RDA Middleton Park Riding Centre. Heather was an inspiration to all who knew her.

Even more remarkable in many ways was the case of Bridie Duggan. She worked in the kitchen of the Civic Hall and I came to love her warm Irish natural charm. When young, she had come to England from a very poor family in Ireland and was met with a very harsh environment. Looking for digs, she encountered sign after sign which said "No Jews, no Irish." Later, of course, there was added to this list "No Blacks". Sad to think that racism was embedded so deep it affected the poorest in the community. Bridie spoke no English and finally found lodgings with an Indian lady who spoke no English either. They communicated by the universal sign language – gesture –and Bridie had found herself a home for at least the time being. From being a young woman to the time I knew her, she had never progressed from being a kitchen worker. She was a lovely quiet homely woman and I adored her gentle character. When I first asked her to be a Lady Mayoress she thought I was joking. Then, as I persevered, she realised I was serious and refused outright as I believe she thought she was not up to it. It was that very characteristic which made me keen to "use" her. After much pressure from her kitchen colleagues and one or two councillors she agreed. Seeing her appear "all done up" for her first foray, I was rather choked by emotion. She looked lovely and so well turned out. I was honoured. After her first event she was more relaxed about doing it again which we did a few times. The Irish press had picked up the story from the British press and soon Bridie was answering questions from the Irish press. Next, they were doing full feature articles of her in Ireland. The next thing I knew was that I was being asked by a TV company for permission to come and make a programme about Bridie. I agreed with the greatest of pleasure and so Bridie's life story was shown all over Ireland, making her amazingly into some sort of celebrity. Once the English press learned of the Irish press and TV interest, they turned their eyes on Bridie, who remained the very calm slow speaking lovely woman she is. She is now back in deepest Ireland with her husband. May God protect her.

Towards the end of my year I held a food and drink party in the Civic Hall for those over 100 years of age. I was surprised there were so many in Leeds and I was amazed when five television crews descended on the party and spent an enormous amount of time recording their interviews. The resulting broadcasts of these produced the most singular reaction in the public as the stories were so varied and fascinating. I hope that this oral history is preserved somewhere.

There are other Lady Mayoresses that I revered. One was the wife of a former Lord Mayor. Someone, I cannot remember who, got me to do a tandem parachute jump to raise money for the for the Mayor's Appeal. I had never done a parachute jump and so agreed. To my amazement, the former Lady Mayoress of well advanced years had agreed to do the same thing. In a tandem jump it is the expert who has the parachutes. You have none. We boarded a small plane carrying a number of us. I found this rather hair raising because, seated on the floor of the plane, as it climbed to get to a suitable altitude, one had the feeling that one is sliding toward the open side of the aircraft, and not having a parachute, this was not unreasonably a matter of concern. I felt that if the pilot banked steeply I would shoot out of the open space which once had been a door. When we got to the required height I felt my partner hook me up to him. I tried to see if he had secured me correctly but not having a head that swivels I could not check this. We shuffled on our bottoms to the open door space and sat with legs dangling outside the plane. This was a significantly different experience from almost any other I had experienced, the other being more exciting even than this, namely paragliding. When we got the signal, my guide pushed me off and we started to fall. Under instruction, I opened out into wide arms and wide legs and enjoyed the experience of free fall. A memory came into my mind of a physics lesson many year earlier when I had learned that a free falling body falls at 32 feet per second per second until it reaches terminal velocity. That may be wrong but that is what I remembered as well as a fleeting memory glimpse of Galilleo. When nearing the ground, my attached jumper pulled the ripcord and we, with a bump, began to fall slowly. We were aiming at hitting a marker about the size of a dinner plate and we got very close but not close enough for the Lady Mayoress and her guide actually touched down on the plate. We all got certificates to say that we had done the tandem jump. In the hut where we had left some gear there was an old man in the corner smoking a pipe. He jumped regularly and he was aged 82. When I heard this I felt a little reassured that life in old age can have its compensations. I am not sure parachuting is one.

Labour relations Protection of Rights and fair treatment

I have always been a strong supporter of the rights of the individual at work. I have seen men sacked on the spot for trivial reasons. The way then was a simple instruction: "Go to the office and collect your cards" or simply: "Get your cards" The cards mentioned were a record of the individual's work, were stamped every week for national insurance purposes and were used to collect unemployment pay. There was no protection for the worker. I was told by a person of impeccable honesty that in the1945 election the owner of a large chemical concern in Huddersfield one evening had seen one of his employees going into the Labour Rooms. He sacked him.

During my youth I heard of innumerable cases of victimisation of individuals at work. Membership of a trade union was at one time a serious disadvantage in some businesses where trade unionists and trade union officers were not welcome. I was very conscious of this when very young because my father and mother were both heavily involved in the trade union movement and we received at home many visitors who were in distress. My mother, before she became a mother, was a fire brand trades unionist in a very large clothing factory – Hepworths. She was a skilled operative whose skills were invaluable when she had to provide for five children. The Singer sewing machine was as integral to the family as was the mangle in the kitchen and the high pitch sound of the treadle working at top speed was just as memorable.

I have, therefore, welcomed the changes to the law relating to work and the current, protection given to the workers. However, believing that justice is even handed, I have been unhappy that unscrupulous individuals take advantage of these protective laws in a way I think despicable. I was particularly concerned about one case where a woman had alleged her immediate boss had made sexist or suggestive comments. She was most vociferous about this which led to the man being suspended pending an investigation. Ultimately after weeks of inaction, he resigned as the strain on him was beginning to damage his health. I wanted him to defend himself against the accusations but the strain was too great for him and his family. I was sure that in this case there had been a serious injustice.

Canny legal advisers often encourage clients to pursue their case even though there is no great hope of success. This is because the lawyers know that the time and expense the accused has to go through in order to prepare a defence and the day or maybe two days spent at the tribunal is a lot more costly than paying a sum sufficient to settle the matter. In these cases justice has not been done.

Acting for the Middleton Park Equestrian Centre for the Disabled, I have encountered this problem. In one case I spent many hours preparing a defence against a claim which was, in my view, an open and closed case of someone trying it on. I turned up to the tribunal in the centre of Leeds prepared to defend the case only to be told that the claimant had just decided that morning to withdraw his case. He had been supported by the union, a representative of which was present when I heard the news. I was angry. The man had been discharged because he had consistently ignored the injunction that smoking in the stables was absolutely forbidden. The union should have refused to take on this case. The man did not deny that he had smoked and he had been caught smoking on the premises.

It is not just staff who try it on. A young woman was having a riding session in the large covered arena. She fell off the horse, a very rare occurrence which is true though surprising. She claimed the instructor had been negligent by making her trot too quickly. She claimed the fall from the horse was the result of the instructor's actions. The chief officer of the Riding for the Disabled Centre was so incensed that such a false claim should be made, she embarked on a series of detailed measurements and timings which, if true, would demolish the claim. The claim against the centre was for negligence and would be heard in the County Court. The chief officer spent a large amount her time preparing the defence and a deal of mine. We won. The claimant lost. It had however involved the chief officer in a serious amount of time and worry for many find appearance in court to give evidence taxing physically and emotionally. It also took up a disproportionate amount of my time but we were not given costs. Most unfair. The claimant was using the law as a means of getting money. My view is simply that those involved in such cases should have an honest commitment to and regard for honesty and fairness or the great reforms to protect workers at work will be eroded. Honesty should be the slogan. The recalcitrant unions should remember this as should employers.

The Drama of Real Life – Cricket in Yorkshire

The drama of life continues and in Yorkshire cricket was at one time almost a religion with saints like Hutton or Boycott. I never met Hutton, one of the world's greatest batsmen and lifelong friendly rival of Bradman, an Australian who could legitimately be regarded as the best batsman in the world ever. I had been involved in setting up a cricket centre in Headingley, home of Yorkshire County Cricket Club. It was situated adjacent to the cricket ground and provided excellent nets for practice. I took the chair for two years and then someone from the YCC became chair for two years. This worked well as I made no pretence about my knowledge of cricket which was nil. The calm at YCC presaged a storm. A stupid decision. in my view. was made by the YCC Committee to set up a cricket school in Bradford. It was a daft decision as the facilities in Bradford for the new school were poor or non-existent in a ground where there was no life apart from a few days when county matches were played in Bradford. This decision caused a storm, the matter being discussed on TV as though the matter was one of national importance. I felt obliged to enter the fray, discussion being a word too bland to match the feelings generated. Headingley is a very important asset to the city's life and to move the proposed school to Bradford when we had invested considerably in the new indoor nets was irrational. I received a large number of letters, some too racy to reveal, but some were typified by a six-page handwritten letter from Mr Stead, a Leeds resident who stressed my ignorance of the world of cricket and why did I not shut up. This is just a flavour of the words in the letter which I still retain with a smile. I also had correspondence with the embattled chairman of the YCC, namely Mr Brian Walsh QC. I had known Brian for some time, sufficient to be on informal friendly first name terms. I felt sorry for him for suddenly he had become the object of countless letters of an inflammatory nature and waspish attacks on his chairmanship. Boycott was perhaps the most effective opponent of the proposed change and in a letter to him in March 1989 I explained that I had discussed the matter with the leader of the council and that there would be substantial funding for the academy if it was in Headingley. I was most keen as was the leader of the council to have the cricket academy in Leeds, adding an important new aspect to our claim to be a city of sport. The academy has flourished in Leeds. The history of its birth is forgotten and gone are so many who were involved in its creation.

Helping the Sikhs

As Lord Mayor I still retained my councillor role in which capacity in 2000 I visited a Sikh Temple and was told that the wasteland belonging to the City Council next door was up for sale and the Sikhs wanted to use it for car parking. The council agreed to the sale at £ 20,000. The Sikhs could not find that money so wanted to pay in instalments. I wrote a letter to the Chief Financial Officer who, doing his job, said paying in stages was no problem but the council would charge interest on the balance until fully paid. They could not have a lease until the final payment was made. The normal rule is: council must get best consideration but there were legitimate means of avoiding this which are frequently used. After lengthy discussions, a lease was finally agreed. This illustrates the impediments to a councillor who, trying to do something sensible and simple, is faced with a long struggle involving considerable officer and member's time. A similar situation arose out of another Sikh request. We have a substantial number of Sikhs in the city. They have proved to be model citizens for whom I have great respect. Apparently the Sikh tradition is and was that the ashes of deceased Sikhs should be cast into flowing waters and I was approached to get them permission to put the ashes into the River Aire in a very lovely part of the Kirkstall Abbey estate. The River Aire was a very polluted river at this point as a result of the out flow from a major Bradford sewage works so the occasional adding of ashes would not cause any deterioration. My support of this very simple request was met by stubborn opposition from some officers and some members of the public who opposed ostensibly on the grounds of the ashes polluting the water but really because they were quite definitely racist. There was a considerable debate on this very simple request. I, however, agreed a spot where the ashes could be cast in the waters which was a quiet and discreet spot, used by Sikhs ever since. I have never had any complaint about this facility. A couple of decades later there is a strong move to purify the Aire now that the effluent from a sewage works has been diverted from the river and the purity has been greatly improved. It remains to be seen if the ashes will be considered a problem in the future.

Junin
An International cause celebre

It is highly unusual for a local authority to become involved in an international crisis. Leeds can claim this doubtful achievement. Junin provides a good example of how something of miniscule importance can become an international dispute and crisis.

In 1984 a perfectly preserved diesel locomotive made in Leeds in 1929 by the Leeds firm of Hudswell Clarke was found abandoned in the Atacama Desert. It was, when made, the first of its kind in the world and was recognised as such. It had been used by a company operating in the nitrate business in Chile which, when the industry collapsed in 1935, it was left abandoned in situ and was preserved almost perfectly by the dry air of the desert.

I am always amazed by the strange interests some people have. There are few more enthusiastic groups than those interested in the railways and their engines. Leeds is a hot spot primarily because Leeds operated a steam engine to move coal before any similar use of a steam engine was developed. It has a splendid locomotive museum almost on the same spot as the original engine which predated all other steam railway engines.

Two very keen enthusiasts decided to get the locomotive back to the place of its birth and started inquiries involving the British Embassy in Chile and the Chilean authorities. A major fundraising effort was launched to purchase the machine, the estimated cost being in excess of £ 20,000. The former owner of the locomotive was employed as an agent and I was approached as the chairman of the Leisure and Recreation department or some such name and I was very happy to give council support to this effort. In 1990 an export licence was granted following a private sale agreement with the owner of the a machine although we could have argued that when it was disposed of propriety rights did not arise. It was shipped to England. On arrival I was asked to sit in the cab whilst it was driven round Leeds on a low loader. I found it rather comical that I stood or sat in the cab and waved to the large crowds which had turned out to see the parade. I was amazed how many people turned out to see this minor event. The press light-heartedly declared that I and my colleagues were the only persons in history who had toured Leeds in a locomotive.

Things almost immediately went wrong. Chile claimed that General Pinochet, the dictator of Chile, had declared the locomotive a National Historical Monument and therefore the removal from Chile was illegal. A Mr Rodriguez who had been involved in the sale and transfer was sent for trial, Leeds City Council paying his court fees. The Chilean authorities demanded the return of the loco and offered the Chilean Navy to bring it back to Chile. Chile claimed: the sale was illegal, it was transported illegally by the trucking company, its being put on a ship for transporting to Britain was illegal, the locomotive belonged to Chile and must be returned.

The next few weeks we were involved in very complicated legal demands, legal rebuttals, counter arguments and very extensive articles in the UK press. Many in the UK argued that this locomotive was as much a national UK article as it was Chilean and returning it would have been very difficult involving the repaying money to those who had so generously given and that the pontoon bridge which had allowed it to get to the museum had been moved and would be very expensive to replace. The UK government became involved as this had descended into a struggle with another nation, albeit one which was reviled as a terrible dictatorship ultimately to be overthrown.

After a little time the furore lost its impetus and public interest and we in the department breathed a sigh of relief. War did not breakout although I received some hate mail over this acquisition. It is remarkable that a clapped-out locomotive could generate such heat and effort as well as money. What I do know for certain is that had we known the loco had been deemed a national icon we would not have agreed to buy it. How the purchase of an old engine which had spent decades abandoned in the desert could become an international cause is beyond me. It reminds me of some of those lovely old film farces like the Titchfield Thunderbolt.

Artistic Freedom

I believe passionately in freedom of speech and the freedom of the artist whether his or her medium is film, theatre, oils or watercolours, photography or music. I received a strong letter from a senior woman member of council to the effect that the hanging of a character in the Northern Ballet, Hunchback of Notre Dame, was too realistic and therefore too disturbing. She asked that that scene be removed from the ballet. She had every right to make this demand. I had the right to refuse.

Another woman councillor, very well respected, complained to me that the Opera North production of Kurt Weill's Threepenny Opera contained scenes of violence and in particular, violence against one woman who is forced to watch the antics of the beggars and is finally murdered by them by cutting her throat.

Her argument was clear precise and demanding of a full and appropriate answer. I left Nicholas Payne, the CEO of the Opera Company, to reply on behalf of the company and I replied as a Member of the Board of ON and a city councillor. She asked that the scene where the woman is murdered at the end of the play be removed as gratuitous violence to a woman. I appreciated her genuine concern but stressed the difficulty of reconciling the freedom of the individual and artist to free speech and the necessary constraints that an organised society feels it is appropriate to impose. I had seen the Opera twice during its run in Leeds and saw the emotional impact the staged murder had on the audience. I am sure Weill wanted to evoke such a feeling because it underlined and underscored the whole animus of the play-cum-opera. Other women also joined in the correspondence with me and all took the same view as the original complainant. This pleased me despite their views being the opposite of my argument because the opera of Kurt Weilll had stirred in these women the very emotions he set out to stir. Without doubt since 1990 when this opera was performed in Leeds, some progress has been made in dealing with violence to women but regular scandals such as the trafficking of women, grooming of children and establishment cover ups show we still have a very long way to go. There is a clear conflict between our mutual opposition to censorship and restrictions on freedom of expression and our mutual desire to prevent the publication or showing of items likely to lead to violence against anybody. My only refuge in the maze of dilemmas is to adopt a quite empirical attitude and to try to be reasonably balanced though this inevitably leads to what looks and possibly are conflicting decisions and views.

It is instructive to remember that Cosi fan tutte was originally the most popular opera of Mozart. Then came a period when strong feelings were aroused by the storyline which involved two men testing their wives' fidelity by dressing up as foreign potentates and returning to attempt to seduce their wives who were totally misled by the disguises. Nowadays the opera is still regarded by some feminists as degrading women and the sanctity of marriage but most look on it as a romp involving marvellous music and lots of laughs. We would have been the losers if someone had come forward and stopped the production. This happened under Stalin in the Soviet Union when composers were subject to the terrible need to ensure that Stalin and his acolytes were satisfied their music was true Soviet music and whether Shostakovich was producing music appropriate for Soviet composers. Woe betide a composer who got it wrong. Similar censorship has existed elsewhere in the most violent way best exemplified by the cultural revolution in China in Mao's declining years. What a tragedy and how important it is for us to preserve this freedom of expression even if it goes close to the boundary of unreasonableness!

WY Playhouse Early History

Post war Leeds was blessed with: the Grand Theatre (a large and beautiful Opera House), the Theatre Royal (another lovely large theatre devoted to running successfully an annual Christmas pantomime which in in some years went on until after Easter and then a weekly rep of dramas by the acting staff of the White Rose Company), the City of Varieties (a historic jewel of a variety theatre) and the Leeds Empire (a very large and beautifully-preserved theatre able to accommodate any show including ice skating by the world famous Sonja Henie. This theatre received the nationally famous artists and a good many from abroad. A generation later, the Empire was pulled down to accommodate Harvey Nicks which made Leeds the only Harvey Nicks outside London. The promise was recorded as agreed that a new theatre would be built to replace the Empire but these were empty words as must have been known then. Developers are prepared to make a similar promise in many other circumstances knowing full well that in future years such agreements can be ignored.

The original idea of a new theatre in Leeds was proposed by a group of university folk and included a formidable troupe of women who proved to be excellent advocates of the scheme. From 1964 when a pressure group was formed, agitation continued until in 1968 when a mass meeting addressed by Peter O'Toole and Keith Waterhouse (both born in Leeds) and the outstanding theatre director, John Neville, a formal committee was formed. The university was heavily represented and a host of very forceful women entered the lists and I believe are the true founders of the current Playhouse. I was supportive but not active initially until I got a visit from a Labour Party colleague. He was the full-time agent of the Leeds Labour Party. Ultimately he went off and later became leader of Birmingham City Council. I was willingly persuaded to join the pressure group for a new theatre. A formal constitution was established and officers appointed. The university was the major moving force, not merely being the catalyst but also the provider of a new theatre. The university offered half a new sports centre for a new theatre. This was accepted with great gratitude. A ten-year lease was agreed as we (I was now involved) thought that it would be sufficient time to build a purpose-designed theatre. The university's generosity was stretched for a further ten years, making the Playhouse tenants for 20 years at a nominal rent for 20 years whilst the search for a site for the permanent theatre was found on Quarry Hill. During this 20-year period, all the offices were situated in temporary buildings (although as they lasted for 20 years, temporary might be misleading) close to the entrance to the theatre. It is surprising to me but heart-warming that this basic make-do theatre should attract such support. One big mistake occurred on the opening night of the new theatre. The play chosen was a very modern play, lots of bad language, dubious double-entendres and dialogue being delivered from a man in a dustbin. It was so avant garde that a significant number of the councillors and many other worthies walked out. The theatre never fully recovered from this lunatic choice. I was appointed chairman when my predecessor, a distinguished university professor resigned. Our search for a suitable site started but now the council was in the hands of the Tories, led by a Leeds solicitor whom I knew well and with whom I had a friendly relationship. I kept pestering him for a site. He would sometime later, often much later, suggest a site which we would visit, find totally unsuitable but then had to prepare a long document showing its unsuitability. This process was designed to keep us busy without making any progress at all. We were assisted by an excellent architect, Houghton-Evans, whom we later betrayed. He gave hundreds of hours of his time assessing each site for suitability. Sometimes it was simply on the grounds of too small, traffic problems, remoteness, no parking space, old mine shaft, etc. He was exceptional in his efforts to help and quite reasonably thought he would be the architect to build the new theatre. This was not be, hence my feelings of betrayal. The Arts Council required us to hold a national competition which attracted some of the most celebrated architects in Europe who chose this as an opportunity to show off their imagination and creativity. Most schemes were quite beyond our resources to consider. We finally settled on a lovely man and wife partnership from Scotland which proved to be an excellent choice.

I had, as a city council member, proposed the Quarry Hill site as a cultural centre and saw the new theatre as contributing to that vision if not actually starting it. The council made an annual grant to the theatre and councillors were put on the board. The partnership between the board of the Playhouse, who were and are charity trustees, and the council has led to the Playhouse becoming the third largest producing theatre in the country with an enviable record of West End transfers. The relationship with the city was so good the new theatre was built on Quarry Hill under an agreement to lease but a formal lease was not prepared and signed until the twentieth anniversary of the "new" theatre's opening. This only happened because the theatre acting in a business-like fashion had agreed a £ 2 m sum for the right of a developer to build a block of flats on part of the theatre site. The council required £ 1 m before they would grant us a lease which would have enabled us to close the deal with the developer who quite naturally felt he/they could not rely on an agreement to lease 20 years old. In short, the Playhouse would never have become a reality were it not for the full and very generous contribution of the council which has never sought to direct or influence theatre policy. The capital cost of the new theatre was met by several million pounds from the former West Riding County Council which was being wound up and fundraising by the theatre and a major grant from the Arts Council and City Council.

Over the many years I have known William Weston, who was appointed manager of the Playhouse, I have held him in the highest regard and affection as a skilled chief executive, a multi-talented individual and someone who observes the highest standards of public and private mores. That the Leeds Playhouse is the third largest producing theatre in the country is predominantly due to Weston's efforts. Before we appointed Jude Kelly as artistic director, the board spent a long time on determining the management structure of the theatre. We considered three main systems: namely a CEO, a dual system of artistic director and managing director, both at equal level and the third a scheme of artistic director, managing director and a third director responsible to the managing director. Weston was keen to play a full part in determining the artistic policy of the theatre. He thought this would be possible if the three appointments were made and he was most unhappy when we agreed to the two senior posts and not three. He saw that in due course the artistic issues would predominate and his role would be restricted to managing a very large business. He wrote to me a longish letter setting out his reservations and concerns which I discussed with board members. He, as a highly artistic person, was keen on being involved in the artistic programme which would become more difficult as Jude established herself. In due course of time, William decided to leave The Playhouse. I was immensely sorry because I so admired him for what he had done to create the present WYPH, more than any other individual and for his gentility, honesty and compassion. He was a genuine friend. Surprisingly, he then proceeded over the years to have three completely different roles and then was awarded a medal which is very infrequently given.

One of the great pleasures for me as chairman was meeting with such luminaries as Alan Rickman, a splendid actor, with wonderful speaking voice. His roles ranged from the utterly wicked to the intensely observed humour. I saw him once again many years later and what he remembered most, apart from the warm reception he had at the Playhouse, was the night when a severe snow storm meant many of the cast including himself and Phyllida Law and the audience had to stay in the theatre overnight. Dame Judi Dench, before she became a Dame, laid the foundation stone to the new theatre. She was a delightful person, full of good humour and warmth. We enjoyed and welcomed the presence of these outstanding performers. On another occasion many years later I walked in to the theatre to see Jude Kelly. She was sitting at a table with Thelma Barlow, who was a fine classical actress, part of the National Company, but had become beloved by millions of TV watchers as a character in Coronation Street. Jude introduced her to me and I said the exact words: "The last time I saw you I married you". She looked blank but her body language said "Who on earth is this disturbed/barmy character?" I explained that in one Coronation Street episode, she married another character in the story in a civil marriage in which I had presided as the person marrying them in the registry office. She looked relieved and very kindly said, "Of course, I remember now." I am sure she did not as I was a fleeting figure in the two-weekly broadcasts but it was kind and typical of her to make that gesture. It was my pleasure and privilege to meet so many outstanding actors, none more outstanding than Ian McKellen who settled in Leeds for a significant period of time taking the lead in a series of major roles. He was superb and he used the variety of different stage configurations we have at the Playhouse. One distinguished actress I do not remember so warmly was Diana Rigg who attended a performance during the opening week of the new theatre. We sat together and during the interval I bought an ice cream which I consumed just before the "curtain went up" for the second half. I carefully dropped the wrapper under my seat. I had discussed with the house manager the need for maintaining a pristine clean auditorium and he made a bet with me that by 10.00 am the theatre on the following day would be totally clean. I thought to test him with my ice cream wrapper as a bit of fun. This was a genial test but I was going to produce the wrapper if his team had failed to collect it and pull his leg about the failure all in good humour. During the supper which followed the performance, Rigg produced the wrapper with the words: "You seem to have dropped this on the floor." I was staggered and highly amused by her playing the strict headmistress and caused some merriment when I complained that she had destroyed my test and now the house manager could claim to have won the bet. He thanked her jokingly for her capacity as a cleaner and offered her a place on the cleaning staff. She was not amused – her pomposity punctured.

The year 2002–2003 is one which is fairly representative of life at the Playhouse. It saw Ian Brown installed as artistic director and CEO, the departure of Jude Kelly who had been with us since our move to Quarry Hill and of Maggie Saxon the distinguished chairman (sic) of the TMA, a number of outstanding productions and performances, record attendances and a surplus for the year, the first for a long time. Ian Brown directed Alan Bennett's The Lady in the Van, achieving 93% of target. The memorable eccentricity of Miss Shepherd was vividly captured by Anne Rye, as were the dual characterisations of Alan Bennett by Malcolm Scates and Malcolm James. Cast members kindly agreed to take part in an Alan Bennett anthology – an afternoon literary event complementing the production. With the added incentive of a cream tea, this event drew a sizeable crowd and set a precedent for similar events. Another great success was an outstanding performance of Geraldine Connor's spectacular *Carnival Messiah*. This stunning reinvention of Handel's celebratory oratorio with a cast of over 100, yet again thrilled audiences, easily exceeding target. With the help of effusive reviews, Geraldine was able to transfer the production to its home country, where it was staged as part of the 2003 summer theatre season in Trinidad and Tobago. The *Carnival Messiah* spectacle was an appropriate production to mark Jude Kelly's departure, forming a resounding climax to her farewell celebration in July. A successful summer was made complete by two immensely popular visiting productions. It was a delight to welcome Pete Postlethwaite to the theatre in the solo performance of *Scaramouche Jones*. This beautifully performed show completely sold out and made 115% of financial target. Another memorable performance was given by Broadway star Claudia Shear in *Dirty Blonde*, the story of America's original blonde bombshell, Mae West. The Playhouse made an excellent decision in choosing to be the British theatre where this Tony nominated romantic comedy would make its British Premiere and there was an excellent turn out by London critics, all very positive in their responses. Ian Brown's artistic tenure kicked off with an intensive period in the rehearsal room. On stage, Ben Brown's endearing play *Larkin with Women* was providing audiences with the first of two dramatic insights into the life of enigmatic poet Philip Larkin. Originally premiered at Scarborough in 1999, this was the play's second outing. Its place in the programme fulfilled Ian Brown's desire for second productions of new plays to have increased profile at the Playhouse and within the theatre industry generally. However, despite confident performances from the cast of four led by Christopher McHallam, it proved difficult to attract many of the major critics, despite the *Daily Telegraph* review which lamented the fact that the original show had not transferred to the West End.

Excitement was high as the opening of Hamlet got closer. The combination of Chris Eccleston playing the Prince of Denmark opposite Brigit Forsyth as the Queen, in what was to be a landmark inaugural production for Ian Brown, created an added air of anticipation, achieving 139% of target. The theatre was buzzing, many performances were sold out and extra seating had to be made available. The critics returned in force to witness Sir Tom Courtenay's compelling portrayal of Philip Larkin in *Pretending to be Me*. The show was compiled from Larkin's writing by Courtenay and directed by Ian Brown. The rare combination of Courtenay's natural stage presence, an immaculate choice of Larkin's poetry and a smattering of early jazz greats, made the evening an undisputed pleasure. Those in the theatre industry agreed and the show made an immediate transfer to the West End's Comedy Theatre where its run was extended for four further weeks. The streets of downtown New York provided the setting for the mock-horror musical *Little Shop of Horrors*, oddly the theatre's festive offering for family audiences! Following the resoundingly successful return of *Singin' in the Rain* in 2001, this show had its work cut out in order to attract similar audience figures, and there was concern at its possibly limited cult appeal. Chris Luscombe brought together an extremely talented cast and, together with them and the wizardry of the technical departments in the construction of the blood thirsty plant, the show won over Leeds' audiences, and despite not making financial target, did achieve 70%. The regional press loved it, as did many of the nationals, with the *Independent On Sunday* describing it as "highly polished and a blast".

Streets of Rage by Red Ladder's Asian Theatre School marked the start of an exciting new relationship between the Playhouse and the idea of an Asian company committed to producing work with young Asian people from Bradford. My position as chairman of the Playhouse and Red Ladder facilitated this programme. Not every year can boast such overall successes.

Jude Kelly

Jude Kelly's departure to take up one of the most important and prestigious artistic posts in the UK would leave a great hole in the way the Playhouse operated. Her imagination, persuasive powers, complete self-confidence, extraordinary energy and ability to see opportunities and grasp them were unlikely to be found in whoever we appointed. To fill the gap she would leave would not be easy. We decided with board approval that we were not looking for a clone of Jude, as there was not one. We should concentrate on getting someone who shared the artistic ambitions of the founders of the Playhouse and its present board, i.e. looking for someone who had the same artistic and cultural vision as the founders of the Playhouse.

In early 2002 we set up an appointments committee to find a successor to Jude.

We knew it was going to be difficult to attract and choose the right person.

A long list of possible possibles was drawn up on the grounds that we wanted to cast the net as wide as was reasonable. As the search progressed it became clear that a number, marked NA on the list, were not available because they were already committed or had no wish to pursue the role. Though we recognised that some of the names we would consider would not leave a major post in a major theatre to come to Leeds we nevertheless put them on our list just in case. This first wish list included inter alia:

Vicky Featherstone, Grandage, Donnellan, Phyllida Lloyd, Warchus, Rickman, Mellor, Loveday Ingram, Dominic Dromgoole, Daldry, Rylance, Howard Davies, Ed Hall, John Tiffany, Brown, Katie Mitchell, Marianne Elliott and Trevor Hands. This was a very ambitious wish list.

David Liddiment was extremely helpful throughout this whole exercise. Because of his senior position in TV, he knew most of the major figures in theatre. For instance, he said that Trevor Nunn strongly supported the idea of a creative leader and Hytner felt it would be interesting to see a theatre led by an administrator of sound artistic quality. Nunn had suggested for consideration Ed Hall and Michael Boyd.

Ian Brown had been with us for some years and had proved to be an excellent director and a personality which attracted the admiration and respect of all who dealt with him. I met him as part of the discussions with staff and said that if he applied and was not appointed I hoped he would stay on as his contribution in many directions was so appreciated. My wish was to reassure him as someone who enjoyed the great confidence of the staff and who is a very good director. I invited all the staff of the Playhouse to a meeting with me to discuss the situation and to ask for their views. There was unanimity of opinion that the idea of creative leadership was the correct one, that we should be looking to appoint someone with flair, a sense of excitement and danger and who would be a good front person for the Playhouse. I promised that I would faithfully represent their views to the board of the Playhouse, which I was most pleased to do.

The vacancy was widely advertised and we received 37 expressions of interest and requests for the details. The appointment committee consisted of myself as chair; Brian Bouttell, a very senior figure in the financial world and a committed member of the small group which planned the new building; Ivor Davis from Yorkshire Arts; Mark Dickson, a board member with a compendious knowledge of theatre in the Metropolis; Peter Gruen, a very successful man of business and local politics; David Liddiment who, through his TV and theatre interests was ideally suited to be an interviewer; Kay Mellor who was established as a playwright and TV exponent and a lovely person; Elizabeth Minkin, a local councillor colleague; and Tony Sharp, an accountant with a passion for the theatre and sound management. Our final list of candidates after much research and meetings included Barrie Rutter, Ian Brown, Phil Willmot, Mark Clements, Steven Unwin and Paul Miller, Vicky Featherstone, Lawrence Till and Natasha Betteridge.

Over two consecutive days we interviewed each applicant. The quality of the interviewees was exceptional, each one a realistic and exciting candidate. To my surprise we all came ultimately to the same conclusion. Ian Brown got five first votes and four second votes. I think we all felt that after the excitement and artistic success of Jude Kelly we needed to ensure that the theatre was in safe hands and the artistic standard maintained which we felt Ian could do. His ten-year reign has proved the wisdom of our choice but in the arts one always wonders what might have been achieved if we had chosen someone else. A member of the board when we announced the decision to appoint Ian Brown asked why we had bothered to go through an extensive programme of interviews, etc., when we could have just appointed Ian. My answer was of course that we had to test him against his peers. I was sorry that Barrie Rutter did not in the end join the interview list as in my view he has a touch of real genius in his work. I am old enough to remember Donald Woolfit and his travelling company. He brought theatre to life across the country where there was no such life and Rutter does the same though Woolfit was something of a ham in some peoples' view. Generations later, though, I remember his Volpone – after sixty years or more.

I can understand why Rutter did not pursue his interest in the position at the Playhouse but thank God he continued to produce and travel performances which are always between very good indeed and excellent. His company, Broadsides, has one of the art world's most atmospheric theatres. It is in the bowels of an enormous old factory in Halifax. Seating is in the round. Acoustics are good. The atmosphere in this dungeon-like space is always to be remembered. I made two unsuccessful attempts to get him a national award. I cannot understand why they were unsuccessful. Subsequently he was awarded an OBE – a thoroughly deserved recognition.

In 2002 I believed the time had come for a review of present governance arrangements and I put the following to the board members. The Current F and GP had gradually assumed the role of the board; the detailed scrutiny of the finances had become less searching and comprehensive than in the days of the old Finance Committee. The board size was a function of the Leeds City Council and other nominees in that the City Council could nominate five trustees and West Yorks Grants one. A board of, say, eight could be, in effect, a board controlled by such nominees which neither the council nor the Trust would wish. It could easily by default become technically and legally, a controlled company of the council with dire consequences.

My proposal for the future organisation WYPH

I proposed that the full board should meet five times per annum, receive minutes of all sub-committees and be legally responsible for all matters appertaining to the Playhouse. It should have a fixed agenda and receive minutes of all sub-committees and reports from the artistic director, finance director and other members of the senior staff. I further suggested we establish a small Finance Sub Committee meeting eight or nine times pa with one function, namely to scrutinise the financial situation of the Leeds Theatre Trust on a monthly basis and report to the board. I further suggested we retain the existing Arts and Development Committee and Audit Committee and establish other sub-committees as deemed necessary. This I saw as returning to the effective procedures we had some years ago. The board would be able to concentrate on the more strategic issues, knowing that more detailed scrutiny was being undertaken by dedicated sub-committees whose work and recommendations will be passed to the board either for noting and discussion if delegated or for approval or ratification if not a delegated function.

I also pointed out that if the normal rules of chairmanship are observed, the size of the board should present no impediment to highly effective working. A national survey published in January 2007 and yearly since then showed that some of the best known charities had boards of 24 or more directors/trustees, that 19% of all trusts polled showed boards ranging from 16 to 35 plus and that the smaller the Trust the smaller its board usually is. I also pointed out that I had been chairman for many years. There is a time when a change may not be necessary but would be beneficial. That time had come now in my opinion. The Playhouse was entering a new phase. We had an excellent artistic director who has maintained and enhanced the artistic reputation of the Playhouse, and an excellent supporting senior management team. For the last four years we managed to produce a small surplus. Ian Brown has signed on for another five-year period. We soon should have one million pounds invested from the development on the car park. Big challenges will come from the developments on Quarry Hill. If there is to be a change of chairman or woman – the time is about now. One of the duties of a chairman or chairwoman is to propose a suitable successor. This I am happy to do in proposing Brian Bouttell. Brian's association with the Theatre Trust goes back almost as far as mine. He knows its operation intimately, commands great respect in the city of Leeds and outside its confines, enjoys excellent connections with major figures in the city, is vastly experienced and has shown over two decades his commitment to the Playhouse.

My feeling was that we needed in the future a widely respected figure capable of keeping a calm but firm hand on the tiller. I would hate to see someone appointed who came in with exaggerated ideas about his or her capacities to develop the remit and modus operandi of the theatre. Our outstanding cast of Ian, Caroline and others in senior management down to the young people who serve on the bar or the staff who clean the place every day, deserve the kind of support and leadership Brian can give. They and Brian can, I am certain, take the Playhouse and its many collateral activities to even greater success. I envy him that opportunity. Summarising, I said that I would hope the board would accept my recommendations and my proposal that Brian Bouttell should follow me as chairman. If that is agreed, I shall not stand for election at the AGM and will resign from the Trust in order to give me the freedom to pursue the interests of the Playhouse in the council and in respect of planning matters in a manner I could not, were I to remain a trustee. I would therefore hope to continue to support the Playhouse from a quite independent position. I had informed Brian Boutell of my intentions before he went abroad on business and he had indicated to me that he would accept the chair if offered.

Brian Boutell was a highly respected accountant in the city and country. We were so blessed because not only did we have this highly respected person in the world of business and finance but another accountant equally respected and influential, David Williams. He had been actively supporting the Playhouse from its earliest days and in the difficult times which followed, acting for some years as the chair of the Finance Committee. He was someone I liked and respected in equal measure. The work he did was splendid. Sadly I have not seen him for a decade or more. Sad really. It would be impossible to put a price on the work he did in support of this great adventure from its inception. God bless him.

Today the board is chaired by a former chief executive of the West Yorkshire Council, Sir Rodney Brooke. I came to know and respect him for the way in which he closed down the West Yorkshire County Council under the legislative orders of Parliament. Neither of us could have conceived that decades later he would be in the chair of the Playhouse after I had vacated it. He has been an excellent choice: genial, approachable and highly competent as one would expect. Coincidences abound: I was attending an investiture in the Palace to receive the CBE. Immediately preceding me was Rodney Brooke in full court regalia, receiving a knighthood which I think he truly deserves for his public service alone. I also understand from the Playhouse staff that he manages to see all the productions. When the time came to appoint a new artistic director I was surprised by their choice, James Brining, as his background was not that of a big name in the theatre world. It has proved to be an excellent choice and the programme of shows has been quite exceptionally well received. On three occasions in three months I have been unable to buy seats at the counter as the house was full. Result – disappointment, but equally, joy at the success in attracting a very large and committed audience which on occasion has drawn in cohorts of young and excited young people. A joy to see. It seeks to enjoy further developments in a £ 15 million scheme, giving it "a new city facing aspect" and a new performance space. I am always a bit suspicious of terms like "a new city face" on the grounds that if the productions are right, a new face is not required. If the productions are wrong, a new face will not attract dissatisfied customers. And what does it really mean? The benefit of such a "new face" can be quantified in the case of retail businesses which look to entice members of the public on the street into their store. I do not see "a new face" increasing the number of paying customers to the theatre. I am not sure what it does to sell tickets for shows. It will put a lot of money into the hands or pockets of architects, building contractors, et al. It is, however, an exciting vision and the provision of a new performance space is long overdue. It is a pity that so many of the pioneers who conceived the idea of the theatre are not around to see the enormous success of their Playhouse.

Northern Ballet

There is a saying which goes back in history: from Hull, Hell and Halifax, may the Good Lord deliver us: Hull because of the danger from pressgangs and Halifax because they used a guillotine for executions. It is also a town which recorded the sale of wives to other men. Halifax was a small town, quite beautiful in its way and was the site of a most remarkable development undertaken by a local entrepreneur, Edward Hall. He bought an enormous, empty, disused carpet factory with the intention of turning it into a major cultural centre which would enliven the town and bring in further investment. This was seen as a bizarre risk and quite impossible to achieve. Others wondered at its optimism but he was widely admired and respected, very much the man of the moment and he was successful beyond anyone's dreams. He became chairman of the Yorkshire Regional Arts Council, being not merely a major entrepreneur but also a very fine concert pianist.

I had seen Christopher Gable dance at Covent Garden a number of times with his equally distinguished partner, Lynn Seymour. I thought him a breath of fresh air as he had not merely a very sound technique but great acting ability so his performance with his outstanding partner evoked not merely appreciation of steps perfectly performed but by its romantic intensity, an intensity which was so different from many dance partnerships. Many years later I went to the Alhambra in Bradford to see him take the lead in the Northern Ballet version of Don Quixote. At the end of the performance Christopher walked to the front of the stage and made a most passionate plea for support of his company. Northern Ballet was receiving a grant from the Arts Council which had stated it was to cut the grant and thereby cause the demise of Northern Ballet. Having been a member of the Sports Council and the Arts Council, I was very aware of the London-centric feeling and that those in London had no deep sincerely-held conviction that work outside London should be fairly treated.

Christopher's appeal was highly motivating. He asked everyone to post a letter to the Arts Council asking for the threat to be withdrawn. This appeal was so successful, it being repeated at every performance round the country, led to the Arts council being inundated with literally piles of bags full of letters. The Arts Council relented and the grant continued but at a level well below other favoured London-based organisations.

I joined the Board of Northern Ballet which Hall chaired at that time and very quickly became very friendly with him. He was a good chairman as one would have expected from a very successful businessman and musician. I have noticed both in the arts and sports and the political worlds there is a phenomenon when all seem to agree in the new person who has everything to offer. So frequently these bright stars, come out, shine and then disappear the light disappearing too. Ernest Hall was not of this genus and I developed a most healthy and warm respect for his integrity, capacity and energy and became a real friend.

As a Labour Party Councillor for many years I had in the ordinary course of business, to meet council colleagues from all over the region. The Halifax lot were the oddest group I have encountered. One of the leading lights seemed to have only one aim in life and that was to get rid of the then chief constable. The Tories were just as bad and I was told by the senior Tory Councillor that if the Tories won the local elections they would stop the grant to Northern Ballet Company and if NBT could not pay an economic rent they would be ejected from their current situation. The political swing was definitely in favour of the Conservatives, both nationally and locally and I saw this determination to remove Halifax's support to NBT as extremely serious.

I went to John Trickett, leader of the Leeds City Council. He had taken over the mantle of George Mudie who had been elected to Parliament and a man who should be given the credit for changing the old vision of Leeds to its new version. Both had the ability to make quick sensible decisions. I said to Trickett that I could get NBT to Leeds which should go well with our support of Opera North and other ventures. He said, "How much will it cost?" I said, "A third of a million." He said, "OK, do it." No reports to committee, time-consuming investigations reports and delays. My only regret is that I did not say half a million instead of a third.

I had a clear idea of how to do it. There was a vacant secondary school in West Park Leeds in a very pleasant environment of green space, with two very large gymnasia with sprung floors which would make excellent studios and more than enough office and storage space. They would only be utilising a part of the school, the rest of the school building being devoted to artistic or social activities. The NBT therefore would become part of a very substantial arts centre with all that that could offer to the community.

I showed Christopher round and he was enthusiastic to be working with me and the Leeds Council rather than the problem Halifax Group group. Ernest Hall, later Sir Ernest Hall, felt that, if Northern Ballet was going to Leeds, I should take over as chairman. He never betrayed any animosity about the changes as he knew the Leeds solution could be long term whereas the position in Halifax was hostile and uncertain. He resigned as Chair and I was elected.

Within a very short time of moving to Leeds, NBT became part of the community in which it was placed. The school building in which they were now ensconced gave them two very large studios, changing facilities room for storage, costumes, etc., and office space. They overlooked on one side a large grassed area as far as the eye could see. My hope was that we would soon have a new home built to our specifications. I should have known better. It took us at the Leeds Playhouse 20 years to get out of a temporary home on the Leeds University campus into the new theatre and it took ten years before NBT could move into its new home. One major step I was able to take in my capacity of Leeds

Councillor was to identify and secure an area on a prime site, Quarry Hill, where NBT would, in due course, be part of the Major Arts Quarter and Community for which I had canvassed and worked for over the previous decade. That was the most significant contribution I made as the defence of the site was not easy, the danger of sale to another being made every few months.

Mark Skipper, the CEO, and I had spent hundreds of hours dealing with developers only to be disappointed every time. We were constrained to look for solutions which would mitigate the cost by being part of local commercial developments. The planners suggested that we build the centre as part of a large apartment block. This seemed so promising that the Arts Council produced a glossy document extoling the way in which we in Leeds were making cooperation with the developers a means to achieve a solution. Developers are, however, only in the business of making money. Unhappily, the developers looked at the cost of a building large enough to house the NBT and produce enough flats to make the scheme profitable. They found it did not give them the profit margin they wanted and so the scheme failed. We experienced the bitter gall of having three potential schemes defeated at the last minute. The developers found that their margin could be achieved in much less costly projects although on one occasion the developers were ready to sign up and had been thanked for their support by HRH Prince Edward, The Earl of Essex, NBT's Royal Patron, when their national board in London decided not to let its regional organisation proceed. We were in this period dealing with some very well respected developers, architects and entrepreneurs such as Rushbond, DLA, Linfoot PL, Carey Jones, Taylor Woodrow, et al. This was quite devastating though we, that is the board, myself and Skipper, were bloody but unbowed to quote Henley, and continued to strive to reach a satisfactory conclusion. Linfoot was one developer I came to know quite well. He had had a meteoric career starting as a joiner and building up a major development company. He was the man of the moment, highly respected and doubtless envied. I, as bit of a pleb, was very impressed by his HQ which I visited from time to time. He enjoyed chatting about a whole raft of topics all of an artistic subject of one kind or another. He was very hard hit by the financial crash which I thought was a great pity as he had the promise of becoming a major supporter of the arts.

Waste of time.

Our original hope in NBT had been to build a new free-standing dance centre but we had been forced to pursue a joint venture with private developers. This had been done at the cost of much time wasted and the enormous effort Skipper had to put in as each scheme evolved, was explored and then rejected.

Phoenix. Our plan was to build a dance centre which would house NBT and Phoenix Dance, a *small company compared with NBT but it had some excellent representatives and was well* worth everybody's support. My feeling was very positive towards this joint objective but I felt at the time that Mark did not share my enthusiasm, though he was never hostile or obstructive. His sole aim was to get a home for NBT. My aim was to do that but also to assist the small but exciting company, Phoenix, which had developed out of the West Indian community. It did, however, feel at times that the tail was wagging the dog as the Phoenix representatives were very ambitious for their accommodation but contributed nothing in concrete help or money, though by being an integral part of the project they brought with themselves the aspirations of the Arts Council. I was keen to support this new company. If we were in a position to help another very fine company we should do just that. We, that is Mark and myself, decided on creating a free-standing building of ambitious proportions and design, something we had wanted to do originally when we were forced, like it or not, to build it as part of a commercial development. In retrospect, I feel a burning anger that the planners had insisted that we could not build on the Quarry Hill site as a stand alone development which had caused us years of delay and an enormous amount of wasted effort. This was the same crew who years earlier had told us at the Playhouse that we could not build a fly tower as its height was inappropriate in the city centre. Such a daft decision was bizarre. It was like the planners saying we could make savings by not providing toilets or have expensive stage lightening. There are in life loons and lunatics and we had them both.

In retrospect, my major contribution to the new building was being in a position to preserve the site during the years of delay. The site for our new building was very attractive to developers and there was the constant danger that given the delay in making progress with the new HQ the land would be sold off.

Mark worked tirelessly on designing the new building. Whereas before I had been involved throughout, I felt that now we were to build our own building we could leave it to Mark and his colleagues. We, of course, had very regular briefing meetings but I was happy in the knowledge that Mark and his colleagues had all the knowledge and experience to design a structure which met the needs of both companies. The only matter on which I adopted a totally dictatorial attitude was in reference to the creation of a dance academy as an integral part of the normal business of the NBT. I had for years been incensed by my inability to help young people, mostly girls, who qualified for entry in to ballet schools which were all in London or the south which put it out of court for all but a few. My years as a member of the Arts Council in London had confirmed my view beyond doubt of the London-centricity of the Arts Council. It was something it always had denied but I felt that there was a sense of condescension when regional issues were being discussed. For instance, in 2000–2001, Royal Ballet had a subsidy of £ 84,76 per individual attendance,(that is the total expenditure divided by tickets sold), BRB £ 66.24, Rambert, a small dance company, £ 35.69, ENB, £ 20.43 and NBT a mere £ 14,76. NBTs foreign tours outnumbered the total overseas tours of all these companies combined, toured more times in the UK than the other companies combined and was the only ballet company which toured to all four home countries.

The New Home

Mark and his colleagues produced an excellent plan for the building. The contract was let and then lo and behold we opened a Dance House which would be the envy of any company. The building is a dream – airy, excellent theatre for dance, six studios, two dedicated to Phoenix Dance which has the full and exclusive use of one floor. It is something of a masterpiece and a tribute to the efforts of Mark Skipper which were outstanding and to the City Council which had made the new HQ possible. This contrasted with our experience at the Playhouse. The company building the Playhouse on completion demanded an impossibly high extra fee for delays which they alleged had been outside their control. We were faced with insolvency before we had started. I knew if the matter went through the courts that would be a period lasting many months and involving us in legal and other fees which we could not meet. We finally achieved a legal "gagging agreement" under which we paid a substantial sum extra and had to maintain the sum strictly secret or else pay a very substantial additional sum in damages. This was a period of intense concern and in my case, great anger. I hated the agreement and the uncertainty but the board of the theatre stood together and we finally emerged from the unexpected dark cloud. The opening of the new NBT/Phoenix Building was, by contrast, not affected by such exchanges. It was a grand affair which I observed from the back row of the theatre. Some months before the opening I had been approached by a fellow trustee with a proposal which, as they say with gusto in old gangster films, is an offer I cannot refuse. It was in effect: would I step down as chairman for the opening and in return be designated a lifelong president and have a room named after me? It was all very nice and I did not mind at all really as what I had wanted had been achieved and once one gets to worrying about how well you are recognised for your achievements, you sink to the level of those around you. I did think, however, that I would be involved in the opening in some way. I could of course have insisted. I did not.

At the opening I had no reserved seat but found a good viewing position on the back row. More than one member of staff and two directors made a point of seeing me to say thank you and expressing concern that my contribution had not been recognised nor mentioned. They were very kind but I reassured them that this was a matter of little import. We should just celebrate a major milestone in the development of the best facilities for arts in Leeds. Sadly, the chap, a banker by profession, who took over the chairmanship from me fell out completely with the artistic director and soon with some of his board and then he too departed the coop, leaving the chairmanship in the hands of the man who had delivered the offer I could not refuse. He is and was a very nice chap and he conducted the meetings as vice chairman very effectively. A search for a new chairman/woman was conducted and an admirable candidate found. The new chairman is someone I hope can assist NBT in getting greater recognition and resources. Sir David Wootton is the son of a Bradford headmaster who, by a strange chance coincidence, I knew from decades earlier and for whom I had retained over more than four decades the highest regard. He was when I knew him the head of a school in a deprived area of Bradford and was an inspirational head, one of the best educationalists I have known. I had the enormous pleasure of meeting him again after four decades on two occasions and was arranging to visit him in the following spring but sadly he died before we could meet again. I was most affected by his parting, having just restored contact after so many years. I should by now know not to wait but "do it now while you can". As a Freeman of the City of London and its former Lord Mayor, his son, Sir David, is well connected and committed and I have every confidence that Sir David Wootton will be a great asset to Northern Ballet. Certainly since he took over the reins the company has prospered.

NBT moves to Leeds

NBT, originally based in Manchester, was tempted to move to Halifax in 1990 as the then Labour Council saw this as something of which Halifax could be proud, it being known for having little artistic activity or sub-culture. This admirable decision was solidly opposed by the Tories, one of whom had several column inches in the local paper with a big banner headline: The Rape of Spring Hall. Spring Hall was a very attractive mansion in a small attractive park in the centre of Halifax which became the home of NBT. The opposition was fierce and sadly even Alice Mahon, a Labour MP, felt constrained ultimately to say that Halifax probably just could not afford to house this ballet company. Initially, the Labour administration had intended to charge a peppercorn rent but a council meeting insisted there should be a proper full annual rent. Councillor Halliwell, Labour leader of the council, had a vision for Halifax and fought hard against the politicians and the newspapers which opposed the hosting of NBT. *The Evening Courier* had supported the NBT in Halifax but felt at the end it had reviewed its position.

Never a dull moment

NBT since its inception has been no more than a moving balletic crisis. It had always been quite unfairly treated by the Arts Council in receiving a subsidy which was unrealistically low when compared with the other companies, though even there one finds a hierarchy. Making ends meet has been a continuous concern, though in 2015 there were signs of a more reasonable level of grant which has continued to grow. I feel this is more the result of Mark's "political" skills than by complaining of the injustice. Money was only one of the causes of crisis. For instance, the company members were suddenly exposed to an anonymous poison pen campaign of some virulence and the author was never found, although strong suspicions were attached to one gifted dancer. This could have been totally unfair. Another event arose when Gable told one of the oldest female dancers, but still one of the very best, that now she was forty she should be looking forward to what she should do next. Good advice but he simultaneously reduced her performances despite she was the finest woman dancer at the time, technically and emotionally. Another crisis was a literal conflagration. When we moved to West Park in Leeds we occupied some offices on the first floor of this former school. Directly underneath Mark's office was a room devoted to Irish matters and also the gypsies' support team. Someone one late evening set this ground-floor room afire. It burned quickly and fiercely due to accelerants, in this case petrol, to make sure the fire was as destructive as possible. To my knowledge the culprits were never found nor a reason for the attack established. It did mean that our room had to be vacated and the floor made safe. We were, thanks to Mark, able to move his office into that of a Leeds business and so amazingly there was little or no adverse effect for NBT. This practical help was invaluable. Mark was also heavily involved in the problems arising from Stephano, who in the months he was with us, upset so many members of staff that there developed almost a path to Mark's door by complainants. For some of the complainants I had little sympathy as what Stephano was doing was insisting on working in a significantly different way than they had been used to. Other complaints were of a different order.

Mark was a very healthy restraint on me and some of my colleagues. I personally found it quite infuriating when some young man or woman or both would appear from the Arts Council or from some consulting company to show us how to manage the business. I always take pleasure in trying to deflate the gas bag of these theorists but that can, of course, alienate them and lead to reports which are damaging. Not quite East Germany Stasi stuff but realistic enough. Mark was excellent in the way he treated the folk who from time to time descended on us.

I have suffered throughout my life in the world of sports, arts and politics by these experts. For instance, they came on one occasion to us at NBT to review our management system as a pre-cursor to the next grant application. They spent a considerable period on how to change the constitution, to set the periods members may serve, on what form reports should take, how often we should meet, what kind of people we should be looking for. On occasions when we have been subject to this experience I have looked round at my colleagues, all of whom were highly successful in their own personal companies or firms and marvelled at their restraint. There is a saying which I do not like but which fits this kind of situation: "You don't tell your grandmother how to suck eggs." One would delight if they gave us some tip which we could use to our advantage. Many voluntary bodies benefit from those who know how to do things and train others to be competent in that area. I admire and like Mark Skipper. The NBT today as a highly successful organisation owes it most to his skill, ability and devotion.

189

Diane Tabern

Diane Tabern has been the rock round which the storms of the NBT's past 20 years have raged. She was the PA to David Nixon and Mark Skipper. If anyone knows the secret life of the company that person is Diane. If we owe a debt of gratitude to someone for the present situation of NBT then that person would be Diane who has served nearly two decades. Diane has been at the epicentre of all the troubles, the joys, the problems the company has experienced over the past 20 years, the change of chairmen, the move to Halifax, the move to Leeds, the fire, the problems, Giannetti, the death of Gable, the transfer of the current HQ to Leeds, the intense hostility of Calderdale, the development of the academy and the two principals, Nixon and Skipper. There used to be an old song: "If you want to know the time ask a policeman." If you want to know the detailed history of NBT over the last two decades ask Diane Tabern. I found her always bright, highly intelligent and extraordinarily competent in her work and situation. She has played a major role in the NBT's achievements over the last two decades. She finally decided to retire and a bumper send-off was organised to send her on her way. Two days later I called into the building and there she was again, this time as a volunteer. What a splendid woman.

› As previously observed, my experience in NBT was like living in a TV series where there has always to be something new to trigger the next story. Just one example is sufficient to explain such an observation.

Poison Pen Letters

On 6th March 1995 I received the first of a number of anonymous letters telling me there had been a meeting with Gable at which he had told them they would be moving to Leeds and that they should petition the new chair to ensure this happened. The letter alleged Gable was able to "twist the board round his little finger" and that the relationship with the new chairman should be objective and professional. It continued: "What worried us even more is the future of the company under Christopher's management and direction. Our main concern is that Christopher seems determined to change the company from being a dance Company and force it into becoming a pantomime and song and dance troupe. Attached is a copy of a very acerbic and damning Dance report of a recent production of Swan Lake by a well-respected critic Mary Clarke." Speaking on behalf of the company (meaning the dancers), the writer wrote that they would be happy to go anywhere which gave them security and stability. The letter indicated that Gable was not very good at choreography "but falls out with any visiting choreographer employed by the company" and said the relations between him and Gillian Lynne over the Bronte Ballet had deteriorated, creating severe problems. (Gillian Lynne is the most famous and widely recognised as the best director of musicals like *My Fair Lady*, *Phantom of the Opera*, *Cats* and *Cabaret*. She is quite unique and was a friend of Gable.) The letter continued, at length, outlining criticism of the classes they took and relating the number of dancers who had left the company. The letter apologised for the anonymity, finishing by saying "most of us are young and at the beginning of our career and our futures are very much tied up with the company. We would ask you to take this matter seriously and take steps to use your influence to investigate the company's problems and ensure its long term future." Christopher averred: "I have never seen myself as management. It has never been my wish to manage anybody but simply to help you achieve your maximum potential." He continued: "Perhaps the best way to proceed is for the company to have serious discussion about the kind of company they really want. It goes without saying that if anybody wants to talk any of this through with me then I can make myself available as always." Further letters followed and in April 1995 I received a letter addressed to me as chairman, the contents of which varied widely: Why does admin always get the money rather than the dancers? Gable is only concerned about his school and not NBT. Gable extremely critical of Gillian Lynne and the meeting finishing by Gable bursting into tears and exiting the meeting in a flood of tears. The next letter, dated 14th May, stated that because of the past problems, three leading male dancers and one female had resigned, rehearsals are being ignored, Pink is too self-confident and restricting his attention to those works he has been involved in, classes and training are at a record low, etc, etc. "The company is floundering and rudderless and the board appears to show absolutely no interest in the company or who cares how it is run."

This series of anonymous letters was leaked to the press which was creating interest in the NBT of a kind we did not like. The last letter in the long line was a public statement by the dancers of their faith in Christopher Gable. The anonymous letters ceased and now are forgotten. When the letters started I was concerned as some of the comments were valid, especially those about breaches of the House Agreement. I was also so very concerned that the trust placed by everyone in Christopher might be false. I made it my business to discuss, off the record, with some of the dancers I knew well enough to single out. It became clear that the majority of the dancers still were strong supporters of Christopher. Some wished to return to the classical ballets classically performed. Gable's *Swan Lake* had included a riotous scene which involved roller skates. I had seen this performance twice and had loved it. I did not see anything fundamentally wrong to be put right. In artistic companies there will always be these sort of discussions taking place but thankfully they do not normally transmogrify into the sending of anonymous letters. Occasionally they do and I have, at different times, received such in my capacity of Chairman of the Yorkshire Dance Centre, The Playhouse, Red Ladder and also in the sporting world of Sports Aid and the Paralympic Association. Systems should be in place which should make the use of anonymous letters unnecessary but that is a platitude. Sometimes the only way of informing someone in power of something which is going wrong or is wrong, is the anonymous letter. There is always the chance it is malicious and untrue. It is up to the recipient to takes steps to validate or not the truth of the accusation As Chairman of the Social Services Committee in Leeds for many years I received numbers of such letters. All were investigated and nearly all were found to be accurate details of behaviour which demanded further investigation. Some of these were allegations of the most abominable abuse. The occasional one was of a malicious intent and unfair and unjust.

The Move to Leeds

When we decided to move NBT to Leeds I had a clear idea of how to do it. There was a vacant secondary school in West Park Leeds in a very pleasant environment of green space, with two very large gymnasia with sprung floors which would make excellent studios and more than enough office and storage space. They would only be utilising a part of the school, the rest of the school building being devoted to artistic or social activities. The NBT, therefore, would become part of a very substantial arts centre with all that that could offer to the community. I showed Christopher round and he was enthusiastic to be working with me and the Leeds Council rather than the problem Halifax group. Ernest Hall, later, Sir Ernest Hall, felt that if Northern Ballet was going to Leeds he felt that I should take over as chairman. He never betrayed any animosity about the changes as he knew the Leeds solution could be long term whereas the position in Halifax was hostile and uncertain. He resigned as chair and I was elected.

Within a very short time NBT became part of the Leeds local community in which it was placed and the local residents were very sorry to see the company move to its new HQ. One major step I was able to take in my capacity of Leeds Councillor was to identify and secure an area on a prime site, Quarry Hill, where it would in due course be part of the Major Arts Quarter and Community for which I had canvassed and worked for over the previous decade.

Wasted Years

Mark Skipper, the CEO, and I spent hundreds of hours dealing with developers only to be disappointed every time. We were constrained to look for solutions which would mitigate the cost of operations by being part of local commercial activities. The planners suggested that we build the centre as part of a large apartment block. This seemed so promising that the Arts Council produced a glossy document extoling the way in which we were making cooperation with the developers a means to achieve a solution. Developers are, however, only in the business of making money. Unhappily, the developers looked at the cost of a building large enough to house the NBT and produce enough flats to make the scheme profitable. They found it did not give them the profit margin they wanted and so the scheme failed. We experienced the bitter gall of having three potential schemes defeated at the last minute. The developers found that their margin could be achieved in much less costly projects although on one occasion the developers were ready to sign up and had been thanked for their support by HRH Prince Edward, The Earl of Essex, NBT's Royal Patron, when their national board in London decided not to let its regional organisation proceed. We were in this period dealing with some very well respected developers, architects and entrepreneurs such as Rushbond, DLA, Linfoot PL, Carey Jones, Taylor Woodrow, et al. This was quite devastating though we, that is the board, myself and Skipper, were bloody but unbowed to quote Henley again and continued to strive to reach a satisfactory conclusion. Linfoot was one developer I came to know quite well. He had had a meteoric career starting by building up a major development company. He was the man of the moment and highly respected and doubtless envied for his success. I visited his office on a number of occasions and, as bit of a pleb, was very impressed by his HQ. He enjoyed chatting about a whole raft of topics, all of an artistic subject of one kind or another. He suffered badly in the financial crash which I thought was a great pity as he had the promise of becoming a major supporter of the arts.

Our aim was to build a Dance Centre which would house NBT and Phoenix Dance. This was a small company compared with NBT but it had some excellent representatives and was well worth everybody's support. My feeling was very positive towards this joint objective but I felt at the time that Mark did not share my enthusiasm though he was never hostile or obstructive. His sole aim quite properly was to get a home for NBT. My aim was to do that but also to assist a small but exciting company which had developed out of the West Indian community. It did, however, feel at times that the tail was wagging the dog as the Phoenix representatives were very ambitious for their accommodation, but contributed nothing at all in concrete help, though by being an integral part of the project they brought with themselves the aspirations of the Arts Council. This was, I believe, a real help to get agreement and more specifically I had a great affection for and I was keen to support this new company. If we were in a position to help another very fine company we should do just that. We decided to create a free-standing building of ambitious proportions and design, something we had wanted to do originally when we were forced, like it or not, to build it as part of a commercial development. In retrospect, I feel a burning anger that the planners had insisted that we could not build on the Quarry Hill site as a stand-alone development which had caused us years of delay and an enormous amount of wasted effort. This was the same crew who years earlier had told us at the Playhouse that we could not build a fly tower as its height was inappropriate in the city centre. Did they not know that a fly tower was essential? There are in life loons and lunatics and we had them both. In retrospect my major contribution to the new building was being in a position to preserve the site during the years of delay. The site for our new building proved to be very attractive to developers and there was the constant danger that given the delay in making progress with the new HQ, the land would be sold off.

Mark worked tirelessly on designing the new building. Whereas before I had been involved throughout I felt that now we were to build our own building we could leave it to Mark and his colleagues. We of course had very regular meetings but I was happy in the knowledge that Mark and his colleagues had all the knowledge and experience to design a structure which met the needs of both companies. The only matter on which I adopted a totally dictatorial attitude was in reference to the creation of a dance academy as an integral part of the normal business of the NBT. I had for years been incensed by my inability to help young people, mostly girls, who qualified for entry in to ballet schools which were all in London or the South which put it out of court for all but a few. Mark and his colleagues produced an excellent plan for the building. The contract was let and then lo and behold we opened a Dance House which would be the envy of any company. The building is a dream – airy, excellent theatre for dance, six studios two dedicated to Phoenix Dance which has the full and exclusive use of one floor. It is something of a masterpiece and a tribute to the efforts of Mark Skipper which were outstanding and to the City Council which had made the new H Q possible.

I made a deal with the leader of the Leeds City Council, when Tory controlled and who uncharacteristically listened to me, that the council should build the new HQ, we meeting the costs of course so long as I did not figure publicly in the deal. This was a tribute to Skipper's skills and the foresight of the then leader of the council, an old protagonist. By the time the building was completed, Labour had taken over control of the City of Leeds and so, quite unfairly, the contribution of the former Tory leader of the council was ignored which I thought most unjust and mean minded.

Gable

Christopher Gable enjoyed and deserved four great careers The first was the star of Royal Ballet where MacMillan and Ashton created for him and his regular dancing partner Lynne Seymour some of the best loved works of the period. He left Royal Ballet to pursue a career as an actor and became famous for his work with Trevor Nunn, Ken Russell and Peter Brook. Later in 1982 he founded the Central School of Ballet with a wonderful lady Ann Stannard and in 1987 became artistic Director of Northern Ballet, a company he transformed. He devoted his efforts to developing Northern ballet which rapidly gained the public's support in making the Company a powerhouse of innovation, the company under his tutelage gaining an outstanding reputation as the foremost company of dramatic ballet. Just as he revitalised Northern Ballet he created in the Central School a training establishment which has become one of Europe's finest training establishments for classical ballet, more than 80% of graduates going to work in companies all over the world.

Sadly Christopher's untimely death meant ultimately that the Central School did not come to Leeds. The main reason for its coming to Leeds was that Christopher would be leading both School and Company. The School he started with Ann Stannard and his wife was a thriving school and its move would dislocate its progress. It made good sense for it to remain in its present habitat but the desire to have a Centre of Excellence in Leeds associated with NBT remained as strong as ever in my mind and so in all the long and increasingly worrying delays we do have a Centre of Excellence in Leeds led by its inspirational Artistic Director David Nixon and his remarkable wife Yoko Ichino. She like he has had outstanding experience of being a star dancer in companies across the continents and both were and are fired to develop dance training to the highest level so that graduating students can go straight into Companies across the world or to complete training elsewhere.

I had become very friendly on a personal level with Christopher Gable and not infrequently met him in London to deal with matters. I was always tremendously impressed by how this very working class boy could have developed such a deep relationship with members of the most influential people in the country. Gable never played on his modest background but he never tried to pretend it did not exist. I visited him in London on one occasion to discuss some issues facing us and saw how easily he could make the necessary contacts. We met the Duchess of Westminster who had been very helpful to Christopher over the years and as the wife of the Duke of Westminster, had access to wealth which is beyond the comprehension of most of us. She also became an NBT Board Member when NBT moved to Leeds and religiously attended those meetings until the death of Christopher. The issue we needed to solve required action from the Education Department in London. One phone call and we were able to meet the Secretary of State for Education that same afternoon. This is not a system of which I approve but like any politician, I can overlook some issues of which I disapprove if the end result is what I hope to achieve.

A similar kind of occasion when this kind of influence was used arose when we wanted a particularly gifted musician to join the orchestra. He was of a standard which made him invaluable and of a standard which we could not afford to attract in this country for the touring and the wages we could pay. One call to the Home Office enabled the visa situation to be settled immediately and for it not to have to wait possibly months before a decision was made. Nothing at all illegal in this – just a cutting of bureaucratic delay. Just another example of how influence and connections amounts to power. I missed this power of influence when I asked in 2004 the Mayor of

Krasnoyarsk to agree to our asking a principal soloist of the theatre in Krasnoyarsk to take the lead in a theatrical extravaganza in the City of Varieties Theatre in Leeds and the New Vic Theatre in London. The show was called "From Russia with Love". The lack of the contacts in the government made this simple request a considerable challenge involving a significant amount of time and energy, exchanges of letters, promises, etc. I would have loved to have had the influence Christopher had in the high places of government.

Christopher's death was reported to the dancers when they were rehearsing on stage. The rehearsal was stopped by a clap of hands. Silence ensued during which a large and beautiful butterfly appeared and settled on the stage in the absolute silence. A brief report of Christopher's death was announced to the assembled dancers, many of whom broke down in tears. Many considered the butterfly to represent the spirit of Christopher attending the announcement to his beloved dancers. This is the stuff of fables but to those present at that rehearsal, the entry of the butterfly is something none of them will ever forget.

To me, the most distressing memory of Christopher is how in such a short time he became transformed from a lithe active creative human being into a grossly overblown very ill man, bloated because of his medication, who bore no resemblance to his former self physically but mentally his powers were the same. He was very honest, making clear that he accepted that choreography was not his forte and he had therefore employed help in this area. Pink, his second in command was a very good choreographer and it always struck me how honest Christopher was in ensuring that Pink's contribution was properly recognised and rewarded. My one initial reservation about Christopher's time with NBT was the technical standard of his male dancers. The ballerinas were of high standard. Some of the men were not and so dancing leading roles, though performed well, there was not the excitement one should expect when the male virtuoso exhibits his skill. However, a Japanese young man, Hiro, developed an excellent technique and played leading roles for two decades. Also in the company were some very good dancers who were excellent in characterisation. Some were quite brilliant as performers. The death of Christopher left us without an artistic director so our full attention was directed to finding someone to take his place. We were adamant that the essential philosophy of Christopher should be retained. We would remain Northern Ballet and we would maintain our direct involvement in dramatic ballets, ballets which told a story and were not just a vehicle as many classical ballets are – vehicles for solos and duets. I love that kind of ballet when well performed. What could be more exciting and lovely than the *Rose Adagio* for instance, but I also love the direction into which Christopher had steered us and one that fitted the company at its level of public funding. Carole Gable was equally determined that we should preserve Christopher's legacy and artistic vision. She was aware of an e-mail exchange between Christopher and Mark Skipper just 20 days before Christopher died, about the future direction of the company. It was prefaced by Christopher expressing "the greatest admiration for your skills and talent and who believes you to be the best administration director that NBT has ever had." This statement coincided with my estimation of Mark Skipper, who at that time, had the title of administrative director. Christopher went on, "it feels as though you wish to take control of the artistic direction by influencing the board. Can that be true?" Christopher had no need to worry. The board was clear in its intention to preserve Christopher's vision though it was not prepared at this stage to agree to a production which Christopher had been working on Nyjinsky j. This suggestion was strongly favoured by such luminaries as Gillian Lynne w ho saw that Cristopher was nearing the end and wanted him to know that his artistic ambitions would be achieved. Another ballet he had been working on was *Carmen* which was put in the repertoire and was a popular ballet devised by Didi Veldman.

Christopher is of divine memory to me and countless others. There were times when he was involved in a war with Halifax Council about changing the promises of earlier years, at odds with his dancers from time to time, and initially at war with the Arts Council, later to become its idol. It seems that in the arts world attitudes can be so entrenched or so volatile that for those involved it can be like living in a TV series, although in this case the truth is more surprising than the fiction.

Mark Skipper

Mark is NBT as much as anyone else can claim to be. He joined the company at the lowest level on the register and progressed through a range of duties and titles starting in 1992 as Company and Stage Manager, 1994 Company Manager,1995 Head of Planning, 1995–6 Acting Administrator, 1997 Executive Director and by 2003 had become Chief Executive. I know of no one who has done more to make NBT what it is now than he, namely one of the nation's four ballet companies and which despite its very modest grants from the Arts Council compared with the other national companies, regularly wins prestigious awards from across the continents. This sounds unlikely because it is so remarkable. I have been fortunate to have been chairman of a number of major organisations and can say without any shadow of a doubt that he was and is one of the most effective CEOs I have known in the world of the Arts or sports or business. It is instructive to remember his appointment to his present position. When his predecessor left and the company was in the doldrums, Mark applied for the post. The position was widely advertised as was our obligation and wish. He was interviewed with others and it was our decision to appoint him. He was in our opinion by far and away the best candidate. The Arts Council representative said we could not appoint him. Withdrawal of grant was considered or threatened. They referred to his first appointment to the company which was a very lowly position for an unqualified person. I was told by one of the Arts Council representatives that we would only appoint Mark "over his dead body". I declared that I considered that not an unreasonable price to pay. My colleagues and I ultimately got round the Arts Council obduracy by treating his appointment not as an appointment, but as a career progression. A facile step which worked. The opposition to our decision smelled of sheer class consciousness.

Objective achieved

Mark and his colleagues produced an excellent plan for the building. The contract was let and then lo and behold we opened a Dance House which would be the envy of any company. The building is a dream – airy, excellent theatre for dance, six studios two dedicated to Phoenix Dance which has the full and exclusive use of one floor. It is something of a masterpiece and a tribute to the efforts of Mark Skipper which were outstanding and to the City Council which had made the new H Q possible. Mark had made a deal with the Leader of the Council, then Tory controlled, who uncharacteristically listened to me, that the Council would build the new HQ we meeting the costs of course so long as I did not figure publicly in the deal. This was a tribute to Skippers's skills and the foresight of the then Leader of Council an old protagonist. By the time the building was completed Labour had taken over control of the city of Leeds and so quite unfairly the contribution of the former Leader of the Council was ignored which I thought most unjust and mean minded. The Opening was a grand affair which I observed from the back row of the theatre. Some months before the opening I had been approached by a fellow trustee with a proposal which as they say with gusto in old gangster films I cannot refuse. It was in effect: would I step down as chairman for the opening and in return be designated a life long President and have a room named after me. It was all very nice and I did not mind at all really as what I had wanted had been achieved and once one gets to worrying about how well you are recognised for your achievements you sink to the level of those around you. I did think however that I would be involved in the opening in some way. I could have insisted. I did not. At the opening I had no reserved seat but found a good viewing position on the back row. More than one member of staff and two directors made a point of seeing me to say thank you and expressing concern that my contribution had not been recognised nor even mentioned. They were very kind but I reassured them that this was a matter of little import. We should just celebrate a major milestone in the development of the best facilities for arts in Leeds. Sadly the chap a banker by profession who took over the chairmanship from me fell out completely with the Artistic Director and soon with some if his Board and then he too departed the coop leaving the chairmanship in the hands of the man who had delivered the offer I could not refuse. He is and was a very nice chap and he conducted the meetings as Vice chairman very effectively. A search for a new Chairman/woman was conducted and an admirable candidate found. The new Chairman is someone I hope can assist NBT in getting greater recognition and resources. Sir David Wootton is the son of a Bradford Headmaster who by a strange chance coincidence I knew from decades earlier and for whom I had retained over more than four decades the highest regard. He was when I knew him the Head of a School in a deprived area of Bradford and was an inspirational Head, one of the best educationalists I have known. I had the enormous pleasure of meeting him again after four decades on two occasions and was arranging to visit him in the following Spring but sadly he died before we could meet again. I was most affected by his parting having just restored contact after so many years. I should by now know not to wait but "do it now while you can". HIs son Sir David has immediately made an excellent start. I could not be more pleased.

Early intentions Calderdale

Looking back is interesting as it reflects the changes or unexpected circumstances that can torpedo the best laid plans of mice and men. NBT, originally based in Manchester, was tempted to move to Halifax in 1990 as the then Labour Council saw this as something of which Halifax could be proud, its being known for having little artistic activity or sub culture. This admirable decision was solidly opposed by the local Tories one of whom had several column inches in the local paper with a big banner headline: "The Rape of Spring Hall." Spring Hall was a very attractive mansion in a small attractive park in the centre of Halifax which became the home of NBT. The opposition was fierce and sadly even Alice Mahon, a Labour MP felt constrained ultimately to say that Halifax probably just could not afford to house this ballet company. Initially the Labour Administration had intended to charge a pepper corn rent but a Council Meeting now insisted there should be a proper annual rent of £ 34.500. Councillor Halliwell Labour Leader of the Council had a vision for Halifax and fought hard against the politicians and the news papers which opposed the hosting of NBT. The Evening Courier however had supported the NBT in Halifax but felt at the end it had to review its position.

Originally part of the deal with Halifax was that the Central School of Ballet led by Gable and a wonderful woman Ann Stannard should move up to Halifax which would be a very significant artistic coup. However as time went on and the years passed Gable felt it necessary to write a letter to the NBT Board on 2th December 1994. "Calderdale through no fault of its own is in no position to facilitate the move of the School in any way at all. The project therefore will fail unless an alternative can be found".

The alternative was my proposal to all the Parties. I proposed the Company should move to Leeds in temporary facilities until the new Building was constructed. Calderdale were not surprisingly difficult at every stage but my proposal was I think extremely fair and reasonable. The NBT Orchestra, I suggested, should be based in Halifax so Calderdale got a very worthwhile cultural asset. I was a great admirer of the competence of this Orchestra despite its being relatively small. It had a splendid conductor, John Pryce-Jones, a first class Leader of the orchestra and quite exceptionally flexible and competent musicians. I strongly endorsed the idea that it should become an independent body acting as the resident orchestra for NBT but free to use their free time when not performing for NBT to undertake teaching and concerts in the area of Calderdale. To achieve this position a number of hurdles had to be cleared. Calderdale was demanding as much as they could no matter what the grounds for claiming were. They were difficult to contact. I was greatly concerned that Spring Hall, the Company's home could be vandalised once the ballet company had left and the cost of refurbishment became the responsibility of NBT. The deal I proposed was fairly complex as it was aimed at appeasing all parties involved but still achieve the goal of NBT coming to Leeds. The Parties involved were inter alia West Yorkshire Grants, Noel (The Orchestra), The Arts Council, the Regional Arts Council, Calderdale and Leeds. There was the problem of financing the whole change, of persuading NBT, the orchestra, the Arts Council and Calderdale all to agree. Fortunately I was a member of the West Yorkshire Grants Committee and on excellent terms with its members. It was during this period too that the chair of NBT, Ernest Hall, a good friend, felt that he should resign as chairman which I fully understood having kept him fully briefed throughout the whole saga. His knowledge and influence was a significant factor in the final solution. Having been elected chairman in his place made life easier in working round the problems. At a Board Meeting of NBT in December 1996 I outlined the plan I had concocted. I think the witches in Macbeth might have been impressed by its complexity.

The Deal: I proposed: Calderdale accepts surrender of the lease. Concurrently NBT pays Calderdale agreed dilapidations of £ 29,000 plus an additional sum of £ 26,5000 in respect of nine months' notice. West Yorkshire Grants would release to Noel (the orchestra) the £ 30,000 it had retained from the grant it would have paid to NBT. Noel pays to NBT a sum equal to the amount of additional rent NBT has had to pay Calderdale less a sum equivalent to one month, namely £ 22,800. This in effect means that to gain surrender of the lease, NBT has paid one month's additional rent to Calderdale. Noel retain the balance between the £ 30,000 less £ 22,800 and NBT does not press for immediate payment of sums outstanding to it from Noel as Noel is experiencing acute liquidity problems. Leeds is informed of the successful conclusion of this arrangement and makes a further grant of £ 30,000 to NBT to cover the sum retained by the West Yorks Grants Committee. WYGrants has to pay the money to Noel direct rather than through NBT. Under the deal I proposed, NBT was to move out to temporary accommodation in Leeds and surrender the lease in Halifax. I agreed to a reduction in the West Yorkshire Grants to NBT of £ 30,000 to be given to the orchestra now known as Noel which was to be based in Halifax and Leeds would compensate NBT by a further grant of £ 30,000.

This whole business was taxing, dealing inter alia with Calderdale, Leeds City Council, the West Yorkshire Grants Committee and NBT. It could not have been achieved had I not been a member of the Leeds City Council and had the support of the Leader of Council. Calderdale was extremely hostile and wanted its pound of flesh but they ended up with a major new cultural asset in Noel, the orchestra, which has been a great asset ever since at a bargain price as roughly half the year NBT uses the orchestra and pays for it. Little did we know it would take us ten years before we entered Elysium, the new HQ for NBT and Phoenix.

New Artistic Director

Our immediate next step was to choose the right artistic director as we realised that Christopher's illness was terminal. We did after his death decide to take all the time we needed to find the person we thought might be most suitable and to listen to the advice or representations of others who were immersed in the Ballet world. A detailed suggestion was approved by the Board of how the search and appointment should be conducted. The first condition for appointment was that the successful candidate had to agree to pursue " the Board's philosophical and artistic approach of Cristopher Gable, namely ballets of strong classical technique, strong narrative and dramatic theatre" Our advert for a new artistic director was circulated world wide by a number of different means. We created a list of Possibles, Probables, the Unlikely but you never know, until we had a very long list of names many of world-wide reputation, some of national reputation and a few wild card names worthy of consideration. The first long list of 61 included only six females.

A small group formed to suggest a short list for interview met at Sadlers Wells and we went through this very long list of names. We had been advised inter alia by Stephen Barry, Festival Theatre Edinburgh, Clement Crisp of the Financial Times, Alister McCauley, a distinguished journalist, David Bintley of BRB, Nigel Hinds of SWT and Emer O'Sullivan of the Arts Council. We also considered the views of others with a direct contribution to make which included Carol Gable, John Pryce-Jones and the dancers who had had made sure in written form their strong support for Michael Pink. The majority of NBT dancers wanted Pink to be appointed. Pink had had a good career elsewhere as a dancer and had been Gable's right hand man doing much of the choreography which other artistic directors. would have done themselves.

During out informal discussions the delegated group gradually eliminated from our list those who would not apply, those who would but we would not interview and those we hoped would attend for interview. Some had visited the West Park Centre to see what it was like.

In the end we decided to interview Moricone, Pink, Brandsrup, Giannetti and Taylor at West Park the new temporary home of NBT. Each interview lasted always more than the allotted hour. After a long discussion we agreed unanimously to recommend to the Full Board the appointment of Stephano Giannetti. His English was excellent, his knowledge of Dickens surprising.

Life with Gianneti

I liked Giannetti but his Latin temperament led to increasing tension with fellow company members. The need for a change became impossible to ignore The words of Lady Macbeth echo this situation. "If t'is to be done then t'were well it were done quickly". This I found a most unenviable task as I was still the only one to have a good word for him. I liked him and felt sorry for a genuinely talented artist who was living now in a totally hostile environment. His one ballet had been "Great Expectations" which reflected his love of Dickens, which I thought he captured well and the orchestra surprisingly given its size earned a substantial Prize for their recording of the music he had chosen.

To ease the situation I agreed he would be the one to cancel the contract to show he was not being sacked and publicly I announced with deep regret the fact that Giannetti was leaving us to pursue a number of very exciting ambitions and opportunities elsewhere. All was sweetness and light on the surface but below was a mass of mixed feelings and regrets.

Being in a Theatrical company one so often feels it is like living in a tv sit com when every week or so there has to be another dramatic turn. During the whole of Stephano's time at NBT there was a daily drama.

One I was very concerned about was a strong difference between Stephano and Diane Tabern. Diane was Marks Secretary and PA and also served the Artistic Director. Stephano's behaviour was such she finally refused to act for him. Diane is one of those persons I shall always remember and cherish. I saw her as pivotal for the Company just as I saw her equivalent in the Playhouse in a similar light. They are invaluable because of their competence, loyalty and memory. I had to deal formally with Diane and tell her she must perform the functions called for and to avoid further arguments with Stephano. While this was going on Stephano had also fallen out with the Stage Manager whom he accused of laughing and talking during rehearsals: "I am not going to take that shit from you or your shit friend" referring to his ballet assistant. Stephano wanted her sacked immediately. He also found the Ballet Mistress not up to the standard required. This led to a meeting I had with her accompanied by Mark with a union rep also present. It was clear that Stephano wanted a Ballet Mistress who had had a fine career at the top level of performance and that she would never match his expectations. I said if she wanted to be made redundant that could be arranged. After discussion an agreement was reached which satisfied the complainant but caused an unnecessary extra cost to the Company. These are just a few examples of the tensions caused by Stephano and our efforts to make his appointment work. I was heavily involved in all these comings and goings but the real burden was on Mark Skipper who was incredibly efficient in dealing with the details.

Finding a new artistic director

The task of finding a new artistic director was taken on by a small group under my chairmanship. A list of 13 was finally reduced to six. The interviewing Committee was large as we wanted every aspect of the work of the Artistic Director to be considered and that having large group would ensure this would happen.

The first set of interviews clearly justified their invitation to the interview They were four quite excellent candidates and after extensive discussion it was agreed unanimously to recommend Nixon. The second interview should have been with Morricone and Mukhamedov but the former withdrew at the last minute leaving us with two excellent candidates to consider. Mukhamedov presented us with a glittering prospect with a world wide reputation but ultimately he decided not to proceed. Nixon did not have the same international reputation but he did seem to fill our specific needs most effectively. He had performed excellently at interview and he filled all the requirements including an international reputation as a dancer. I was particularly impressed by his enthusiasm for developing a school for ballet dancers and his ideas on strong narrative ballets were exactly what we were looking for. It was a pleasure to offer him the post subject to the usual qualifications. After the loss of Gable, the period without an artistic director, the sad experience with Stephano Giannetti we looked forward to a period of relative calm. That was too optimistic. Michael Pink not unreasonably felt he was the ideal person for the job. His choreography was good which he had proved over and over again when working with Gable. The dancers had declared their support for him and many could not understand how he had been over looked. He was not overlooked as I for one certainly had seen him as a possible artistic director to follow in the footsteps of Gable. I suppose most of us at some time feel we have been unfairly treated and so I appreciated Pink's anger and frustration stoked I feel by members of the company who wanted him and not another Stephano. With Pink they thought they would have an easier ride. They knew him, respected him and liked him. Very valuable assets.

A duopoly

The contract I made with Nixon created a duopoly. He was responsible directly to the Board as was our CEO Mark Skipper. My experience in the theatre and elsewhere led me to believe that if one is given the top spot the company will go in one direction – his or hers. We did not wish to have a company run by an artistic director who could run the company into bankruptcy. We did not want a CEO who ran the business solely with an eye on what was commercial but someone committed to the artistic aims and ethos of NBT. In discussion of this scena at the Board I agreed that tensions could and would arise. It was the job of the chairman or woman to deal with that situation and if necessary refer matters to the Board. In the years that I have been involved with NBT there have been difficult times but the last decade has seen some wonderful work on the stage, the skill of the male dancers now matches the skills of the females, the business is run as a successful business, the Academy is expanding, the NBT or as it is now officially called NB is making a serious contribution to the social life of the city and its environs and Mark and David I am sure have for the other a deep sense of comradeship and the happy feel of joint success. At least that is what I hope. I was delighted when David was honoured by the Queen when he was awarded the OBE. I was equally delighted when Mark was given the title of Deputy Lord Lieutenant. The Company has benefitted from this aggregation of the talents. NBT has been blessed with success and recognition. For instance A Midsummers Night's Dream and the Three Musketeers were nominated for an Olivier Award, the latter receiving the Manchester Evening Post New Theatre Award. The Great Gadsby was recommended for a National Dance Award. David was voted Director of the Year by readers of Dance Europe in 2003 and 2006 and for the successive years 2004, 2005, 2006 and the Patrons Award in 2009 and 20014. NB received the audience award at the Critics Crcle National Dance Awards for three successive years. In 2014 Northern Ballet won the award for Best Company at the inaugural Taglioni Ballet Awards. When we appointed David Nixon we also agreed his wife would become Ballet Mistress and a Principal of the proposed Academy. Yoko Ichino was a dancer who as a soloist danced with the great names in ballet including Nureyev. She has developed her own technique to prepare dancers and has been an outstanding success in developing the Academy.

By comparison with the other three major ballet companies the Arts Council grant is financially poor. NBT tours more than the other three major ballet companies combined. The grant is such as the number of dancers is restricted. This puts major burdens on the Principals. What has always amazed me has been David's ability to get all the dancers to learn different roles in the ballet they are performing so that in a week they can play less physically demanding roles. The importance of this was seen dramatically in a production of *Romeo and Juliet*. During the sword play between the hostile families, Romeo was injured by a sword, survived to the curtain for the end of the act but was too injured to go on after the interval. A colleague rapidly changed costume and took his place for the second half but that change had a chain reaction causing two other males to dance the parts of others. There have been other occasions whereby the importance of principals knowing a variety of roles can be invaluable if the show has to go on. The past financial strictures are illustrated by the occasion when the board had to decide to employ a physio or appoint a new dancer. We could not afford both. The decision was to appoint the physio which was necessary to keep the dancers fit to perform.

Further dramas

NBT since its inception has been no more than a moving balletic crisis. It has always until recently been quite unfairly treated by the Arts Council in receiving a subsidy which is unrealistically low when compared with the other Companies though even there one finds a hierarchy. Making ends meet has been a continuous concern, though in 2015 there were signs of a more reasonable level of grant. I feel this is more the result of Mark's "political" skills than by complaining of the injustice. Money was only one of the causes of crisis. For instance the Company members were suddenly exposed to the anonymous poison pen campaign of some virulence and the author was never found although suspicions were attached to one of the gifted dancers we had. This could have been totally unfair. We never found out the author. Another event arose when Gable told one of the oldest female dancers but still one of the very best that now she was forty she should be looking forward to what she should do next. Good advice but he simultaneously reduced her performances despite she was the finest woman dancer in the company at that time, technically and emotionally. Another crisis was a literal conflagration. When we moved to West Park in Leeds we occupied some offices on the first floor of this former school. Directly underneath Mark's Office was a room devoted to Irish Matters and also the gypsies support team. Someone one late evening set this ground floor room afire. It burned quickly and fiercely. Accelerants, in this case petrol, were used to make sure the fire was as destructive as possible. To my knowledge the culprits were never found nor a reason for the attack established. It did mean that our room had to be vacated and the floor made safe if damaged. We were thanks to Mark able to move his office into that of a Leeds business and so amazingly there was little or no adverse affect for NBT. This practical help was invaluable.

Mark was also heavily involved in the problems arising from Stephano. In the months he was with us he upset so many members of staff that there developed almost a path to Marks door by complainants. For some of the complainants I had little sympathy as what Stephano was doing was insisting on working in a significantly different way they had been used to. Other complaints were of a different order.

Mark was a very healthy restraint on me and some of my colleagues. I personally found it quite infuriating when some young man or woman or both would appear from the Arts Council or from some consulting company to show us how to manage the business. I always take pleasure in trying to deflate the gas bag of these theorists but that can of course alienate them and do reports which are damaging. Not quite East Germany Stasi stuff but realistic enough. Mark was excellent in the way he treated the folk who from time to time descended on us.

I have suffered throughout my life in the world of sports, arts and politics by these experts. For instance they came on one occasion to us at NBT to review our management system as a pre-cursor to the next grant application. They spent a considerable period on how to change the constitution, to set the periods members may serve, on what form reports should take, how often we should meet, what kind of people we should be looking for. On occasions when we have been subject to this experience I have looked round at my colleagues all of whom were highly successful in their own personal companies or firms and marvelled at their restraint. There is a saying which I do not like but which fits this kind of situation: " You don't tell your grandmother how to suck eggs". One would delight if they gave us some tip which we could use to our advantage, Many voluntary bodies benefit from those who know how to do things training others to be competent in that area.

I admire and like Mark Skipper. The NBT today as a highly successful organisation owes it most to his skill, ability and devotion.

The Labour Group at fault

If the Labour Party stands for anything it is honesty and probity. My colleague, Councillor Illingworth, had done nothing wrong when he was suspended by a full Labour Group Meeting in a process which breaks all the proper processes of natural justice. His appeal which was rejected was a farce in terms of justice. Illingworth had the support of Kirkstall Labour Party and the ward and constituency in which he resides. This is a constituency which we should have won given the poor rating the LibDems possessed at that time. This dissention along with the incomprehensible decision to introduce trolley buses to the city however was a conclusive and fatal element in seeing a Lib Dem win the seat again. There was widespread cross-party opposition to a planning application to build on the last remaining playing field that could serve a deprived area of inner city Leeds. The issues were debated at Area Committee Meetings, the Executive Board and the Health Scrutiny Board in May and there was common cause in opposing the proposals but the main concern was whether on Appeal, given the Government's policy of deliberately appointing Inspectors of a particular hue, the decision could be reversed. at a not inconsiderable expense. Notwithstanding this concern the Plans Panel voted to refuse the application. It is sad that many local authorities including Leeds decided they would not go through the time and money meeting challenges from developers when they knew the Inspectors were quite biased in their judgements and consistently favoured the developer irrespective of the facts. Secretly the Executive Board Member invited the councillors from the three wards most affected to a confidential cross-party meeting with the Planning Chairman plus planning, asset management and legal officers. The Ward members reluctantly agreed to a deal to accept the profits from the demolition of a property to fund new urban green space elsewhere and in return withdraw their objections to the planning application. This meeting was kept secret and consequently some Councillors continued publicly to oppose the Victoria Road planning application in line with agreed policy. On 26 March 2014 a Planning Officers' report was published recommending members to ignore Public Health objections and accept the application. Being unaware of the confidential meetings Illingworth, as Chair of the Health Scrutiny Board publicly challenged the report, and suggested it be referred to the Health and Wellbeing Board or the Health Scrutiny Board for possible revision. No criticisms of Labour members were made. Comments on Planning Applications are public documents; they cannot be made in secret and Scrutiny and Plans Panel business cannot be whipped in theory at least.

The then Chief Whip failed in his duty to ensure that Labour councillors knew of any agreements, confidential or otherwise, between Planning Officers and the local Labour and Lib Dem councillors. He has since been replaced. Illingworth continued to promote the existing policy, which had been debated and endorsed by the Executive Board, Health Scrutiny Board, Plans Panel and by the Inner North West Area Committee and its Planning Group. A Special Group Meeting was convened and Illingworth was charged though with what it is difficult to state as there were initially three versions of the charge and so far as I can ascertain no formal written charges were provided to Illingworth at the meeting. There are now four different iterations of the "charge". In effect the meeting was called to approve the recommendation of the Advisory Committee to suspend him. This was not a fair trial. It resulted in a quarter Page article in the Evening Post, a paper with a wide readership, headed "Heart Surgery Hero Suspended over e mail row." Illingworth had taken on the National NHS Management in London and won a Judicial Review to enable child paediatric surgery to continue in Leeds. I understand that at the Group

Meeting, which I could no longer attend, there was a proposal to suspend him which was agreed by a majority in a ballot which was as bizarre as I have known. This was not a " fair trial". It is Kafkaesque and is not consistent with the Party's ethics or rules. The decision was made by a small group of individuals in the Advisory Committee, sure in the knowledge that no one can remember when the Group overturned an Advisory decision whether it was about the closure of old people's homes, sport centres, community centres et al. An appeal was agreed. It took place and to my best knowledge the following statements are true: Illingworth was not told in advance what the charges were against him and for which he had been punished. The then new Chief Whip produced a fourth version of the charges despite the fact that this was an appeal relating to the decision of the original hearing not a new trial. The new Whip produced without warning two witnesses Gruen and the Planning Chairman. Illingworth was not informed of this in advance nor of his right to call witnesses. It transpired that the Regional Labour Party Officer had not sent all the documents to Illingworth and so a brief adjournment was called, a very serious fault on the Regional Officer's part and to the great disadvantage of Illingworth.

Any lawyer would say this appeal process was fundamentally flawed as was the first meeting at which the Group decided on the withdrawal of the Whip. I am appalled at this show trial when the rules of the Party are ignored and personal vendettas are pursued by these means. I am appalled that we were using our energy and time in pursuing personal vendettas in a manner which is a disgrace to the Party when we should be doing all we can to win a seat from the Lib Dems. Sad to say the faith in some of the Councillors has been shattered and a sense of ill will was poisoning the atmosphere when we should be fighting not ourselves but the Tories and Lib Dems. Illingworth, an exceptional individual, modest, high principled and highly intelligent seems incapable of holding a grudge. If I were he I should be looking for blood for this dishonourable behaviour.

He bears no such feelings. I find it ironic that I see myself as a Catholic and as such believe in forgiveness but would be seeking redress and apology if not blood on the carpet. Illingworth, an agnostic or atheist I do not know what he is, has an unlimited capacity to forgive and not to stick pins in a figure in in his cupboard.

Police

A massive change to the organisation of police forces in the country was decided by parliament. The Leeds force would disappear and become part of the new West Yorkshire police. There were sound reasons for this change but the police would lose their close relationship with the communities they had previously served.

I wrote, in my capacity as Chairman of the Leeds Watch Committee (the name of the Leeds Police Committee), to the Home Secretary expressing my concern about the way in which the Chief Constable of the new amalgamated police force was being appointed. I had the honest suspicion that the decision to appoint a particular person had already been made and what was to follow a sham process. Mr Gregory of the West Riding Force and Mr Angus of the Leeds City Police Force were invited to appear before the newly constituted Police Authority for the new area. Mr Gregory was appointed. I believe this was a foregone conclusion and the result of informal decisions but one which it is impossible to challenge in the absence of firm evidence and the methods employed leave little room for that to appear. Almost immediately Mr Angus was asked if he would be Deputy Chief Constable. Naturally, and with my support, he wished to know what the compensation figure would be were he to go. As these had not been devised and as he was required to answer immediately, he was put in a position which had no like across the country. The situation was worsened when Mr Gregory, the new Chief Police Officer, asked for letters of interest from other senior officers for this post and insisting that a decision would be be made on 5th December, that is approximately four weeks before the terms of going or staying were published. My view was that what we needed was a good and honest copper as the new Chief Constable who was capable of meeting the challenge of the new force. Instead we got a person who, in my opinion, had all the social skills for self-advancement but not the abilities to deal with crime in Yorkshire. This inability was demonstrated with awful consequences as the Yorkshire Ripper's activities started in 1975 until his capture in 1981. Gregory's failing in this period led to many changing their views of him. My challenging the way in which the appointment had been managed led to some fairly tart exchanges of views with the Home Office. As chairman of the Watch Committee I could stand on the rules and regulations which were effective until the date of the creation of the new police force. I used the existing law to be very awkward for those who I believed had made a decision to appoint Gregory irrespective of anything else.

My obduracy led to my receiving an invitation to meet The Home Secretary and this led to a silly little vignette. The Chief Constable of Leeds, the Chief Executive of Leeds City Council and myself arrived at the House of Commons and were told to which floor we should go. We used the adjacent lift, not knowing it was to be used by Members of Parliament only. Before the door closed, in rushed Jeremy Thorpe MP with his hat on at its usual jaunty angle. Thorpe was at that time a most significant political figure who featured regularly on radio and early TV. He was what is now termed a personality. He looked at us and then quite deliberately barged into me without a word of apology. I resented this arrogance and barged him rather more generously than he had barged me. The result was that he fell back against the wall of the lift and his jaunty hat adopted a quite unjaunty rake over his eyes. We could have been two primary school children in the playground. It was so stupid that the idiocy of it was more than we three could contain so there were a few moments of barely controlled laughter. Thorpe said nothing, possibly in view of the fact that the Chief Constable was a big chap.

Thorpe was a successful politician who became leader of his Party. Homosexual practices in those days were criminal but in political circles his appetites were well known as he inclined to boast about his successes and even wrote incriminating letters on House of Commons paper. It transpired that he rather preferred what he called the lower orders, rough stuff, and it was from this sociological group that he met his fate. He formed a relationship with a stableboy which broke down. An apparent attempt on his life led to his dog being shot and killed and he was saved because the intended assassin's gun jammed. The trial in the Old Bailey was a significant public event, providing the press and the public with a show which was both hilarious and tragic. Homosexual activity was not merely dismissed as disgusting but it carried very serious legal consequences. His behaviour was strange. From a position of substantial political status and public recognition he fell to being an object of fun so damaging his Party, which in my view was the most heinous part of his story. Although his Party was one I could never support, I know that there are so many people who devote their time and efforts to put people like Thorpe into their very privileged positions. They deserved better.

Savile/child abuse

I knew Jimmy Savile over many years. I disliked his public persona as a disc jockey and later his flouncing about in odd regalia with a big cigar in his mouth. When I met him out of the glare of publicity, I found him intelligent and a very easy chap to get along with. The admiration the public held him in was quite remarkable. When he died, his coffin was placed in a ballroom in The Queens Hotel, remaining there for three days, the public flocking in in great numbers and scenes being recorded by a host of TV cameras and reporters. I made at least three broadcasts from roving reporters as having been known to have been friendly with the deceased. All in all, it was highly bizarre like a staged Royal or Churchill-like state funeral. What was to follow was even more theatrical. Within days of his funeral, a story broke which showed him as a sexual predator. Asked by the BBC what did I think of these allegations, I said quite honestly that I had never heard a whisper of such behaviour over the years and did not believe the rumours I had just heard. The rumours quickly became reinforced by facts which showed his character to be that of Dr Jekyll and Mr Hyde. Never in human history, with few exceptions, can a man's reputation as a benevolent saint be so rapidly changed to become an arch fiend. Saint to sinner in three days.

I find it difficult to understand how he could have got away with what is now alleged. Of course, the riotous Sixties saw a great change in public attitudes and often film stars were feted because of their female or male conquests. All a bit sick but by the end of the Swinging Sixties there had been a massive change in public attitudes; the pill was offering safe sex, HIV was not diagnosed, censorship standards were being relaxed, smoking pot was seen by some as the acme of sophistication, marriage was out for some as old fashioned as social attitudes changed. Had some of Savile's victims complained, the accuser could so easily have become the accused. "Best not to make a fuss" were words often given as good advice. As many men of the so-called Establishment took full advantage of the change in mores, making a complaint against someone in high places became more difficult. The accuser became the victim. We now know that was the case. Certainly when the name of the gross Liberal MP Cyril Smith came up in conversation there were sniggering asides which clearly indicated the speaker(s) knew of his taste for young boys. He was a sick pervert. Many knew. Nobody had the courage to blow the gaff or if they tried, they were somehow silenced. The threat of legal action is very persuasive to all but the very rich as the cost, even if one wins, can lead to bankruptcy and enormous mental strain. In Leeds, my four year stint as the chairman of the Social Services Committee brought me into direct contact with the victims of this plague of child abuse. The public attitude was bizarre. How many times was I told: "You can't stop it" or "Most takes place in the home and so you can never stop it". Such was the view of two politicians I greatly admired. One was Alice Bacon MP who was a minister at the time as was Merlyn Rees. Fortunately, the Director of Social Services in Leeds was a man of splendid mettle. Honest and committed, he ran a very efficient department. Derek James was one of the most easy going individuals except in relation to his job. He was dedicated to serve the poor, the ill and the mistreated. A fine man and one whose memory I shall always cherish. I had the honour of delivering the valedictory address at his funeral. I felt a deep personal loss. In 1983 and in contravention of specific DHSS instructions not to record/register sexual abuse, he started recording and in some detail. He also, with colleagues, looked at the very good work being done in the USA and he began training staff on a multi-disciplinary basis. In all this he was way ahead of any other similar services in the UK. As early as 1985 he asked the Social Services Inspectorate at the Department of Social Security for extra money to meet what he saw was the need for extensive measures to stop or reduce child sex abuse in Leeds. He was told by letter that it was not possible to meet his request for money to finance the child abuse scheme. This response was typical of the Establishment's attitude to what they must have known was a sink of iniquity. Moreover, among many in the community there was a reluctance to discuss a matter so unpleasant as child sex abuse. It was easier to look the other way and most perversely, those who wanted to expose the scandal were often regarded as dubious and disgusting.

Leeds had been early in the field in its dealing with child abuse. Two remarkably brave consultants at the Leeds Hospital, Dr Wynne and Dr Hobbs, had been treating and recording cases of child abuse and reporting it but with little success. They had discovered a test for anal penetration called anal dilation. It was a simple test but only one test among the others. In other words, this was not conclusive in itself. Their article in the *Lancet* led to their receiving some of the most unfair and venomous reaction from many medics who perhaps were annoyed that these two, by revealing the extent of the problem, clearly indicated that they themselves had failed to identify child abuse. I was used to this venom in the world of politics. This surpassed any level of venom I had experienced previously. The two exceptional characters did not receive the applause and recognition they deserved. They were damned by their peers and this affected them both in terms of their health. They nevertheless worked in close cooperation with Derek James, Social Services Director, and from 1983 recorded child abuse separately in the abuse register. There were just five entries in 1983. Four years later the number increased to 223 cases, exceeding for the first time physical abuse in number.

The press was uncertain how to treat this growing phenomenon. *The Guardian* was excellent, reporting regularly and conscientiously whilst some at the opposite end of the moral spectrum reported some of the cases with a lascivious undertone. I was cautioned by political friends not to become involved with the issue as "some of the dirt always sticks". One old sweat who had survived the war as a Tommy and being a prisoner in Japanese hands, said: "If you are digging a latrine you are sure to be covered in mud and possibly something more foul." I appreciated the friendship this advice suggested but I felt that if you take on a job you have to do your best and without exception. This is not liquorice allsorts, to pick the ones you like and leave the rest.

As Chairman of Social Services I received a letter from a woman expressing her views: "I have been treated simulator (sic) but I am 25 years old now and married with two children. From 14 to 18 I was a foster child to a family who had a son three years older than me, everyone was so good. The foster parents were always saying that there (sic) son was like a brother to me, buying me small things, taking me to parties. If they only knew. I was glad to return to my parents. I could never say anything. I was scared of him. I had to sleep with him when he came into my room, he got me to go on the pill, yes, after a while I wanted him to make love to me. I have never told anyone before. I couldn't."

As I looked at the reports, the picture drew darker than ever. During the autumn of 1984, social workers investigated a physical assault on a small boy by a 12-year-old girl who it transpired had been sexually abused by her mother's boyfriend. The investigation began to uncover evidence of very young girls offering sexual favours to men for money or other consideration. Led by James, the police to their eternal credit, agreed to create a small team of policemen to join the social workers in the investigation of this phenomenon, namely young girls acting as prostitutes. This police early involvement was unique in the country and was made possible because I had always maintained good relationships with the police, supporting them on a number of major occasions. The team revealed a web of child corruption in that very small area of Leeds known as Holbeck. It was estimated that 160 children aged between eight and 16 were involved and their sexual experiences ranged from simply observing to masturbating their clients and to sexual intercourse including anal and oral.

These are some of the examples produced in Criminal Court:

› Girl 10: involved with at least seven known men over a short period.

› Girl 11: intercourse with a pervert known to be a danger to children.

› Girl 8: enforced buggery with one known man.

› Girl 12: intercourse with at least four men and suspected incest with the stepfather.

› Girl 12: sexually involved since the age of 10, seeking money for whatever was required by the man.

› Girl 13: sexually involved with at least seven known men over a long period.

Child sex abuse falls into three basic categories, the first of which is abuse within the family. The majority of sexually abused children are victims of an adult or older person whom they know well as father, stepbrother, stepfather, uncle or other close relative. The second form of abuse is where children sell their services for small rewards but here a caveat must be entered as infinitely more subtle factors are present such as a sense of power over an adult, precocious sexual gratification or excitement and status within the group. The third category is the experimentation in which most normal children engage whilst exploring their developing sexuality.

By its nature, sexual abuse within the family is the most difficult to detect and to solve. By definition, it is almost always secretive, the child has a strong deep sense of guilt, often retracts an allegation, dare not say anything as it could break up the family, and often still loves the close relative despite the abuse. Child abuse in the family is so often a self-perpetuating cycle.

The revelations coming out of social services attracted the interest of the television industry and one or two programmes were devoted to the Leeds problems. I was interviewed on these programmes often as though I was responsible for the horrors they were revealing, which I thought was wrong but I welcomed the fact that these programmes were highlighting an abuse which had been ignored over the past decades or longer. I received a very hostile reception when I met the members of the Holbeck Community Association. They accused me and the *TV Eye* programme of defaming Holbeck, a very poor and working class area, which saddened me greatly as I had been Holbeck's councillor for ten years or so in the Fifties and early Sixties. It was an area for which I had the strongest affection. Another handwritten letter was caustic, telling me to get my facts right, "child prostitution – rubbish". "How dare you discuss a problem when there isn't one." This was not untypical of a number of letters I received. I cannot remember one which praised the social services and police for their work in Holbeck.

The abuse, of course, was city-wide though the Holbeck situation was unique. A very sad case illustrates the difficulties social workers have. A lovely young teenage girl was found to have been sexually abused by her father. She was told never to see her father unaccompanied as this could be dangerous. This message was repeated to her and she made a promise never to see her father alone but only as a part of a protective arrangement. This lovely young person wanted to see her mother and knowing that her father would be at work, she went back to her home against her detailed warnings not to do so, expecting to see her mother there. Sadly, the father was there too. He killed his wife and child and then committed suicide. This naturally attracted media attention which resulted in the most unfair vilification of the social workers involved in the child's protection. This angered me and I was very aggressive in defending the reputation of the ladies involved. They had behaved impeccably and short of maintaining 24 hour control of the child absolute protection cannot be effected. I was supported in my defence of the social workers by Derek James or more accurately, I supported him. After detailed inquiries, the social workers were exonerated but I felt sure they had felt to be in great danger. Their bulwark and defender was Derek James, the Director of Social Services. As always, he acted promptly, honestly and with force.

Sexual abuse of children and young adults today remains an unsolved problem. The unwillingness of the police in West Yorkshire to pursue child abuse in Rotherham was a disgrace. When they did react, they revealed a real conspiracy of illegal acts which it is pleasing to note sent handfuls of abusers to prison. That work goes on but it should have gone on a generation earlier and those responsible for this monstrous delay should be shamed for their inaction.

Dealing with child abuse is very taxing. In Leeds we had the two outstanding clinicians who were at times put under the severest pressure from all sides including the media and the medical profession, to its shame. Dr Wynne and Dr Hobbs suffered from this pressure but continued with their work. We owe them a special debt of gratitude.

Speaking at an open meeting of the Association of Metropolitan Authorities in 1986, I suggested a number of propositions which included the following: the government must acknowledge the scale of this problem and the need for adequate resources. Local authorities must devise a strategy fully resourced to deal with this problem. The substantive law must be codified to make it more comprehensible and relevant to today's situation. The adjectival law must be reviewed to ensure that rules of evidence do not preclude guilty verdicts while protecting the innocent accused. Family courts should be introduced. Special training for social workers involved in child protection is essential. MPs and Members of Councils should give regular information to the press, avoiding the use of euphemisms which hide the horror of the trauma to children. The treatment of offenders should be reviewed as it currently achieves not one of the aims of punishment – not even that of retribution. The apathy of society must be destroyed. The taboo should be removed. Ignorance dispelled.

A council colleague some years later was convinced of serious child abuse in a named school. He wrote over the next two or three years to the press, the Prime Minister, The Queen, a number of MPs, the Chief Constable, Archbishop of Canterbury and the Roman Catholic Cardinal and to many others. His accusations were not investigated and he was rather disturbingly treated as disturbed. Thank God the situation has changed. A handful of successful prosecutions has been achieved in Rotherham where the child abuse had long been recognised but nothing was done to stop this horror. Amazingly, many very well-known individuals in the entertainment business have been tried and found guilty. The next step is to go after those members of the Establishment who treated children as their sex toys. A public Inquiry was established and it was with pleasure and relief when I heard that the first named person to lead the Inquiry was Lord Justice Butler-Schloss. She had to resign before she had started as she almost certainly would have to consider decisions made 20 years earlier by the then Attorney General, a close relative of hers. This was a pity in way because Baroness Butler-Schloss was a fine judge and had presided in the inquiry into child sex abuse in Cleveland. Her decision to resign from the position indicated her commitment to absolute propriety. Since then two others have resigned from that position. It is difficult to diagnose sexual abuse. Some families embrace a lot, hugging is normal and heathy. Abuse is difficult to discuss in public. It is often too lurid for TV or film or too unsavoury or disturbing and difficult to suggest an answer. An unfair and untrue allegation against a parent can have devastating effects on family relationships. Possibly the biggest difficulty resides in the fact that children are not believed. This was no problem when two children under two and a half years of age were diagnosed with gonorrhoea.

A very up-to-date attitude was revealed when Microsoft refused to let me open a draft of an article on my computer which

I was preparing on child abuse. In it, I quoted facts and figures in some detail, anonymity being preserved. More than an hour's work lost because of what I presume to be an automatic system which acts as a needed censor.

One case illustrates the complexity of such cases. This letter is a good example of the emotions and problems which affect those connected with allegations of child abuse. It was addressed to me as Dear Mr Atha and the names of the three children I have changed.

Dear Mr Atha,

I am writing to ask for your help to get my two youngest daughters out of care. I have three daughters, Karen, Emma and Ruth. Dr Hobbs told me that he thought Emma had been sexually abused but he could not be certain. He told me to talk to her and see if you can get her to tell me anything. I talked to her that evening and she told me that my uncle had been touching her in a way she did not like. I wasn't sure what to do. On April 10th I contacted Social Services in Rothwell about it, and Mr Dobson arranged for the children, Karen and Ruth, to be examined. Karen was medicled (sic) by Dr Wynn in Clarendon Wing of the LGI and thankfully she hasn't been abused. Ruth was medicled (sic) by Dr Hobbs and he said he thought she had been abused but she denied it. There was 2 Social Workers with us MXXX and GHXXX. They contacted the Police and DC Backhouse from Morley told me he would arrange for 2 policewomen to come from Millgarth Police Station to my house to take a statement from Emma. The two policewomen came on 12th of May and EXXX gave them a 7 page statement. Three weeks later my uncle was arrested. He denied everything and because the Police had no corroborating evidence they had to release him. On 9th May I had a letter from Dr Hobbs asking me to go and see him on 12th May. Because he'd said that he thought that Ruth had been abused. I took her with me and asked Dr Hobbs to examine her again He did then told me she had been abused since last time he had examined her. I just could not believe it as I'd not noticed any change in her behaviour. She had no bed wetting problems etc and was a very happy care free little girl so I asked for a second opinion.

Dr Hobbs arranged for Dr Winn to examine both Ruth and Emma that afternoon at the Clarendon Wing. Mrs Howe took my 2 daughters my husband and I to the Clarendon Wing and Dr Wynn examined our daughters. She confirmed what Dr Hobbs had said about her but did not think in Emma's case it was going on. By the time DR Wynn had finished her examination Mary Cousens had arrived with PC Backhouse and two police women. My daughters were taken in to care and we were given a 28 day care order. Both my husband and myself have been interviewed by the Police and have been told that the police are satisfied that we have not abused our children. After five weeks in care we were told on 16th June who had been abusing her. My uncle has been taking her for car rides This is where I need your help. We told the police straight away and were promised that the three police women would go and see Ruth and get a statement from her then the Police at Morley could arrest my uncle and hopefully charge him then see about getting my children back. But here we are 10 days later and so far the police have done nothing. The longer my daughters have to stay in care there is always the possibility that my uncle could abuse some other little child. Can you do anything to help me. I would be very grateful. Also Ruth will be 8 years old on July 11th and I would like her to celebrate her birthday at home. Another thing I would like to ask you, is there any reason why my husband and I should not be able to visit our daughters every day? It is heart breaking enough that our children are in care but it would ease the pain if we could see them more regularly. We asked Mrs Howe but she told us that if she said yes

she would get into terrible trouble her from her boss. Will you
please ask Social Services for permission to see our daughters
more regularly her.

Thank you for reading this letter,

Yours Sincerely,

HXXXX

I was moved by this letter and was very happy to get in touch
with the department and get some answers and actions. The department has the obligation to be careful and this can lead at
times to unreasonable decisions but on the whole social services
are charged more with neglect than over activity.

Gross stupidity Trolley Bus

In 2013 a very extensive discussion of a plan to create a trolley bus service in Leeds occurred. The scheme proposed was very expensive and every month which passed by, the costs increased. The motivating force was a Leeds councillor who also chaired the regional Transport Organisation which had been established to look at transport regionally. There was almost universal opposition to the scheme which failed every test yet continued to be driven forward by this scheme. Had it been implemented it would have meant massive destruction of properties and effectually damage the Headingley community and centre. It simply was a completely daft proposal, a bit like the old story of the king who wore no clothes because no one told him he was naked. Labour members were constrained to defend the indefensible. This enabled the one Liberal MP to have an enjoyable time lambasting the Labour administration and all for nothing as subsequently the leader of the council, under pressure from many of his colleagues, determined that the scheme had to be formally discarded to stop the discussion of a scheme which he felt would never be built. What a crass episode in terms of wasted time, and large amounts of money spent on the scheme and most importantly of a feeling in the local population that they had been constrained to defeat a barmy Labour Party scheme. The Leader could have put a stop to this crazy scheme. He did not and the Party felt the impact His unwillingness to act against his close colleague gave the one Liberal MP in the city the chance to win countless supporters by his open objection to the scheme, sufficient for him to retain his seat in Parliament which a few years later he lost.

Leeds Film Festival Le Prince

I was approached by a very enthusiastic woman, Janice Campbell, with a most gorgeous gurgle of a laugh who suggested we should develop a Leeds Film Festival. She pointed out the role Leeds had played in the development of film from an erratic cause to wonder at the flickering screen to a developed fine art. Her enthusiasm was infectious and her arguments logical and sound. We agreed to set up the Leeds Film Festival which has now become the second largest Film Festival in the Country after The London Festival.

Leeds has played a very significant role in the development of cinema in this country. Many of the very advanced projectors were made in Leeds which later caused me some headaches as there were a host of Leeds made projectors which we felt should be preserved as museum pieces but they were very large and storage of large objects is very expensive particularly if they by their nature do not attract hordes of people to see them in an exhibition. Projectors do not have the power to attract large crowds. We tried one exhibition and it was a total failure in every respect.

Leeds had also provided the world with a major "Who dunnit" scenario which still attracts attention. Opposite the Fenton Hotel in Leeds where the former BBC building was and which is now part of the Beckett University Louis le Prince worked on making a revolutionary new movie camera. He it is claimed without serious contention to have succeeded in his ambition to have been the first person to invent a useable moving picture camera and he proved this by making two brief films on paper film using the single lens camera he had invented. As big commercial interests in the movies as our US colleague would call them were growing. Le Prince claims were received with great interest especially in the USA where similar ambitions existed, the big name Kodak and Edison being familiar to all. Anyone able to produce a good working movie camera was going to make a fortune. Louis le Prince was many months ahead of his competitors such as the Lumieres and Edison in the USA who a year or more later took their claims to court, claiming the patent on their camera.

The first film clip made by Le Prince shows Leeds Bridge in 1889. It is a 30 second film, which had been looped. It shows the view of the motning traffic on Leeds Bridge looking North from the window of a building at the end of the bridge which is still there today. It was shot on sensitised 2–1/8th Inch paper and is reputed to be the first actuality film to have survived. Le Prince shot this brief film with a revolutionary camera. He disappeared in mysterious circumstances and others were able to patent his inventions and so make a fortune. This film was reshot to start the first Leeds International Film Festival using an exact replica of the originall camera and shot from the identical position with a descendent of Louis Le Prince standing on the bridge in the place of one of the individuals seen on the original film. This was the idea of Janice and required all traffic to stop whilst the film was shot. This caused massive grid lock in the city as the Leeds bridge had to be clear to produce the film. The figures on the bridge were dressed as they had been shot by Le Prince and I was asked to be one of the people in shot. This film is still in the archive.

Louis le Prince was known to have taken a train on 16th September 1890 and had not been seen since. No trace of where he had gone could be found. He simply disappeared as did his luggage and his body was never found. The suspicion arose when the question was asked; Who would benefit from his disappearance? Were the profits to be made by someone making and patenting a workable movie camera sufficient to justify murder? The gravest suspicion was of competitors in the USA who did succeed in making such a camera and enjoyed thereby ever larger profits as the Film Industry expanded with remarkable rapidity.

The Leeds Film Festival has gone from success to success thanks to those remarkable enthusiasts who held the post of Film Festival Director, namely Janice Campbell, Kath Baker and Liz Rymer and an equally inspirational lleader Chris Fell who have been able to attract such luminaries as Ken Loach, Peter Ustinov and Lord Attenborough. The latter was well known for his use of the term Darling as a mode of address. His explanation to me was that as he met lots of people whose names he could never be able to remember he called them all the same namely Darling so achieving equality of address to all but the Almighty. Lovely fellow and I did enjoy being called Darling when we met. First "Hello Bernard" and then always Darling.

Alan Bennett

The Leeds City Council decided to honour Alan Bennett with
the highest honour it is able to confer, namely the Freedom of
the City which must have amused Alan as the Freedom of the
City confers no freedom nor any right to drive sheep across
Leeds Bridge. I was nominated to make the conferment speech
in Council which was an honour in itself for me. In my speech I
pointed out that Leeds had produced a number of distinguished
writers such as Hoggart, Waterhouse and Willis, the classic story
for children of all ages, *Swallows and Amazons* written in Leeds
and Barbara Taylor Bradford. I said that none is more illustrious
as he whom we honour today. He had pursued an exceptional career as performer, writer, playwright, diarist, TV presenter, film script writer, broadcaster and occasional director. He
has scooped more awards than the promises any three politician
make in a year. His work whether it be plays, diaries, prose or
TV is imbued with a genuine compassion for others, an understanding of human nature and concern for the human condition.
It is at the same time gently ironic which makes his work so po-
tent. His career as a performer in Beyond the Fringe with the
highly educated, intelligent group of young men, produced incredibly silly and nonsensical sketches which are as uproariously
funny today as they were three decades ago. They took America
by storm and revolutionised comedy. I suggested that his prose
works commands equal public appreciation. Diaries and memoires evoke for many of us waves of nostalgia as we recognise
the places which he paints so economically but accurately, the
forgotten vocabulary, words like sculleries, middens, ginnels,
long-departed picture houses, the pictures rather than the movies, odd things like the Kennedy Latin Primer, a copy of which

book I still retain today and from which I learned the magic rules of grammar and the order or ranking of the floor cloth. Despite the success which takes so many away from their roots, he has always retained an affection and an interest in Leeds. Some years ago he wrote to me expressing fears about the future of the reference library. "It's a library I'm very fond of since I was virtually educated there and I'd be sorry to see it dispersed." He wrote to me: "Could you let me know what the situation is? I am sorry to land you with this but short of the staff in Hertz Car Hire and one or two ladies in Marks and Spencer, you're the only person I know to ask about Leeds matters. I had other occasions for correspondence. As chairman of the Playhouse, I had asked him if we could name one of the two theatres we were building in the Playhouse after him. He replied to the effect that he was greatly honoured but that as most theatres seemed to be named after dead people, he thought he had better not risk it. He has, however, been a great friend of the Playhouse as whenever we put on one of his plays we do excellent business.

In my view a recital of his successes, his skills, his perceptiveness and the causes for his celebrity provide only a partial explanation of his popularity. I think we really like him for his genuine concern for others and for his eccentricity. Who else would allow an obstreperous old woman to park her van in his drive and live there for years? Who else would later enshrine her in immortality by writing a play about her van and him?

I concluded my conferment speech by saying: "If you ever feel you are running out of inspiration, do come to a council meeting when you would have enough material to write a dozen more articles or plays."

Uganda and Save the Children

In 1988 I had an experience which I treasure because it exemplifies the remarkable potential and character of young adults. I was invited to join a small group to visit Uganda to report on how children were suffering and how we can help. The expedition was organised by the Leeds Give for Life, an outstanding charity. Our group of five consisted of Anne Pickles, woman editor of the *Yorkshire Evening Post*, one of their most effective cameramen, a representative of the Church of England, a lay member of the Catholic Church and myself representing the Leeds City Council. The aim was to raise a million pounds in Leeds to aid the devastated children In Uganda. I was asked to join as I had led a similar very successful major appeal in Leeds. Our visit would precede a visit by the Princess Royal, a person whom I hold in the highest regard for her charitable work. I had by then travelled extensively in Africa and understood the terrible life so many millions of Africans were forced to experience. When we arrived in Uganda we were met at the airport by an African driver and the senior white representative of the charity in Kampala. We were taken to a large house in a small compound guarded by a large gate and a guard. The guard was an old man and he carried a rifle. I looked at it, recognised it as a very old single-shot rifle and pretty well no real weapon of defence. He was a cheerful old guy with whom I made immediate friendly relations. The house was home to a small group of young idealistic women and men working for the charity. They were lovely committed young adults with a great sense of humour and the capacity not to be overcome by the realities which they dealt with daily. I was full of admiration for this small group of volunteers.

We visited the main hospital. It was primitive in this capital city. The staff seemed totally dedicated; the facilities were pathetic, if not actually appalling. I had seen horses better housed back in the UK. So much was primitive and old. Its strength as a hospital lay in the dedication of the staff and ancillary workers. I felt like crying at some of the sights I saw. One has to be inhuman if one is not to be seriously affected when one sees a small child on the point of death because the services are inadequate. Mothers were allowed to sleep under the bed of a seriously ill child serving as nurse and mother. We were shown a freezer which contained a large number of dead children. The hospital kept them for a period of time to allow relatives to collect, and if not collected they went into a communal grave. Much of the medical equipment was antediluvian so I resolved when I got home to visit all the major hospitals in the area and collect any small equipment which I could send when discarded by the Leeds Hospitals. In one children's ward the cots were, in fact, small tin baths normally used for bathing young children. Here, they were cots with ill children in them.

I became very friendly with our driver, a most jolly fellow, always ready for a laugh but also excellent in his job. One of his roles was to find a home for orphaned children. He would drive round small villages with two or three children asking at every stop for people to come and look to see if they recognised the children. On one of his rounds he had found in one village some of the locals who said they knew the children and that their parents and family had been killed in the troubles. One lovely occasion which still fills my heart on reflection was when we took this young girl of probably 11 or 12 with a much younger sister to a tiny village in the bush. We brought with us a large rabbit which the little girl held tightly and possessively and a cooking pot and some food. We arrived at the village and were taken to the mud-walled, thatched roof, single room hut which was to be their home. There we left them and I felt an enormous sadness as I envisaged what kind of life they faced.

Driving round with my friend the driver with two or three children, was always fun and interesting. We visited little settlements – really often nothing more than a few primitive houses built in a circle so the space in the centre became quite hard. On one occasion we arrived at a larger settlement perhaps 20 or more huts. We were warmly welcomed as my driver was well known and obviously respected. I saw a three-legged stool and went over to sit on it whilst the driver did his spiel. I had no sooner sat on the stool than a subdued low cry came from the mouths of the women present and they all looked at me with anger. I did not know the cause of this sudden interest and hostility but did see the sign of what seemed to be strong hostility. My driver intervened and told me the stool was a birthing stool and only women could sit on it. I had broken this taboo. I rose with unaccustomed speed, leaving the stool in situ. In a moment of concern I wondered if the stool could have any effect on my sexual life. The driver apologised to the angry women in a loud argument and in some heat. He later told me why. Because I had desecrated this stool it had to be returned to the state it was in before I changed it. This would take time and ceremonies which were time consuming. No male is allowed to sit on that stool.

I felt safe with my driver going where the authorities would strongly suggest we did not. Our safety could not be guaranteed. The truth of this statement was reinforced by three events. The first was when we were driving along a path in very high elephant grass. We were driving quite slowly until we heard a short volley of light arms which we assumed was directed at us as no one else was around. It came out of the blue. A quick burst and then another. My friend put his foot down on the pedal so we disappeared quite quickly in the opposite direction from which the shots seemed to come, using the tall elephant grass as cover. He made me promise that I would not recount this episode back at the house as that could mean he might be prohibited in the future from going where he pleased. The second event showed an aspect of there being no enforceable law. Our local colleagues gave us a lot of good advice. They warned us that out in the bush or on the main roads there were groups of young lads with arms who often stopped cars pretending to be security forces and would demand money. We were advised to carry just a small sum in our pockets and hide the rest in the car. We were stopped by a handful of lads in a kind of uniform who appeared to be in their early teens. They purported to be official safety staff, a kind of territorial army and demanded to see our money. The young men were carrying guns which looked like Kalashnikovs. As these are capable of rapid fire they are particularly dangerous in the hands of the non-expert. The expert has his finger extended but not on the trigger, until he or she wishes to fire. The non-expert has his finger on the trigger so just a non-expected jolt or shock can produce a burst. This small group had their fingers on the triggers. This did cause me real concern. However, we let them search us rather perfunctorily and take what money we purported to have and then were allowed to go on our journey. The third indication of the lawlessness of the time came a day or so later. We had agreed to take a plane from the airport and fly in it to the north to where there was another isolated Giving For Life station. Travel there by road was too dangerous. We arranged to meet the other workers in the organisation and be able to report back when we returned to England. The pilot of our small plane phoned the remote air field we were to land on to meet our colleagues and use their car for us to look around this outpost service. The pilot handed the phone to one of my colleagues who spoke to the people we were going to meet. He told us that bandits had just stolen their vehicle and all their money at gunpoint but no one was hurt. Our visit had to be cancelled as, though we could land as planned, there was no means of moving off the airstrip.

Life in Uganda at that time was very uncertain. For considerable periods there was no effective national government. Everything was uncertain, be it electricity, the phone, safety in the street or in the bush, etc, etc. This made me even more honoured to have met the young folk who help others and who were our hosts for our stay. They went out six days a week on their good works, aware of the dangers which no matter how careful they were, remained omnipresent. In the relative safety of their "home" they were a jolly, spirited, splendid a group of caring young people, full of enthusiasm, fun, direction and spirit. They were delighted we had come to see for ourselves the problems they were attempting to solve or at least ameliorate. They made us, the visitors, feel rather humbled.

One abiding memory of the trip remains with me. It is the recollection of the piles of human bones in so many "villages" – the bones of the men who were so mercilessly murdered in the so recent days of horror. Man's inhumanity to man evidenced.

Europe

In late 1992 the European Community, through two of its major divisions (DG V and DGX), decided to establish a European Community Committee on Sport for People with Disabilities in each member country. It is difficult to realise how backward so many countries were in developing sport for people with disabilities and I welcomed this move, knowing how difficult this was going to be in so many ways such as the wide range of languages, the disparity in the way nations dealt with the disabled, the cost of meetings and the necessary bureaucracy, etc.

The guidelines for setting up this central committee were very simple and sensible. Each country would elect two persons to attend meetings of the EC Committee. Voting at meetings would be on the basis of one vote per member with no postal votes or substitutions permitted. This autonomous committee would advise the Commission of the European Committee on Sports for People with Disabilities and devote itself to stimulating, developing and organising sports for disabled people and importantly to evaluate applications for grants. All very fair and sensible. The aim was to encourage participation in the interest of social cohesion, good mental and physical health and fair treatment, and above all, because sport is good per se. The proposal set out very clearly issues like the involvement of disabled people at all levels and how the national committees must operate to be party to this development. Of particular interest was the proposed guidelines for applications for subventions.

A year later, in September 1993, a meeting was held chaired by an old friend and colleague, Bob Price, who had significant connections with and experience of, the EU Commission. The minutes record that Price admitted there had been some problems but "he had done his best to smooth down the problems encountered during the transition period." I had been involved, dealing with a number of these difficulties which were inevitable in this kind of operation – issues like should the organisation become an NGO (Non-Governmental Organisation) or an Advisory Committee? There were profound consequences involved in the choice. I was happy to second a resolution which was carried for the creation of an advisory committee and also to propose successfully that "The commission will request advice of the European Committee before implementing a policy on sports for people with disabilities" and that votes could only be cast by members attending. It would be wrong to think that the commission had not previously aided sport in the then limited number of countries in the EU. The UK led with 20 events supported and only one other country got into double figures. Perhaps the most successful event was an event organised by the UK Sports Association for People With Learning Disabilities (UKSA) and INAS, the International Sports Federation for persons with a Mental Handicap. The event was a conference attended by nearly 60 delegates from 20 different countries and more than 200 others who joined in the workshops and discussions. It was organised primarily by a man called Roger Biggs, a Londoner by accent and a brilliant organiser and advocate. He was Chief Executive of the UKSA of which I was chairman. I would have loved to take the credit for this but cannot as it reflects my modus operandi: if you want something done well, find the persons to do it and then sit back and take the credit.

In 1993 the UK received substantial support for 20 projects. Belgium was the only one to achieve double figures for schemes supported. The UK had 25% of the grant available as against the other 11 States.

In 1994 the 10th World Transplant Games were held in England with more than 1000 competitors from 35 different European countries. It was a tremendous success. To qualify, each competitor must have received a transplant of one or more organs – kidney, heart, lung, liver or pancreas. Public interest was very high, which of course is one raison d'etre for the Games. It helps people who may have to face having a transplant to know that this procedure really does work.

In 1995 the Greek organisation, Special Olympics Greece, which seemed to qualify perfectly for membership of the European initiative, was denied membership as the body representing Greece. The members contacted me to intercede on their behalf. I was surprised that their application had not been accepted and looked for a reason. It seemed that the constitution of the Special Olympics did not permit its inclusion in or membership of the Greek organisation on the ground that Greek law prohibited membership because Special Olympics in Greece was "owned " by the American organisation. It was not a free organisation. I took the matter up in May 1995 but it was not before the end of the year that the Greek committee was allowed into the Garden of Eden with the other countries. I have no doubt at all that there had been the strongest pressure on the officers of the EU. The Kennedy family had started and developed Special Olympics and their interest in the organisation was, and is, retained. It was, in those days, organised like a multi-country business, very proscriptive and organised. The Kennedy family remain closely attached to their baby and well they might for they have done an enormous amount to help people with a learning disability.

At that time, Special Olympics (SO) treated people with a mental handicap as children. For instance, they had a system which meant that at the end of a race they were hugged by huggers. As someone observed: "They may be mentally handicapped, but they are not daft." This arose out of a colleague hearing one lad saying to the other that when he finished the race he would make for the woman with the big bust. Better hugger than the lady by whom he should have been hugged. Special Olympics had a strong following in parts of Greece and during a meeting in Athens Bob Price and I were invited to go for a sail by a very forceful, very engaging woman who was a senior member of the Greek SO organisation. I did like her, despite acknowledging that we were the subject of a very pleasant inducement. The lady wanted Special Olympic Greece to be the official member representing Greece. The sail was in a very large boat, the sort you associate with the very wealthy indeed. We were entertained most generously and that sail is a memory I shall never forget. It was a glorious 12 or more hours of sheer sybaritic excess. Every now and then I have the privilege of seeing or experiencing occasions which are quite outside any reasonable expectation. This was one. We were not suborned and my enchantress did not succeed in her ambitions then for Special Olympics. The law in Greece changed and this permitted me to propose successfully that it should become the Greek member, albeit as one of a new wider membership.

In 1995 we had a meeting of the whole committee, 17 nations being represented and a report received of those events and initiatives supported. It was quite impressive even to me, a critical person by nature in these matters. There was a lot of talk but people do need to say something or they and their interests are ignored. We had immediate translation in four languages normally which gives the English-speaking members a distinct advantage and is possibly one reason why Bob and myself were so involved, he far more than I.

There is a common complaint at the cost of the EU organisation and I am sure that a more pro-active management of affairs could lead to some savings. The reality is, however, that if one is to be fair and impartial to all nations, great and small, each with its own language, the enormous cost of employing large numbers of highly-skilled translators, produce reports in a variety of languages, maintain buildings, meet extensive travel and phone costs, etc., the basic costs of the organisation can be and doubtless are enormous. This makes it so easy to be unreasonably critical of the system.

Cadet Fighter AFFN Church Fenton

I joined the Air Cadets at school as soon as it was permitted on the basis of age. It was a fascinating experience. We visited regularly a number of RAF stations in Yorkshire as a group but it was possible to visit a station on one's own initiative and were always received without difficulty. In addition, we went on a week's attachment twice a year which gave us a fascinating experience of seeing Bombers being loaded up with bombs and watching them take off on missions. They would taxi out and wait for a green flare to set them off. It was, even then to a young teenager, an emotional sight knowing that some would definitely not be returning. The air crews were to me of outstanding bravery as each one would know that the chance of completing a full tour was very slight, most not getting past ten sorties before being shot down.

We were able to visit RAF stations quite frequently and we all managed to fly in one or more Lancasters, Halifaxes, Airspeed Oxfords, Ansons and Whitleys. On one Easter holiday, the school magazine records, every cadet had at least one flight and most had two. Very occasionally, the pilot would let a senior cadet take over the controls. This was a practice of which we passengers did not approve but of course the skill of the instructors was such that there were no nasty surprises. The most exciting experience we had was being taken up on training or testing flights. The supreme experience which I had on two occasions was something called fighter affiliation. This was, in my case, a Lancaster taking off and then engaging with a Spitfire in a mock attack. The aircraft would be proceeding as though attacking a target and then was subject to attack by the Spitfire. We heard the WOP/AG (Wireless Operator Air Gunner) call out "corkscrew port or corkscrew starboard" which caused to pilot to undertake a manoeuvre to evade the attacking plane. We could not see what was going on but were able to hear the various commands and hold tight to anything in the plane which we could grasp. This process was recorded by a senior member of the cadets in the school magazine called the Owlet. I still have the copy.

"Our Halifax went upstairs to about 6,000 feet and then a Spit hurled itself at us. The driver (pilot) warned the crew over the RT (we all had earphones) and proceeded to jink. "Bandit coming in on starboard – 1000 yards – 500 yards – jink," called the rear gunner. "Corkscrew dive, port to starboard. Here we go," shouted the skipper and we went with a vengeance. The horizon leapt up. The dial, showing the rate of climb and descent, told us that we were diving at 5,500 feet per minute and turning all the time. Next came the worst part of all – the climbing at maximum rate. This climbing puts a terrific amount of pressure on you. You become unable to lift your arms, your mouth is forced open, you remain helpless, unable to think coherently – benumbed in mind and body until one becomes insensible. This jinking is the approaching doom. I just sat there in my misery and waited but thanks to a light dinner I managed to stave off disaster."

Another fellow cadet described the same exercise less graphically in a later report in the magazine without a schoolboy's hyperbole but equally detailed.

One outstanding memorable experience was a flight in a large glider. I remember the names of two types, Hansa and Horsa. We collected our parachutes from the store and were ferried across to this very large glider. We got inside and had to sit tightly attached to the seats, No walking about or movement no matter how necessary it was. We were towed off from a long runway by a Stirling Bomber. It was a strange experience to be taken airborne by being towed and the experience came more personal and concerning when the glider detached itself from the Stirling and we were flying without any means of propulsion except gravity, which seemed to me more a threat than a benefit. My genuine concern was minimised by the thought that if it was dangerous they would not have let us go up in the first place. The pilot was, of course, a highly trained pilot and he was teaching servicemen to become the pilots in those amazing and deadly raids towards the end of the war, the difference being that we landed on a long runway with a crack pilot and there was nobody firing at us. I look back and wonder at the bravery of those men who parachuted into the enemy territory or arrived by glider landing on sites which were most often of rough terrain or protected by posts stuck in the ground by the Germans against glider attacks.

As a rather gauche teenager, my close school friend, Richardson, and I enjoyed the fun of the ATC. Where else could you be shown how to shoot a Lee Enfield 303 rifle at targets a hundred yards away or shoot a Sten gun. "Be careful how you hold it as if you hold it wrongly you will shoot your finger off." This stern warning I remember more than 70 years later. We were shown how to throw hand grenades, initially and thankfully all without explosives, as some of us were not as effective at throwing them as others. Then we had to throw one live grenade when all but the thrower and the sergeant in charge took safe cover. This training served me well when I was conscripted into the RAF and sent to OCTU – Officer Cadet Training Unit. We Air Cadets had at least one week's camp per year. Our Commanding Officer was our chemistry teacher who had been trying for two consecutive years to teach me chemistry. As I look back I was quite possibly an insufferable young student in his class and so our personal relationships were strained. To get his "own back" as it were, he designated me his batman and then as we were under martial rule (we were covered by King's Regulations) as it were, he made the most of making my life very busy. One duty I had to perform was to take him his morning tea at 0650 hours exactly. I saw one possible method of chalking up one success against him to balance the entries he had on his register of me, things like clean his boots, make his bed, clean his rifle and bring him his morning tea. At 06.50 hours exactly I brought him his tea in a mug in which he kept his false teeth overnight and his teeth in

254

his drinking mug. His eruption is what I wanted and received though it did not improve relationships. A couple of years later when, as a sixth former and prefect no less, I apologised to him and he remembered the occasion with a resounding laugh.

Richardson and I often at weekends would put on our uniforms and cycle to one of the local air stations and sign in at the guard room and then go to "Flights" to see if we could cadge a lift. This generally was unsuccessful but sometimes we were lucky and a plane was due to be tested after maintenance and we heard the magic words: "Get your parachute." What a wonderful instruction that was. Such informality today would not be countenanced much less permitted. Pity in a way that we have become so meticulous in drawing up policies which do protect but do also rule out a bit of imaginative freedom. Such is the cost of a compensation culture. It has not prevented my silent voice telling me that I am one of a very small number of individuals still alive to have flown in a Lancaster, Stirling, Hampden or Whiteley. My heart goes out to those extremely brave young men who went out on raids from which they had in some cases little hope of returning. God bless them and shame on Churchill who prevented Bomber Command from participating in the magical VE Day parade in London. What a disgraceful decision and all to do with the bombing of Dresden which suddenly had become an attack, being challenged for its unimaginable destruction and strategic importance. Churchill gave the order to bomb and did not want later to be associated with the horror of the destruction.

Many years later, as vice chairman of the National Sports Council, I was asked to visit a gliding club in North Yorkshire. Again, I found the informality of matters surprising and exciting. I was offered a flight in a two person glider which I accepted most willingly. Then came the informality I love. A chap came up to my host and offered to tow us off. He was an Air Vice Marshall in mufti and had to ask the owner of the towing plane details about speed on take-off and landing and a number of technical questions about the plane. This quick and almost laconic briefing of our towing pilot took very few minutes and then we were hooked up and being towed by this small aircraft. I was surprised how rapidly we were airborne and how quickly we were able to cast off and enjoy the amazing feeling of freedom in circling over updrafts which my pilot knew very well. It was exhilarating and almost religious in its effect. I had a few concerns about the landing because in a glider you cannot "go around" if you are making a mess of the landing. My pilot, however, was skilled and we landed perfectly on the grass. It had been a most splendid experience and I felt a sense of gratitude to God for being so generous with His favours.

My love of flying was, I think, started by reading the Biggles books which were popular in the 1930s and 40s. It was singularly enhanced when I was posted as a most junior officer to RAF North Luffenham which occasionally gave me the rare opportunity to fly in what was then the finest jet fighter in the RAF. The Meteors had been modified to carry an instructor and a trainee. After repair or servicing the plane was taken up by a senior flying instructor to test the plane before returning it to the training programme. This enabled me on rare occasions to fly in the trainee's seat while the instructor put it through its paces. The rule was "If you are sick, you clear up the mess." I was not sick and will always remember flying up the Great North Road at 2000 feet and then climbing at what in those days was at a remarkable speed. I remember, too, being allowed to fly the plane for a few minutes, possibly three or four, on hearing the magic words: "You are in control." We, of course, were doing no more than flying straight and level.

Many years later I saved up enough money to have flying lessons. They were expensive but great fun. It was a singularly remarkable feeling to fly a plane and, the best was a Chipmunk, an agile plane used to teach RAF pilots. It was quite aerobatic which the other training planes were not though they were easier to fly for a novice than the Chipmunk. The senior pilot at the Aero Club was a splendid chap, exuding competence. There was, however, an RAF pilot based there for liaison reasons who helped out giving flying lessons to people like me. He knew from conversation that I would love to do aerobatics and so when he stood in for me he asked: "Aerobatics or straight lesson?" I always opted for the former as that experience could not be enjoyed elsewhere. He would let me take off and fly to Ilkley Moor and then he took over. There was an outdoor swimming pool which from the air looked like a bright blue dot. He used that as his fixed point and then did loops, turns, showed me how to get out of a spin and do rolls. He then handed control back to me to fly back to Yeadon, leaving enough time for the instruments to settle after the aerobatics. This reminded me of my riding a horse from a stable in a nearby village. I would hire a horse, give it a good gallop and then walk it steadily for 20 minutes so it did not arrive back hot and sweaty. Yeadon then was no more than a local station and so there was not the rigour of the present day. For instance, I was doing a landing and the immediate rolling take off. I got to about 50 feet in the air when the plane, caught by a sudden gust of wind, blew me off course towards the control tower. It was only a slight deviation but over the wireless came the dry observation: "You missed!" Such intimacy or informality are long gone. It was some years later when a close friend of mine, Caroline, who worked at the Leeds and Bradford Airport, took me up to the tower which I found extremely interesting and a privilege which would not be tolerated now.

Sadly, my training to get a private pilot's licence became too expensive for me to continue and so I with reluctance, gave up the idea until I had reached a greater state of financial security. Since then I have been offered and accepted flights in a Tiger Moth, a very venerable aircraft, and was promised a flight in the only Flying Swordfish which was due to come to a nearby airfield, Church Fenton, but sadly the weather was poor where the plane was based and so it did not come up to Leeds and I was denied the great privilege of flying in the renowned Swordfish which, for a plane so old fashioned, slow and steady achieved some astounding success in the Second World War. On my 80th birthday I was given a surprise present by my lovely family. It was fifty minutes in an aerobatic plane, the like of which fly in those amazing flying contests. We took off and the pilot would show me a manoeuvre a couple of times and then let me have a go. The first item was rather naturally a loop and when I put the nose down to gain speed for the loop the pilot said: "Not necessary, just pull back," and the amazing little plane shot up in a manner reminiscent of the flight in the Meteor. He showed me how to do a flick roll and fly upside down and it seemed only minutes before he said we must get back. He gave me the compass bearing to follow as I had no idea where we were and then he took over for the landing which, because the plane had a high nose like the Spitfire, one could not see forward for landing. For this reason, he flew in a line parallel to the runway and put it down so softly that it was not immediately clear we were actually down. It was a birthday gift I shall always remember. The pilot, a commercial airline pilot enjoying a morning off and indulging his love of flying a small high tech plane designed for aerobatics, was impressed by the number of high Gs we had pulled, the plane recording these automatically.

I sincerely hope that if I reach the age of ninety they, my family, will offer me a similar surprise. I may have to drop an innocent remark or resort to some other devious subterfuge which I do not think will fool them, but who knows?

RAF

I had been fortunate by having my compulsory national service delayed to allow me to graduate and be called to the Bar. My first week in the Royal Air Force was a shock. I was instructed to go to a large RAF Station, Padgate, through whose portals all new conscripts were sent. It was an unpleasant introduction. We were issued with a knife, fork and spoon, referred to as "our irons" which we used at meal times and on exiting from the dining place doused them in boiling hot water in a large tank, making sure that one did not drop them by accident in the water. Fortunately, my stay was short, and I was given a pass to the OCTU (Officer Training Unit) at Wellesbourne Mountford just outside Grantham. I enjoyed this experience because we were treated as though recruited for the army in that discipline was severe. We were taught how to fire a rifle and being officer cadets, how to shoot a revolver and throw hand grenades. We were regularly made to go through the outdoor tests like climbing walls with our rifles and kit on, climbing ropes and using them to fly through the air to land on a sand pit. This was physically quite taxing but many like me were very fit and took to this experience as a pleasurable challenge. There were others who struggled and did very badly, thereby losing a number of OQs – officer qualities. There was a good feeling of togetherness and so we aided our less able colleagues when we could, though this had to be done surreptitiously. I became very friendly with a very pleasant young man who did find the physical aspects beyond him. He was taken off the course and went as an AC2, the lowest rank in the service for two years. I enjoyed all the running, swinging on ropes, climbing ropes, going through water holes, climbing high fences and, shooting on the range, etc. As a lover of the cowboy films I enjoyed shooting the revolver. It was a heavy firearm and hardy anyone scored hits on a figure 20 or so paces away.

Our physical training was in the hands of the RAF Regiment. This was a bunch of soldiers wearing blue and not khaki. They were determined to be as tough on recruits as the army, something I saw as a weakness. They always had to prove their equal competence instead of just accepting it as something which did not need to be proved. We had one final foray to make before we completed the course and that was a three-day military manoeuvre. Carrying our rifle and ammunition we had to dig foxholes, set up perimeters and exist on hard rations only. This could have been a pleasant game to play. It was not because the three days were three days of heavy rain. I remember the misery sitting in a foxhole of our creation as it filled with water so that if standing the water came half way up to the knee. It was an awful three days which I remember quite clearly. It did tell me something, namely that in the real war, men of all nations were living in conditions even worse and in a game where the killing was real and not pretend. I have been doused in water and frozen in the far north but nothing do I remember more clearly than those three days and wonder at the capacity of those soldiers who faced this kind of life for years.

One final episode I remember with distaste. On our course was a unique figure. It was a very handsome young man who was a qualified pilot and proudly wore the coveted mark of an RAF pilot –the wings. He was arrogant, scornful of the plebs as he saw us, and remained very much a loner despite well-intentioned efforts to bring him into some kind of comradeship. He was extremely good looking, a fine figure and sported the most perfect big moustache – Kaiser Wilhelm would have been outfaced. His arrogance finally caught up with him. Some members of our intake decided to deal with him before he left this station. They apparently jumped on him en masse and shaved off half of his moustache. I did not like him at all but felt extremely sorry for him when, the following morning he appeared for breakfast, he having shaved off the moustache completely. The arrogance and presence had gone with the moustache. He looked like a boy, a lost boy.

I was posted to a large working station, RAF North Luffenham in the Midlands. It was then in Transport Command, its planes flying all over the world. I reckoned that in due course I could cadge a lift to far distant places. My selfish hope was dashed when the station moved from Transport Command to Fighter Command. This simple change caused an enormous change to life on the station. The group captain in Transport Command insisted on the pre-war kind of behaviour. I understand that he had been shot down at the beginning of the war and so had risen through the officer ranks whilst a prisoner of war. He loved the pre-war ethos. For instance, there is a ritual when an officer joins a new station; he leaves his card at the homes of the married officers. The card had to be genuine copperplate and not printed. When one undertook this ritual you simply left the card without personal contact until sometime later when it would be appropriate to call.

He also insisted on having regular dining in nights when every officer except those on duty would appear at the mess for an evening meal in their best uniform. As the meals were cooked under strict rationing regime, dinner was not so attractive. Formal dress rules involved three levels. Full dress uniform was very expensive indeed and only worn on very formal occasions by senior officers. The usual dress for formal occasions when uniforms were to be worn was the Full Blue (blue trousers and jacket). The Cinderella garb was the blue ever-present battle dress which was for working and not for evening wear in the mess. This meant that the Full blues were to be worn on dining in nights or formal officer mess occasions and the senior officers, i.e. Squadron Leader and above, wore the full ceremonial evening dress. I wisely had bought a Full Blue uniform (second hand) for £ 27.10.00.

Formal dinners always followed a pattern. For instance, when the meal was concluded the most junior officer on the station, which was me for my whole time at Luffenham, had to propose the toast: "Gentlemen, the King." This was symptomatic of the

RAF at this moment in time, the old guard trying to recapture the peace time punctilio of the pre-war period. The pilots and other members of the RAF had been demobbed and their practical but informal ways had gone with them so many of the senior officers in the immediate years after the end of the war tried to bring back the old outdated social norms of the Thirties. National Service officers like me were looked on disparagingly by the Group Captain but as I had bought a second hand Full Blue uniform, I was treated as one of them in a number of silly ways until I crossed sword with the CEO. He voiced a few uncomplimentary views on the Labour Government to a group of officers of which I was one in the precincts of the officers' mess and I had the temerity to say that I could not comment, sir, because one is properly declared to be committing an offence by introducing party politics in the mess. He nearly went apoplectic and I found myself doing a number of extra duties. One thing I did like about him was that he invited me – an order in reality – to join him in an old fashioned aircraft, an Avro Anson, which he would fly from time to time to get his flying hours in. This was necessary for GD officers and men, i.e. General Duties, which means trained aircrew, had to keep doing a minimum number of hours flying to ensure their flying abilities were not lost.

When we became Fighter Command we gained a new and dynamic station commander. The whole temperature and ethos changed. Our purpose now was to train former RAF pilots to fly initially the Spitfire and later the Meteor. Many of those called back had been bomber pilots and not fighter pilots but they quickly became versed in the modern RAF and there was a high record of success. These ex-war hardened pilots brought back with them the experiences of the war years. The mess became a lively fun-dominated organisation with an almost crazy fun atmosphere and behaviour patterns. When, for instance, we held a dining in night, the dinner itself was lively but contained but thereafter it turned into a very chaotic night of physical fun. One game played was to pile the furniture, which was extremely solid and heavy, in a heap and then play "Cock of the Heap".

That is, you tried to knock down the chap at the top of the pile and then rebuff others attempting to dislodge you. There was only one rule and that was: the Medical Officer, now a close friend from Scotland, had to remain sober so that if accidents did happen he would be able to deal with the injuries. This was terrific fun and as I was very fit then, and though a lightweight was often more agile that the attacker(s), I did rather well until one or two veterans decided to "Do the little b...." It did not work as the general Mess members decided to enter the fray and defend me or in some cases to attack. Another mess game was to put someone light in a carpet held soundly by the others who would try to get the person on the carpet to bounce high enough to get his feet to touch the roof. This was fun but when I was conscripted to the carpet my worry was to get my feet below me in case the carpet was to touch the floor with me in it. A favourite trick of the Wing Commander, a pilot with two decorations along with the campaign medals, was to frequently enter the bar walking on his hands. No one took any great notice of this aberration. These pilots had reverted to the kind of life they had experienced in the war years, activities which took their minds off the loss of close friends or young men killed on their first mission. One night I shall always remember with a chuckle. We had extended an invitation to a small army unit nearby. One of these officers was a most unpleasant arrogant character, noisy and loud spoken. That night the buffet table was beautifully set out; the centrepiece was a very large salmon which had been given by a local titled gentleman who was very kind to the RAF officers. Things got very loud and jocular and this idiot picked up the salmon by the tail and swung it above his head, the fish simply disintegrating, showering all in the vicinity with cooked salmon. The world stopped for a moment and the army major, the senior army officer there, told the idiot to stand to attention, apologise in a loud voice and then go back to his unit and come and see him at 09.00 hours the following morning. The shaming was deserved. I enjoyed it but regretted that the salmon had been shared so indiscriminately.

One RAF officer I particularly admired though he was a little distant with me was a flight lieutenant called Daffy who had had been an acting wing commander in the war and was the most decorated airman on the roll, DSO, DFC and DFM, the latter being awarded when he was a sergeant. When he heard I had been offered a permanent commission which I had declined he quite definitely did not like this which he made clear to me. I had no difficulty with this aggression as he had obviously done so much and I could well understand his feelings as he had been turned down for a PC (permanent commission) previously. He was my hero and I only wish I had been able to make him a friend so I could hear of what he had done in the war to deserve his outstanding record.

The whole station was driven with an intensity with one aim in view – namely to train these called back war veterans to fly the Gloster Meteor which was one of the two jet fighters in the air force. Everything had to contribute to that objective. As a result, the many jobs that on a normal fighter station officers would have been given were not given. These were passed on to the supporting staff. As I was not operational, I gradually had heaped on me, a most junior officer, a host of other jobs. For instance, I was made responsible for the station bicycles and officer in charge of blankets. This appears a little silly. In fact, they were responsibilities the officer cadre avoided when they could. There were more than a hundred bicycles on the station, each with a unique number. They had to be checked regularly as bicycles were valuable and worth a few pounds on the illegal market. This involved me in a weekly count and the power to approve or refuse an applicant for the bikes which were so needed on the vast area of the base.

Blankets were a bane of my life. Every week I had, with the flight sergeant who under me and was in charge of blankets, to undertake a count of the blankets in store and reconcile numbers with those out on loan to airmen in the blocks. I learned to feel the piles of blankets as a clever thief could steal one and then hide the theft by getting another blanket, cutting it in two and then folding it with newspaper inside to give it the full-feel thickness of a blanket. This was a trick shown to me by the Flight

Sergeant who also would have faced a criminal inquiry if blankets had been found to be missing. The blanket store was inspected without notice at irregular times to prevent the blankets leaking out into the black market where they brought a good price in those very austere post-war years. I also acquired two other jobs, one of which was that of deputy mess secretary and the other, officer in charge of the residential blocks for the non-commissioned ranks. Every station had an officer's mess often in a large building providing sleeping quarters for the officers and a bar. One had to be at least a flight lieutenant to hold the position of mess sec but as the current mess sec was operational, I was given the position of deputy. This was a serious job as although all the accounts for each officer were managed by efficient clerks, I had to reconcile the accounts completely each week and sign it off when done. This was then checked by a senior accounts officer who warned me that the most frequent offence followed by being cashiered was to do with mess accounts. He was very helpful and supportive. I hated the job but in fact it provided me with some of the tools to be used later in civvy life.

The responsibility for the blocks where the non-commissioned lived proved also to be demanding. These buildings were two storeys high and were based on two wings. Each wing on each floor contained a room for a senior NCO and the men slept in barrack-like dormitories. Each NCO had the duty to keep his floor in good clean order and I had to inspect each dormitory with the NCO responsible. The aim was perfect cleanliness, ablutions especially. It was not good enough to wander through and have a look. One had to really inspect for if you did not and the station commander decided to do his own inspection which was a common experience, the men in the offending area could have privileges denied and be ordered to have a full cleaning session when they could have been free to do whatever they wished. The officer responsible, now me, would also be held to account and ordered to attend the offending block until the extra cleaning was completed. All this was in addition to my real job as education officer. The group captain when I first arrived would inspect the barracks wearing white gloves so he could detect dust more easily. He really was what the Americans call "a real pain in the butt".

I look back on my extra responsibilities: officer i/c bikes, officer i/c blankets, mess secretary, officer in charge of barracks et al with a wry smile. As the station education officer I found my centre very pleasant. It was part of a building half of which had been destroyed in the war but the remaining half was quite large, an office for me, an office for my sergeant and a substantial library and classroom. The rest of the staff were two young West Indian fellows, twins who were a constant source of laughter to me. I think they had been posted to education merely because they were quite useless for any serious business. It was like having two mischievous monkeys as helpers. They were good fun, very stupid and at the same time very acute but quite lacking any malice in their tomfoolery. They did keep the unit extremely clean and tidy. I tried to get them to embrace some study which might have been helpful but in this I failed. They were two coloured lads, the appellation used at that time, and what they were doing in the RAF baffled me. I did greatly enjoy their sense of fun and humour and I was very sorry to say goodbye to them when I got my next posting. I was quite moved when they gave me a present on the day I left – a small bottle of whisky.

I spent little time in the education unit as I was so involved in other activities, as say orderly officer. This was a position where under an executive officer whom I never saw I was charged to deal initially with any problem which might arise on the base and take such action as necessary which, if the problem was one I could not deal with, then I would report to the officer of the day who would always be of senior rank. Part of the job was to go into the large mess hall where the non-commissioned ate and ask the standard question: "Any complaints?" of one or two eating breakfast, lunch or tea – the evening meal. I must have asked that question innumerable times and never got anything but "OK, sir or NO, sir."

Another task I enjoyed was to take the pay to personnel who were based in small units around the base. This was quite exciting as I had to wear full uniform, white cross belt and waist belt with a revolver with counted rounds, six in all, in a holster attached to my belt. I would then be driven in a staff car to the outlying units, pay them their weekly sum and get them to sign the receipt and then return to base. It is silly that I felt so splendid with a loaded pistol. I had seen on the range how hard it is to hit a target only 20 yards away with a pistol and so I doubt I would have used the pistol had I been held up by some modern Turpin. On one occasion I picked up two US airmen to give them a lift, a breach of standing orders. I was amused to hear that their pay for one day was what I received for one week. They were privates.

I had two good friends in the station. One was a bright lad who had an engineering degree and was only a pilot officer until he got his wider stripe of Flying officer just before I did and he loved to play my superior officer. My other close friend was the station MO – the medical officer. He was a Scot who had been deferred until he had finished his medical studies and then posted to Luffenham soon after I arrived. We found our feet together and were helped by our engineer comrade. In the early period under Transport Command, the mess held parties of a restrained nature as we invited the great and good from the area. On arrival, the guests were offered a small drink of punch from a large bowl. This was a concoction that the doc and I produced. We got a lot of tins of fruit, as fresh fruit like oranges and lemons were very hard to get, and mixed them in a large bowl into which we poured a bottle of gin or sometimes something a little more alcoholic. The alcohol level was low and so the doc produced a small quantity of alcohol from his surgery which he assured me would not be harmful in any way to those drinking it. Certainly we were frequently complimented on the preparation of the welcoming drink and the doc's applications for pure alcohol from group stores were never challenged. At this stage, the commanding officer of the station who had been an officer in the pre-war RAF copied many of the esoteric attitudes and customs of that period, one of which involved inviting junior officers to a brief soiree. There was a young newly-commissioned pilot who loved the old customs, the social divide and was a frightful snob and someone on whom we could not rely. A small handful of junior officers were invited formally to have drinks with the CO and his wife. The group included this pretentious pilot office who flaunted his public school education. He was a genuine pain in the neck so my two colleagues and I devised what Blackadder would have called a cunning plan involving the CEO's very large but amiable dog. We took the "best blue trousers" of this chap from his room and rubbed the legs of the trousers round the basket in which slept a bitch which was on heat, as I believe the condition was called. We then returned the trousers to the owner's wardrobe. Later that evening we presented ourselves at the CEO's home and were invited to sit down in a rough circle with a small sherry in hand. In came this very popular large dog for its customary patting but not this time. It sniffed and went straight towards our target, mounting his leg as though it were a mate. Great embarrassment. Great fun. The dog was taken out only to reappear 15 minutes later, going straight to our target and simply refused to be moved from its excited humping activities. Peace was restored. The CO was in full flow, apologising to us all. I enjoyed every moment of his and our target's embarrassment.

By one of those remarkable coincidences in life I was to meet the CO again though he did not recognise me. I was vice chairman of the Sports Council and we were in the process of replacing our chief officer, Walter Winterbottom, a legend in the world of sport, especially football in which he had excelled. We advertised widely and received a large number of applicants. We received a well written CV from an air vice marshall retired. We interviewed and though he interviewed well, he was simply not suitable for the job. It was my old CO who had made my life a bit of a misery at times but I did not harbour any ill will, almost a sense of pity that he was looking at taking on such a job.

The three of us spent a large amount of time in each other's company. One night we decided we would go out. I told them I would work in my office until they rang me to say they were ready. I had the key to a back door which opened out into the very damaged building to which my office was attached. There were no lights in this half a building and I always felt a frisson as I passed through it in the dark thinking back to the time when several people were killed on this very spot by a bomb. I left by the backdoor because the keys to my unit had to be handed in every night to the guard room. I could have called for them without at any problem but to save the bother of signing out and then signing in I had a lock fitted at the rear for my entry and exit. This was not in accordance with the station's standing orders but such minor infractions were ignored if kept secret. The night we were going out I left by the back door, and walked the route I knew well in the total dark. Passing through one of the empty door spaces I felt a hand grab my head and in my already excited state I nearly stopped breathing. I did, however, grab for the hand and my hat without success until my two good dear friends shone a torch enabling me to find my hat and my composure.

There was one incident which has remained with me. A nice fellow, one of the experienced pilots who had survived the war and now was on the conversion course, took off as usual in a Spitfire. When he came back he could not get his undercarriage down and so under instruction by radio, he made a belly landing which he did very expertly. He was naturally shaken but proceeded with the training only to experience on another flight a loss of power and barely reached the station to land on the grass when his engine stopped as he approached the airfield, something they called a dead stick landing. He was a married man with two young children and he refused to proceed with his training. He said that the third emergency might be his last and that would leave his wife and children bereft. He was finally discharged with the designation LMF-Lack of Moral Fibre. This was a frightful note on his record and I think quite unworthy of the RAF. He went, branded a coward and any decorations he had won during the war had to be returned.

Another strange duty was passed to me. An airman from our base had been found breaking into a shop and attacking a policeman. He was being held on a charge of attempted murder in Winchester. I was told: "You are a lawyer – get on down there and see what the position is." I rode my motorbike down and visited the accused in a cell which really was an old-fashioned/ancient dungeon. The airman was very frightened by the charge of attempted murder of a policeman but after listening to his account of what had happened, I could assure him he had no need to worry about the initial charge. I have no doubt it was a charge made to frighten the miscreant and to teach him a lesson. Old-fashioned policing but often very much more effective than the current system. I understand the charge was reduced but I never heard of the final charge and prosecution.

There is one custom I did find very strange. When the whole personnel of a station was paraded, we officers stood in front of the non-commissioned ranks. The CO in charge of the parade gave an order to a senior officer who called out: "Fall out, Roman Catholics and Jews" whereupon we Catholics and Jews turned sharply to the right and then quick marched round the assembled personnel to their rear. Then, when the announcements and prayers were said, there came the shouted order: "Fall in Roman Catholics and Jews" and we Jews and Gentiles marched quickly back to our places in front of our troop. I found this excessively strange but in no way offending. It was on such a parade that the death of the King and the ascension of Elizabeth to the throne was announced rather dramatically. I do not know when and if this order is still called. I doubt it. Perhaps the most warmly held recollection of Luffenham is that of being allowed to fly in a test flight in a Meteor. The CFI (Chief Flying Officer) or a similar colleague was required to take up any plane which had had a serious repair done to check it had been done properly and was airworthy. I had done such an officer a kindness which I cannot remember and he phoned me on the internal phone system to say if I wanted he could take me up on a flying check of a Meteor, then the fastest fighter in the world. I was delighted and shall never forget the incredible power of the plane nor flying up the Great North Road at 2,000 feet or the dramatic feeling of being crushed when the pilot pulled the stick back. When flying level he handed over to me with the words, "You have control."

I knew better than to try any trick and was quite happy to hold the controls until he took back control after a couple of minutes. He had undertaken all the tests required and ticked off on a document and I returned, dazzled by the experience. What a marvellous experience and one I shall never forget.

My legal background was used on a number of occasions when I was ordered to assist senior officers in preparing serious cases involving serious charges against individuals. This was always an interesting break in my usual work.

My great life at Luffenham was broken when I got a posting to a station in Chigwell on the outskirts of London. I had hoped and had requested to be moved nearer home, given my parents serious health problems but the RAF decided otherwise. In some ways this was a very comfortable posting. This was a small station, no aircraft, and was deemed to require a high form of security because of the technical work done there to radar and similar developments. Again I was the education officer, mess secretary and security officer. This latter was taken very seriously because post war, the need to bring our radar and related scientific developments up to date was essential. Some of the work and hardware were top secret and this involved me in a good deal of work as security officer. We were often subject to inspection to check on security and on one valve in particular which took radar and related technology to new heights. I had to sign off each demand for this device.

There were some advantages being posted here. First we had a WAAF unit based on the station and this I found very congenial. As I was mess secretary I could appoint me a woman and so I appointed a splendid looking young WAAF to be my batman. She was splendid – great sense of humour and took relations close to the wire in terms of RAF custom and informality. Social intercourse and any other kind of intercourse between commissioned and non-commissioned ranks was contrary to King's Regulations – the RAF Bible or part of it, for the other half was the ACIs i.e. Air Council's Instructions. These two massive tomes were the Holy Bible to the Royal Air Force. The

271

officer I had most trouble with was a squadron leader who was the most narrow-minded miserable fellow. I saw he got a batman of similar nature. At one point he told me to change the batman as his was unsatisfactory. I willingly agreed as there was another who lacked any of the social graces. Petty revenge. Quite satisfying. The chief WAAF was a most delightful young woman who was the object of lust in every male breast. She was a delightful, extremely beautiful young woman, both temperamentally and physically. She and I got on well because we both had been through the higher education system and found we had much in common, though that did not permit of any closer relationship.

The great prize for me was how close the West End was – a short tube (Chigwell) or bike ride. I was particularly fond of opera and ballet which meant the Royal Opera House. More important than that: I had an old friend from Leeds who had become the person who made the costume jewellery for Fonteyn, Moira Shearer and others. She, Jeanne, was highly skilled and later in life became a Freeman of the City of London. Then she was a lovely sparkling young person who had access to free tickets. In "civvy dress" I would drive my bike to her flat, she would get on the back and we would arrive at the Royal Opera House, leave the bike close by and enter the front entrance like the wealthy punters also entering this temple of the high arts. I treasure so may happy memories of this incredible good luck. To see Fonteyn and the red-haired Moira Shearer was a delight. The women were excellent but the men were poor by comparison. For instance, Helpman was the leading male but at his best he would not rank with today's best dancers. He did, however, partner well and was quite celebrated. One night I remember with absolute clarity. Jeanne and I went to see *Norma*, a most beautiful opera which contains a masterpiece – the aria *Casta Diva*. This quite ample young woman came on and sang *Casta Diva* so well the applause went on for some minutes. The name of the soprano was Callas who went on to have a star-studded career marred by personal tragedy. What a voice! Opera at its best and her life like a romantic opera itself with a very sad ending.

On the station at Chigwell was a man well into middle age. He was an oddity as he was both civilian and RAF and wore the uniform with the very coveted wings which indicated he had been a pilot. I, as everyone else, called him ADJ, short for adjutant. He had an old open Austin 7 car and each weekend would drive down to his 32-feet-long boat or yacht moored on the river behind a magnificent old sailing ship, the *Arethusa*. He regularly invited me to join him and I enjoyed the open car ride, the car being excellently maintained by the technicians on site. I enjoyed the sailing enormously and the lessons which one learns, often the hard way. On the first time I went sailing with him, we came into the area where we tethered (wrong verb) the boat. We were travelling very slowly and he told me to grasp the ring on the top of the buoy to which the boat would be moored. For this I went to the front of the boat, grabbed the ring and held on. A bad move, as the inert energy of the boat was too much, the boat sweeping by skilfully directed by the ADJ who had anticipated the consequence of Newton's laws of motion. I entered the water among much laughter from the ADJ and some of the lads on the near by *Arethusa*. Thus, one learns one's lessons. The boat had bed space for four people so after a meal cooked in his tiny galley and a modest drink, we bunked down for the night. Sleeping was induced magically by the lapping sound of the boat and its gentle rocking movement. I loved going in this boat. We could get up a considerable speed and one day we sailed right down to the mouth of the river. We did not enter the open sea which was a mere couple of hundred yards away because our insurance only applied to the estuary and river.

I left the Royal Air Force with regret and sadness as it had been a marvellous two year experience for me and I had been privileged to experience something of the professionalism and bravery of the Royal Air Force crews. I had also made some good friends whom I was unlikely and sadly ever to see again. Reminds me of the poetic line – "parting is such sweet sorrow." The poets do know how to pack a lot in few words.

Algeria

Tony Baxter and I decided having just finished serving in the forces, to visit his sister Patricia who was living in Cairo at that time. The money we could spend in the sterling area had increased from the original post-war figure of a nominal £ 5 per annum to just £ 25 per annum. We decided that there would be sufficient for us to get to the border of Egypt which was outside the sterling area and so could use our sterling to buy a ticket in Libya to get to Cairo and after a stay there, take a boat back to the UK. We set off by train to the south coast, bought a ticket to cross the channel and then started to hitchhike to the south of Spain to cross over to Algeria. We each carried a full haversack, mainly food and a very flimsy lightweight tent.

Our travel through France and Spain was fairly easy as in those days, immediately after the war, hitchhiking was for many, the main means of travel. At night we would find a suitable place to erect the tent and then sleep like logs in as many clothes as we could comfortably put on in the absence of sleeping bags which we decided not to carry as, though light, they are bulky. Our water bottle was just an ordinary hot water bottle which gave the water a very odd taste. However, it served us well. Additionally, almost every village in France had an old-fashioned hand-operated cold water pump, something we never see today. Also in France there was a very warm attitude to us as coming from Britain who had helped to end the German occupation. We met very generous and warm treatment, as foreign hitchhikers were something of a novelty to the French so soon after the war.

The Spaniards we met on our travel were also very friendly and interested in these two chaps walking and hitchhiking to the south. Sadly, my Spanish was limited to a few phrases, whereas in France my schoolboy language came back in a way that surprised me. We reached the port of Ceuta and bought a steerage ticket across the short trip to Algiers. I had as a boy been fascinated by the books about the French Foreign Legion by authors like A E Mason or A G Hales and so was fascinated by the thought of visiting Algiers. We were warned on arrival by a French official that it was dangerous to visit the Casbah in Algiers but that is where we wanted to go. We were fortunate to meet a middle-aged American who knew Algiers well and he offered to guide us through the tortuous streets of the old city. It was fascinating and quite matched my anticipations. Seeing a street called Rue de Diable (sic) was so exciting to me which is a bit pathetic as I was then no longer a boy in my estimation. After a day spent wandering round the city we decided it was time to depart as we were aware that our very modest financial resources would soon run out before we got into Libya. It took us some time to exit the city, arriving at a concrete area on the outskirts of the city in the late evening. We decided to sleep there as, though it was hard, we would not be bothered by insects and other live creatures. We were just putting on our extra clothing for the night – nights were very cold and days very warm – when the most evil-looking one-eyed Arab came up and sat down immediately adjacent to us. He was really an ugly looking villain but he spoke good French and we conversed with him for a little time, I translating for Baxter. I was concerned for a number of reasons, one of which was focussed on a long curved dagger/ sword in his belt, the size of a large sickle. I said to Baxter that we had better sleep in turns. I would stay awake for four hours and then he could take over the watch for four hours. I was sure this wicked-looking scruffy chap was after our kit and I was equally determined he would not get it. Our fears were groundless as though we did keep the four hour on and four hour off routine and sleeping with our heads on the rucksack so that any interference with it would have woken us, he quietly left us at some time when we must have had both dropped off to sleep.

We had looked at the map and had decided the route we should follow would take us to Constantine. This proved to be a lucky decision. I found the city most exciting, worth a long stay but that was a luxury we could not afford in time or money. We found hitchhiking difficult in Algeria. We were told by one person who gave us a lift that the French banned hitchhiking and enforced the law, thus driving everyone to use the buses which were far from regular, always jam-packed and owned by the French who had managed to have this made the law. Thus, when we did get a lift we had to duck down out of sight when passing through a village or small town. If we got a lift towards a large town we had to get off the cart or wagon long before we got to the city limits. There was bitter hostility to the French residents which they transferred to us until they learned we were English. Then their attitude changed. It was difficult to see why, as GB was at that time still a very self-conscious empire and willing from time to time to engage in actions which today are simply seen as totally unforgiveable. We were seen then as an example for other nations to follow.

Getting a lift across sparsely populated areas where traffic was negligible or none at all was a joy. We were happy to jump onto the back of any cart going our way. On those days when we had no lifts, we tried to ensure that every day we would cover 25 miles; an argument about what that meant in kilometres would always be good for a long dispute as to who was right or wrong. On one occasion we were stopped by the French police who wanted to see our passports, search our haversacks and were extremely unpleasant. They arrested us without charge put us in their jeep and to took us back 25 kilometres to a town where we were put in a cell which was a filthy mess. I hate spiders – an irrational fear which I can manage without problem but I did not like them then and I do not like them now, though I would not kill them now. We were sitting on the floor of the cell, there being no seats, when a small newspaper page on the floor began to move, but there was no wind to move it. Baxter picked it up to reveal a spider which seemed enormous. I was up in a trice and ready to kill it but Baxter, with his Buddhist-like attitude, thought we should not kill unless we had to, so he steered this vicious looking spider through the cell bars, the cell being made of iron bars so that the person in the cell could be seen at all times. We were kept in the cell for some hours. No food or drink. Then a ridiculous time was spent explaining to the French officer who we were and what we were doing in Algeria. We were returned to the cell unsure as to what was going to happen next. I feared that we would be taken back to the capital. However, ultimately we were released and told to go. I asked if they would take us back to where they had picked us up but that nearly got us put back in the cell for such insolence. We had perforce to repeat the whole 25 miles and in my soul was burning a deep hatred of colonial domination and the absence of proper procedures and the rule of law. I could see then as I can see now, why the independence struggle would be inevitable and so bloody.

Our journey across country meant we went for hours in an empty area, until we came to a village. This might be just a few houses and tents or a substantial settlement. There are two memories I have of these small settlements. On more than one occasion, some sort of leader would come out of the village which was just off the highway and talk to us as it was most peculiar for them to see strangers in this way. Like the police who had arrested us, the local population could not understand that individuals from the UK would wish to make such a journey on foot. There must be some reason we were hiding. We normally would try to get our heads down near to water. As such villages had water in a well this is where we would like to kip especially because the ground round the wells was well trodden and bare, meaning the many little beggars that can give you a bite were not encountered. On more than one occasion we were asked by the person who came formally to talk to us not to spend the night in their village or nearby because if anything terrible should befall us the village would be punished most severely even though they had done nothing. This I saw as another French Colonial misuse of power and showed in a tiny parochial way why the indigenous population would, in due course, raise its standards of freedom and home rule so leading to a terrible and bloody period in a country which deserved better.

On one occasion we were approaching a small village just off the main highway. A lad about 11 years of age was riding on a donkey and hitting it in the face with a twitch to make it go faster. Needless cruelty by any standard is appalling but those standards were not to be found in such places. Baxter was enraged. I believe that Buddhism is the nearest faith to which he would subscribe if asked. He hated killing anything; fly, bug or animal. He shouted in his cultured English accent to stop and the boy not understanding the words but, looking at us with great interest as something not seen before, continued to strike the poor donkey in the face. Baxter got more excited and to deter the boy, picked up a stone and threw it at him. This he repeated as long as the boy was in range. The boy stopped hitting the donkey on the face and hit it on its rump which seemed to encourage it more. He just could not understand why this odd-looking white man had suddenly started throwing stones at him and his donkey. I laughed at Baxter and his over-excitement and we went on walking. I heard a noise and I saw a small crowd of young men or boys coming after us and throwing stones at us. Thankfully they were well out of range which gave us time to move as rapidly as we could to distance ourselves from the group. They, to my relief, gave up on our expurgation and we continued on our way. This is a simple, rather daft anecdote which I treasure as it encapsulates in a way the character of a dear friend, Tony Baxter.

We arrived at the border in the middle of nowhere. It was a place marked on the map, Bou Chebka, and consisted of a few buildings and a barrier which could be lifted manually, barring the road. It was a formality, as if one so wished, one could simply pass it on either side. It was no obstruction. The person in charge was a local in uniform. He said the real person in charge was a French officer who was at lunch and we would have to wait until he reappeared later in the day. He could not raise the barrier without permission. This I felt was getting more like a silly sketch about a dead parrot. It got better or worse however, when he said conspiratorially that the officer was busy and would I like to see him? I answered yes and so he took us to a small building, all the buildings were small, and then "shushing" us to absolute silence, he let us look through a hole in a window shutter, to see the officer in charge engaged in what looked like serious passion with a lady. I could not see much of her and did not want to. I just wanted to get away from the place. If we had been seen by the officer we would be in trouble. All I wanted was our passport stamped which apparently the officer could do for both sides of the barrier but our new friend said it could be days before the officer would sign as he might have to contact authorities on both sides. Baxter and I decided that we would not wait and so, with the blessing of our new-found friend we left, our friend saying he could not raise the barrier without permission so we would have to walk around it. This is one of the most bizarre experiences I have had at a border crossing.

Crossing that part of Tunisia was equally interesting, and in my case, satisfying. I had always had a stereotype picture of what an oasis looked like. On this leg of our journey I saw this mental image appear in reality. We were always treated very cordially by the locals, if at times they indicated that they thought us a little deranged. Another phenomenon I wanted to experience was "to see" a mirage. This I am happy to say occurred twice and I can well imagine that if lost, one would assume that what one saw was reality rather than a vision.

We finally arrived at the border post, Ben Gardane, between Tunisia and Libya. We were delighted to get so far and felt a sense of real excitement that once we got into Libya we could travel by conventional transport, be able to buy a proper meal and have a bath. Alack and alas, our hopes were dashed. We were told that Libya now required a visa before one could enter the country and the only place to get a visa was the Embassy in London. This was a disaster of seismic proportions. We had spent almost all the money we had, so going back to the UK would present us with serious problems about food. After discussion we agreed that we would wait until dark and then walk the 20 or more kilometres to the border and simply cross it in the dark. We felt confident we could do this and settled down for a rest before dusk fell. A Tunisian man in some form of uniform came and sat down next to us. He was very clear in his French and additional words in English. He said he had worked for the British during the war in North Africa and was now part of the Tunisian Border Force. He very kindly assured us that he knew what we would be planning to do. So did the officers whom we had met when we tried to get our passports stamped. They had queried the lack of an entry stamp or an exit stamp from Algeria and told us to come back the next day. Our new friend said that many others had tried to cross into Libya by unauthorised routes. They were all picked up as the distance from Ben Gardane to the border was a very long walk or ride and well policed. He professed the warmest feelings but said we could be sure that we would be picked up, we would be put in jail and held for trial. As a friend, he advised us against what we were planning. He said we would have been better avoiding Ben Gardane as now the French knew we were there, they would expect to pick us up just before the actual borderline. He impressed us both and the reality of the situation was clear. We could go back and find a route to enter Libya but without a stamped passport we could not get access to our sterling to buy food or meet travel costs. The only route we could take would be to return to the UK in the way we had come so far. The only difference was that we had spent nearly all our foreign currency. We set off northward through Tunisia which is a gorgeous country full of history and antiquities. The Arab population was consistently very friendly and we found that in the small villages or oases we could sell off articles we possessed. The flimsy tent we carried went quickly. I had taken three shirts and so we sold two of them and later the third. We both sold our socks for a pittance but enough to buy a loaf of bread or in one case exchange it for a small loaf. We both had a spare pair of trousers which brought in a substantial sum in relative terms. We even sold our walking boots, Baxter's from his army days and mine from my RAF days, leaving us both in open sandals. The only item I refused to sell was my university blazer which I had intended to use in Cairo for more formal situations. The Leeds University blazer was bright and colourful but not too exaggerated. It attracted a lot of offers. Baxter kept urging me to sell, putting on a great dramatic act equating the sale to a question of life or death. All good fun which made us both laugh but I kept the blazer even though later I had no shirt to wear under it. I felt a bit like the character in *La Boheme* who sings an aria to his old coat which he prepares reluctantly to sell to get money to buy medicine for Mimi.

Travelling north along the coast was relatively easy as there was a lot of traffic on the roads and getting a lift, though never easy, was easier. Interestingly, wearing my blazer in its bright colours seemed to be a device to get a lift. In Souse, a major port, we saw for the umpteenth time an opium den. I thought we should try this as the price on the bar showed the price about the cost of two or three cigarettes. I had never experienced or tried drugs which in those days was seen as a matter of adventure fiction. I made a deal with Baxter. I would have a go smoking the opium pipe while he remained alert in case something happened when I was away on the opium trip and I needed his assistance/protection. Then he would smoke a pipe and I would stand guard as it were on him. We entered the den and there was a handful of men lying on bare bunks smoking pipes. It was all very quiet and restrained, a bit like a film setting. I smoked a pipe lying on a similar bunk and experienced nothing spectacular except the sight of the others calmly puffing. I think it was because I puffed it in and out without inhaling. I am not sure what I was expecting though I did think of Coleridge who found inspiration from this drug but Kubla Khan did not arrive. Then, as I was compos mentis, Baxter had a go. He did experience some dream while awake but perhaps he inhaled, even though he did not smoke tobacco at all whereas I did smoke a pipe, trying to look perhaps like the film stars of the time who purported to smoke a pipe to show their rugged and manly features. Sadly, I think I failed in this respect too.

At each port we inquired about getting a boat back to Europe but were not successful until we reached Tunis. There, scouting round, we finally found a ship which was going to France and we got a trip for a nominal sum as we were to do the journey in one of the holds, no bed or such facilities and no food. The journey was expected to last 24 to 36 hours depending on circumstances I did not know. What I did know was that we were to share the hold with a substantial number of soldiers returning to France. The journey went without incident as the news vendors say. One thing I do remember with absolute clarity. I got to talk to the soldiers who, learning of our predicament of no food, offered us large bowls of hot soup. It seemed like heavenly intervention. Quite soon after that I felt a severe attack of antiperistalsis i.e. being sick, coming and raced up the ladder to the deck and was thereupon violently sick over the side. I put the reaction down to my own personal delicacy as the soup had no such effect on our soldier colleagues and Baxter who had consumed two bowls of the same soup without incident. It did, however, instil in me an irrevocable hostility and hatred of garlic.

I did do something dishonest mea culpa, mea maxima culpa. When on deck I saw that the galley where food was prepared had a back door leading directly to the deck. I could see the food being prepared and most inviting was a dish full of baked potatoes. I waited until the man in the galley went out, opened the door to gain entrance, one pace to the dish, half a second to grab two potatoes and close the door after me – a perfect crime perfectly performed. The potatoes were very hot but delicious. Thus, adversity creates crime as I think Hegel said.

We arrived in France in winter when even the south coast was cold and inhospitable. We began our hitchhiking immediately, dressed bizarrely for the winter conditions. I had open sandals, no socks, shorts and blazer but no shirt. Baxter was equally poorly clothed which accounted at times for the drivers who on the highway saw us thumbing conventionally with the hitchhikers thumb would slow down, and when close enough to look at us, shoot away. Baxter unkindly put this phenomenon down to my blazer. We nevertheless made good time but encountered considerable discomfort when we met snow and icy conditions.

We were frozen and hungry and dying to get home, get warm and eat. We were fortunate in getting one or two lifts by large lorries at night which gave us the incredible delight of warmth in the cab. The French in Algeria and Tunisia were examples of the worst standard of colonial rule. The French in France were then as I have always found them, friendly and warm.

Calais to England ended our foray except for the trip home. This was winter and we were dressed as for high summer. We both had passes for the trip from London which we had received on leaving the services, both of us being demobbed in London. Quite why Baxter had a first class pass I cannot remember but we both travelled first class from Kings Cross to Leeds. Midway, the conductor came along to check the tickets and saw us two tramp-looking fellows in the First Class. It was a pleasure to see him puff up in shock at such impertinence and then deflate like a punctured balloon when he saw our passes. I found his discomfiture very satisfying. I required him to address me as "sir" and not "You". Baxter, however, being funny, told the conductor it was Sir Bernard. I have a strong adverse reaction to little Hitlers. Home sweet home was never more deeply appreciated than when we arrived home feeling ready for the knackers yard (yard used for slaughter of useless horses, Oxiford Dictionary). Baxter would have been poetic – bloody but unbowed. (Henley) It had been a great experience.

China

I loved foreign travel and have visited China on a number of occasions, the first by train from Hong Kong to Canton. I was travelling alone and was shown to an armchair by a window so I could watch the passing countryside in real comfort. There were very attractive Chinese waitresses who were there to supply any refreshment I wanted and to hand out damp towels as the air was damp and humid. I had never travelled so luxuriantly. Canton, as it was then known, had been a fictional site on Hollywood film stages for films involving the exotic and dangerous gangs and gangsters. Peter Lorre frequently played these gangsters from a different world. The West had not been introduced to the true martial arts which the Chinese had embraced.

I was in Canton for only a few hours before having to return to Hong Kong as at that time the Chinese authority only gave one day visas. I was greatly impressed by its size, apparent affluence compared with other sites in the world and regretting that day-only passes are permitted. It was many years later when the Chinese did start to give visas and saw the economic benefit of tourism that I decided to make a grand tour of China. To do this I combined in part three trips properly organised by my tour operators. Knowing that I cannot stand foreign food, I decided I would be hungry for three weeks unless I took with me enough food to keep me going. I took ten small tins of corn beef, ten small tins of salmon, ten tins of beans, two packets of butter, two loaves and a variety of other food to keep me going. This amount of tinned food presented a problem for me as I normally just took a rucksack. I borrowed a Samsonite case from a friend and felt this would enable me to take my stock of food without difficulty.

I arrived in Peking with the rest of the travellers on my trip, about 30 people in all. They all passed a rigorous search. I did not. When I opened my case the officers saw all these tins and thought I was trying to sell them to the Chinese public. This was commercial and needed the appropriate permit which they were very reluctant at that time to give. I was arrested for a breach of my visa which was tourist and not commercial. I protested my innocence without success. I was put in a room with only one chair and that was for me. I was held for about 30 minutes in silence and then in came two very official-looking types. I explained to them that I was not a foreign spy or businessman. I had brought the food to eat as I did not like Chinese cooking. I was searched again and the case inspected with rigor and then my food and surrounding clothing put back in the case. The two officials engaged in a little conversation and they left me just under two hours from being taken into custody. Another, apparently more senior official, came in and asked me why I was carrying all this food. I told him I was staying for three weeks and had to have something to eat because I did not like Chinese cuisine. He could not believe it. His English was fluent but heavily accented. He said in English: "I do not believe you do you not like our famous meals like the famous Peking Duck." I said I did not like foreign food which rather foxed him as here I was saying in all the worlds different forms of cuisine I only like the British. I could have restricted these further and limited it to Yorkshire but decided against any levity in this particular circumstance. Finally he shook my hands, took me and my now refilled case back to the world where the rest of my group were waiting very impatiently. My reappearance was met by a small but ironic cheer as they had been kept waiting until my position had been cleared. They were quite flabbergasted when the official asked them: "Do you like Chinese food?" There was a dubious yeah which seemed to satisfy him. Later they were keen to hear of my temporary incarceration but I, to add to the interest, said enigmatically that I was not in a position to divulge the nature of my interrogation. In doing this I tried to look like a James Bond figure but I am sure I failed to so impress.

285

The trip I embarked upon covered a substantial part of China, much of it in the very old-fashioned but totally reliable aircraft, the Dakota, which had first flown in 1935 in the USA, served throughout the war and later did fine service in the Berlin Blockade. In some of the places I visited like Shanghai, my European appearance aroused little interest. Elsewhere, away from such places, I was often surrounded by young children who obviously found this chap in shorts very interesting. I wished I had been able to speak to them. They had not seen a European ever and so I was much of a zoo exhibit and sometimes a frightening one as quite often in the depths of China children would look at me and then if I approached they would run away.

Life on the Stage
Pamile-Dame, Anna Markova

On being told that my arches as a small ten-year-old boy had dropped, my mother took me to the Pamile School of Dance where my sister was already a pupil. My mother was a friend of the two principals, Pam and Noni, who assured me that the ballet training would soon raise the arches. Initially, when forced to go to the dance school which I thought was "cissy" for a boy but OK for girls I resisted strongly until I was introduced to my first class and my attitude changed. The room was full of lovely looking girls in tights and leotards. My conversion to dance was immediate, being hormonal rather than aesthetic. My conversion to ballet was almost biblical in its suddenness. I was ten years old and taken to see the ballet. The curtain went up and there was Markova, still in her dancing prime, and her partner, Anton Dolin, who was getting on a bit. The ballet was *Les Sylphides* and to me, at the tender age of ten, pure magic. I rapidly became a lover of my ballet training and my tap dancing which Pam taught. Pam Hudson was one of the two owners of the Pamile School of Dance. It was not long before I was given little dances to perform at the shows which Pam and Noni Brown, the other partner, ran in a number of outposts like the neighbouring town of Wetherby or village of Adel. Being at that time the only boy, I was given a number of roles to play. One I enjoyed was singing an old variety theatre song also sung with great comic effect by the wonderful woman, Gracie Fields. Its words were: "Why am I always the bridesmaid, never the blushing bride, etc., etc?" I was made-up to look like a panto dame with appropriate wig and long bloomers. This act went down well whenever I played it though in retrospect I wonder if the applause was so warm that it was a way of getting me off. These shows I enjoyed but I enjoyed more the hard graft of the ballet training. I remained a member of the Pamile School until I was conscripted into the air force. I had passed the RAD (Royal Academy of Dance) exams up to and including intermediate and had been promised by the Royal Academy of Dance that I could take the two final stage exams, advanced and solo seal, together as I was to be conscripted into national service as soon as I had finished my degree at university and the Bar. I was training hard to do these two exams, when I received my call-up papers so I never got to take the two final exams. I enjoyed my time with the Pamile School of Dance and have the happiest memories of my time there. It certainly had given me strength and aerobic capacity which served me well subsequently but it also instilled in me a long-standing passion and love of classical ballet and also a deep appreciation of all performers of no matter what species: singer, knife throwers, adagio dancers, acrobats and above all, comedians. When in the RAF in 1951, I was posted to a station on the outskirts of London which enabled me to see, on a regular basis, the Royal Ballet at Covent Garden and also from time to time have a class with professional ballet dancers. I remember one occasion. I had been told of the excellent classes Dame Anna held in Central London. On my motorbike I had to deliver in uniform some files to the Air Ministry. I decided to call in on Dame Anna and ask if I could join her classes. She seemed a bit dubious, almost suspicious, but agreed that I should join her class the next day. I turned up and found the class she had put me in was a beginners class for young children. I was the only adult and male. Dame Anna quickly realised I was not a "funny" as she later explained and so, thereafter, I joined the main classes which were large in number as there were a number of established ballet companies now long gone and forgotten, the dancers of which needed to hone their skills. One occasion will remain with me forever.

I attended a large class of advanced dancers one morning and just as we had been put into lines by Dame Anna, in walked Margot Fonteyn and Moira Shearer ready for class. Here were two of the world's top ballerinas attending a mixed class of dancers. It was a great tribute from them to Dame Anna without being overtly flattering and done with extreme courtesy and a good bit of fun by them to her. I enjoyed the class greatly because I managed to get into the back row so I could see them both. I often think of this beautiful little tribute these two marvellous dancers paid to a marvellous teacher.

In later life I got to know another great, Alicia Markova, very well. She was patron of a summer school for classical ballet which was an annual feature in Yorkshire for more than a decade and one which I had been in the position to offer substantial help. It was headed by a very pleasant chap, not much of a great dancer himself but with a passion for dance which was infectious. He somehow had managed to get the aged Markova to be resident president or some such term. His passion and knowledge made the summer classes very well attended. I found it fascinating to listen to Markova, remembering her meeting such individuals as Fokine, Prokoviev, Stravinsky, Picasso, et al. If only I had had the foresight and knowledge of how to operate the sound recording equipment of the day, I could have preserved these memories of a great star.

When I was demobilised I had a number of choices to consider. One big one was the Bar. I knew how difficult it was to get into Chambers, the route to a career at the Bar. I had one serious offer by a young barrister, E J Paris, who was making a successful career appearing in a number of notorious cases. It was really too good an offer to resist. However, the stage offered more excitement to me as a young man. My sister Sheila had achieved success as a dancer and I was self-persuaded to join with her as a double act. We could have looked like twins as we both had flame-coloured hair and similar complexions. She was very professional by this time and I was not. The professional has a patina which is quite clearly recognised by the public and can only be acquired over time and experience. This she had. I did not.

When a student, I had done some work for a rep company based in one of the large theatres in Leeds. Half a year the theatre offered a pantomime which ran for a long run annually – it was intensely popular – and then the theatre was taken over by a distinguished rep company. In one of their shows, *Ramona of the High Seas*, they needed a dancer to appear as one of the locals. I had been spotted by the director when I performed a solo piece in *Oklahoma*. This role required that I be covered with a brown make-up which involved me to stand in a bowl while two ladies from the make-up section covered me in a dark brown colour. The White Rose Players – if I remember correctly – had three theatres in the vicinity of Leeds and so I danced the piece three times. Having established that relationship, I was called upon on rare occasions to do very small parts.

The stage

When my sister Sheila and I decided to pursue life on the variety stage it was essential we got an agent and on advice I went to one of the top agencies in London who had on its books a list of the then major celebrities. I was frankly surprised when the partner of the agency agreed to put us on his list. Of course, he would receive payment for each gig he fixed up for us. This would be minimal compared with the very substantial stars he had on his books. I rather think he hoped that he and I might share the same physical interests but in that respect he was mistaken. The casting couch is something that did exist and sadly still does. One thing he did for us was to suggest we changed our names to accommodate billboard proportions. We had proposed to be billed as Sheila and Bernard Atha. He pointed out that that was far too long for the billing space we would get, Bernard is reminiscent of a shaggy dog and Atha made us sound like aliens or from Greece. I agreed we would become Sheila and Peter Bray, few enough letters to get on the billboard.

At that time the variety theatres did two complete performances: a First House and a Second House with a half hour between them. That is, the show was performed twice nightly. It was customary for the show to open with a dance act unless the dance act was top of the bill. This was because dance acts were generally lively and established a warm, lively and untaxing opening. Also, if there were latecomers the act would be unaffected. We were required to produce a first act number of about twelve to fifteen minutes for the opening of the first half and a short four or five minutes to open the second. Doing fifteen minutes as a dance act presented a problem so we did what other acts would do. We devised a routine with the two of us in a costume which covered another costume which we revealed to do a semi-ballet piece followed by a hot tap routine. The two pieces were developed largely by Sheila who had experience in this field with my making such contributions as necessary – the amateur helping the artist.

We also had to provide the band parts for the orchestra which was also a problem as orchestras varied in size and one had to have enough to cover a band of 20 to a group of five or six. My father's connection with the Musician's Union found us someone to produce the band parts exactly as required. The costumes were made by my mother – very expertly. We also had to get photos for the billboards and in sufficient numbers to replace those that got torn or damaged.

Our first showing of the act or the major part of it was in a nightclub opposite the famed Windmill Theatre. The club had a large dance floor ideal for tap but not for other forms of dance and was the haunt of agents looking for acts for which they claimed a fee of course. This is the first time I really felt nervous. A frisson is always present before entering the stage but nerves are different. We must have performed well enough for it did lead to some work which was our great aspiration.

Sheila and I hired a flat in Mornington Crescent in London. There we waited for jobs and it was splendid having a base, the rent for which was derisory by today's standards or lack of them. In the same Victorian house, in the large bottom flat, was a family of very competent athletes which did a very exciting act of balances, human pyramids and great tumbling. In summer I enjoyed looking down on them as they practised in the quite extensive back garden. We did a few weeks touring to different towns doing our act which rapidly improved, doing it twice nightly and practising in the day when we would hire for an hour a studio very near to where the Chinese Market is in the centre of London.

The kind of act we were doing meant that one went to a town, found the theatre, found yourself digs, awaited the Monday morning band call. Each act, as it came in, put their music down on a pile of music at the side of the stage. The conductor would take each act's music from the bottom of the pile and play it with the orchestra. Some required considerable attention if say the comic was going to burst into song at some time in his act, possibly a number of times or required a drum roll and cymbal crash.

My first experience of this was a cause of early fright and lack of confidence. All the acts seemed so professional, talking in a professional sort of shorthand which they all understood. By comparison, I felt like a very raw beginner and this was only the beginning of "my career". I was so nervous I kept taking our music out of the pile and putting it back on top so our band run through was delayed to the last.

At that time there was a hierarchy of theatre chains. Possibly the most famous was the Empire Chain. These theatres were generally pretty palatial and very well run. The one in Leeds was a magnificent theatre, very large and doing excellent business until a bigger business came along. The theatre was pulled down to be replaced by shops. There was a lot of opposition to the destruction of this very big, popular and beautiful theatre to be pulled down to build shops. Planning permission was given for the destruction of the theatre on the promise that a theatre of similar quality was to be built not far away from the original site. It was of course never enforced and no new theatre arose as a consequence. Ultimately, the site of the theatre is now the site of a Harvey Nicks as it is affectionately called which mirabile dictu produced more profit per square foot than its senior in London.

Sheila and I generally got work on one of the lesser well-known circuits, our act becoming increasingly professional in execution. No nerves but still, thank God, that essential frisson before going on remains.

Our agent came up with a proposal. An impresario was setting up a revue i.e. a touring variety show. It would have a lead entertainer, an established comic and specialty acts and, of course, a troupe of lovely looking dancers. After discussions with the entertainer who greatly impressed me, we signed a contract for a longish run. The entertainer was a man called Bob Grey. He was called entertainer rather than comic or comedian because he did

293

far more than do stand up. I watched him many nights trying to catch what it was that made audiences eat out of his hands. He made them laugh, engaged them in conversation, sang extremely well in variety of modes. He had a very good voice and had obviously had it trained. I enjoyed doing this type of show, called a Revue as we knew we had an income for the whole of the run. On one run in 1953 Foster Agencies secured for us a weekly income of £ 17 pounds 50 pence and took a weekly commission of £ 3.10. We could make friends in the cast and there was the opportunity for me to do dance pieces with others and learn the art of feeding. When doing sketches, the comic has to get the laughs and the others participating feed him the lines which he then turns into laughter. Feeding a comic is an art to be learned. If not done properly one can speak over the beginning of a laugh, or you wait too long or you forget your line or you try to get a laugh yourself. You must not ad lib and get laughs yourself. The comic has to get the laughs. One of the best feeds I have seen was Morecambe of Morecambe and Wise. Originally their turn consisted of Wise feeding Morecambe to great effect and it was only later that Wise was also getting the laughs from Morecambe's feed. We happily agreed to terms, which meant in reality accepting what the backers proposed. We had ten days rehearsal before going out on tour.

We visited Bedford and the following article appeared in the local paper which is, of course the very kind of note which one wants to read on Tuesday. "Appearing at the Royal Court Theatre in Bedford Mr Bob Grey, suave honey-toned performer bills himself as "Britain's Ace Showman." He can sing delightfully, anything from Al Jolson to operatic excerpts, has a nonchalant comic pulse which brings a responsive throb from the audience and is without doubt an excellent character actor. But what enhanced his ambitious claim most was his ability to throw cigarettes to one section of the audience and then to recoup his losses by talking to other sections of the stalls, pit and circle into giving him back all he had dispersed and more besides. The audience loved him and the rest of the show. What the Butler Saw

Show is without doubt one of the most accomplished productions at the "County" for many years. Last night the theatre was packed to the doors. More shows like this – even though one was left in doubt as to what the Butler did see – and the management will have to rush forward their plans to increase their accommodation. Backing up Mr Grey to the hilt was comedian George Beck, Billie Roche, Sheila and Peter Bray, Al Perry, Batty Allawy, Ramena and the Del Rosa dancers."

Bob Grey was a most accomplished performer and I admired his skills and tried to assess the special ingredient which made him such a splendid performer. All the others in the production were of vast interest to me too, a novice in the business as they were so finely tuned to perform to the audience with a slickness and professionalism which I admired and wished to learn. They were of great interest too as individuals. Billie Roche was a lesbian in days when such a term would never be used. She had a polished act, dressed immaculately as a man in white tie and tails singing some of the famous old songs like *Burlington Bertie*. I had a number with her and it was a pleasure. Ramena was a lady of West Indies' extraction and was billed as an exotic dancer. The finale of her act was tassel twirling. The tassels were attached to her bra and her trick was to make the tassels twirl first in one direction and then the other and then in opposite directions. She kept herself very separate from the rest of the company and I decided I had little to learn from her speciality as I did not see myself as a twirler. George Beck was a relic of the past music halls. I heard his routine twice nightly for the length of the run and again was fascinated how he delivered his act – a professionalism honed over years of use. The Sheila and Peter Bray were my sister Sheila and myself under the soubriquet of Bray, a name now short enough to fit in the modest space allowed on the billboards for supporting acts.

This was a most enjoyable tour as we visited places which I found so interesting. I remember visiting a museum in Lincoln. Right at the entrance was a magnificent bust of the great Paul Robeson. I found it mesmeric and visited the museum on a number of occasions to feel the magnetism of that head. We were also within range of the glorious Broads and I spent some very happy hours accompanied by a number of the dancers. in a hired boat. I remained in touch with a number of these girls, young women, and even today regularly correspond with one of them. Maureen Reynolds – a great character who was the head girl. I toured on my motorbike, Sheila travelled by train. Life was quite hard as one finished a week in one town late on Saturday, packed one's cases ready for an early start on the morrow, travel to the next town on the list the next day i.e. Sunday to your pre-ordered digs and prepared for the music call on Monday. Getting digs in the next town never seemed to be a problem, the system being well-established. Often the girls would book me into the same billet that they were in which I did find quite congenial. They found out that 27th August was my birthday and that evening when I had gone to bed I was invaded by six or seven females, decently attired but in clothes suggesting ready for bed.

They brought in with them a cake and some bottles of pop and beer. I was very surprised and quite delighted. They all settled comfortably on or in the bed. Conversation was very *sotto voce* with lots of subdued laughter but then the bed collapsed under the weight of eight bodies causing a hell of a row. The quiet was banished by almost hysterical laughter. The landlady burst in, thought that this must be a sexual orgy which had caused the bed to break and under threat of calling the police she told me to get out. I dressed in my motorcycling clothes for warmth and went out of the back door and tried to sleep on the step. I did manage to do this without too much bother as the night was warm. Unknown to me the girls had a camera and took photos of me on the back step fast asleep the following morning. I thought it one of the best photos taken of me. The next day peace was restored with the chatelaine and I was allowed to sleep on my bed which was now on the floor waiting repair. I greatly enjoyed the tour with Bob Grey and the opportunity to work up good dance routines with dancers other than my sister; a favourite was the Apache Dance which the audience seemed to like.

We made a similar tour with a couple who had taken on the character of Old Mother Reilly which had been a very popular and major act, touring to all the number one theatres and had been featured in a number of comedy films, though now I doubt they would raise a titter. Old Mother Reilly was a long established male comedian in this comedic role as were others mainly in the north. When the original Old Mother Reilly died, another comic assumed the role playing to non number-one dates. His act was just part of a revue and Sheila and I were very happy to be joining an established company. I also was pleased to have to join in the sketches – all excellent training.

There was a comedian, Ted Lune, who did one spot which consisted of his sitting at the front of the stage, legs dangling, reading a letter from his mother. I watched in some mesmerised state as each time he did the act it was word for word the same, extremely droll, getting laughs always at the same place in the letter reading. He was a nice working class man, quite reserved who suddenly got a life-changing chance to get a permanent role in a TV comedy show. Sadly and ironically at this magic moment in his life, he died suddenly. I learned this later and felt deeply sorry for the man and his mother's letter. Quite surprisingly, I was watching TV recently and I saw a man doing exactly the same old-fashioned routine almost word for word as I remembered it, so in a way his memory lingers on.

One occasion I will always remember with mixed feelings reminds me of him. We were playing at a London, theatre, Collins Music Hall, which was one of the few historic music halls remaining. The Leeds City Palace of Varieties was another. It was at the bottom of the theatre venues list and had a small band of about four to five musicians. The conductor role was taken by the woman pianist who was a remarkable character, very proficient, who smoked almost continuously whilst playing. One day I was late getting back to the theatre, a serious breach of the protocol. I had been visiting a friend, Maureen, whom I had got to know during a previous tour when she was acting as top girl. She was appearing nearby in one of the then large circuses. I had only a few moments to dress for the opening scene which was a short comedy sketch in which the comedian, Ted Lune, came on gun in hand and demanded the lads to take off their trousers. We three lads in the scene took off our trousers and continued the dance. In my haste I had not put on the customary dancers' jock strap briefs and therefore had to complete the number totally exposed. The pianist looked up as she did as leader of the orchestra with a fag in her mouth as usual. It dropped from her mouth as she saw the extent of my exposure. The number ended and I dashed off to put on my normal ballet dancer briefs. My nakedness had apparently not been seen by the audience, my shirt giving some kind of protection from startled eyes. The story caused a lot of amusement and when one of the orchestra who had not seen my situation told the pianist he had not seen anything she said: "You did not miss much" and so my private parts were dismissed.

It was a strange life being on tour. Being a member of a revue was much more fun than just travelling around doing the act and then going back to the digs although this did give us the opportunity of seeing many fine acts. One I remember was a magician whom I watched twice nightly for the one week we shared the billing. Looking from the wings enabled me to see how some of the tricks were done but not all. One that fascinated me was how he produced a handkerchief, floated it out of his hand and watched it float in the air. Our itinerary for one show was Bedford, West Bromwich, London, Walthamstow, York, Grimsby, Skegness, Scunthorpe, Lincoln and Norwich.

We were booked to play in a show starring Diana Dors. She was very handsome blonde with a well-rounded figure and her act was basically singing to a grand piano accompaniment supported by the band which this being a number one circuit was a sizeable orchestra. Basically, it was a cabaret act. In the short time we were in her show I got to know her reasonably well. I found her quite lady-like but without any artificial effort to be anything but herself. She later proved to be a very good actress as she appeared in a film which portrayed the life of the last woman in England to be hanged. I thought her performance outstanding as this doomed woman and dramatically, most effective as she portrayed the last two days of the woman's life. She later starred in a soap based on the famous Quarry Hill flats in Leeds. I was pleased to meet her again in Leeds, something of a surprise to us both, I having left the stage and was now a member of the council.

Dors had a husband, who was very personable, very friendly to me, very interested in my academic background, particularly in the law. One night when Sheila and I were in Mornington Crescent, he phoned, inviting me to come and join a party they were holding in their home. I was not keen to go but it is at such parties that one meets people who might be able to offer work. I arrived at their very palatial premises on my motor bike. The place was full of lovely-looking females and a lot of middle-aged men. It was abundantly clear what they were there for. I secretly felt that I was unshockable, that I was not a person to be shocked or disturbed by the kind of thing I was watching but I did feel a strong feeling of disgust which I took great care to hide. I remember being invited into one room where I and others were able to watch the activities of a man and woman on the bed in the adjacent room having an energetic and adventurous sexual experience not knowing that we were looking in on them through a one-way mirror. I was shocked that Diana Dors had presumably approved or allowed this kind of sex shop. "You be good to me and I will be good to you." Although the latter promise was not always honoured. I was disgusted, not so much by the sexual depravity which was being evidenced but by the constant realisation that females are grossly mistreated, that they are always the exploited and have to pay heavily to succeed in the entertainment game. I saw no reason for staying so I politely made my exit on the basis I had to be in good shape for a rehearsal that morning.

There were periods when we were not booked and so I "signed on" (that is: registering as unemployed and seeking work) giving me the experience so many millions had to meet. I was directed to a book store where, for £ 15 per week, I worked for 48 hours parcelling and sending books to all parts of the kingdom and abroad.

This is my sole experience of going to the Labour Exchange as they were then called and asking for work. A very salutary experience for me. I wish I could make all MPs go through this routine and be made to live on the handout they might receive.

It was during this period when we had a week resting, the euphemism for being out of work. I went with friends, Hartley and Richardson, to the Woodhouse Feast. This was an invasion of a large area of a cinder-surfaced park hosting the major roundabouts, shooting galleries and various ways of losing your money on kicking goals or testing your strength. In those days there were travelling boxing booths. These were large tents holding a boxing ring. The proprietor in this case was a Mr Sullivan, an old pug, whose son, John L Sullivan, was a major contender for the middleweight championship of Great Britain. Mr Sullivan had a number of professional boxers whom he paraded and challenged any man to come forward and fight the pugilist selected for £ 5 if he won and nothing if he did not. No one would challenge his son, the championship contender, which was very sensible as he was a class fighter. In desperation, the old Mr Sullivan offered a pound to anyone who would go in the ring with his son to box an exhibition three rounds. His words: "I promise he won't hurt you." I remember and cherish those words. Looking at his son on the front of the tent I can see why no one responded. I, however, was interested, not that I was even remotely of a standard to go into the ring with a well-trained, very fit boxer at least fourteen pounds heavier than I. I was, however, persuaded by the promise that he won't hurt you that I volunteered and was immediately whisked into the tent before I had the time to change my mind.

When my time came I entered the ring, took off my shirt, rolled my trouser legs up a bit and waited for the bell. If you are to succeed in boxing, you must have a punch hard enough to at least make the opponent wary. I had no such weapon. What I did have was speed at moving backwards. I survived the three three-minute rounds ending up covered in blood, all mine. I had been encouraged by the spectators with admonitions like "Stand sideways, lad and he won't be able to see you." No sign on this occasion of sympathy with the underdog. At the end of three three-minute rounds, Mr Sullivan came over to me and offered me a ten shilling note as pay. I strongly refused to accept just half of what I had been offered. The old man was less than pleased but JL came across the ring and said, "Give him the pound, Dad," and that was it. I got a pound which I felt would be poor compensation for the loss of blood. This was not one of my physical achievements but I could tell myself I went three rounds with JS Sullivan. Unbeknown to me, two Labour Party friends had seen the whole pantomime and later had a good laugh with me about the boxing mismatch. One of them later became a very well-respected author of three major tomes on the history of the working classes and the trade unions in Leeds and the UK.

Then came the bad news. My father was diagnosed as having cancer of the spine. I was fortunate to be born into a very happy family, each member loving the others although such views would rarely, if ever, be expressed by the male children. This awful news cast a pall over us all. My father had gradually lost the use of his legs and so was admitted to the Leeds Hospital. The surgeon opened up my father's back to reveal an advanced cancer of the spine. Inoperable, we were told. They stitched up my father. Amazingly, as the pressure was relieved, my father found he could use his legs as well as before. He thought he was cured. Sadly, we knew to the contrary. We felt pessimistically that all that had happened was that the opening up my father at the site of the cancer had removed temporarily the pressure which was affecting my father's legs. He did not know of the diagnosis but just felt he had been cured by an operation. We were bombarded with expressions of deep regret by so many who knew him and amazingly the secret was maintained, my father being the only one not to know of the prognosis. As days passed and turned into weeks during which my father got to walk quite normally, our hopes were raised and in due course the medics became very interested in the case and after some months they recommended that he go to a cancer radiation centre for treatment. It was this that made my father realise the true position. He went to Cookridge

Hospital which was the centre for radiation treatment, a lovely hospital of which my father became very fond. My father ended up with amusing radiation burns. In those primitive days they attempted to restrict the radiation to the area required, to prevent collateral damage by placing square lead mats around the area to be treated. He received radiation on his front and back. For the rest of his life, and he lived to almost to ninety, when sunbathing one could see very clearly a "patchwork quilt" of burns on his back and front. They at no time caused him pain or irritation.

There is one aspect of this story which I remember vividly. My mother had a deep religious conviction and a belief in the power of prayer. She asked everyone she knew, whether Catholic, Protestant, Jewish, Muslim Buddhist and non-believers to pray for my father. She was unrelenting in this campaign. I was surprised how well her request was received. I wished someone else had the same conviction when later my mother succumbed to the same disease.

Mam death Teaching CBM Students

My life has been enhanced by my long contact with students, whether small children in my early years or young adults or old adults. It is quite a privilege to teach people of all ages and to share with them ideas, concepts and theories.

I have been blessed as so many are when they find an occupation which satisfies their beliefs and ambitions. I found teaching as an occupation purely by chance. I took up teaching temporarily during a period when I felt obliged but happy to remain at home. My father had been diagnosed as having an inoperable cancer and now my mother was seriously ill with stomach cancer. In all the very loving family of brothers and sister I was the one who could most easily undertake the function of staying with them. I loved my parents as thank God the majority of children of no matter what age normally do. That did not offer any consolation when my mother. who was dying slowly at home in her own bed. We had an excellent doctor, Dr Fernandez, initially from India and a friend of the family through close contact in the political field. He was a member of the local Labour Party. Today there are excellent systems of palliative care to allow someone to die without suffering the tortures of hell. That is now. It was not so then. The cancer was diagnosed as advanced and terminal. No cure or respite was available. Then the only respite from the pain was an injection of morphine delivered religiously every night by our friend Dr Fernandez. My mother was tough but even she suffered the tortures of hell despite this alleviation. The injection once every 24 hours meant that she was afflicted by the pain for a substantial part of every 24 hours. I asked Fernandez to give her two injections per 24 hours but he told me she was being given the highest amount of morphine permissible. Anything more could cost him his professional practice licence. It would be seen as causing her death. Her ultimate death finally granted her the termination of the pain. How I loved my mother and father. Here I am, a so-called grown man, lost in a whirlpool of sadness like a small child. This same sadness was felt by my two brothers and sister, all part of the Atha cell of love and protection. All were bereft though I for some reason cannot remember the funeral or any events about that time. Complete erasure. Possibly nature's way of helping.

As the one who could easily stay at "home" I did so without any regrets or feeling that I was making a sacrifice. As it turned out I found a vocation in teaching. I found great satisfaction as so many teachers do. I got on well with my pupils, requiring high standards of behaviour but in an atmosphere that we are all in this together and learning can be fun. As a supply teacher I spent periods of different times in a host of different schools in the West Riding of Yorkshire.

I did a lot of supply teaching which gave me a very wide experience quickly. One of the most demanding experiences is the one you would least expect. I more than once had to "stand in" in primary schools in different parts of the West Riding. Children at this age are like sponges in that they can absorb ideas, concepts and views so well. When they are very young they can be exhausting too, for as soon as you stop, the thirty or forty infant children in the class stop and then go off to do something that strikes them at that moment. You simply had to maintain momentum and light touch control. I have ever since had the most high respect for teachers of the very young.

I had a stint to cover illness in an RC primary school in Castleford. The headteacher was a character out of fiction. He had a glass eye and was reputed to warn the class that when he left them he was leaving his glass eye to see how they behaved when he got back. This was apparently a very effective way for retaining control at a distance. I learned a lot from him about teaching very young pupils and only once did see him take out his glass eye in front of a class. I did note that during the early afternoon he always took a little time off to drive with the left overs and dinner scapings to where he kept and fed his pigs. Today he would be sacked for such behaviour. He was a good head and someone worthwhile keeping. That was the view of the parents who knew of his foibles.

The great thing about young children is that they are not afraid to express themselves. I did a two-term stint in a small school in a large village called Ardsley. I had to take gym with these young nine or ten-year-old children. This became very popular with them as I based most of the lesson on dance technique which was very physically taxing and also good for posture and balance. I often used music from an old-fashioned record player to extemporise and after a short time reluctance disappeared and enjoyment of movement became apparent. I was very happy at this school as it was the heart of the little community but after two terms I was posted elsewhere and so said good bye to my class. The teachers there were very kind and supportive and in an English class the children in my former class were given the task of writing a letter to me. These I received with great pleasure, they were so honest and direct. One such letter I still have illustrates the honesty of these young children. Joanne said in her letter how "Much the class miss you. Mr Brown has taken your place. We all like you better but Angela prefers him to you." Older children can be equally expressive. I received a letter from a lad I had taught at Castleford Boys Secondary Modern School. It was written in well-formed italic script. In his letter he says (sic) at one point: "There is one thing worrying me Sir, that's finding a job when I leave school, there's still 80 on the dole in Castleford from last August, things look bad for me. Is it bad in Leeds. How are the boys taking to your bat at the new school. Yours truly M Champion". Michael Champion clearly knew there were such things as apostrophes and commas but was not quite sure where to put them. He refers to the bat. This was a little child's bat which I used on the backsides of serious miscreants. In those days corporal punishment was widely used as the norm. Difficult to imagine today. I personally thought the cane was pretty barbaric, an application of considerable energy/force over a very narrow area of thin flesh. When forced to use corporal punishment, which I awarded for serious bullying, theft or heinous behaviour, I preferred to use a child's bat which gave off a good sound on contact with the rear of the boy and was not really painful as the energy was dispersed over a wide area of the boy's rear. Bye and large, the lads did not feel this was untoward and so over the years the bat had innumerable signatures of lads who had had it and those pretending to be in that small group. Interestingly, when teaching in a mixed school, the girls thought it unfair that the boys got punished there and then and it only took a minute whereas if a girl misbehaved she could be kept in for more than half an hour or refused breakouts or playground breaks. I was consistently told: "It is wrong, sir. It is unfair." At another school I had a colleague with a warped sense of humour. His punishment was a board ruler, i.e. a piece of wood about four inches across and four feet long or thereabouts, He had this hanging on a wall. When stationary, it rested vertically at "6 o'clock", marked by the word guilty. On the wall at about 15 o'clock and 45 o'clock were the words "innocent". When a boy said to the teacher he had not done something wrong the teacher would say he would let the ruler prove innocence or guilt and "you, young man, have two chances whereas there is only one chance for guilty." He would then give the ruler a good push and it would swing for some little time, watched by the children.

Of course, the child was always found guilty despite his "having two chances" to prove innocence and of course the lads would object but the teacher insisted and execution took place. He was a popular master among the boys.

Another letter came from a Shipley girl, dated 21 July 1960:

"Dear Mr Atha,

Sorry about not being here at school because I particularly wanted to be. Tonight you will see all the girls crying their eyes out. A little word Please do not read it out to the class

306

as the boys will think me stupid. All the girls including me think you are very nice. Thinking to myself, the boys like you too, I imagine. But this is not the last you will hear of me because Ruth and I are coming to the school on Wednesday afternoons and will look forward to seeing you. Yours sincerely Annie or Hastie or just Ann.

PS.: Please excuse the writing and punctuation."

Elaine Myers, a young girl from Ardsley, sent me a well-composed letter in a good hand:

"We all miss you for English, because we have to have Mr Hxxxxxxs plus his claw, which is pretty terrible but to relieve the tension we usually have forty winks in the middle of the lesson while he is muttering about something uninteresting.

PS.: We are still a rum lot. Elaine"

One of my favourite correspondents was Jennifer, a delightful, rather reserved girl when I met her as a pupil. I liked horse riding and she "worked" at a local stables. She invited me to visit and I became a regular rider with her leading. She was quite expert and the rides were always exhilarating. She very expertly took us at a fast canter through a large wood with quite low branches where the danger of being knocked off one's mount was very real. She exuded mischief on these occasions. She became a real friend over the next few years, my going back to Shipley to ride and enjoying meeting her mother and the lady who owned the stables. The latter had been very impressed with my horsemanship. I had been galloping at speed towards her at the other end of the field when the horse shied and stopped abruptly, frightened by a large sheet of tarpaulin which moved in a sudden gust of wind. I flew off the horse, landing on my feet holding the reins nose to nose with the excited horse. She thought this as so expert. I did not disabuse her faith in me by telling her it was not deliberate, just lucky. That was in the early 1960s. Another memory is for me unforgettable. Every day there was an assembly in the school hall of Castleford Boys Modern, each form having to organise a message of some sort. On one occasion I chose the mad scene from Lucia di Lammermoor which lasted for three records, the old large size record of many decades ago. The singing was superb and as it took three records to play it all. I suggested that the assembly should lie down stretch out and listen – go to sleep if they wished. Amazingly, many of the lads said how much they had enjoyed it but I was not sure of the real reason why. This freedom extended to a whole raft of issues aimed at getting the lads to make decisions after careful thought and not necessarily selfish ideas.

There was a girls' school next door to the boys school, but never the twain should meet. The headteacher of the girls' school seemed to think any social intercourse would lead to its other forms. A new lady came in to establish cordial and supportive arrangements. She was bright, and as practical as she was experimental. Two of the results of the fall of the wall were that I was taught how to jitterbug by one the girls, which has served me well in the past and to help produce Humperdinck's Hansel and Gretel. This was a formidable task but fortunately our music teacher was an excellent pianist and was very keen to help us have a good production. The girls' school also had a good pianist and so the music was ensured. We had to prune the full version of the opera which ran for two nights. On both nights I was quite definitely affected by what I saw and heard. In the opera the lost children sing a prayer for their safety. I have seen the opera three times in professional productions over the years and for me it is the high point of the opera. Seeing these two lovely lasses singing the night prayer with utter conviction was truly moving and one I shall always remember seeing one or two women in the audience wiping their eyes. It was a magic moment.

By contrast there were amusing letters explaining the absence of: her son from attending school because she was under the doctor or at home expecting a carpet Such sayings enshrine a truth. Pythagoras said the "The shortest words, yes and no, are those that require the most thought." How right he was. Some letters I found quite disturbing or moving. I have a small piece of lined paper obviously torn from an exercise book. It read "Dear Mr Artha, Please may Elizabeth and I sing in him sining when you take us because I like to sing I think you are fab but I no you do not like me all the lads in this school does not like me". I deeply regret many years later that I did not record what I did to assist this poor child.

I received the following from a former student at the Huddersfield Technical College.

Dear Bernard,

I was a bit like Billy Caspar when I started in HTC (Huddersfield Technical College) in 1963 at age fifteen. Mine had been a hard-luck story up to then. Left school at 13 – two years in a reformatory – escaped from there – father died – no educational qualifications whatsoever. I was a mental and physical wreck bristling with resentment of the world and especially of adults. After having experienced so much ill-treatment it was a very welcome culture-shock to be treated as a human being for a change. The HTC (Huddersfield Technical College) staff actually addressed me as Mr Bxxxxx and not as "hey you". I do not exaggerate when I say that the General Studies course delivered by yourself were my salvation. As much as anything else I learned from you chaps how to teach properly – a skill that served me well. I spent most of my working life in the education business. Why I wondered at the time did a fifteen year old thrive at HTC when the school system had rejected him as a failure. I con-

cluded that students succeed in a system that treats them with respect. A bit of kindness goes a long way. You may never know the good you did Bernard.

Thanks again and best wishes,

Jim

My connection with former students varies. For instance, every Christmas I send at least 20 cards to former students in reply to theirs and at least ten cards to those overseas, mainly in the far East. Sometimes a message comes out of the blue. For instance, some years ago I received a letter from a wee girl I had taught in Woodend School. Sylvia Hudson and her husband. She and her husband would drive to Leeds for a chat and a yearly lunch we both looked forward to. We still do meet twice a year for a meal and a chat.

One of my "favourite" friends was a young dark-skinned boy from Kuala Lumpur. He was extremely bright, played badminton with me, winning regularly, who went to Leeds University for a degree before returning home where he has clearly been highly successful. To use an ancient and arcane term, he has become a buddy. He was an excellent student. My only complaint to him was why did he have a name as long as an essay; Thanneermaliai Somasundram, to which he has replied that Atha sounds rather like a sneeze and does not deserve to have the title of a name. He paid me a greatly appreciated compliment. He I am sure would deny this. In the spring of 2016 he flew all the way from Malaysia to the UK, stayed overnight with a friend in London, took the early train to Leeds next day where I met him after a couple of tannoy calls over the Leeds Station tannoy, spent that day and part of the next – about 36 hours in all –in Leeds and Haworth and I took him to the London train for a flight home the next day. I could not ask him outright why he had come all that way for just two half days in Leeds. He just said it seemed a good idea. I did, too, but I feel sure he must have thought, Bernard will be ninety in two years' time. If he exists so long so I better see him while I can. I take this as a most heart-warming gesture and one I appreciate greatly. Thannee is a great friend and former student of mine.

A very similar person from the same background is another who ranks with Thannee for intelligence and scholarly achievements. Harish Pankhania was one of the most gifted students I have ever known. He seemed to pass examinations so easily. I referred to this as his hobby. I was his course tutor and found his ability quite outstanding. He was very quiet and reserved but willing to assist any fellow student having a problem with accountancy lessons. My contact with him and his family has been intermittent but I know that his many generous offers to provide me accommodation when in London are genuine. He, like Thannee, is a lovely fellow with a charming family which I have met on two occasions.

I regularly meet former students by chance. For instance, I recently attended the opening of a new Hindu Temple in my ward. A young early-middle-aged lady came up to me and said what many say: "You are Bernard Atha, aren't you?" I always resist the desire to say yes I do know who I am. I did nothing so ungracious. She was a former full-time student of mine and very generously invited me to meet her parents and sister who was over from America who had also attended my lectures. I visited the lovely Shah home in Huddersfield where I met the mother and father of the two Shahs I had taught. They were two sterling women, both obviously successful but with quite endearing attitudes and generous feelings towards me. Their ancient mother spoke English but not as well as the daughters. The even more ancient father was present the whole of my stay, not understanding any of our conversation but seeming to enjoy it nevertheless. This meeting was just typical of the warmth of feeling with student and lecturer if the social environment is right.

I received a call from a former student who invited me to a reunion of former students on one of the courses I had run at college. I said I was now Lord Mayor and I could offer them a nice place to have the reunion. This is a beautiful room in the Civic Hall reserved for important social engagements. They were a most lovely bunch of young folk, all now about 35 years old. It was a most enjoyable occasion, full of laughter, reminiscences and pathetic hilarious humour. They were a credit to themselves and I feel quite proud to have been their mentor for two years when they were very young adults. My recollections of the cohort of students I knew are very happy ones. I would have liked to know, for instance, how Helga got on. I have still in my possession the answer paper she did for her final exam in law. It was of a quality, especially in its remarkable number of relevant quoted legal authorities, which would have satisfied a degree examiner. When I was not advanced from deputy head to head of the department which had seemed inevitable over the very many months I was acting as head of department, the Students Union came to see me with a proposal to have a major protest in the centre of Huddersfield. They were very supportive and relished having a major protest, flags posters and all. I thanked them but said the protest would be of little value and would not effect a change in the decision.

Over the years I had become well known to students outside my department which led me to become involved in matters of great delicacy. The college had rightly attracted young people across the local authority which included a large number from the Indian subcontinent. As the girls grew into women, many refused to accept the norms of their parents in such matters as the parents choosing a husband for their daughters. On something like twelve occasions during my time at Huddersfield, I was introduced by fellow students to a teenage girl who did not wish to marry a selected individual. I felt obliged to help and put them in touch, via a complex security provision, with an organisation which could help the girl by giving her secure accommodation elsewhere. I was able to reassure myself that this was a safe haven and not a conduit to something too unpleasant to contemplate. The whole process had to be done in strict secrecy. I did, on each occasion, inform my lady colleague who was the senior woman in terms of looking after female students. Peggy, as I knew her, was splendid in her duty and reassurance. Then one day the college was invaded by a small group of angry Muslims armed with knives or swords looking for the daughter of one of them. She, so far as they were concerned, had just disappeared and they thought the college was hiding her. Unbeknown to them, I had settled her safely in a distant city. A porter rushed into my room and told me of the invasion and that its members were asking for me or rather Mr Atta. The police had already been called and so I did a diplomatic move and disappeared from my room and department until I got the all clear.

This problem I found upsetting as in the culture clash, both parties are nearly always adversely affected and unhappiness caused.

Word gets around and I was from time to time approached by a group of two or three lads because one of the them thought he had "contracted a disease". So it was on a number of occasions I drove a lad off to the hospital in Bradford for an examination and relevant treatment if necessary.

In a way I was flattered that students I had not taught had the confidence to come to me rather than use anyone else in the large college but I often found it burdensome. The worst were three occasions when a group of girls/young women came to see me because one of them was pregnant. They did not know what to do. This was particularly worrying in the case of one girl as she was from the Far East and was feeling suicidal so far from home, from family which would have been horrified by the news of the pregnancy and could have led them to cut all connections with their daughter or worse. I was able to get her out of that awful despair by talking to her at length but handing over the case to my friend and colleague Peggy, the senior woman lecturer responsible for this area of female students. I never knew the outcome as I insisted on strict confidentiality that I should only know something of this personal nature if I had to know.

There is one student, Peter, who stands out above all the others. On a Friday night I ran a two-hour class aimed to prepare students for the A level in law within the year. Friday night would not appear to be the best time to hold such a concentrated course but the regular attendees averaged from 55–60 each Friday night, causing me to have to use three registers to accommodate the numbers and names. On the whole they were a lively mature group of men and women. One stood out negatively. He was physically of modest height and diffident demeanour and I instantly warmed to him. He had a car and earned a living giving driving lessons. I made a point of talking to him when I could without being too obvious. I always set the class an essay for me to mark and return the following week. He was reluctant to submit work and when he did, after much cajoling, I saw why. His writing abilities were very limited, the result of having left school at the age of 13/14 He attended this same class for three consecutive years during which time I could see he was improving in his understanding and written work. I spent some time with him, helping him with his essays and after three years I could count him as a "friend" and as a successful friend as he took the examination and passed. I was delighted and so was he. He continued to attend the class for another year "just for pleasure" which I take as a serious compliment. When I retired early to concentrate on my other activities, I said good bye to Peter and hoped we could keep in touch. I was surprised to hear that he had gone to the Leeds Polytechnic, now a major university, and was delighted but surprised that he actually was awarded an LLB although it took him four years. In my view, this was a major achievement for someone who had left school at fourteen and had no other formal education until he came to the college on a Friday night. I was delighted to send him my congratulations. Ever since I left college we have kept in touch at Christmas time when I regularly receive from him by post a bottle of whisky.

I still am very fond of this quiet unassuming man and am delighted we still keep in touch although it took me some years to persuade him not the send me a bottle of whisky any more although he still seems to forget this every Christmas. I am full of admiration, respect and warmth for my most dedicated student.

The Friday night A level law class was strange because it attracted a strange cross section of society. On one enrolment night, for instance, three rather generously proportioned middle-class and middle-aged ladies settled down in a line abreast. They explained that they had "done" History and got an A level and then English Lit and now wanted a change and the Law looked promising. They were very able despite their advancing years and all three passed. I never had the chance to find out what they were going to do next.

I did so enjoy Friday night's class. The students were genuinely nice folk. It was a privilege and a pleasure to know them. Another course which I similarly enjoyed was one designed to educate in a general sense police cadets. These were a fine group of about ten youths, fit, healthy, bursting with testosterone and tremendous fun. After just one year, two female cadets joined the group. I ran this course for some years and aimed at puncturing the superman feeling some of them had. I, for instance, talked to them about food and then took them off to the slaughterhouse. I asked the girls if they wanted to duck out of this trip but they were almost insulted by my asking. Quite right. I was pleased with their attitude and respected them for their indignation. Seeing animals killed in this heartless and mass-produced process can be disturbing. Seeing a perfectly healthy animal enter a stall, be shot with a bolt to the head and within a few minutes being disembowelled and skinned can be disturbing. It was ironic that it was one of the lads who fainted and another CBF i.e. caught before falling. Both were male cadets. The girls took it all in but accepted that what they saw was as humane as it could be if we as a nation continued to eat meat.

Another visit I shall not forget was taking them down a working mine. I deliberately opted to visit a mine which had a very rich but narrow seam of coal which was so rich it was being cut by hand, the kind of method used for centuries before mechanisation. I had been down a number of working mines and so was not unfamiliar with the experience. I did notice a change of posture of the lads (no women allowed down the pit at that time) as we got into the cage and dropped to the appropriate level like a falling stone. I heard two ejaculations: of "Jesus" from the lads which I presume was a brief prayer. In making the arrangements for the trip, I asked the officials in charge if they would do the exciting cage drop and not the one used for normal purpose. This system involves letting the cage fall freely before the excellent and highly competent staff in the winding house slowed it down and brought it gently to a rest at the appropriate level. The initial walk took us some minutes before reaching the seam. Here, were men using pick and shovel like their ancestors. It was necessary to crawl along the cutting and all of us were happy after a long crawl to stand up on one of the pit's roads and make our way to where machines were working. The noise was extremely harsh and the atmosphere polluted by dust which is why some of the workmen had a scarf round their heads and mouths. It reminded me of the vision in *Dante's Inferno* though here there was no fire but it seemed like hell without the flames. The visit triggered very forcible discussions among the lads, all of whom were so pleased that they had come on this trip despite initial concerns.

One of the great privileges teachers have is the excitement of creating interest in something which would otherwise never be there. I asked a large class if anyone would like to go to the opera in Leeds to see *La Boheme*. There was a short riot of laughter and derision. Nevertheless, a group of teenage students on the night dressed up and boarded the mini bus driven by me. Only one of the ten students had been in a theatre before. I unfortunately had an unscheduled meeting at the Civic Hall and so told them that I would pick them up outside the Grand Theatre and drive them back to Huddersfield. After my meeting I returned to the theatre in time to see the very moving end of the opera. I stationed myself at the bottom of the stairs down which they would have to come. The first were the girls, all of whose make-up and mascara had been affected by tears. I felt a genuine thrill for this could mean the effect of seeing this opera might open the door figuratively to similar life enhancing experiences. A first step to what many of us enjoy and benefit therefrom as a matter of course.

I received a letter from Malaysia asking about two young people being sent over to Huddersfield to study. I replied and in due course two delightful young women, Fei and Yen Chin, arrived. They were so innocent and unworldly compared with the local girls of the same age. They were two very lovely individuals who had been "put in my care" by their father and so I felt an enhanced personal sense of concern. I met them at the station and took them to where they were going to live whilst in Huddersfield. It was a Yorkshire-style family and I felt confident in leaving them in the hands of the lady of the house. She had assembled her family to greet Fei and Yen and introduced each one in turn. I left feeling quite happy about our first two overseas students. A day later I called on the two and took them by car to where they would be studying. Fei asked me if everyone in Yorkshire started their name with "Ar". I was a bit confused when they told me that a Welshman they knew in Malaysia called his sons Ab or Ap. I then realised that the landlady had, whilst I was there, introduced the family by saying "and this is our son, our Harry" or "this is our Cis" which came out as Ar Harry Ar Cis. They stayed with the family for some time when the question of the loss of some valuables arose and in consultation with the two girls I arranged for them to take over and rent a small flat which was ideal for them and cheaper, though money never seemed to be a problem. They remained essentially unchanged in regard to worldly matters – protected by their ignorance of the world they had come to live in. My colleague, Peggy, the senior lady responsible for female issues, was as always totally helpful.

MPEC – The Middleton Park Equestrian Centre – Riding for the Disabled

MPEC was the child of John Tinker, the chief officer in charge of Parks in Leeds and Charlotte Bromet, a quiet but most effective member of an extra-ordinary organisation, Riding for the Disabled i.e. RDA. She discussed with John the possibility of creating a Riding For the Disabled centre and he supported this very positively. Tinker was renowned for being a "doer", someone who accomplished things and did not just sit back and run a very efficient organisation. I was a great admirer of John Tinker who was my ideal of a council officer. Brisk, clever, kind and totally honest. I was then the holder of the Parks portfolio and John discussed this idea with me. They both knew of my commitment to the disabled and that I also rode on a very regular basis and true to their instincts, I was most happy to take the lead as Chairman of Leisure Services. The plan was for us, that is the RDA activists, to fund raise, for the council to grant us a lease on an undeveloped area in South Leeds and to create a full-sized centre planned so additional units could be added as part of the whole as funds permitted. We were ambitious and confident which is the only way to achieve something worthwhile even though the confidence might prove to be displaced. I, however, had in mind some serious possibilities to assist in achieving the dream.

Charlotte Bromet, the chairman and wonder woman in my view, raised £ 400,000 personally. I raised £ 200,000 from the FSA and Bev Backhouse, who ran the centre, raised £ 76,000 personally. The new building was erected so in a reasonably short time we had made positive progress. The building was designed to enable further planned development to take place and Princess Anne, a strong supporter of Riding for the Disabled, opened the new facilities. This made us more keen to build the centre to the original full ambitious plan.

The English Sports Council advised by the Sports Lottery Grant Committee awarded us a grant of £ 838,448 towards the total cost of £ 1,010,178 for the extension. This involved further fundraising by Charlotte Bromet obtaining £ 132,000 from RDA National and giving £ 23,428 personally plus £ 76,000 raised by Bev Backhouse.

I had no part in determining the Lottery grant although I had been a member of the Sports Council and the Lottery Panel. I did not know of the generous grant until we received a formal letter which set out a very considerable number of prior conditions which were absolutely right and appropriate. The new development was again managed very skilfully by council officers who were quite splendid. This major grant had to pass through the council's accounts but surprisingly we were told that for technical taxation reasons the management structure of the organisation had to be changed to preserve the VAT position of the council.

Since then, the centre has been developed further so we now have the very large covered hall, one of the biggest in the country, another covered hall nearly as large, a smaller outdoor arena and an isolation stable, all funded by donations from generous sources like the Wooden Spoon. Often modest gifts by comparison paid for items like the hoist which is used to put riders on to the horse when this is necessary as it is in many cases. To help meet increasing costs, the centre offers rides to non-disabled people whose fees and often small donations help to meet the annual running costs. The centre also attracts considerable use by other equestrian organisations which pay substantial sums to have a very large area to work in. From time to time the site is used for dog shows and other events, anything which helps to meet rising costs.

As a centre, we do more driving sessions than any other centre. As so many of our guests are so disabled they cannot ride on a horse, the centre provides driving. This involves having a horse which can be driven in shafts and a carriage which is stable and has all the means necessary to keep the driver safe. Carriages are very expensive as they have to meet very exacting standards of design and build. Also, for safety reasons, the driver has to be accompanied by a trained driver and another staff member has to walk alongside the horse in case it is frightened and might bolt. This makes driving very expensive but it is the only way we can be fair to the multiple-disabled who enjoy the drive so much. The horse, driver and staff drive out of the gates of the centre, turn right and immediately into extensive gorgeous woods and park lands totally isolated from traffic. The drive on a fine day can be idealistic. The Centre became a football or even a punch bag. This was quite odd as the Conservatives of my experience before them was of a group of men or women with whom there was mutual respect and who often became strong allies in certain issues. This however was a different era and my colleagues and I felt under attack. An example of this attitude can be seen in the annual reports. Efforts were made by the Council to take over the Centre and bring it into one of formally the Council's functions. After immense waste of time the Chief Officer of Leisure had to advise the Council that this was not possible for legal reasons.

Dirty tactics were employed. For a period the Council cancelled the insurance which protected us all at the Centre without informing us. It was only because a council officer anonymously tipped us off to this that we learned that we had had no insurance cover for some months. Had there been a fire or personal injury the Trustees would have been liable and possibly bankrupted. During this bleak period the legal advice we had from the Council was stopped and I as the obvious trustee to do so had to deal with three legal cases brought against the Centre, one in negligence and two which were industrial tribunal cases. This is not my field and so I found it very time consuming and worrying. Happily we were successful in winning each case except for one. This was a complaint of unfair dismissal for a severe breach of our safety rules. I spent hours preparing for the tribunal only to receive on the evening before the day of the tribunal a phone call from the tribunal office to say the man had just called them to withdraw from the case. I suppose this was his way of getting his own back on the Centre and I suppose this added up to a victory but at a cost.

The extent of the animosity displayed during these turbulent times of Tory dominance in Council is exemplified by the fact that the Tory spokesman and member for Leisure Services, was in my estimation, a person of modest intelligence, high personal ambition and viperish disposition. In one Council Meeting the verbatim report records in his own words that I Councillor Atha and the trustees of MPEC personally owed the City Council over £ 100,00. The next year he is recorded as saying we now owed over £ 200,000 and the third year his claim was that we owed the Council £ 300,000 plus. As our liability as trustees is not limited this should have caused us deep concern. I knew however that when the accounts would be completed the Council would owe the Centre more than £ 100,000. I say when the accounts were completed because this same bumptious creature had the effect of frightening people. He was a bully by natural disposition. As a result the Council Accounts Department would not complete the financial records until the matter became too dangerous and the Chief Executive or some one determined the accounts should be completed when I pointed out to him that the Chief Finance Officer of the Council was legally the Secretary of the Charity Company with a high level of responsibility for the three year delay. This naturally concerned him as his reputation was on the line. When reminded of this he ensured that all three years accounts were submitted to Companies House pdq and the last showed the Council owing the MPEC a sum in excess of £ 100,000. My little Hitler never apologised and said in Council that he would never apologise. Perhaps he was more a Benito Mussolini, in puffed up vanity and posturing but whatever he was he caused me to send 183 e mails on the matter and endless hours writing letters and having meetings with officers following his instructions, all of which should never have been necessary.

The actual legal owner of the site where MPEC is situated is technically one of the oldest charities in the country going back nearly six hundred years and still the owner of a very wide areas of land including a substantial part of the neighbouring public park, and large areas across the city. During this bleak period the legal advice we had from the council was stopped and I, as the obvious trustee had to deal with three legal cases brought against the centre, one in negligence and two which were industrial tribunal cases. This is not my field and so I found it very time consuming. Happily we were successful in winning each case except for one. This was a complaint of unfair dismissal for a severe breach of our safety rules. I spent hours preparing for the tribunal only to receive on the evening before the day of the tribunal, a phone call from the tribunal office to say the man had just called them to withdraw from the case. I suppose this was his way of getting his own back on the centre and I suppose this added up to a victory but at a cost.

IFI The Inclusive Initiative
A Resounding Success

The Garry Jelen Foundation was a small charity set up by a wealthy business man who had a son with intellectual disabilities but was an outstanding weightlifter. The foundation instituted an inquiry into the provision of sports facilities for people with a disability which showed what every person should have recognised that in sport it was society which turned the disability into a handicap. It highlighted the lack of provision, the lack of disability awareness, the social barriers to provision and the ignorance of the value of sport for the disabled. The English Federation of Disability Sports (EFDS) of which I was chairman responded to the report and established the concept of an Inclusive Fitness Initiative. The aim of the initiative was to ensure that disabled persons should have access to inclusive fitness equipment in a target number of local authority facilities thereby increasing the opportunities, training and ultimately an improvement in fitness and health of disabled people. The initial objective of the IFI program was: to ensure that in 30 local authority areas disabled people would have access to fitness equipment; to train the staff in those facilities; to market the facilities to the disabled, the aged and temporally disabled and raise the profile of the value of sport for all, hence the word "inclusive" in the name of the initiative. The aim was to have fitness units used by all those without disabilities alongside those with disabilities, along with older people along with anyone wishing to enjoy the advantages of exercise.

As chairman of the English Federation of Disability Sport I put the proposal to the EFDS Board members who were enthusiastic and agreed to make a million pound bid to the Lottery. In January 2001 we received a £ 1.3 m for the initiative. We were promised that if the scheme was successful a further £ 15 m would be available to extend the scheme countrywide. The plan was to use the £ 1.3 m to fund pieces of accredited inclusive fitness equipment, i.e. equipment suitable for both the "able-bodied " as well as the disabled, the training of local authority staff, marketing professionally the scheme and a sport development programme to provide pathways and opportunities and access to new and existing sport and training apparatus. More than ninety local authorities applied, a short list with reserves drawn up, targets set for the launch of the scheme and the certification of the thirty sites; the first being two sites in September 2001, 10 sites by December 2001, the 30th by August 2002 and a final report by December 2002.

When embarking on this scheme I was very aware of the hidden hostility to disabled people training alongside the wider public, the reluctance of some disabled people to enter a facility where they were not sure of a welcome or when they could not operate some of the equipment. From some quarters there was genuine hostility and our stated aim of getting the manufacturers to adapt their equipment so that it could be used by all was seen as unrealistic pie in the sky. It was clear that if the IFI initiative was to be successful we would need an organisation to run the scheme. We widely advertised the post of manager and received a number of applications, a number coming from the best known businesses in the country in this field. After exhaustive and exhausting interviews and presentation we chose a firm in Sheffield Montgomery Leisure Services which turned out to be an excellent choice. Our decision was challenged rather viciously by other companies wanting the job but we had operated with complete integrity and the appointment was confirmed. The pilot scheme was acknowledged to have been more successful than originally anticipated and like many schemes which turn out to be successful, it began to receive support and commendation even from those who had been either sceptic or hostile to the scheme, a perfect example of the phrase success breeds success.

It was clear to me and some of my colleague that the IFI was a major programme and required its own organisation. It had to be run as a business. The English Federation of Disability Sport (EFDS) which I chaired, was a new body, riven by conflicts within the board and in my view and that of my colleagues, had too many issues itself to manage a major scheme like the IFI. Indeed, some of the members of the board were antagonistic to it. MLS, the Sheffield firm appointed to carry out the IFI scheme, had proved to be absolutely committed to the scheme and had worked extremely hard to get us where we were. We were particularly lucky to have Sue Catton of MLS managing the scheme. She was devoted to IFI, was tireless in its pursuit and seemed able to persuade or charm all those with whom she had to deal. One of my favourite Atha aphorisms is: if you want to be seen as successful, get someone really bright to do the work. She fitted that position perfectly. She was quite splendid, tireless in her work, ultimately highly expert in the technologies of the equipment and had the confidence and respect of the manufacturers and local authority officers, an epic achievement in itself.

My immediate colleagues and I decided to create another company wholly owned by EFDS with its own directors called the EFDS Operating Company. This enabled the new board members of this company to focus on one scheme alone, with all its ramifications. Despite its great success as a scheme, getting substantial publicity and approval by senior politicians the main board of EFDS would pass without comment the regular reports submitted to EFDS by the operating company. They were not interested. An indictment in my view.

By 2007 the IFI had worked with 180 facilities, initiated a scheme with three private establishments, and achieved 6% of users of the IFI Centres being disabled, meaning 3,000,000 visits by disabled across the 180 sites. 12% of all new inductions at IFI centres were disabled i.e. 17,000 new disabled individuals being introduced to IFI equipment and services. More than 1,100 outreach officers were appointed to increase the use by disabled people. Over 1,400 instructors had qualified after advanced training and over 4,000 staff had received disability equity training. By 2009 it was time for me to relinquish my position as chairman of EFDS and thereby of the operating company. At this stage IFI could record 180 facilities established with the full participation of the world's largest fitness equipment manufacturers, a PhD research project to investigate problems of inclusive equipment design and had its standards included in European Standard EN57. There were regular exhibitions of inclusive equipment organised by the industry under the direction of Sue Catton who had established connections with other European countries and the USA which had become involved in, or committed to, the ideal of inclusivity and had developed £ 1.4 million partnership funding from operators, can claim circa £ 2 million extra investment in the scheme. IFI established a buddy scheme to enable people without the confidence of trying the use of facilities to gain that confidence, a Kite mark accreditation scheme which has become an industry standard and organised a national conference in the Queen Elizabeth Centre attracting more than 250 delegates, the Minister of Sport and the Minister for Disabled People and other MPs as well as delegates from abroad, including the USA which established its own IFI Scheme. We held one of our "public" sessions in the House of Commons where there is a fitness suite which attracted a number of MPs and Ministers who are of course always ready for a good photo opportunity.

Today, many years after I ceased to be involved with it, IFI is under the direct care of EFDs and not a separate company and seems to be marching on with great success, with more than 400 IFI sites established and operating with the IFI Kite Mark which means the equipment and staff are up to the required high standard and that every effort is made to remove social or psychological barriers. An electronic newsletter goes out to 800 contacts and 103 products have been approved from 16 suppliers of equipment.

I enjoyed those few years with IFI, most of the pleasure coming from feeling we were doing something most worthwhile but also because the small number of the board members of the operating company were a close-knit group of individuals who knew the business. For instance, Mel Welsh was a well-respected academic in this field, David Heddon, a former regional director of Sport England and Colin Chaytors, then Chief Executive of the EFDS. Martin Jelen, who had started the whole process, attended all board meetings without exception, travelling first class from London, having breakfast on the train and dinner going back. It amused me that for all his wealth, he claimed his full expenses which was a constant joke among us including Martin himself who was of substantial physical proportions. He was a most determined and forceful character and an outstanding advocate for the scheme. I remember one occasion when we suspended our meeting for an hour whilst Martin bought a new Rolls Royce. I have not had contact with him since I ceased to be chairman of the IFI.

I account the development of IFI, one of the most successful ventures in which I have been involved, bringing a new means by which to remove those barriers which face people with a disability. Long may it continue its work for much remains to be done.

The landlord experience

I learned that my Aunt Janet, whom I had not heard from for many years, had recently lost her partner after decades together. She was living in straightened circumstances in London. My brother John and I hired a van and drove down to see her, pick her up and her furniture, which easily fitted into the van, and brought her back to Leeds to live temporally with me. Temporarily proved to be a inaccurate term. I found her exceptionally good company. She was a bright person with a splendid sense of humour. She was also very hardy and no problem at all. That winter was exceptionally cold and for a few days we were without water and, therefore, the central heating system was not working. Not one complaint.

I looked round for suitable accommodation for her near to my home so that I could maintain regular contact and finally found a terrace house up for sale in Horsforth, ideally situated near to the shops. I bought the house in April 1982 for £ 17,950, taking out a loan to do so. Janet lived there and being gregarious, quickly made friendly contact with neighbours. I was deeply impressed with this old lady and called regularly to see how she was getting on. She often stayed up late and on the evening of 16th March 1998, about 9.30 on my way home from a meeting, I called on her. She did not answer although the lights were on. As she did not reply to my knocking I presumed she had gone to bed and forgotten to turn off the lights. I drove off to my home ten minutes or so away but felt a lingering unease so I turned back and looked through her letterbox when my loud knocking was not answered. Through the letterbox I had a very restricted field of sight but thought I saw what looked like a foot on the floor. I broke one of the small glass panels in the door and put my hand through and found she had left the key in the door. I entered to find her lying on the floor at the foot of the stairs. She could not communicate and I immediately concluded she had had a stroke. I phoned for an ambulance which appeared to my relief extremely quickly and they rushed her off to the Infirmary four miles away. I followed and waited until the medics could give me a report. They diagnosed a stroke and she went into intensive care. I returned to her home, locked it for safety and then went home, arriving in the early hours and very depressed but so glad I had returned to her home or she might not have survived. She did survive and after a period was fit to be moved. Unfortunately, it was not possible for her to remain alone in that state and a place was found for her in a council-run home nearby at a weekly charge of £ 32.90 per week. The staff were excellent – just very ordinary ladies with a very extraordinary capacity for care of the elderly. There Janet stayed for a quite a time, enjoying the care of these remarkable women and becoming quite a "character" in the home because of her sense of fun and badinage. Ultimately she became ill and died. I felt that in the end she decided enough was enough and had given up so death could relieve her from a life which did not offer anything more than the Grim Reaper.

I know that my mother would have been happy to see Janet being looked after. Genuine love in the family is something which should be treasured. Not interested in becoming another landlord, I decided to sell the house in Rose Avenue as soon as possible but my cousin John, who was vice principal at the Catholic College, now a university with an excellent reputation academically, asked me if I could let the house to a student whom he wanted to help. She was apparently a girl who had become pregnant and had a small baby. She needed accommodation desperately as her attempts to find a place to rent had been unsuccessful as landlords did not see her as a suitable tenant – a student without resources but with a baby. I was not averse to helping someone in these kind of straits and so I let the house to the girl/woman at a rent to be set by an independent appropriate authority.

She was an unfortunate person and the baby was not a very healthy child. She was not a good tenant due to her inexperience and so I was not infrequently called to deal with some problem or another. The one I remember most clearly is unblocking the sink. She had it seems poured hot fat into the sink which had then solidified at the u-bend and blocked the sink. I took me some time to clear this. I also had twice to deal with fitting new fuses when she overloaded one of the plugs. I called on one occasion to collect the rent and found her accompanied by another young woman, a colleague at the college. This female was a bit of a virago and approached me as if I was Rachman himself. I would have been very tart with her had I not felt that she was doing what she thought was right in defence of her friend. I felt angry which was tempered by my respect for someone who would come out fighting for the underdog even though my tenant was being treated very sympathetically, much more so than the average landlord who is letting for money. Ultimately, the tenant left on completing her course successfully and I decided to sell as quickly as possible before John produced another case which needed help. However, in retrospect, I did well out of what I had considered an act of charity for when I came to sell I had made a profit and had a sum of money I could invest at a time when interests were high by today's standards and subsequently so high they were excessive.

The English Federation of Disability Sport

The Memorandum of Association of this organisation, EFDS, lists a host of objectives, a to z, which can be summarised as developing sporting facilities and opportunities for people with a disability to engage in sports of their choice. One of the subscribers was Roger Biggs, someone I knew well because he had been heavily involved in creating an organisation, UKSAPLD, which was starting on the path to gain some sort of parity for people with a mental handicap as the phrase was then. He was a terrific advocate, worker and visionary and one individual whom I would rate to be the most effective, honest and successful operator in this field. I felt a sense of great loss when a decade later he took a post in the Far East, Cambodia, to take up another most worthy cause. I did later have the pleasure of calling on him for a few days as part of a holiday. A great experience.

The board included British Blind Sport, British Amputees, Les Autres, British Deaf Sport, British Wheelchair Sports, C P Sport, Disability Sport England, The English Sports Association, Three Regional Representatives and an observer from Sport England. It started in 1998–1999 with a Sport England grant of £ 170.340.

In February 1999 I was asked to become the president and chairman. I felt genuinely honoured and willingly accepted. We all had great hopes. These were unfounded as our meetings, despite my position as chair, became more difficult as so many representatives were keen to pursue their individual ambitions rather than consider the whole picture. The deaf later withdrew, having decided they were not handicapped in the usual connotation of the word. They merely spoke a different language. Some were keen to have fully active regional organisations. Some were keen to exclude the people with a learning disability for a number of reasons.

The organisation set off on a blissfully optimistic note which was soon dissipated. Board meetings became more of a battleground than a place to reach accord and big issues arose. One of the concerns was an organisation called Disability Sport England (DSE). This organisation had a splendid well-deserved reputation for organising competitions for disabled people. Unfortunately it had accrued a very significant deficit of approximately £ 130,000. Sport England wanted us to save the organisation which I considered most certainly deserving of saving as its performance record was excellent if one ignored its financial woes. After much time and effort, aided by Colin Chaytors, the Chief Executive of ESAPLD, and a substantial sum from Sport England, DSE was saved and became an arm of EFDS.

Colin Chaytors was a registered disabled person. He was a kind, very competent and effective person as chief executive. I could have not asked for someone more kind and competent. His was a quiet reserved approach with none of the bombast some CEOs acquire. Over time he became most unfairly more and more under attack by those wishing to steer a course of their own choosing. He was not helped by the officer delegated by Sport England to attend our meetings. His attendance was irregular and his contribution negligible which, in effect, was a serious problem for maintaining an understanding with Sport England which was so important. He was an engaging black African officer with a great smile and I attributed his irregular attendance to his knowing he was going to be attacked by those who felt Sport England was not helping enough.

As a politician of sorts, I was familiar with the knife in the back between close friends, or personal rather than community advancement, dirty tricks et al and for much of the time our board meetings were refereed by me rather than chaired. We did make ultimately some progress as evidenced by the return of CP Sport as a member after withdrawing some years earlier. It was this turbulence and back biting that made me decide to run a major IFI scheme via a separate company from EFDS. The IFI was successful beyond our most optimistic expectations. I cannot remember the scheme ever being discussed when its minutes were presented for the record by EFDS. A report dated March 2007 records that, of the 55 objectives set out in the Development Framework, the EFDS fully achieved 94%, partially achieved 4% and deferred 2%. Over the years, board changes led to a more sensible approach and objectivity. It is reasonable to see the work of my colleagues, particularly Colin Chaytors and his finance officer, as leading to significant changes in terms of understanding and execution.

The report for 2008, the year leading up to my ceasing to be chairman, lists planned and activated schemes of a variety and challenge of which anyone could be proud. I was and so were my colleagues. It was a bit like a major symphony, all *sturm und drang* and then the struggle over, all peace and calm in a relaxing last movement.

My going meant we had to find a successor so the Chief Executive of EFDS and I, plus a board member, advertised and interviewed. One or two applicants seemed just right until one leaped out at us. It was a curriculum vitae which was quite exceptional. I had reservations as the extent of the list of appointments, past and present, seemed so substantial that one had to wonder was this chap just using posts for self-advancement. He was interviewed along with others and impressed me despite my concern and my two colleagues, the Chief Executive of Sport England and a member of the board. We were unanimous; the appointment agreed. I met the chap a few times, briefing him and he was quick to pick up the jargon and details. Sadly, the appointment came to be seen as the wrong one as he almost immediately fell foul of those he was going to work with. What a pity as I am sure either one of the two whom I had originally favoured would have slotted in perfectly. I am pleased that EFDS survived the turmoil after some difficulties and is now operating successfully.

INAS 2016

I had established a UK Sports Association for People with a Mental Handicap (UKSAPMH) following my running the Sports Council's Year of the Disabled Campaign aided and abetted by Liz Dendy of the Sports Council. The UKSAPMH Board was a large and highly regarded body with representatives from bodies like the Directors of Social Care Organisations and the Sports Council.

One Social Services director was particularly interested in the formation of an international body to represent the sporting interests of the people with a mental handicap. I felt he and his similarly-interested colleagues were more interested in the foreign travel than in any other thing. Despite my lack of enthusiasm, this small group went ahead with discussions which would later lead to the formation of the international organisation INAS FMH – International Sports Body for People with a Mental Handicap, later changed to Learning Disability or Intellectual Impairment. I was wrong to assume their motives to be more selfish than idealistic and now look back with admiration on their enthusiasm and commitment.

There were just 14 nations represented at the first meeting of INAS in January 1986 but the new organisation soon received recognition from the international organisation of that time which ran the Paralympic Games, namely the International Coordinating Committee (ICC). This was a remarkable achievement in a very short time though none of us at that time could conceive of an organisation which now has more than 70 national members, 15 annual events worldwide and 3,500 registered athletes.

I became part of the UK delegation to INAS and over a very short period of time came to know a host of individuals from all over the globe. Some of them were the most committed members one could hope to meet. The general concept was based on a theory of a distinguished and highly individualistic academic of an international reputation from the prestigious University of Uppsala, Bengt Nirje. In condensed form he preached "Normalisation", a theory that people with a mental handicap should be treated as normally as possible, enjoying the passage of each day, week and year exactly as other people of the same age and gender. My view is very similar, namely that a person with a mental handicap should be entitled to enjoy all the opportunities that everyone else has. In short, no discrimination, no matter how well intentioned.

A small town in Sweden called Harnosand offered to meet the central costs of INAS and this included providing the salary of the general secretary of the organisation. This was an exceptional example of generosity and enabled us to employ a very competent young man, Mats Hamberg, who served the organisation splendidly for a number of years.

In 1980 the First World Games for athletes with a mental handicap were held in Harnosand which was a major first step to have our athletes competing exactly as everyone else competes, i.e. normalisation. Had Harnosand not been so generous it is doubtful if the organisation would have survived. Meetings in Harnosand however, required expensive air travel which was outside the competence of some countries to meet and therefore attend. INAS had started off as a very open and democratic body but it changed when Fernando Vicente from Spain became president. He seemed to have limitless resources to spend and he was more of a General Franco by disposition than a Saint Francis. His term of office lasted four years and he stood for re-election for a second term at the AGM in Harnosand. Fernando arrived with a sizeable entourage. He was very unpopular with many of the countries represented there who found him bombastic and dictatorial. He was seen by so many as a dictator and not a democrat. As there was no one prepared to stand against him, I was put under great pressure to stand for president, something I was keen not to do given my already full calendar of responsibilities, one of which was earning a living and meeting the very considerable expenses of travel, though the Sports Council did pay some of these expenses as it did for other organisations.

After receiving great pressure to stand, I finally agreed but counselled all the conspirators not to reveal my challenge before it happened in the meeting. Strict secrecy was enforced and we all felt a bit like kids enjoying a game. Game, however, it was not. When the chairman called for nominations, Fernando expected to be unopposed and he was completely taken aback when after the Spanish delegate nominated Fernando, someone nominated me and that was quickly seconded by a number of delegates in chorus it seemed. Fernando was furious and even more furious when I won with a great majority. He got up, waved theatrically to his entourage to follow him and made an exit of which Bette Davis in her prime would have been jealous. Fernando left Harnosand without paying his hotel bills and other bills he had accumulated which fell on the town to meet. Quite despicable but in keeping with Fernando's way of working.

Fernando was an enigma. I was told that he had started off as a social worker with little or no fortune. At his height before his fall, members of INAS were invited to visit his home/farm. They were amazed by the opulence and wealth displayed. It reeked of wealth – great wealth. The question immediately raised in one's mind is, how did he do it? We were to find out later.

He was a man of ambition. He told me he wanted to stand for the EU Parliament and thought that as chairman of a major charity like INAS, that would help. He sent over to London two of his henchmen who explained Fernando's ambition and promised me substantial financial benefits if I were not to seek re-election as President of INAS. I naturally refused but was impressed that Fernando could set such store upon becoming President of INAS once again. He was very well connected. He seemed to be able to call on two Spanish princesses to attend competitions and even meetings and I ended up on first name terms with them. They were very genuine people with a real interest in people with a disability and it was always a pleasure to meet them.

The first Paralympic Games for people with a mental handicap took place in Madrid. A large number of nations competed, the majority coming from Europe. The Games, without qualification, were successful. They had shown that our athletes with proper training could compete at a high level and that it was only the mental handicap which prevented them from vying for a place in the Olympics. Fernando had, of course, been crucial in organising this event and quite rightly bathed in a warm glow of real success. He was particularly keen to meet Prince Edward who very kindly came over to Madrid and made a great impression on our athletes whom he met for prolonged periods on a number of occasions in a four day visit. Fernando was quite determined to become President of INAS once again. On Monday 17th February 1997 I met the the brother-in-law of Fernando in London. He offered me a deal on behalf of Fernando. The plan was that I should not stand for the presidency but allow Fernando to be elected without a vote. Fernando would then set up an office in Madrid and send me on a long trip to canvas nations in the third world with Fernando meeting all the costs. Fernando would pay for delegates to come to the General Assembly if they promised to vote for him. If Fernando was not successful he would set up another international organisation in competition with INAS, something he had tried three years earlier and failed. I responded by pointing out the illegal nature of the proposition and that for four years Fernando had not played any part in INAS and indeed, had been two years behind in paying the annual subscription. The next General Assembly met in Germany and the vote for me was 18 and Fernando 19. Fernando had bought tickets for a number of individuals who had promised to vote for him and had been lavish in providing entertainments for all. He was jubilant but being the great performer, he could not have been more generous in his praise of my presidency. Most of those who voted for him came from countries which had no significant schemes and in some cases no schemes of any kind to develop mentally handicapped athletes and who had never sent athletes to an INAS event. As someone who has all his life been involved in politics, local, national and international, I am a bit case hardened but I did feel by letting this happen we were going to put back our cause significantly and that made me sad. I, however, accepted defeat despite the dirty tricks and promised to remain fully involved in the future. Two women delegates from West Africa came to see me and apologised for voting as they did. They said that a number of the delegates including themselves had come because Fernando had agreed to meet all travel expenses and if they voted for me they would have to pay their own fare to back home. This they could not afford, I reassured them that I understood. They were two very nice individuals coming from countries which have very few public services and extremely poor standards of living. That they were able to do anything to help the mentally handicapped was in itself very impressive. I was, however, disgusted when Bob Steadward, the Chairman of the IPC International Paralympic Committee, paying a courtesy visit to the General Assembly, virtually directed the delegates to elect Fernando. This was not so explicit as it appears in these words but it was exactly that. This surprised me because I had been much involved in the early days of the IPC and indeed had helped to get him elected. I understand that Fernando had promised a large sum to an organisation in Canada which Steadward would lead and carry his name. I liked Steadward despite seeing him as a person devoted to the elevation of himself at whatever cost.

In due course, Fernando got his "comeuppance." He was determined that Spain would do well in the Paralympics in Sydney so he picked, as part of the Spanish team, a total of fifteen athletes or more who had no mental deficiency and who had not been examined for eligibility at all but were good athletes in their chosen sport. This could happen because Fernando had taken the registration of athletes into his direct control. Only registered athletes could compete. The Spanish team indeed did do well but the problem for Fernando was that he had picked as one of the illegal team of athletes, a man who was a journalist who had been researching Fernando's life and lifestyle. He broke the news and this was a tremendous body blow to INAS because it was their president who had engineered this quite atrocious subterfuge. He could do this by his bribery which took many forms. He controlled the registration of athletes' eligibility, paid the expenses of some of the countries which could not afford to send athletes or representative abroad if they promised their vote using every aspect of the work of INAS FMH to his glorification. When the story broke Fernando suddenly and wisely felt compelled to visit his second wife's country, Columbia in South America, most urgently. A detailed police investigation of his business in Spain revealed a very profitable, if not always a legal, business. Two years later he appeared before a Spanish court to answer criminal charges. On 7th October 2013 the Spanish court fined Fernando 5,400 Euros for his role in the scandal and he was ordered to return 142,355 Euros. It was confirmed that at least 15 members of the Spanish team were not mentally impaired in any way and had not been given any test which was an essential part of the establishment of the impairment. The journalist provided all the evidence to justify criminal charges against Fernando quite apart from the Paralympic scandal. Fernando had put back the movement for inclusion of the athletes with a learning disability (the term adopted for mental handicap) and which led to INAS athletes being barred from Paralympic and World Championships for ten years. This may not sound too awful but it meant that many countries ceased to support the mentally handicapped athletes and their organisations and so for nearly a decade, athletes with a learning disability/mental handicap had all financial government support withdrawn. All the athletes who could have competed on the world stage at Paralympics and international events could not do so. A lifetime's opportunity lost for ever.

Fernando did enormous damage to our cause for athletes with a learning disability. It provided all the arguments needed by those who did not want "these people" in the Paralympics. Their opposition was based on the need to maintain the sanctity and purity of the Paralympics, something I strongly support. I do not approve in any way, however, if it is used as a tool to exclude INAS athletes. I have no doubt in my judgement that this disgraceful episode was used over the years as a weapon to exclude learning disability athletes from any IPC event. The antipathy this attitude shows is attributable to any number of causes. For instance, if the learning disability athletes are admitted to the Paralympic Games and given a full calendar of events, they will be taking up space in the programme and in the physical resources that their athletes, blind, Cerebral Palsy, amputees and wheelchair, etc., could fill. The resource to finance the elite competitors is relatively small and if the LD athletes are admitted, everyone else would get less. Others still have the "Does he take sugar?" syndrome. That is, if you are in a wheelchair with your helper or friend who is engaged in conversation, you are left excluded and diminished or even worse, talked down to as though mentally deficient. I concede without reservation that this was a widely-held view and that it was a real hardship for many people in wheelchairs. Thank God the position is now quite changed thanks to the great success of the Paralympic Games in London and Rio.

It was with some pride when, for the first time since the Fernando tragedy, INAS athletes were permitted to compete in the London Paralympics. The events were very few, insultingly so, but they set the precedent for INAS athletes to participate in the world of the IPC. One must not forget that in Atlanta it was the medals won by the learning disability competitors which put GB near the top of the medal table and indeed there was one exceptional track athlete, Kenny Colaine, a black mentally handicapped sprinter, trained by Linford Christie, who was awarded an MBE.

He clocked 11.33 sec for 100 m and 22.90 sec for 200 m, times better than some of the non-disabled Olympic runners at that time. It is also only fair to say the INAS athletes were excluded for ten years from international competitions organised by the IPC because INAS had to accept the blame corporately and not individually. The INAS organisation had allowed a small number of Spaniards to obtain the control of INAS organisation. A vocal group of countries including the UK tried their best but they could not and would not use the illicit tricks which Fernando could apply – primarily bribery. The dishonesty was that of the people who controlled who was eligible or not. The LD athletes all over the globe were denied their right to compete through the dishonesty of those who were elected to be their champions. History tells us of the danger of allowing power to fall into the hands of a few powerful people. We allowed this to happen in Germany, Italy, Russia and many other countries and the effects are always dramatically horrible. Fernando is a good example of the stereotype "baddy" who is at the same time endearing. Fernando could be a most generous host, liked a laugh and high spirits and could be as convivial as anyone. Half of me liked him enormously. The other half would have wanted his head for the damage done to our movement. Prior to the scandal breaking he invited all the delegates attending a meeting in Madrid to an evening at a bull ring which is used to train bullfighters. The conviviality was extreme and so when it was suggested that we could try out our skills in the ring with a small bullock without horns, the chance was too good to miss. The animal I was provided with was the size of a donkey and did not appear to be aggressive, more puzzled, I thought. I knew that one held out the red cape to one's side so the bull would charge that and not you. My problem at that moment was that having quaffed immoderately, I could see two bulls and chose the wrong one to excite. Little the little bull might be, it charged me, sent me completely apex over base, performing a backward somersault and landing more or less on my feet having executed 360 degrees involuntarily. I received great applause not for my athletic skill, but because I was still pipe in mouth smoking. The next day I had a knee the size of a football. The price one pays when Bacchus replaces sobriety.

The UK has been very well represented at the international level by the UK Sports Association for People with a Learning Disability. In the early days of UKSA we were fortunate to employ Roger Biggs, one of the most effective CEOs I have known.

He was extremely sharp and intelligent and had one of the most persuasive talents I have known. He really put the UKSA on the map and was widely respected even by the "enemy", whoever they might be at any time. I was profoundly sorry when Roger decided to take a job in the Far East but the loss was lessened by his having left someone to fill his place, a highly intelligent woman who, during her time with us, obtained an LLB and was called to the Bar. We could not have found a better replacement for Roger than in the current CEO, Tracey McCillen. I have been equally blessed by the good friends I have made across the globe through our international relations. Outstanding among these is Jos Mulder, a Dutchman of incredible honesty and integrity, totally reliable, highly intelligent and committed. I was delighted to nominate him and see him elected as chairman in Acapulco to replace Fernando as what INAS needed most was someone who was palpably honest, fair and incorruptible. Another star in that firmament was a splendid Australian lady, Marie Little, who was a permanent knife in Fernando's side. INAS is now a very effective organisation and offers a wide range of events worldwide but it lacks in the UK the support other similar sports organisations receives.

There has been another problem from the very beginning of the formation of INAS FID. Special Olympics is a worldwide organisation with HQ in the US and is most generously funded by the Kennedy clan. It is a very worthwhile organisation and commands my respect and support. The Americans, however, saw INAS as a competitor and were very obstructive, so when I was elected President of INAS I felt my first task was to make some accommodation with Special Olympics. I asked for a meeting and was given a date and time in Washington. I booked a return flight, arriving in Washington in time for the meeting which lasted under an hour. I spent the rest of the day sightseeing and flew back the day after. Special Olympics operated on the principle of letting everyone participate. Thus, at an athletic event there could be several 100 metre races, each one with a first, second and third winner. The aim, most creditably, was participation. Thus, at one major championship there could be a small handful of winners of the 100 meters or other event and several second places and a similar number of third places. It also operated on the basis of rewarding runners with a hug at the end of each race. The huggers were ladies offering their services. One incident comes to mind. A colleague at one big SO Games in England heard two young male participants talking before they raced. One said to the other that he was aiming to get to the hugger in the next lane as she had bigger boobs than the hugger in his lane. Such well-intentioned ideas of having huggers have long been dropped in the UK.

The Paralympic movement was a marvellous aspiration with an aim which was totally honest in intention but also riven by politics. For instance, there was concern in the ISODs – The International Sports Organisations for the Disabled – that Steadward, the chairman/president of the International Paralympic Committee, was attempting to make the IPC the supreme body for sport for the disabled and reducing the authority/role of the ISODs which did the work of sport development on the ground. He seemed to many, me included, as a man determined to pursue his personal ambition and be another Samaranch. I knew President Sanz, who represented the blind, well and was frequently in touch with him. He had close Spanish connections not least with Samaranch, President of the Olympics. Sanz also appeared to be financed very substantially by ONCE with whom Samaranch had, so I was told, business connections. ONCE was a very rich charity in Spain. Sanz was very concerned that IOSDs were being side-lined. I shared that view as did the presidents of the other IOSDs. We pointed out to Steadward that all the athletes competing in the Paralympics came from one IOSD or another. It was the IOSDs which provided the athletes for the Paralympics and other IPC events, yet they were being threatened with an ever-reducing role by the seemingly megalomaniac desire of Steadward and others to be the world organisation of all sport for disabled people, being responsible for regional and international sporting events as well as the Paralympics and be the sole voice of sport for the disabled. This ambition was seen as a real threat not merely to the IOSDs but to the development of the sport itself as clearly IPC could not undertake the development work and development events that the IOSDs did.

It was this view that fired Sanz up with the support of the other IOSDs although we did not support his threatening to withdraw from IPC. Sanz, however, showed his influence by arranging an agreement that Samaranch would meet the IOSD presidents individually. We were invited to meet Samaranch collectively in Geneva to express our concerns. We were later individually invited to meet Samaranch in what amounted to a show of support for the IOSDs from Samaranch. He clearly showed this support for the IOSDs which Bob Steadward could not ignore. Each president of an ISOD was given the "privilege and honour" to meet individually with Samaranch which was always something like dealing with a god. Samaranch wielded enormous political influence outside disability sport as well as the Olympic world. He was accorded international diplomatic status but was later proved to be not as perfect as he should be, thereby finally losing his position as President of the Olympics and his status as a world president. I had three sessions with Samaranch and found him personally a positive individual who promised more than he effected. I was, however, pleased to see him go.

The IOSDs were not sporting Luddites but concerned about all their athletes, not just those who went to IPC events. It also illustrated the power of the Spanish sport mafia, almost all of which was beneficial. For instance, ONCE handsomely supported INAS FID in its development work in the third world. There was also great concern in each IOSD that the specific needs of the individual disability would not be met if Steadward was successful in his ambitions. These concerns were among those which, in the end, led to the withdrawal of the deaf from the Paralympics. I was genuinely honoured when I was invited to their world championships in Bulgaria.

During this period there was growing concern about the role of the Steadward as president. From the position of commanding almost universal support, his authority and views were coming under increasing criticism although this change of attitude was not expressed in any public forum. Steadward also suffered from a gradual erosion of the trust which had existed between himself and his executive director, Andre Raes, until it led to a total breakdown of relations. Raes was a stickler for correct procedures and meticulously accurate reports. I had to visit him from time to time which I did by driving to Hull, getting an overnight ferry to Belgium, driving to the meeting in Ghent, then returning the same evening to catch the ferry home to Hull. Steadward was much more of a pragmatist and freewheeler which got him into trouble when he tried to get Bonn selected as the home base for the IPC without following the correct procedure. This gave Craven, a former wheelchair athlete, the first opportunity to appear as a significant figure politically which ultimately led to his becoming president and a very effective one, although I had no help from him to establish the rights of people with a learning disability which did not stop me from liking him for what he had achieved.

Hospitals

Over the years, I have been deputy chairman of all the Leeds hospitals and for two long periods the acting chairman. Originally there were two governing bodies, one for the west and one for the east. Originally I was vice-chair of the west which included the Leeds General Infirmary. The chairman was a very decent substantial businessman in Leeds. He attempted to make some significant changes which were strongly opposed by the senior clinicians. He was a businessman and unused to politics and how political systems work. In the end, the senior clinicians passed a vote of no confidence in him and he felt it necessary to resign. This meant I took over as acting chair and went out of my way to create a less confrontational climate so that some reforms could proceed. I was told informally that the Conservative Government was not happy to see a local Labour politician take the chair but it found considerable difficulty in getting someone to take the departed's chair. I was paid approximately £ 3,000 per annum and, following my earlier promises to myself, I accepted the salary but then gave it over to the restoring of a unit in St James named after a Labour politician, David Beevers, who had been a leading figure in the development of the hospital. I was asked to formally reopen the centre. The ceremony took place in a large room in the refurbished unit. On the wall wherein I was to make the opening speech was a large copper plaque which listed those who had created the centre when it belonged to the people before nationalisation. I knew nearly all of those earlier Labour activists whose names were recorded on the large plaque. I was reminded, and reminded all present, that when the NHS was established against great opposition, more than half the beds in the nationalised NHS came from local authority hospitals. This was quite a moving moment as I thought of those pioneers but I felt it necessary to point out that the names included some dedicated members of the Conservative Party.

In due course, my time ran out in West Leeds and I was then asked to become deputy chair of the East Area by the chairman. He was a Tory, well respected by all political parties and so I became a vice chairman once again. Then Sod's Law took over and I became acting chairman for a substantial period, my chairman having been moved to a Regional Board. I was sorry to see him go as he was an excellent chairman, always looking to see how we might be more efficient.

Certain memories remain with me. The current view was that clinicians tended to hide or bury their mistakes. I took the chair at a number of investigations of alleged medical mistakes or misdemeanours. The committee was made up of the most senior clinicians and I merely acted as an independent chairman of the meetings. I found that these specialists were quite prepared to deal objectively but with considerable force. There was no question of the hiding of any mistake or omission. I was deeply impressed by the attitude of those clinicians who were judging one of their colleagues. They were quite prepared to express, in the strongest words, their disapproval of the clinician's work where and when criticism was required. Patient safety was paramount and clinical errors had to be addressed.

I also sat as lay chairman on the appointment of senior clinicians. We were on one occasion appointing a senior surgeon in the Breast Care Unit. I was full of admiration for the quality of the young folk who were shortlisted. Each was required to make an initial statement for ten or so minutes and then be subjected to a cross examination which was most searching. One young woman devoted her ten minutes to an acerbic denunciation of the Breast Care Unit. She could not have been more damning. I admired her for her incisive severe censure, knowing that it might have upset members of the committee. She did not get the job, being narrowly beaten by a slightly more experienced person but her words concerned me and so soon afterwards I visited the clinic and found that her critique was justified. I determined to raise money for the clinic to be upgraded. I asked Liz Dawn, who was a nationally recognised figure and liked character in Coronation Street, if she would join me on a fundraising effort to make the necessary changes to the clinic. She agreed and so I set up the Liz Dawn Breast Cancer Appeal. Within months we had raised nearly £ 200,000 which enabled the centre to be completely modernised in terms of environment and equipment. I asked Liz if she would do the formal opening. This was a public awareness opportunity and given that Liz was one of the most loved characters in Coronation Street, the opening was a great public event carried in newspaper, TV and magazines. Later we changed the appeal to the Liz Dawn Cancer Appeal for having had success with the Breast Cancer Unit I could see many more opportunities. The appeal went on until I ceased to be involved with the NHS in Leeds many years later, the appeal having raised more than one and a quarter million pounds. There is an old saying: for the want of a nail, the shoe was lost, for the loss of the shoe, the horse was lost, etc., up to the statement – the kingdom was lost all because of a nail. In this case because of an honest and fierce critique of the failings of the unit, a brand new unit was created. The criticism was the nail which saved the shoe, etc. There are many hundreds of women who have been through the centre since who owe Liz a great big thank you. The appeal was also important in the creation of the Leeds Molecular Institute, now a worldwide respected research unit. The whole concept of creating a Molecular Institute which would have worldwide recognition was so exciting but when the sums were done, there was a shortage of £ 200,000 which was holding up progress and every month that passed costs would grow. Liz and I, there were no other trustees, decided to provide this sum. A floor of the LMI is named after her which must confuse some visiting it today, knowing nothing of the Liz Dawn Appeal.

The General Infirmary at Leeds and St. James's University Hospitals were amalgamated in 2000. The Special Trustees of these two hospitals were replaced in 2000 by a new charity headed by a distinguished clinician, Hamish MacDonald, who command-ed great respect across the NHS. The funds of the two previous charities were transferred to the new charity which was com-pletely independent of the hospital board. These funds amounted to £ 25 m, 90 % being restricted funds, i.e. could only be used for the specific purpose for which it was given. As almost every ward and every clinic had some funds, this required us to main-tain accounts for each fund – a momentous task as there were more than 500 separate accounts. Twelve years later, income had totalled £ 72 m and £ 51 m had been given to the hospitals for capital/medical equipment, staff amenities/training and patient amenities. £ 22 m was awarded to research. By the end of the 12-year period, reserves had increased to £ 41 m despite two of the worst financial crashes in recent times. Schemes to enhance ser-vices included £ 2 m towards a new Molecular Research build-ing, £ 1.3 m for a Da Vinci surgical robotic system, the third to be used in the UK whereas in other advanced countries they were comparatively common. Possibly the best deal Hamish did with his colleagues was to get us to agree £ 7 m to fund a Research Linear Accelerator (LINAC) for treatment of cancer in the new Cancer Wing and the establishment of a Professorial Oncology unit to develop it, making Leeds General Infirmary a world-wide leader. The deal was to get another LINAC free and in re-turn all the technical research knowledge gained by its use by research medics would be shared with the manufacturer. That deal has put this unit at the very leading edge of research world-wide. Each trustee undertook to be responsible for some aspect of our work. I was responsible for fundraising. We had a small group raising money for cancer and another small group for all other purposes. This was a small team compared with other large hospitals but we were successful. Our success was not always ap-preciated. The Chief Executive of the Hospitals received a for-mal written complaint from a small group of women who had been raising money on a very small scale but with great intent and commitment for breast cancer. The complaint was that my raising money made it more difficult for them to raise money. It was as though these no doubt very worthy women resented The Liz Dawn Appeal's success rather than welcoming the radical change for breast cancer we had made possible. Had they asked, they could have been very useful and I would have welcomed their active support.

When the time came for Hamish Macdonald to go, a ballot was held by the trustees and I was appointed in his place as chairman. The work continued as before, our concentrating on a number of projects. I became concerned that in late 2012, four of the six trustees would retire in 2014 and this was not in the interests of the charity. I made a series of recommendations to the Appointments Commission which, after much detailed discussion, accepted these proposals, staggering the dates of retirement and acknowledging the danger to major fundraising plans if extensions were not given. This was recorded in the minutes of the board in January 2013. Given this early assurance, the trustees embarked on a number of major initiatives in 2013. We were surprised when the TDA, which had succeeded and replaced the Appointments Commission, revoked the decisions of the Appointments Commission and a six-month extension only substituted by TDA. I appealed this decision, stating that we were embarking on a number of very ambitious projects and that plans at risk would include a multimillion pound appeal to establish a centre for the study and treatment of diseases of the central nervous system and the major development of the listed buildings of the Leeds General Infirmary planned to become a Heath Science Centre, both of which would attract grants from outside trusts. Also at risk would be: a very substantial sum – as much as £3 million pounds – from a charity wishing to remain anonymous at this moment, a new and innovative campaign to increase the annual million pounds from legacies and the cost of a new senior appointment to fundraise for the central nervous system proposal. In addition, the hiatus caused by the loss of four of the most involved trustees would inevitably impact on fundraising generally and thereby reduce the assistance which can be given to the NHS Hospitals.

When we set up the new Trust more than a decade earlier, we agreed we would not raise money, just to deposit it with the hospital board as part of its income stream. We determined we would devote our resources to make a big difference which was so clearly seen in our work with the Cancer Centre and the LINACs or the third Da Vinci robot system in the country or for specific research programmes. This was a reasonable decision as we wanted the charity to make identifiable differences which were needed and for which raising money was much more effective than for raising money to hand over to the hospital board as a supplement to their government grant. Despite this decision, in 2013–14 the Trust came to the rescue of the hospital board which was in a financial crisis. We made grants of £ 6 m to support staff costs, new equipment and research and an additional sum in 2014–2015 of more than £ 2 m extra to help the Hospital Trust to meet its financial targets. The hospital had a problem and we tried to help. The unique position today of the Cancer Centre at St James' Hospital can be traced back to the grant of £ 3 m plus to acquire two of the world's most modern LINACS which have given Leeds such prominence in the development of radiological treatment. A similar effect was achieved by grant of £ 1.4 m to purchase the Da Vinci robotic system some years ago which made Leeds a leader in "keyhole surgery" and robotic surgical skills. Another example is the £ 2.5 m grant to fund the recently appointed chair in Clinical Oncology gained by personal contacts with the Burton Charity which could be lost. The TDA refused to accept these arguments, referring to the Nolan Principles. I pointed out Nolan's rubric is not legally mandatory and Nolan himself said that "these recommendations should never be allowed to displace common sense and sound judgement." If judgement in these matters is ruled out there is no need for a committee to sit and make decisions for any clerk could do that. The TDA insisted new appointments should be made. An interviewing group was established consisting of a TDA nominee and three trustees appointed by the Board of LTHCF: myself, a former chief education officer and a very senior former employee of the NHS Trust responsible for the development and construction of the Leeds Cancer Centre and the Leeds Institute of Molecular Medicine. Initial shortlisting was done individually and without consultation *inter partes*. The shortlists of the three trustees proved virtually identical. The TDA member opposed most strongly, in reality hysterically, one candidate, nationally recognised for winning a judicial review against the NHS proving strangely wrong statistics had been used improperly to close the children's paediatric centre in Leeds. He, Councillor John Illingworth, was a senior PhD lecturer at the Leeds University, lecturing *inter alia* to medical students and was Chair of the Health Scrutiny Board of Leeds City Council. He was an ideal candidate. He had led the fight to keep open the child surgery in Leeds when threated by closure on grounds which he proved to be totally false and made by individuals who had recommended their units to remain open. He had beaten the NHS Mandarins twice in cases going to the Supreme Court and he was target number one for these managers of the NHS. The TDA member also wanted an applicant living on the west coast to be included although the TDA had previously insisted that the persons appointed should reside in Leeds or its area. Her application was very poor and not in the same class as all the other candidates and she lived at a significant distance from the local area. This was the very reason the TDA had used for not appointing one of the current trustees as he had no longer a home address in the area even though his work brought him to Leeds more time than he was away from it. This double standard reflects badly on the TDA. It suggests a specific motive, namely to get on the board a friend of the chief executive. On a vote it was agreed by the trustees to invite an impressive shortlist which included this PhD academic, despite the violent opposition of the TDA representative. His reaction was bizarre, bordering on the hysterical and when asked for the reasons for his recommending the lady from the sea side, he did not reveal what was later established that this was a person favoured by the new Chief Executive of the Hospital Board. He denied acting to previous instructions. Interviews took place and recommendations to appoint included the PhD individual in dispute, despite the TDA representative's highly emotional, even hysterical, opposition in which he claimed he would "not permit" the appointment of the candidate. I asked him again if he was acting on instructions. This he denied. It was also agreed, against his wishes, not to appoint the individual who lived on the coast, a friend or colleague of the Chairman of the Hospital Board. Asked directly whether he had the right to veto recommendations made by the majority vote he finally said he had not this power. However, when the appointments were referred to the TDA it decided not to appoint the senior lecturer on the specific grounds of the TDA's representative's opposition, thereby in effect granting him the veto. His experience had never been at the level of the others on the panel and the very reasonable suspicion was that he could have been acting under instructions. The behaviour of the TDA representative could have led to our thinking he had come with a predetermined agenda or was acting on instructions, real or imaginary but in the end we concluded most charitably this was possibly not the case but was possibly due to poor judgement and little relevant experience or to ingratiate himself with his superiors in the TDA.

I welcomed the intention of the Conservative Government to create "as soon as possible" free and independent charities, i.e. not subject to the Appointments Commission, as this will prevent this kind of situation occurring again. A legal colleague interested in governance sent in a freedom of information inquiry re the process outlined above. He sent me the results, more than two hundred pages, every important detail redacted – no indication of who wrote what to whom and a large number of pages totally redacted. Every word obscured. How to make freedom of information a farce or hide something they wish to keep secret! There is an old saying which I have just made up. "If it is worth hiding, it is worth finding." I did not bother.

Leeds Industrial
Co-operative Society i.e. the COOP

My experience on the council and in the health service had made me accustomed to six or seven digit figure budgets. My experience had also involved me in sums a fraction of these big figures but large in their own context. The first was my most worrying – The Leeds Co-operative Society.

The Leeds Industrial Co-operative Society was a major organisation in the decades following World War One. It offered decent simple food in a large number of shops dotted around the City of Leeds, and a major central shop which was situated in one of the busiest streets in the centre of town. I imagine that if any octogenarian was asked for his old Co-op number, he or she would remember it just as an ex-serviceman would remember his "last three" i.e. the last three numbers of his identity disc. Every year the Co-op declared a dividend, the divi as it was called. In one year, I remember as a child it declared a dividend payable to members of half a crown i.e. two shillings and six pence in the pound. That is for every pound recorded as paid, one received a half crown paid out in dividend. A half crown was one eighth of a pound. Many reserved their spending until they received their divi – a lifeline for many of the families where the father was unemployed and the welfare state did not exist except in the minds of some intent on creating a fairer society. The Co-op nationally and locally was seen as a friend of the Labour Party, both having similar aims of a society which is fair and which supports the weak, poor and unemployed.

I was asked to stand in the election for Directors of the Leeds Co-op by the then Chairman of the Board. Eric Brierley was an old-fashioned socialist with very strong convictions. He was, in addition, a successful businessman. I stood and was elected to the board. I had always been a strong co-operator as I remembered how important the "divi" was in my youth. We always looked forward to hearing what the dividend would be and how much we would get. Nearly all our spending was at the local Co-op shop, a ten minute walk away in Carlton Hill and in the big shop which was situated in the heart of the city on both sides of Albion Street. For many in the working class areas, the Co-op was a central part of so many lives. I remember as a small child going to pick up the groceries from Carlton Hill and being served by a man who from time to time would give me surreptitiously a broken chocolate biscuit, broken because he had just broken it so he could give me it. Biscuits, like everything else, were rationed in the war but biscuits had to be sold whole as people would not accept broken biscuits as part of their rations. So he broke one so he could give it to me. The memory of this little kindness to a little boy remains warm in my memory. He was a Labour man, later elected to the council and after many years, elected Lord Mayor. His daughter followed in his footsteps, being elected to the council and ultimately Lord Mayor of Leeds also.

The Board of the Leeds Industrial Co-operative Society when I joined it was riven by incredibly stupid asinine political differences and ambitions. The elections to the Co-op were contested on Labour versus Conservatives terms and this led to the election of some incompetents and worse. Often decisions were made on Party lines as the Conservatives regularly managed to elect a handful of directors. Some were downright destructive. One, however, a very old-fashioned true blue Conservative, was an excellent board member with the good of the Co-op his aim and ambition. On the Labour side there was considerable competence but some odd characters from time to time. One I remember well. On one occasion he spent the large part of the board meeting lying down on the floor of the boardroom contributing his views from the floor for most of the meeting. In addition, there were always one or two Co-op employees on the board which was in accord with Co-op principles but did not provide any independent voice. They were not of the calibre of earlier staff members who were confident enough to express views which challenged or tested the views of the CEO. I strongly support members of the work force joining a board of any business. The danger is they can be absorbed by the other board members or that they feel it essential to object to developments or that they did not understand fully what was going on or they were aware of the results which might follow if they decided to speak out about sensitive issues. When I joined the Co-op, it was a major commercial force in the city. It possessed two large dairies, factories, an enormous number of milk rounds and retail food businesses, a major coal business, barges and a city centre coal stathe, a large number of horses, a fleet of heavy vehicles, a host of small stores throughout the city, a large department store in the heart of the city, a substantial television sale and repair business, a number of workshops and a large number of premises spread across the city, then of only half a million people. The Fall of the Roman Empire was a book often in my thoughts as I saw the Leeds Co-op gradually bleed to death, not through an endemic corruption but quite simply because of crass stupidity, incompetence and ignorance.

Unfortunately, Brierley decided he had served long enough and persuaded me to step into his shoes when he retired. I was elected and shared for a short time the benefits of working with the much respected chief executive. I was very concerned when he decided to retire as I could see the need for a major restructuring given the changes which were taking place in the retailing world. I knew that major changes would have to be made to meet the competition and for the Leeds Industrial Co-operative Society to remain an independent company. Such a major restructuring needed a man of his quality and it was possibly the magnitude of this task which decided him to go whilst the Co-op was turning a sound profit every year. His loss proved to be a major factor in the years of decline to come. The new chief executive was a competent member of staff but his promotion from the relatively small business of running a number of successful pharmacies to running a surprisingly large conglomerate proved to be too great. I liked and respected him as a person and understood the pressure he was under to succeed. We were late in the large stores proliferation and the two we opened were most attractive but in the wrong place and both were without the needed car parking. They were doomed to failure. Bit by bit, our assets were sold off. The two stores in Albion Street were sold, prime sites worth a fortune, and the Coal Stathe was sold and the Hilton Hotel built on it. All over Leeds, premises which were once Co-op stores were sold off and if one drives round the city one can still see innumerable buildings with the stone carved sign Leeds Industrial Cooperative Society.

As someone committed to the Co-operative movement, I was intensely worried. Any effort I made to induce a sense of reality failed. When it got to the point where we had a debt of £ 12 m I formally proposed we should join one of the other Co-operatives lock, stock and barrel. The CEO, seeing his job at risk, got to the members of the board and preyed on their loyalty to the Leeds Co-op. I indicated that this was an issue which was fundamental in my view to continued trading. I was defeated by the board, the Tories joining up with the employees' representatives to defeat even the question of investigating such possibilities which I had suggested as a compromise.

On 4th May 1996 I wrote to the board members of LICS a letter of resignation, something which without being in any way dramatic, was a soul-searching experience. I was lost in a pool of regret and despair. Such reactions come to us all when faced with a major problem we cannot solve as we see a cherished institution flounder. My letter went: "The recent decision of the board to refuse to commission an outside independent firm to review our recent past commercial activities, the decision not to meet to discuss the future of the Society plus the decision not even to discuss the possibility of exploring the advantages and disadvantages of a possible merger are decisions I cannot support." I pointed out that between 1981 and 1994 the "Society had only twice produced a profit before distributions, had sold each year substantial assets and still had to transfer from reserves seven years out of thirteen and how total assets less liabilities declined from £ 17.9 m to £ 14.1 m in 1993–94." I went on to say that I thought that I was, in effect, a trustee of the LICS which was in effect a conglomerate of small businesses some of which are successful others are not which every year for the past 15 have failed "to produce an adequate return on capital and meet the considerable overheads of the Society."

It was rather revealing when some colleagues said we must be alright as the banks seem very keen to lend. I pointed out that was true because we had assets which would cover any debt and that is no way to run a successful business. In the letter I made the following point. "Last year showed a transfer to reserves only because of the multimillion pound sale of our coal wharf and a windfall return of tax of £ 332,000 which really should have been returned to the customers. Our assets for sale are running out. The unwillingness of the board to act in a manner which I consider to be consistent with prudence, good business practice, its unwillingness to consider a variety of options open to it and its determination to proceed on the course of remaining an independent society without assessing the feasibility of the future effect on our employees leaves me with no alternative but to cede the position of president to another. I am sure you would agree that it would be quite inappropriate for me to be involved in the appointment of a chief executive feeling as I do." I felt extremely sad in large part because I must be fundamentally soft, partly because I hate to be beaten when I am right and am sure of it; because I would have loved to see the Society grow and serve the public and because for many years each fortnight I had had a meeting of the board. I felt for the poor dear Co-op which was once of such great importance to the working class in Leeds. In the words of the poet "Parting is such sweet sorrow". Some years later the Leeds Industrial Society was absorbed into the main Co-operative movement and to my disgust the board members all received a considerable pay out for so doing.

I felt extremely sad in large part because I must be fundamentally soft. I felt for the poor dear Co-op which was once of such great importance to the working class in Leeds.

Hartley and Co

At the other end of the scale, I enjoyed the pleasure of working with my friends to create a business from which we would benefit. My commercial business experience over a long life has extended from the minimum to the maximus, from a business earning over a few thousands to the Leeds Co-op which was worth at one time more than £ 40 m and the hospitals which have infinitely greater figures.

In 1962 my friends, Peter Powney, Alec Hamburg, Bill Strutt and Nigel Hartley, over a drink decided to form a partnership which we hoped would save us or make us some money. Powney was an affluent owner of a garage and taxi business. Hamburg was also a taxi business owner as was Hartley. They realised that between them they were paying a substantial sum to insure their various businesses. Strutt was an insurance salesman for a big company. We decided to set up a business selling insurance and we named the business Hartley and Co. My role basically was to chair our meetings, sign the cheques and produce weekly and monthly accounts as well as participating in all discussions. We were all equal partners though in the end the business depended on the work Strutt and I did. Our first audited accounts, 1960–1961, showed an income of £ 190.16.5 and a loss of £ 329.1.6 largely due to setting-up costs.

Year on year the business developed until within a few years we had a successful and profitable business sufficient to require full time application by Strutt. If he took over the business full time that would mean that the benefits to the rest of us would be minimal after paying his salary and expenses but as good friends we agreed to hand the business over to Strutt so he could develop it without consideration of others. The move was a success and his business prospered. We, the others, of course put our business in his way which in my case was limited to house and car insurance, but in the case of Hartley, Hamburg and Powney, their insurance requirements were very substantial.

This was for me a good experience as I learned first-hand how demanding it is to set up a successful business but how rewarding it felt and how to cast a long row of figures like an accountant, a skill much more needed then as we were pre-decimal – everything in pounds, shillings and pence. The farthing had disappeared but there remained: 240 pence in the pound, coins of a value of one half penny, a penny, a shilling, half crowns, ten shilling and pound notes. Five pound notes were still very rare.

Bill Strutt developed a sound business which he later merged with a larger concern. He was honest and a social individual, one on whom one could rely without concern. Nigel Hartley was a card to use an old-fashioned and ambiguous term. Alec Hamburg had a substantial taxi business. He was a Jew and I had met him through my Jewish connections. We often joked that he would say a prayer for me in Hebrew if I would say a prayer for him in Latin, at that time the language used in RC masses. He remained a good friend until he died. Peter Powney was happily married to a lovely woman whom I greatly admired. His business interests developed and he bought an enormous old manor house and lived in just a wing of it. Occasionally, I and Hartley and Strutt would call for a drink or meal and we would explore like teenage boys the other wing which was boarded up. It was quite eerie as we had only hand torches and the desire to do something unexpected to shock the others was in the mind of each one of us. In effect, we adults behaved like silly boys and felt better for it. Alack and alas, all have now left this world. Sadly, the inevitability of losing old friends is the concomitant of growing older. May they rest in peace.

Dave Barker

Among the many who have enriched my life are those who never receive the acclaim they deserve. One such in my life is a former adult student in Huddersfield, David Barker. He was a most enthusiastic lover of the outdoors, in long walks over the moors and activities like potholing and rock climbing. He enjoyed and looked forward to challenges. His enthusiasm was catching and soon he had a number of young students as adherents to these activities. I joined him and his entourage and enjoyed a new set of experiences. One was climbing. This is a demanding activity. With him and a couple of talented climbers I was able to join in some exciting climbs well above my skill level but made possible by the other highly skilled climbers led by Dave. This was a new passion for me which I enjoyed greatly. Less attractive but equally demanding was potholing. My introduction to the sport if that is the appropriate term was to be led after a long walk from the cars to a hole in the ground which one entered with difficulty. At first I thought this was a joke. It was not. I had to force myself "to take the plunge" and so, directed by Dave, I effected an entry via the hole to an underground passage through which we wriggled for some time before entering a large cave. The feeling of relief was substantial. I joined him and his entourage on a number of such trips underground, some of which involved one in crawling through passages which had water running through them. On these trips I wore an old boiler suit which I used when working on my cars. On one trip we crawled through running water for a substantial time and my boiler suit became totally soaked. When we finally exited I was shocked to find my body covered in oily water which required the use of strong detergents to remove when I got back home. I think what I got from these excursions was the satisfaction of overcoming a general feeling of concern about safety. Potholing was not my favourite sport but that did not stop me from joining such trips on a regular basis. The pleasure of being with a group of young people who shared the sense of challenge on these trips was intense. Our long hikes like climbing Snowdon in cold and blustery weather presented physical challenges which it was a pleasure to overcome. Every time I use the M62 to Manchester or Liverpool I inevitably feel a sense of pleasure that we had undertaken long walks across the boggy moors before the M62 was built. No one who has not walked on these boggy moors can appreciate the physical effort required and the pleasure of overcoming the hardship involved. Now in my late eighties, I look back with feelings of great gratitude to Dave and his friends for giving me the chance to experience these activities and challenges. I remember them as great fun which I was privileged to experience. For instance, on one occasion we, that is David and a group of male and female students, set off to visit North Wales. For many, this was the first time they had camped in this way. They had separate tents and so far as I know there was no intercourse other than laughter and conversation. I did not sleep in a tent. I slept in the back of my car, a Maxi – a Leyland production. When the seats were put down I had a large, totally flat area on which to sleep. On the Friday night we went off to "bed" aware of the imminent rain. The rain came. Torrential. It was heavy enough to wake me. What next roused me was a banging on the car by three bedraggled females who asked me to let them in. Their tent had collapsed. I let them in and they stretched out in some comfort. Not for long because we were again roused by three other female members of the group and so they were admitted to the back of my car. The only advantage at this time was the cover from the rain. The six girls/women were in wet clothes but I assured them that their clothes would dry out on them more quickly than if taken off. I did my best to sleep but finally sought refuge by sleeping on the driver's bench seat. Some months later the same group went on a night out. The conversation was all about that night in Wales when "we" invaded Atha's car. Another occasion comes to mind. A group of us had completed an under the ground route, emerged soaked to the skin on this bitterly cold winter's day and walked to our cars. We, male and female, stripped off all our soaking clothes to towel our bodies and then put on our dry clothes. All of us were in the buff effecting this change in this remote spot when a group of walkers suddenly emerged to our surprise. We continued our dressing as though this was an everyday activity. The walkers had the difficulty of being very interested in this group of naked or semi-naked individuals without wishing to look at us as voyeurs. This caused us some merriment, and as Dave pointed out, it was difficult to distinguish which of these naked individuals were male or female without looking very hard at us as being so cold reduced the male apparatus to nearly disappearing point.

Dave was a magnet for the more adventurous students and I feel that they benefitted by being students in the college whilst he was there for those who joined Dave on his expeditions would store up memories which will be there on their dying day and many joined the group long after they had left. Dave, in retirement, undertook a series of studies and exams and ended up with a master's degree and finally a doctorate. Another member of the gang graduated from Leeds University and being an outstanding student of the sciences, went to work in America where he enjoyed major success in academia. Another close friend in the group became an airline pilot.

Personae

Seneveratne

I made a great friend at university in a most handsome and genial man of my age, Tony Seneviratne. He was dark skinned and as handsome as any film star. He came from Ceylon where his father was, as I remember it, a distinguished lawyer. Tony was a Roman Catholic as I was and am. He was always a welcome visitor to our home and was a great favourite with my mother.

To become a barrister one had to join one of the four Inns of Court – very ancient organisations. I joined Gray's Inn and on a first visit to Gray's to "keep term" he and I went together. In London we were met by a lovely lady who for some reason was attached to the Seneviratne family. She asked where I was staying overnight and I said I hoped to get into the YMCA. She insisted that I stay overnight at her home to which I readily agreed. What I did not know was that she would put us up in a large double bed. I remember feeling it most strange to wake the next morning and find myself in bed with a person of the same sex, not that I had had any experience of sleeping with any female. In Leeds Tony stayed with his grandfather, a white working-class Yorkshire man who lived in a very working-class and impoverished area.

During the holidays in summer Tony got himself a job working in a local iron and steel foundry and one awful morning, whilst carrying liquid hot steel in a crucible, he tripped and the molten metal engulfed his leg and foot. He was rushed off to hospital where he was a patient for some weeks. According to my belief in life's double entry system, the damage to his leg and foot was the debit balanced by his being nursed by a most kindly woman, the credit. The relationship grew during his convalescence which took some months, so bad was the damage to his foot and leg and the two agreed to marry. She, Bunty, was the best thing that could have happened to him as they have remained in the warmest human relationship over the several decades since they first met. They became a most happily married couple much to the angst of his family in Ceylon and his brother who lived in England. He was totally opposed to the marriage on a number of grounds, one of which was that Tony, a Catholic, was marrying someone who was not a Catholic and another was that Tony was marrying someone low on the social scale. Sheer snobbery. This did not stop Tony and as the children's stories end, he and his Bunty lived happily ever after. Tony's proposed legal career was to be jettisoned and he took up other opportunities including a long spell in the secret establishment at Aldermaston. Tony was highly intelligent, terribly British in the most likeable way and full of the social graces that made him liked as well as respected. Of the years he spent at Aldermaston I learned absolutely nothing. He simply said he had signed the Official Secrets Act but that, more importantly, he had sworn an oath of loyalty. On retirement he went to live in a small town in Turkey in an area I have visited three or four times as a tourist. I never got to find his home when I tried and was extremely worried when, well into what we call old age, he fell into his empty swimming pool and suffered severe injury. In the end he recovered and I was delighted to go to his 80th birthday celebration organised by his grown-up children in England. What a pleasure it was to meet them. A quite lovely family and Tony beaming all over. I was fortunate to have had him as a friend and confidant. God Bless Tony and Bunty. Bunty remained the same throughout her life. Totally honest, not afraid to express a contrary position, kind, no nonsense, down to earth are all descriptions which applied to her. I just loved her Yorkshire "down to earth" approach to life. She and I got on famously over the years, maybe because I always seemed to agree with her.

Howell

Denis Howell MP had had a successful period as a councillor in Birmingham and when elected to the Commons became in turn Minister for Sport, Local Government, Education and Science and was, from time to time, given jocularly not merely the title of Minister for Sport for Recreation but for Snow and the Floods when Britain suffered an arctic winter. I had known him for many years and was one of his greatest admirers. This did not prevent our having a very public argument as to who should follow Walter Winterbottom as Chief Executive of the Sport Council. I wanted to appoint a cleric, the Revd Nicholas Stacey, who was also an athlete of the highest quality. He also had the strong support of the Oxford and Cambridge sporting gliteratti. The press was very interested in our exchanges which were often broadcast over the wireless as it was known then. He won and we could not make the appointment that I and my colleagues wanted after a proper search and interviews. In retrospect, his decision was seen as reasonable and led to a successful appointment of which he could approve.

Howell was a great lover of sport, not merely of the elite but of the whole population. He recognised the many social and health benefits which come from a nation which is keen on sport. He also recognised that the only way to meet the call of Sport for All was to help the local authorities. He saw them as absolutely crucial if Britain was to become successful internationally and the whole of society benefiting from participation at all levels in terms of health and social cohesion. With his local government background he decided that each region would have a regional Sports Council to ensure the sport for all strategy could be achieved. He appointed me as the first Chairman of the Yorkshire and Humberside regional Sports Council which I remained for ten years. Each region was instructed to draw up a ten-year plan for sport facilities. We in the Leeds HQ of the new Regional Council, using the incredibly motivated staff, many coming directly from the old CCPR, produced a plan which was extremely ambitious. It was ridiculed by Tory politicians as being totally too ambitious and would come to nought. The two TV stations, BBC and Yorkshire, shared this doubt but were very willing years later to advertise the fact that the Regional Council had achieved virtually all the developments we had planned and which had been ridiculed initially as impossible. This was made possible because Howell had the power to allocate or approve government resources or permission to borrow to build facilities. He engineered a law which gave to regions the right to approve schemes for government grants or approvals. There is talk today about regional government. We need to look no further back to Howell's power and influence to show that if the will is there and regions are allowed to determine whether a scheme is eligible for capital approval without which the scheme could not proceed, delegating this decision to the regions is a system which can work and which did work. This delegation of Central Government control to Regional Councils worked extremely well. Sadly, Howell's imaginative and extremely brave decision has not been followed by either Tory or Labour Governments. It seems that when one is elected to the Commons one is immediately affected by the belief that "We know best and those in the regions and cities are not capable of making sound decisions." When Howell made the rule that Government approval for the making of capital grants or permissions to borrow be devolved to regions he was breaking brand new ground. It took courage and ability to get this through. The progress stemming from this decision of Howell was an enormous surge in sports development both in terms of facilities and numbers participating in sport. Later, as Britain experienced enormous snow falls, he was given the role of dealing with the crisis. Later, he had a similar tasks in relation to exceedingly damaging floods and was jocularly known in the press as the Minister or Snow and Minister for Floods. One of his major achievements was the creation of Sports Aid. My colleague, Cyril Villiers, and I had set up three centres of sporting excellence in Leeds and were setting up a fund to assist the needy to meet the cost of travel to attend the centres. We called this fund Sports Fund for the Gifted. He was very interested in our proposal asked for more information which I sent to him and within a period of a year or so he had set up Sports Aid UK which has served sports people so well up to the present time.

I look back with great pleasure that I knew Howell so well. I admired him enormously and felt a great sense of loss when he died as a member of the House of Lords in 1998. May he rest in peace though I do not doubt that he may still be active in heavenly reorganisations.

Kevin Linfoot

During the year's-long efforts to build a new home for NBT I had dealings with a number of chief executives of some of the best known developers in the country. One man I came to know in this way was a remarkable individual, Kevin Linfoot. He had had a meteoric career starting, as I have been told, as a joiner and building up a major development company. He was the man of the moment and highly respected and doubtless envied for his success. I visited his office on a number of occasions and as bit of a pleb was very impressed by his HQ. Quite exquisite. He enjoyed chatting about a whole raft of topics all of an artistic subject of one kind or another. He was extremely devoted to the concept that the arts were uplifting and should be open to all down to the poorest in the community. He once said to me in conversation that the poor can enjoy beauty as much as the rich individual if given the chance. He suffered by the financial crash which I thought was a great pity as he was a dedicated supporter of the arts and had the promise of becoming their major supporter. For instance, In July 2008, I received a letter from him telling me he was organising an exhibition of two most amazing paintings, Whistlejacket and Scrub – the great horse paintings of Stubbs – in Leeds Art Gallery. These life-size paintings are exceptional. On entering the S-studio reserved for this exhibition one got the initial impression that there was a horse there. Linfoot had negotiated the loan of Scrub from the Earl of Halifax as advised by Sir Nicholas Brooksbank, the art adviser to Linfoot as well as to Halifax. The letter to me concluded: "My reason for writing to you about this is that I thought you might like to hold an event during the run of the exhibition in aid of your own favourite charity. If you would be interested please give me a call."

Linfoot pointed out to me that hoping to get a truly splendid Dance House as part of a residential development as envisaged and highly recommended by the Arts Council was going to be too expensive and would not lead to what NBT really wanted. He thought a free standing building was the answer to our prayers. A free standing building was my hope for a solution though, if that became impossible I would happily go into any deal which sited the HQ in a residential block of flats. I had decided that I would propose his election to the Board of NBT if all went well. Alas and alack, things did not go well I regret to say. I had the greatest respect for Linfoot and was sad in the extreme when his business collapsed as so many did during that frightful period of economic turmoil and disaster.

Mrs Thatcher

Mrs Thatcher is a person whose politics I hated. I could not, however, do other than admire her many outstanding qualities. She was very intelligent, a grocer's daughter but with the deportment of the upper class which she certainly did not come from, and a determination to have her own way no matter who stood in her way. She was to me as right wing as any of the old Tories. She was also always well-groomed and a good-looking woman. On one occasion I was invited to a "do" in 10 Downing Street. It was a hot and humid summer's evening and I was standing near one of the windows overlooking the street. She floated over to me and asked me to help her open the window which required her to stand on a window bench. I agreed and had the awful thought that just one push would change history. She smiled and thanked me for my assistance and floated off around her guests. I am still ashamed that I had had that thought even though it would never have been followed by the push. To have thought it was a sin. I also remember that occasion for another reason. Standing alone and not part of any group was a good-looking chap whom I immediately recognised as Group Captain Leonard Cheshire VC. He was a man I most admired for his outstanding bravery, his enormous skill as a pilot and someone who after the war turned his talents to helping the very poor and those in need. I looked and wondered but had not the courage to go up to him and voice my admiration.

Many years later when Margaret's best friends booted her out of office she came to Leeds to address her followers. The Town Hall seats over a thousand people and it was jam-packed with standing room only to hear her speak. They were a very dense crowd of fanatically-devoted fans of this woman wishing to worship at her feet even though no longer PM. After she had performed she came into a large reception room for refreshment in the company of a small specially invited entourage. I often see an animal in a person. Some suggest Boxer dogs or poodles. Some suggest an elephant, others a mouse or cat. As she entered the room after an amazing endless round of applause I thought of an old hen pecking her way along. We engaged in a few pleasantries and shortly after she pecked herself off. I felt sorry for her which was quite stupid but for some reason that is how I felt, albeit for a very short time.

Alan Bennett

As I left Leeds Modern School Alan Bennett joined. His recollections of school were not dissimilar from mine except he was very bright and I was not. In his books he refers to his school days and the Gym Master who used a slipper or some other item to whack the boys who were not trying or not trying hard enough. He was regarded as an upper-working-class lad as he came from a family which was in business – a butcher's shop. The Groococks, by comparison, who ran a substantial grocery business in Headingley, were regarded as lower-middle-class. Such fine declensions existed. Britain was a very class conscious nation. I was clearly working class but as a fee payer I was in a class well above the scholarship boys.

I do not remember the first time I met Alan Bennett but over the years our paths have crossed many times to my delight as I am a tremendous admirer of what he achieved. I played a modest role in one of his televised plays. It was shot in the Morecambe area and he was there, not directing but commenting from time to time to the director. Over the years I have met and exchanged pleasantries with him. I achieved immortality, however, when in one of his books he stated, *ex cathedra* as it were, that only two people knew the true story of the raid on Temple Newsam House, me and him, or he and I.

Temple Newsam is a magnificent Tudor house with historical connections. When I was Chairman of the Leisure Services or Culture Committee, the names changed the job did not, I was technically the Member of Council responsible for the house and its contents which included a collection of gold and jewelled articles of great beauty and value – insured for, if I remember correctly, around £ 300,000. A very professional gang, we never knew how many were involved, it could be just two on the night, came cross country to the house by motor bike, effected an entry and then got the collection by the use of a sledge hammer which created a hole through which the jewel boxes, etc., could be collected. The method of making the hole in the very burglar-proof case of inches thick plastic was brute force. It was supposed to be impregnable to all brute force but the makers of the cabinet had not realised that the brute force technique employed would have the effect of changing the nature of the plastic so effecting an opening. The miscreants were never caught.

On one occasion I asked Alan if he would support a nomination for honours of a very distinguished clinician who had a great respect for the ordinary working-class individual, a Professor Losowsky whose list of academic and social records were outstanding He readily agreed as he knew Losowsky well. He also very kindly hosted a dinner as part of my fundraising efforts for the Hospital Charity Fund. It was not possible to accommodate all who wished to join the occasion. It raised more than £ 7,000. worth £ 14,000 today.

I admire him as a performer. He became a member of a small number of Oxbridge University educated entertainers and anyone who has done a live performance knows it takes real courage. The courage required to do a live dance routine or musical number is substantial. To act in sketches live on TV requires greater courage. There is nothing worse for a comedian than to "drop dead on stage" and this is always a possibility. It takes real courage to do this and Bennett had this courage but also the skills which matched those of his co-actors, all of who whom went on to international success.

As he is so popular he must receive a torrent of letters, cards, etc. In defence, he has adopted a way of communication by writing answers on the back of a postcard. This allows just enough space to send the essential message but no space for the niceties which a full letter would demand, a very clever but obvious way of communicating. I was given an absolutely splendid dinner to mark my departure from the council and the organisers invited Alan. I knew nothing of this. He replied on a postcard, thanking them for the invitation "to Bernard's farewell dinner. I can't I am afraid but I enclose a contribution to his presentation. I wish there were more like him (mind you he was at the same school as me.) The infrequent occasions I have met him or been in his company I have always regarded him with some awe and great affection. He is not merely a successful man of remarkable talents: he is as the Irish Say: "A lovely man". I concur. Leeds City Council decided to confer on Alan the Freedom of the City and I was deputed to make the speech of conferment. I made the point that his diaries and memoires evoke for many of us waves of nostalgia as we recognise the places he paints so economically but accurately. The same effect is achieved by the deployment of a forgotten vocabulary like wireless, scouring stone to his mother's hierarchy of cloths. Alan, despite the success which takes so many away from their roots always retained an affection for and interest in Leeds. Some years ago he wrote to me expressing fears about the future of the reference library "It's a library I'm very fond of since I was virtually educated there and I'd be sorry to see it dispersed. Could you let me know what the situation is. I am sorry to land you with this but short of the staff in Herz Cars and one or two ladies in Marks and Spencer you are the only person I know to ask about Leeds matters." I have had other occasions for correspondence. Many years previously I was asked by the Board of the Playhouse, then under construction, to ask him if we could name one of the two auditoria after him. He replied to the effect that he was greatly honoured to be asked but that as most theatres seemed to be named after dead people he thought had had better not risk it. He has been a great friend of the Playhouse as whenever we put on one of his plays we do excellent business.

A recital of his successes, his skills, his perceptiveness and the causes for his celebrity provide only a partial explanation of his popularity. I think we really like him for his genuine concern for others and for his eccentricity. Who else would allow an obstreperous smelly old woman to park her van in his drive and live there for years? Who else would later enshrine her in immortality by writing a play about her and him. I concluded my speech with: "God Bless you Alan Bennett. May you long continue to amuse and above all stimulate and challenge us by your works. And if you ever feel you are running out of inspiration do come to a Council Meeting when you would have enough material to write a dozen comedies or more talking heads".

The Freedom of the city is the highest award the council can offer but confers no tangible benefit – not even the right to drive cattle and sheep across Leeds Bridge. His prose works command equal public appreciation, his diaries and memoires evoking for many waves of nostalgia as we recognise the places which he paints so economically but accurately or the forgotten vocabulary like sculleries, middens, ginnels, long departed picture houses, the pictures rather than the movies, odd things like the Kennedy Latin Primer a copy of which I still retain today and from which I learned as my cohort learned the magic and almost incomprehensible magic rules of grammar: Genitive, Dative Cases, Auxiliaries, Subjunctive Mood etc. Alan, despite the success which has taken so many away from their roots has always retained an affection for and an interest in Leeds.

Mandela

One of the highlights of my year as Lord Mayor of Leeds was to host a council meeting to award Nelson Mandela the Freedom of the City of Leeds, the highest award it can give. For years, members of the Labour Party had espoused the cause of "Free Mandela" whilst the leaders of the Conservative Party retained their original view of him as a terrorist and fully deserving being locked up. I find it incomprehensible that members and leaders of the Conservative Party could support the White Supremacy Government in South Africa. They opposed a proposal to name a small new urban plot Mandela Gardens. When Mandela was released the world seemed to rejoice and this left the Tories in a bit of a quandary: how had this man with the amazing power of bringing peace to a divided nation be a terrorist? However, they managed this transformation. I received countless requests from all sections of the council and the wider city that they would be able to shake hands with Mandela. I was amused by the insistence of the Tory leader who now wished to be involved in the ritual forgetting that only a year or so earlier he had described Mandela as a terrorist who should not be freed. The Free Mandela movement was a campaign over many years before his final release and was unfairly treated by opponents worldwide as a left wing plot.

A show was put on in Millennium Square to celebrate Mandela and the new South Africa. People like me who had boycotted South African exports were now able to buy South Africa's wine or oranges. It was at the big outdoor concert that Mandela, making a short but passionate speech of thanks, thanked the people of Liverpool for their kindness rather than the City of Leeds. His error was not corrected and to many thanking Liverpool was simply his way of showing how much he travels. I am sure the majority, however, realised he had made a mistake but that did not seem to affect the joy of the moment. For me, meeting him and having the chance to have a few quiet minutes of talk with him was a lifetime high. I rank him along with those outstanding individuals like Ghandi and Nehru who, through their remarkable personae, achieved so much, albeit at a terrible loss of life. Newton famously said: "We stand on the shoulders of great men." He was referring to the world of the natural sciences. It is true, however, of the world of politics. Having visited South Africa a number of times over some decades I felt sure that the political pressure cooker would explode into an enormous blood-letting. There seemed no other sensible prognosis. It took an amazing person like Mandela to show how an alternative method is possible. On his visit to Leeds he, at one point, addressed me as Bernard. I felt enormously honoured by this simple word. Daft but real. We humans are an odd lot. We all know of and speak extensively about the evil men and woman who have existed, names like Napoleon, Attila, Hitler, Mussolini, Stalin, Henry Vlll, et al. I doubt whether many could give the name of the person who started the Salvation Army, the NSPCC, the National Trust or the Welfare State. Mandela reminds me of the lines of Longfellow:

"Great men all remind us we can make our lives sublime.
And departing leave behind us footprints on the sands of time
Footprints that another sailing over life's solemn main
A forlorn and shipwrecked brother Seeing shall take heart again."

May Mandela rest in peace but remain a beacon of hope and inspiration for us all.

Pele

I met another ikon figure, though not in the same category as Mandela but capable of gaining almost sanctified status by his millions of admirers. I was attending a meeting in Brazil in my capacity of Chairman of INAS, the organisation which represents athletes with a learning disability. As part of our campaign for these athletes, the Brazilians had arranged for Pele to attend our football matches. Though not being a strong supporter of football I nevertheless knew of this figure. The Brazilians had arranged for me to fall under his wing as we watched game after game. Wherever Pele went crowds would gather in a way which was miraculous. I was amazed that this rather unimpressive looking man could earn such affection and adoration. Everywhere we went crowds would gather. He clearly enjoyed this adoration and was always ready to call me up to his entourage during which time he could not have been more warm and concerned to support the idea of INAS Football. The only other time I have seen such expressions of support for a national hero is when I see the Pope addressing the crowds in Peter's Square. When I got home I would occasionally drop into my conversation with the football world a phrase like: "Pele said to me ..." This immediately prompted disbelief in the question. " Did you meet Pele? What is he like? What did he say, etc?" In retrospect, I was extremely lucky to have had this remarkable experience.

Trueman

Pele was almost deified by his football followers. In England, Freddie Trueman enjoyed almost the same veneration in the world of cricket. I cannot claim to have known him well but we had met a number of times very convivially. The Sports Council of which I was the vice chairman had adopted a strong anti-smoking campaign which caused a high level of interest – for and against. I appeared before the BBC TV cameras to discuss this matter with Freddie Truman who was a pipe smoker and was opposed to a ban on smoking. I greatly admired him as a cricketer *sans pareil* (as he would not have said) and he was strongly arguing against the proposed restrictions on smoking. Fred was smoking a pipe of substantial proportions, leaving all of us in the studio in a haze. I had put my pipe down some time earlier. We got the 10 second call before the cameras opened on us and Fred said to me quite casually: "Hang on to this for a moment." Like a sucker I took his pipe as he asked. This meant that as the cameras came on I, as the voice for the ban, was the one holding a large and smoking pipe. His skill in playing this trick is something which has amused and impressed me over the years. A simple trick done with great skill and timing. We both had a good laugh after the interview when we both were smoking our pipes. It is difficult to remember just how extensive smoking was in or outside buildings. It regrettably took us a long time to take the first steps to ban smoking in public places and buildings but I have no time for those absolutists who would ban smoking in public open spaces such as the nation's parks.

Henry Moore

The Leeds College of Arts and Design has over the past few decades produced some outstanding artists of which Henry Moore and Barbara Hepworth are the best known. The list is long and distinguished, including Frankie Vaughan who later played opposite Marilyn Monroe in a film, Damien Hirst, Jacob Kramer and many other glitterati. Less famous was my sister who also studied there for a short time before leaving for a stage career.

Moore was interested in developing a centre which would be the focus of future training and research in the world of sculpture. He had been born in Castleford, a small mining town close to Leeds and had trained at the Leeds College for which he felt some emotional connection. At the height of his worldwide reputation he indicated his wish to establish in Leeds an institute devoted to modern artists and his work. He knew and had great respect for Robert Rowe, Director of the Arts in Leeds who inhabited the finest chief officer's office in Leeds. He ensconced himself in a wonderful large room in Temple Newsam, a Tudor Great House, with a desk large enough to a land a light plane on it. (This is something of an overstatement made for effect). He was a friend of Moore and instrumental in Moore thinking of a Leeds Institute rather than something elsewhere. As the idea began to form itself into a possibility, I became increasingly involved as a close friend of Rowe and I asked the Lord Mayor if he would host a dinner with Moore as chief guest. There is in the Civic Hall in addition to the Banqueting Hall, a very beautiful room large enough to accommodate up to thirty people for a formal meal. The Lord Mayor at that time was a fun loving Tory who loved playing the role of a broad Yorkshire-speaking man and he agreed to hold a formal dinner in this Blue Room.

On the evening of the dinner we were standing having a drink when the Sergeant-at-Mace called for silence to receive the chief guest, Henry Moore CH. Moore entered the room smiling and was greeted with the Lord Mayor's welcome and then his words: "I thought with all that hammering on stone you do, you would be a big guy." I shuddered, thinking, "Bang goes our plans." This, however, seemed to amuse the diminutive Moore who was normally accorded venerable respect. This was just the opposite. It set the tone for a most convivial meal which cemented relations between Moore and the council. Ideas for the Leeds Centre were discussed most extensively and the ambitions grew larger and larger. This delighted me as this was a new experience. In trying to do any major project by the City Council the biggest restriction on ambition was always money. In this case, money seemed to be no problem. The criteria for decision was: Does it enhance the scheme? Is It artistically sound? Money seemed no object. And so it was, on a day I shall remember, I was given a cheque made payable to the Leeds City Council by a most friendly Irish lawyer acting on behalf of the Henry Moore Institute. The cheque was for half a million pounds, which in those days was not a small fortune but a big one. It was the first instalment and the centre was magically developed in old premises adjacent to the public gallery and accessible from it. It has a worldwide reputation attracting students and the public in equal measure.

This development made me wonder if we could not do something similar with Barbara Hepworth, another locally born artist of international repute. I confess to being quite unable to appreciate the work of Moore which I have found too abstract for my taste. Barbara was equally abstract but for some inner reason which I do not understand, I quite like her work which sounds a little condescending from someone like me for someone who had gained a worldwide reputation. In discussions with her, progress seemed very possible until her quite appalling sudden death in a fire in the artists' colony in St Ives. I was horrified and deeply saddened, She seemed to me to be a lovely person and quite unaffected in my experience. There is now in Wakefield a new gallery named after her so her name and work will be preserved as is that of Moore in Leeds. If one travels abroad, one can come across Henry Moore's work which seems to have tapped a vein of appreciation worldwide which I regret to say has avoided me.

The Institute in Leeds is of immense artistic value which attracts visitors and students from across the world. It is physically connected to the Civic Art Galleries so one can move without difficulty from one to the other. It is a pleasure to have been involved in the development of something which attracts such worldwide visitors and artists.

Royals

Prince Philip

As Vice Chairman of the Sports Council I was tasked with running a year's campaign: The Year of the Disabled and I needed a big name to launch it.

For some time The Duke of Edinburgh was thought to be less than enamoured of the Sports Council, not quite a hostility but a certain coldness for what reason I do not know. However, by the good offices of Lord Rupert Nevil, a senior member of his staff and a member of the Sports Council, he agreed very warmly to launch the Year of the Disabled on 3rd December 1980. Lord Rupert Nevil, an aristocrat, performed a role in Buckingham Palace managing the Duke of Edinburgh's very heavy list of functions. In preparation for the big day, I had recourse to visit Rupert Nevil in Buckingham Palace on a number of occasions. I was met at the door on arrival and ushered to his office through a minor labyrinth. On leaving, I was shown the way out. Having done this route a number of times, I told Rupert that I did not need him to see me out as I was now familiar with the route. I made a wrong turn and was horrified to see three Corgis emerge from a corridor and I thought, "Oh hell. It's the Queen." Fortunately, it was not or they might have taken me off to Tyburn or burned me at the stake. It was "a lackey" exercising the dogs and he showed me the way out. I confess to finding my having to visit the palace an ego supplement. I was conscious of being watched walking from the steps of the palace to the gate of the grounds by the inevitable hundreds of voyeurs and I felt at times like doing something silly like a couple of grand jetes or a pirouette or two just to create in them a sense of bewilderment.

The launch of the campaign was scheduled to be in Saddlers' Hall or to give its actual title, The Hall of the Worshipful Company of Saddlers. The saddlers are one of the ancient guilds or trade unions though they would probably have the vapours at the thought of being given such a description. I love history and find entering these ancient buildings and establishments quite a thrill. The saddlers, to their very great credit, have for very many years been supporters of riding for the disabled. They provide a marvellous venue for meetings and for social and public occasions. Were all such institutions as generous!

During the period before the formalities I went to the loo to spend a penny. I was standing doing what one does in the gents' toilet when the Duke came up, stood in the next stall to mine and said to me quite gratuitously: "You should always go to the heads (Navy talk for the Loo) when you can because you never know how long it is to the next suitable break." I nodded at this wise suggestion and frequently remember it as good advice. Go when you can or you might regret later not doing so.

I was to open the meeting and had been schooled in how to do this: "My Lord Mayor, Your Royal Highness, Minister, Sheriff, Master and Ladies and Gentlemen." The punctilio on these occasions is both a burden and a pleasure – a bit like a pantomime. The day went well. No acts of *lese majeste* and having started at 10.45 it finished with the departure of HRH in a bright green vehicle which he used to remind all of the need to save the environment, and that was decades ago. We all should have listened harder and earlier.

If he had any antipathy to the Sports Council he did not show it to me in any way. In the many years since then, I have had a number of occasions to meet him on visits and respect him for giving substantial parts of his time to organisations which do not rate high on the Richter scale of organisations and are often working to assist the poor, elderly or disabled. He has always been polite, asked intelligent questions and appeared to embody the tenet: Let's get on with it. My respect for him has increased by his visits to a small Leeds club meeting every Friday night for people with disabilities. The club is organised by a splendid group of volunteers who collect disabled people from a wide area, provide them with a lot of fun, company and assistance on that evening which for many is the only event they can rely on to get them out and about. Prince Philip opened the club in the distant past and has returned at least twice since, where he meets the members and then says a few words to them collectively. He need not do this. The club is hidden away. It meets just once per week. Nevertheless, he religiously visits every few years as his calendar permits. This is a surprising energising occasion for the helpers as well as the group members.

Princess Margaret

Princess Margaret was the Royal sponsor of the Northern Ballet Theatre when I became involved with NBT. I feel she was under the spell of Christopher Gable who was very much the adopted child of the "Great and the Good". She was still an attractive woman when I first met her socially and later it was my pleasure to meet her when she came to the Leeds Grand Theatre for a performance by NBT. In the interval as a devoted disciple of the genie, tobacco, she lit up. In conversation she was clear, concise, bordering on abruptness and had no inhibitions about expressing her feelings honestly. This I found praiseworthy as it is so often missing in the art world. She told me that she did not particularly like the ballets produced by NBT. This was very frank, direct and said without any passion to which one might take offence. As Chairman of NBT I might have thought it inappropriate to the occasion. I, however, liked this honesty in her because so many in the Arts are not so honest. I quite understood her reservation. She loved the Petipa-type ballets, lots of tutus, tights and classical technique of the highest order and gorgeous classical music, preferably Tchaikovsky but Finkus would do. I share this same love.

I met her on a number of occasions not associated with NBT on which she made a point of having a few words with me which always excited the interest of those not so favoured at a large event.

One memory abides with me, each recall creating an internal smile. Many years ago there was a song "Can I have a light boy, can I have a light?" sung by some unter mensch group who became very successful with this song which was a good bit of fun. It still remains with me decades later. I was attending an occasion in one of the big London parks. During the interval, we VIPs were ushered to a large marquee for drinks. I picked up my glass of red wine and went and stood just outside the entrance to the hospitality tent. I lit my pipe and was puffing to my satisfaction when Princess Margaret appeared, holding a cigarette case in one hand and a glass in another. She very courteously asked me if I could give her a light. The words of the song immediately loomed in my mind enough to make me have to conceal an involuntary laugh with a very false cough. The pantomime continued: I had to put my drink down on the grass to operate my lighter; she had both her hands full so I had to relieve her of her glass so she could open her case to take out a cigarette. She produced the cigarette, I produced my lighter, combustion was achieved, her glass was returned to her and I picked up mine. She lifted her glass in a silent word of thanks. All the time I was hearing in my deepest mental recesses, "Can I have a light boy? Can I have a light?"

Sadly, she died and I had the duty of writing to the Queen conveying the condolences of NBT and myself. It is strange that life seems to create for some an equilibrium. On one side there is great affluence and influence and on the other, deep personal sadness. Princess Margaret has had all the adulation and benefits of being a royal princess yet one does not feel she has achieved much happiness. It is also true I believe that she made little difference to many of the charities she technically supported, unlike Princess Anne. All rather sad.

The value of having a Royal Patron depends very much on whether the patron has the willingness to help or is just willing for his or her name to be used on an annual return. I am by intellectual persuasion opposed to hereditary monarchy where the

Head of State is someone not chosen by the people and is often there by accident. The successive British royal families of the past have been largely a murderous bunch with no consideration for the villein, serf, peasant, freeman, et al. Very often the king or queen came from a foreign country and retained their deep connection with it. At one stage, our monarchy was more German than British and later the term, House of Windsor, was adopted and House of Saxe Cobourg Gotha dropped. Our social history is one of suppression of the majority by a small group for their own interests. Some would say with some truth that nothing much has changed.

However the UK modern monarchy is a different animal from its predecessors. The Head of State is the Queen. When she shuffles off the mortal coil it will not be her husband but her eldest son who will automatically take the throne. Were he to die before the Queen, his son would take the throne. This is a mechanical process and guarantees succession without dispute. The people of this country have no influence on this succession. However, when those dedicated to a more democratic system advocate the election of a Head of State one looks at those who hold that title. The list includes people like Stalin, Putin, Ghaddafi, Franco, Amin, Pinochet, Mugabe, Hitler, Mussolini and a host of others across the world not to mention Chairman Mao. Our system seems to work very well by comparison and long may it continue.

Prince Edward

Having lost one Royal sponsor, Princess Margaret, we at NBT had to look for another. Prince Edward and I had met and been on first name terms (he called me Bernard and I called him Sir) when he visited in Madrid the First Paralympic Games for People with a Learning Disability, which in those days was normally referred to as a mental handicap, the term used by the WHO whose definition of that condition we used as our benchmark for inclusion in the Games. Prince Edward stayed for a few days, much of which he spent with me and my colleagues. He was excellent in dealing with the mentally handicapped athletes and gained the respect of the various team managers from across the globe. He could not have been a greater success. There was one afternoon when there was no competition and he invited me to join him at a concert to which he had been invited. I remember Respighi's *The Pines of Rome* being a substantial part of the programme. It is a piece which I find unmusical "full of sound and fury, signifying nothing" and tedious besides, and when asked by Edward what I thought of the programme as we shared a drink after the concert I was frank about my inability to appreciate the piece. It seemed he shared my opinion but was too royal to state it so succinctly. He was accompanied by a super chap, ex-Army Senior Officer, with a sense of humour, a liberal attitude to life and very committed to his charge whom he guided most expertly and discreetly when and where necessary. I found them two very companionable individuals.

Years later, I met Prince Edward and his wife, the Countess of Wessex. They very generously visited a showcase evening of The British and International Festival of Festivals Organisation of which I was then president. The evening consisted of young people displaying their musical, dance and speaking talents. The performances were excellent, showing enormous talent in the performers, primarily young people but not exclusively. Ever since Madrid I had had the warmest feelings towards Edward. I now found that his wife, the Countess, was a person of boundless energy and good will to all. She never adopted the airs and graces of some in her position, was always dignified but gregarious and fun at the right times. Prince Edward has always been inclined to the Arts and at Northern Ballet he seemed the perfect person to fill our need for a Royal sponsor. Mark Skipper and I went down (Southerners would say go up to London) to Buckingham Palace where Prince Edward had a suite. We were received most warmly and he agreed to accept our request for him to become our Royal Patron. This position he has filled admirably and is retained today.

Sycophancy is sickening and one sees too much of it. At the risk of being accused of this weakness, I have no hesitation in expressing my respect and admiration for what they do. His wife, the Duchess, visited a marvellous development in Leeds. It is a large charitable development on a site which was formerly a medieval grange of Kirkstall Abbey. The religious body which runs this establishment and a number of homes for the disabled is an example to all such bodies. The Duchess, who addressed me by my first name, was quite splendid, spending some hours at the centre, most of which was with the workers and the handicapped. She exuded informality, energy and a great sense of humour which went down well with the disabled folk there in their numbers.

Princess Di

Princess Di was a remarkable woman. She had the ability to create a deep affection in those she met and those she had not met. I did not know her at all, having had only one real opportunity to exchange views with her. She had obviously a strong personality and she was genuinely interested in "doing good". I especially regarded her highly for her interest and active participation in mine clearing in areas where men, women and children, not to mention valuable cattle, were being blown up by crossing old mine fields. Her interest in the brave men undertaking this dangerous work was clear. She admired them and their work and was eager to make this obvious to all. She also took a leading role in emphasising the need to combat the terrible effects of HIV which in the circumstances of those times, was highly unconventional and she showed remarkable and genuine compassion when meeting those affected with a short life expectancy.

I was at some significant "arty do" in London. I cannot remember what it was but can only assume it was about the Arts. Peter Palumbo, Chairman of the Arts Council at that time and a very effective chair in my estimation, made a point of introducing me to Princess Di. His introduction was very flattering and we spent some 15 minutes in discussion of the problems facing the Arts. I knew of her interest and love of ballet but did not know of her admiration for Wayne Sleep. I *en passant* referred to him as the most highly-skilled technically-brilliant male dancer this country had ever produced – technically quite brilliant. This apparently chimed with her view and we rapidly exchanged our individual views about the role of ballet, how the big organisations were too metropolitan bound and the need to expose more people across the country to this particular art form.

I was impressed by her. She obviously had a passion to see more people benefitting from the millions spent on the Arts, but she in no way showed any condescension during our 15 minutes or so. We exchanged opinions and views rather than what some in her position do, that is monopolise the conversation outlining their views. I felt the circumstances of her death were what her life seemed to engender. May she rest in peace. The efforts of the two sons to preserve memories of their mother are wholly admirable.

Princess Anne

Princes Anne is the most active Royal. I first came to know her when Leeds City Council pledged to raise, and did raise, one million pounds for the Save the Children Fund in one year. She visited the city three times in that year to help in our fundraising. I was given the role of running the year's campaign and so met her at each of her visits which were not brief but lasting on one occasion well into the evening. One school which came from a very poor area won the prize for fundraising. She was excessively good talking to the children and complimenting them on their efforts. She commented to me that she did not find it surprising that the poorest children had raised per capita more than those from the more affluent areas – this was something she had noted for some time.

Normally royal visits operate to a strict timetable. On one occasion when it ran into the evening for a show at the Grand Theatre, there were gaps when conversation automatically took place which is most unusual. This can cause a problem but not in this case. There were no longueurs. All went well. It was a success as she had been briefed so she knew of my involvement with the British Paralympic Association and she had competed in equestrian events in the Olympic Games. Having seen the Olympic course, and how taxing if not actually dangerous it was, I admired her guts. It was her guts which possibly saved her when her car was stopped one evening during an armed attempt to kidnap her only a mile from Buckingham Palace when she refused to get out of her car even though threatened at gun point.

She presided over the splendid Riding for the Disabled Association which held its meetings in the Saddlers' Hall. As a national trustee I found these meetings extremely convivial. A room full of hearty outdoor-type women committed to Riding for the Disabled and a very small group of men of which I was one. Princess Ann chaired the annual meetings with calm efficiency, making sure that the diffident were heard as well as the rest of us. They were very pleasant occasions and I was sorry when my time came up for me not to stand again for election. She has visited on two occasions the RDA Centre in Leeds which is now one of the biggest in the country. On such a visit the great and the good assemble to be introduced individually or in numbers. Princess Anne always makes sure each is addressed, however briefly, and then she moves off to spend her time with the women who run the centre and the disabled riders who were there to perform their routine. This I think is an appropriate division of her time and she does recognise that some individuals play a crucial role in supporting the centre she is visiting and having been told who they are, they get the royal treatment.

The Queen Mother

I have been introduced to the Queen Mother on two occasions with no obvious effect on her. I cannot say I have ever known her, a quick hand shake not qualifying for that status. One thing I did know from personal observation was her amazing strength. This was a real admiration. On three occasions I have been in a large group awaiting her appearance. One is requested to be there by a certain time to ensure all are present before the Royal arrival. As many of those present were getting on in years, a euphemism for old and decrepit, standing for a long time is a kind of purgatory, but standing we remained on all three occasions. One of these occasions was in the Banqueting Hall in Whitehall in the very room that Charles I entered before stepping out on to a specially constructed stage for his public execution. The Queen Mother entered and for an old person remained standing or moving round the group being introduced to the specified individuals. This went on and on and I could see some of the folk there were beginning to cave in. It was absolutely bad form to depart before she did and I was truly amazed at her resilience. She was obviously enjoying the warmth of her reception from those to whom she was introduced and when everyone thought that was it, she continued moving round speaking to those to whom she had not been introduced. I expected calls for an ambulance so tired were we that only stood and waited. She finally left to the most palpable relief of her loyal subjects. How I admired the strength of this old lady. And how glad I was to sit down in a taxi immediately thereafter and how relieved so many elderly folk were who made a dash for the toilets.

Sarah Ferguson

I have always found her good fun, relaxed and not playing the superior Royal female role adopted by others less entitled to such vanity. She became the Royal Patron of Sports Aid National of which I was vice chairman. She took this seriously, not just as some paper adornment. Meetings with her were always fun, direct and effective. She was obviously highly intelligent.

I attended one of her fundraising efforts. She held a dinner for some of the country's wealthiest individuals, about 12 in number. It was a very convivial affair and then she went round each one asking him, there were no women, what he was going to do to help our fundraising. It was superb gentle "arm bending" which led to some very substantial donations. When her period of time elapsed as Royal Patron, a farewell do was arranged for us to say thank you and goodbye. I had to make the valedictory address which was fulsome but genuinely meant. The occasion was a sell-out. A large crowd showed its appreciation of her active support of Sports Aid and there was a very definite regret that we were to lose someone who had contributed so much.

I did meet her once more when she visited the St James Hospital of which I was then acting chairman. Her sense of fun remained. As we walked towards the main building on a bright summer's day, some workmen on the roof gave her a piercing wolf whistle. She responded by giving them an even more shrill wolf whistle in return. The workmen nearly fell over laughing at being beaten by a woman. A small crowd of the "great and the good" had assembled for the customary set of introductions. As we entered the very large main concourse where the large official group was waiting, she saw a bunch of women, clearly cleaners or domestic staff, peering round a corner and clearly not part of the proceedings but just a group of cleaning ladies eager to see the princess who was forever in the news. The princess saw them and immediately started to walk towards them. When they saw her coming they shot off and I had to ask the chief executive to call them back. The princess had a good laugh with them and shook hands with each one in turn. We then resumed the more formal introductions and then a two hour tour of the hospital in which she showed considerable understanding and interest. In retrospect, I look on her with a deal of affection for the forthright nature of the woman, her sense of humour, and her no nonsense and lets have fun approach to life.

Personae

Carol, JKR, Maxwell, Poulson, Waterman

Carol

As we all go through life one meets so many characters that most fade into total obscurity, unremembered. Others stick in the mind and will be there when we take our dying breath. Just such a woman was a most dear friend, Carol. She was a pretty young woman, a Doris Day lookalike. I met her at a party of friends, she being invited as she "did the hair " of the hostess, Pam Constable, who in her own life was a force of nature, a delightful hostess and friend. I got to know Carol well and we saw a lot of each other, I becoming very friendly with her father and mother, two very working-class folk though they voted Conservative. They lived in a working-class district. I do not know if they owned their own house or rented it. It was immaculately kept.

Over the years we remained close friends and it was with deep regret she told me she was off to the USA to become an air hostess, as they were called in those days, with United Airlines. I admired her courage in taking this step and promised to keep in touch. She stayed in the US for some years and I was pleased to visit her in the flat in New York which she shared with two other hostesses. They were a splendid trio – very beautiful, immaculately dressed and so well behaved except when they doffed the air hostess cover and just relaxed and became enormous fun. The three became very close friends which I was so pleased to see as in a city like New York and in the career they were following, it was good to have a solid base from which to go to work.

In due course Carol came home on leave and we decided to visit a pub on the outskirts of the greater Leeds built on the top of Otley Chevin, a remote high point among the surrounding valleys. It was a pub we used to visit for a quiet drink but on this occasion the pub was filled with rather raucous but friendly predominantly male customers. Carol attracted the immediate attention of the crowded bar – crowded because some cricketing enthusiasts were holding a party to raise money for Boycott's benefit, Boycott being not only a Yorkshireman but without doubt one of the world's greatest batsmen in history. I knew Boycott to say hello to but no more, though our paths frequently crossed and I did admire his skill as a batsman. A man came over to our table to sell some raffle tickets. The crowd shut up and watched this subtle advance. He asked Carol if she would buy a ticket. Pure silence. She said: "What is it for?" He said: "It is for Boycott's benefit." She said: "Who is Boycott?" Total silence then the biggest burst of laughter all round. We could have stayed all night drinking the drinks they offered us. I had to explain to Carol what had sent them laughing. A night to remember for no reason other than at the time it was hilarious as a put down.

Carol stayed many years in the USA and came home when her father died. She decided to stay with her mother who otherwise had no kith or kin and again that is something which enhanced my respect for her. She and her mother moved to Scarborough and I visited them very regularly on a Sunday. Her mother was such a nice person, a Geordie by birth with a number of phrases from that region. One was "Cum on bye" which translated meets come and pass by or "after you, Claude. No after you, Cecil" to remember that catchphrase from the enormously liked ITMA show of an earlier time.

In due course, the mother died and Carol remained in Scarborough in apparent good health and we often went on substantial walks when I called at the weekend. She had a problem with her foot and I kept nagging her to see a doctor. In the end she did. One day she phoned me in a voice as calm as could be and said, without preliminaries: "Bernard. Should I let them take my leg off or not?" I shall never forget that blunt question with no preamble. She told me that the doctor had detected cancer and that he advised her to have an amputation from below the knee as soon as possible. She repeated the question: "Should I have my leg taken off from the knee?" It was one of the most awful questions I have had addressed to me. I knew from experience that such an amputation is traumatic, especially for a handsome woman with lovely legs but once cancer was established there was no alternative to that or the spread of cancer would be fatal. I reassured her that it would not stop her walking which she enjoyed with proper prosthesis and that it need not be obvious given the progress made in developing artificial limbs. There was no alternative. I went immediately to see her and lend her moral support which she appreciated and after a brief discussion she decided to go ahead with the amputation. This took place and Carol, in her hospital bed on her first day after the amputation, received a visitor unknown to her. It was apparently a very fit looking and handsome woman who came in unannounced. She showed Carol two elegant light pumps and said: "These are the shoes I wear when I am relaxing." Then she showed another pair: "These I use for hill climbing." The third pair she showed Carol was a pair of high heels, very *a la mode* and she said: "These I use for formal "does" and ballroom dancing and I had the same operation as you only six months ago. So do not worry. You can do the same." She then exited the room as abruptly as she had entered. I have no doubt that that woman, whoever she was, was someone who helped Carol enormously to get over the loss of her leg. In due course, with an artificial limb in place, it was impossible to tell which was the real or the manufactured limb.

She moved to an old cottage which needed extensive repair in a small village. She bought it in its broken down condition as she was keen to refurbish it herself. It was in an idyllic beautiful spot with a small stream running a few yards from the cottage door. It was ideal – a beautiful picture for any artist. She

met a local man who shared an interest in "doing up" old houses. He and Carol became friends and that developed in to a genuine high octane love match, enhanced by their common interest in doing up old homes. It was to me an enormous pleasure to
see how these two individuals drew so much pleasure just from
being together, repairing the staircase, the chimney, the kitchen
floor, etc. It is always for me a warm pleasure to see people who
genuinely love each other and become almost as one.

Most tragically, just when everything seemed to be just perfect, a most unfair fate struck the two of them. He was diagnosed as having cancer, well advanced with no hope of recovery. They both faced this death sentence bravely but it must have
been emotionally draining for them both, she desperate not to
lose him and he desperate not to lose her. Sadly, the disease won
and suddenly it must have seemed to Carol that the "lights had
been turned off". She was distraught. I had never seen her so
desperately unhappy. I could see as she looked round her kitch-
en where we would sit when I called on her, that every board,
window, step had a connection with her husband. I shared her
desperate unhappiness but could do little to alleviate it. Even
calling on her was difficult as I was heavily involved with work
and a number of major projects and just driving over and staying
for an hour took up a third of the day and half of the working
day. This I did on most weekends as I hoped to support her in
her deep sorrow. It never occurred to me that she might consider suicide. Not the Carol of old. She was as tough in some ways
as she was lovely as a person. Self-harm did not even present itself as a possibility to me. How wrong I was! Carol was found
dead in her car by a walker, apparently asleep with her little dog
in her arms. He then noticed that there was a pipe running from
the exhaust into the car. He called the police and a day or so later I was informed of her death.

As I mentally reconstruct her last few hours, I feel a poignancy
which now, many years later, brings a lump to my throat. I envisaged her going round to buy a pipe which would do the job she
had in mind. It seems she had bought two gallons of petrol the

day before she died to ensure the car would run for a long period. I can imagine her, locking the cottage door for the last time, putting her lovely little dog in its customary seat and setting off from home for the last time. She had clearly selected a remote place where her suicide would not be noticed possibly for days. How late in the evening she stopped at the place she had chosen, fixed the pipe to the exhaust pipe, got back into the car, started the engine, made sure the windows were closed and finally, taking her lovely little dog in her arms, she closed her eyes and drifted off into unconsciousness and then death.

I was quite devastated as I would never have believed Carol would take her own life. She was too powerful a personality and character to do so. That she was such a strong personality, full of fun and vivacity indicates just how deeply she was affected by the loss of her husband. May she rest now in peace, poor dear Carol.

I have often wondered whether if I had by some miracle arrived at the site of her death and been able to resuscitate her, would I have been right to do so? Or would I have been better letting matters take their course? I am grateful I did not have this problem.

Tony Baxter

Tony and I met at our first school at the age of five. We quickly became good friends and like most small children went "adventuring". He was the son of a tyrant father, Harry Henry Baxter, who was always gentle in his words to me but he made it quite clear he did not rate Tony and Tony was quite aware of this. Harry Baxter was a man of modest stature who, on occasion, put on the uniform of the Legion of Frontiersmen. This was an association of old soldiers who liked to dream the dream. Baxter's uniform consisted of a hat reminiscent of the early cowboy films, a tailor-made military uniform jacket with lots of chains, riding britches and expensive riding boots with spurs. He carried his dreams further by stabling a very good horse in the garage of the pub and possessing some side arms which, to his credit, he kept under lock and key and he the only key holder. He had an odd circle of friends and when I was a small boy, possibly 10 or 11, I was walking through the bar to the stairs which gave me access to the family home above when Mr Baxter stopped me to introduce me to an old friend of his. The gentleman was clad like a comfortably-off working-class man. We shook hands formally, something I had not done much before. Mr Baxter, doing the introductions, introduced me as Bernard, Tony's friend and he was announced as Mr Pierrepoint. I went upstairs to see Tony, unaware that I had shaken hands with a man who got paid for executing condemned men and occasionally women. He had operated more than once this medieval custom in Armley Gaol in Leeds which is a substantial Victorian prison. He racked up his score by despatching a number of Nazis, condemned after the war was over.

Tony had a sister, Patricia, a beautiful girl who later made her career as an actress then a television presenter and finally a major position in the US as the TV producer and editor of a German/US English-speaking television company, mixing with the cream of American society which she included in her TV programmes. As a small boy I thought she was adorable as was her friend, a girl of similar age and with an equally independent approach to life. Pat Baxter was independent and she let her father know it. She refused to be bullied and so Mr Baxter gave his attention to Tony, but rapidly seemed to write him off.

My mother simply adored Tony as he was a very polite, shy, almost withdrawn individual in company but this reticence did not last under the glow of my mother's warmth. It got so Tony would call on me as a small boy even though he knew I would be out and then my mother would ask him in. She became an almost surrogate mother to him. Baxter and I became what was called "Best Friends". We had gelled when we met on the first day we attended school and the friendship started there and remained for the rest of our lives. I felt protective of him as he was at that time regarded as backward – i.e. he was behind the rest of the class in reading, writing and arithmetic. He was also very shy. I certainly felt very protective of him. Pat, his sister, was also protective of him and as he grew into an adult she more or less abducted him to stay with her. She was an actress in a repertory company along with a number of young artists who became famous and in some cases making a successful jump to appear in the booming film industry. Baxter stayed with his sister and learned that he was very good at painting flats, i.e. the curtains or back cloths which are painted to represent a castle or farmyard or country road as required by the play. He established a good career as an artist, something which quite amazed me, especially because the army had classified him as colour blind.

Baxter was a complex character. He was almost Buddhist in his desire not to kill any living thing yet when he was conscripted he joined the Paras. I could not understand how such a kind, diffident lovely, peaceful man as he was could decide to join one of the most tough and demanding forces. National Service lasted for two years and it was a matter of record that private Tony Baxter had spent two Christmases not in the Guard House where petty offenders might be incarcerated, but in a genuine army penitentiary, which means he must have done something pretty bad in the eyes of his superior officers.

He made a living in Civvy Street painting scenery which is quite an art and then he made a surprising decision. He enrolled for one year's duty as a soldier in Korea where war was raging. The deal was that he enrolled for a year as an infantry man and then would be demobbed. He went to Korea for the one year contract but never spoke much about what he did. The most remarkable thing he mentioned was the cold but more than that he said nothing. On his return he decided he did not want to stay in the pub and so rented a flat adjacent to Woodhouse Moor which I would drop in on when anywhere near. He finally moved to Christchurch, near Bournemouth, bought a dinghy and settled down in a small bungalow in a quiet street. Although he had attended a Catholic school when very young, I do not think he had any deeply religious feelings. If anything, he seemed to be more Buddhist than anything else. I found this belief which involved not killing anything disturbing when lying in bed in his front bedroom I noticed a most remarkable sight. There was a whole army of ants forming a column three or four inches wide coming up from the floorboards and reaching up to the top of the windows. When I told Tony and suggested getting a spray to kill them he demurred, saying they were doing no harm and we should not kill unnecessarily. He also built a number of large garden ornaments such as one would find in the Far East or Japan which he had visited on leave when in Korea.

I visited him regularly, staying for a week or more with him in Christchurch. He loved Great Danes and had at one time three. The biggest and best in terms of temperament was Satan, a very big black beautiful animal with a beautiful temperament. In order that the dogs could freely come and go into the garden, he knocked out a "cat flap" in his rear bedroom covered by nothing more substantial than a large piece of canvas. It must have been the biggest dog flap in the country. I could get into it by just bending down low. It was an entrance to the house which I used on one occasion when I arrived and he was out. I entered by the hole in the wall and was subjected to a quick licking by the dogs who, thank God, knew my scent. We enjoyed going out in his boat and on one occasion he, me and another friend, Hartley, went out from Christchurch harbour in the boat and were caught in a severe thunderstorm. Tony's seamanship was rudimentary and as we tried to enter the harbour the waves battered us against the stonework of the harbour walls and we had to use the oars to stave off the battering against the harbour walls. It was quite exciting and we found we were the object of interest from a small but growing crowd which had gathered to witness this attempt to reach the safety of quiet waters. The oars gradually grew shorter as we used them to push back from the harbour walls. We finally achieved a safe arrival to the rather ironic cheers of the crowd who had gathered to witness this less than magnificent example of British navigation. We had to buy two new oars as the two we had used to save the boat from being battered by the waves against the harbour walls when entering the harbour were much reduced in length.

There are many other memories which warm me as I remember them. I had a motorbike and he bought one. He was possibly the worst motorcyclist I have ever known. Sadly, that led him to have a most serious accident. I got a phone call from the hospital in Winchester that he had had most serious injuries and had given the hospital my name and telephone number as next of kin, which of course I was not. I raced down to Winchester on my faithful Velocette motorbike and arrived at the hospital. Tony was not conscious, being sedated whilst his treatment could begin. The surgeon asked my advice as "next of kin" whether he should amputate Tony's most damaged leg or wait and see if it could be repaired. They were alternatives, each of which carried advantages and disadvantages. Tony was in a coma and delays could further endanger his life. It was a nightmare scenario for me. I found this a very hard decision to make but finally decided we should try to see if both legs could be saved. The surgeon was pleased with my "decision" and by effective surgery and introducing a metal support in the leg, he saved it. In due course, Tony was discharged with one leg in a pot and one in very heavy bandaging. When he got back to his home in the pub he was hopping down stairs when he slipped and put his hand through a glass pane in a door. He was taken off to the Leeds Hospital where his wounded arm was sutured and bandaged, leaving him with two bandaged legs, one in pot, and one bandaged arm. I pleaded with him not to do anything which might affect his one good useful arm. Throughout this period he was of unfailing good spirits. On one occasion he and two of my friends, Richardson and Hartley, took the front seats of the rear stalls in a large cinema so Tony could sit in comfort, his leg in pot stretching out. During the interval some girls of raucous nature passed by and one tripped over the legs of Hartley. They swore in an unladylike fashion and when they came back, one kicked quite hard the first leg they came to. It was Tony's but his leg was in pot so the girl cussed and swore and limped off, presumably wondering what his leg was made of.

We remembered the days when we were young and I would call on him at the pub as a small child getting some passing adult to lift me up so I could reach the bell. He would come down to let me in when the pub was closed. We would then go in the bar and get a drink of wine from there and if there was a large enough cigar stub in the ashtrays, have a smoke. We would be about ten years old then so that is when I began my drinking alcohol. We never had much but we did feel very grown up for kids in short trousers. We often played a trick with the cat. The bar had a central money till on the top of a cupboard which could be spun so that it was accessible to someone serving the three bars. If the cat was about we would put it in the cupboard and then set it spinning and we laughed as the cat jumped out, quite dizzy, not being able to walk in a straight line. How can I remember something so minimal and trivial but not remember a host of things of infinitely greater import?

Tony's mother used to visit him in Christchurch for short periods and sometimes for some weeks. She had run the Fenton Hotel – a pub still in existence and not changed in the slightest degree – since her husband died. I liked her but she was idiosyncratic. She loved to take out Satan, the big black Great Dane and then call him back shouting: "Satan. Come here, Satan" to the bewilderment of the rather staid residents.

Later, a friend of Tony wrote to me to me to say she was worried about Tony. She was the wife of a retired C of E priest and a near neighbour of Tony for whom she had developed a motherly affection. She was perhaps his best friend in Christchurch. I drove down and it seemed Tony had formed an affection for a lady who had led him an emotional dance. She was very attractive but had severe problems of her own. There was little I could do except talk things over with him. Some months later, I got a call from this neighbour to say that Tony was dead. She had not seen him for a couple of days and the dogs were playing up. She entered by the dog flap as there was no answer to her knocking on the front door. She found Tony dead on the floor. He had suffered a fatal heart attack and could have remained there indefinitely had it not been for this good neighbour. I found this news heart-breaking. A dear lovely lifelong friend gone in this way. His funeral took place after the necessary investigations were completed. I cannot remember any details of the occasion. It is as though the mind can mercifully blank out details of occasions which could return to haunt one. I am grateful for this phenomenon – just like pressing delete on the modern computer – but still feel a deep sense of loss of a dear and respected person whose personal life could have been so much happier. Knowing him enriched my life. I just wish he had not gone so far south that contact could only be fragmental. The one comforting fact was that the medical evidence showed the massive heart attack would have struck him down and he would have felt nothing further. Writing just this brief history is still painful. That, I suppose, is the case for us all when disaster occurs to a loved one. I have one constant reminder of him. He painted a view of the Madelaine in Paris on a piece of canvas cut from his army kitbag. On the reverse side is his service name and number. It is a very well executed picture and shows high technical skills, reminding me how many times I had suggested to him that he should paint such pictures and make a living selling them. My advocacy was obviously ineffective. May dear Tony rest in peace.

Richardson (Charlie)

John Keith Richardson was a child of the same age as I and we made friends, as the phrase was then, as classmates in the Modern School. He was a quite athletic lad, very keen on football which he would play ad infinitum. Football was mandatory for our form on a Wednesday evening which was the same time as the school orchestra rehearsals. This meant I did not play much football but that was no loss to the sport. It has never as a sport excited me and in my life. I think I have not been to see a professional game more than five or six times, and most of those were my attending Leeds United as Lord Mayor, a duty for all Leeds Lord Mayors. Football can be useful at times. One such time occurred when I and two friends, Charlie and Nigel, were travelling abroad in North Europe. One evening we had engaged too long in eating and drinking in a small French town and we had not found a hotel. The bar owner told us to call on a lady at the given address nearby as she put people up. We went hoping for the best. She opened the door, saw three fellows wanting at that late hour to stay the night. She did what I think any sensible woman would do and said, "Sorry. No room." As she was closing the door on us she asked us conversationally where we were from. Hartley said, "Leeds" and suddenly the closing door opened. The woman become quite excited. "Leeds?" she said. "Do you know Leeds United?" I did not know much about Leeds United and I am not sure the others were so well versed as they presented. We said we were friends with John Charles, a football ikon worldwide and this sent her into ecstasies of enjoyment, being able to quiz these three English men who know all about Leeds United. Her commitment to Leeds United was so very intense. She let us in gave us coffee and we stayed the night. Over breakfast her questions about Leeds United recurred and the task then was for my two lying miscreants remembering what they had said the previous night. Richardson was a very good friend throughout my years to and including the 5th form. He was a regular at our house and became one of my mother's favourites. Besides football, he had another keen interest and that was motorcycles. He had a good bike. Hartley, another friend had a better. Mine, when I got one years after them, was an old but serviceable machine which I looked on as a human. The motorbike riders tended to gather together to talk about bikes and some of the group had really splendid machines including a Square Four which had four cylinders and not just one or two. For some reason, Richardson was given the soubriquet, Charlie. Why, I know not, but it was a familiar nickname which he carried for his short life. My mother prohibited anyone referring to him as Charlie in our house. She insisted on John, as I did mainly but not always, when with others. John was loved by my mother who was a bit like a mother hen to my young friends who were always welcome to our house.

Then Richardson/Charlie fell for a young girl and in a whirlwind romance they decided to marry. She was Catholic and JKR readily agreed to a church wedding and after the honeymoon they settled in Leeds. His new wife was not very keen on riding pillion behind him. She did not like the cold or getting soaked if it rained and so dear Charlie decided to get a sidecar. He purchased the bike and sidecar so that she could sit in comfort and warmth and dry if it rained. Sadly, that was to prove fatal. He was a very sensible rider. I had been on the back of his bike innumerable times and never had any qualms about his driving except once. This was when he called to pick me up at the steps outside the university Students' Union. It was a splendid bike and attracted much attention from the young male students. The moment came for us to depart so I nonchalantly cocked my leg over and sat on what passed as a pillion but which was just a large slab of foam rubber. In order to make an impression, a polite way of saying he was showing off, Charlie revved up, shot off at speed when one of Newton's Laws was proved yet again because as Charlie shot forward, I shot back, head over heels. Good old Newton. I was unhurt except for my pride, though I tried to make it look like a trick. I am sure no one would have believed that. We had another similar episode. Charlie took me on his motorcycle to a smallholding where we purchased a dozen eggs which were still on the ration and so these were black market eggs. We put three eggs each in our jacket pockets and drove off with me on the pillion. Charlie usually drove quickly which was our undoing as we hit a patch of oil deposited on the highway. We both came off, ruffled but unhurt, which was not the case with the eggs. We both had our jacket pockets filled with the remains of three crushed eggs. Not one egg of the original twelve survived. The loss of the black market eggs was not seen as a Divine Providence punishing us for our sin of breaking the rationing laws, but more a hilarious little episode enjoyed in retrospect with a friend.

Poor dear Charlie/John. He was taking his wife in the side-car for a drive one sunny day and at a point about a half a mile from Wetherby, he was overtaking a car when another car travelling towards him crushed him and his bike in a major accident. Richardson had let himself get hit so that there would be less impact on his wife in the side car. The irony of this is that had they been on a solo machine there would have been no collision. Poor dear Charlie was lying on the road, mortally hurt. The first person to get to him was by the most remarkable co-incidence, someone who knew him well, Donald Foakes, and so poor dear Charlie died in the arms of a friend though I doubt whether he would have known anything given the force of his impact with the car. I never pass that part of the road without saying a moment's prayer for the soul of a dear friend snatched away long before his time. "Snatched away in Beauty's Bloom" in the words of the poet. I still have his wallet with the inscribed initials JKR – John Keith Richardson. May he rest in peace. I have never used it and it remains year after year in a drawer. I cannot imagine giving it away or throwing it away. It is almost a bond with me in this world and he in the next.

Robert Maxwell MC MP

I never knew Maxwell very well. Many years ago, when I was a young man very much involved in politics and he was emerging as a major commercial force and also a politician of some consequence. I do not remember how we met but I developed a very friendly relationship with this rather left wing socialist and entrepreneur. I admired him and his courage. He was a Czech Jew who had escaped Hitler's annexation of that country, joined the British Army, rising through the ranks and finally being awarded a top military honour, the MC – Military Cross. We corresponded over a period of a few years, largely when he was an MP for Buckingham but as his commercial ventures, which were monstrous in scale, took over his life, my contact with him was lost. As the picture of him as a capitalist entrepreneur emerged, I lost the respect that I had had for him and ultimately the extensive correspondence I had accumulated with him was dumped, with some regret now. The best tragedies on stage or film or opera tell the tale of ambition leading to destruction. This applied to Maxwell who mysteriously drowned when on his yacht facing bankruptcy and more serious legal proceedings. What a pity and how different from another Czech I came to know.

Leslie Silver OBE

Leslie Silver was a Czech Jew in Prague when the Germans invaded his country. He determined to fight the invader, made his way to the UK by a route which is the tale of the incredible. Having arrived in England he joined the Royal Air Force in which he served with distinction, having achieved high marks when winning his wings. On leaving the Royal Air Force with a nominal gratuity, he started a paint making business. This was in a garage initially but by hard work and mental ability, he finally ended up with one of the biggest paint producing companies in the country. I got to know him quite well and he gave me a tour of his works when they were at their zenith. He was on first name terms with many of the workmen and women in his factory which had very well developed amenities for his work force. He also showed me a house on his factory estate in which the Brontes had lived for some time. He was retaining it in its early form as a tribute to the sisters and a place of resort for the Bronte followers. His aims and values were very similar to other very successful Jewish entrepreneurs in Leeds – Burton, Marks of Marks and Spencer and the Ziffs. I was chairman of the Leeds Playhouse at that time and was looking for one big donation to kick off the appeal I and others were going to launch to build a new theatre, what is now the Leeds Playhouse, one of the finest in the country. I have not the courage needed in this situation, namely to ask someone for their money – I would rather give than have to ask. However, I did speak to him and he made a very substantial grant which enabled us to launch our appeal from a most advantageous position. We had become friends over the years and so I was reluctant to ask him. He later gave me some advice, knowing of my hesitation in asking him. This was: "Never worry about asking or "making a pitch". Just worry about what you are asking for." He was a man greatly admired and liked. As a jew he was generous to Jewish causes but he was equally generous to non-Jewish causes and he gave magnificently and generously to the Leeds Metropolitan University, now known as the Beckett University Leeds. His donations were in millions, making it seem a long way since he started his paint empire in a garage after the war. I look back on him with great affection. May he rest in peace.

Poulson

Poulson was a remarkable man who had an international reputation at one point as an architect when in fact he was not qualified as one. His multimillion empire was said to have been built on bribes and more bribes. His corruption extended across the kingdom and abroad where he built a number of spectacular public buildings. One I saw for myself on a visit to India. His corruption extended and he might have remained an internationally successful architect with unblemished reputation but for his greed which finally brought him down when he could not meet financial obligations. Rumours of his duplicity were general and quite soon the police were involved and the consequences were surprising. One of the most prominent civil servants in Scotland who moved in the most elite circles was arrested and brought to Leeds for trial with Poulson. As the story unravelled, the Tory Home Secretary, Reg Maudlin, had to resign as did a splendid fellow I got to know quite well, Mr T Dan Smith, who in his work as a Labour Councillor made heroic efforts to enhance the City of Newcastle and elsewhere. It was in connection with big cities like Newcastle and Leeds that I came to meet him and join in joint political initiatives. The press absolutely loved this great scandal story and they did a lot of probing themselves. Around the time when Poulson was operating I was involved in developing Sport for All, the mantra of the Sports Council, across the kingdom. I was one of the group which got the Leeds Swimming Pool built which made it the first 50 metre pool with a proper diving platform in the UK and Poulson had built it. I was legitimate game for the investigative journalists who wanted to uncover other irregularities which would provide them with another allegation – all good for the press but also of course for the good of society. Investigative journalism is essential for a good society. Things got silly. A former Labour minister had accepted a request to open some sports facility and was presented with some very nice wine glasses. The press reported this, making me feel that there was possibly some hidden corruption. In reality, it was a present of the kind that many public figures get on such occasions and to assume dishonesty is unfair. I was lucky in that Poulson had made me an offer to visit some of his major buildings across the world at his expense as a generous social gesture. It was very attractive but I felt that there was no reason for me to be given a trip of this kind without the expectation of a return which is something I could not consider. Thank God all this was supported by the letters I had received and so it was to be used to show the means by which Poulson gained local business. Bribery. Poulson was tried in Leeds along with others and received a stiff prison sentence. Three MPs were indicted but because of legal technicalities, they escaped this retribution. Not fair and just a bit too unlikely.

Fanny Waterman

Fanny Waterman is one of the most impressive individuals I have had the pleasure of knowing. Her family were immigrants at the beginning of the last century. Her father was a most lovely old man when I got to know him, a calm and friendly individual. He had a jewellers shop opposite the Grand Theatre where, from time to time, I would drop in for a few minutes to say hello. He had, as I remember, four children, one of whom I came to know well as he was elected to the Leeds City Council which I joined sometime later. He was a generous caring person who gave me every support as a new councillor. I was honoured to be counted as a friend and was deeply moved when he died by his own hand if I remember correctly. His sister became a distinguished violinist. In all the years I have known Fanny, I never heard her refer to her brother or sister. She was a distinguished pianist with an international reputation but, thanks to the gods who bless music, she decided to concentrate on teaching. Because of this commitment and ambition she, with the then Countess of Harewood, decided in1961 to create a piano competition to match the best competitions in the world. The Countess ultimately became Mrs Thorpe MP. They were heavily and generously supported by another Jewish family, the Lyons family. In Leeds we owe a great debt of gratitude to the Jewish families who have made Leeds their home and have been so generous towards it.

The first competition took place two years later in 1963 with Fanny as artistic director. Her husband, Geoffrey de Keyser, very greatly respected as a local doctor, was her great support. He was a person steeped in classical music and had an amazing memory which was invaluable to Fanny. In many ways he should be equally revered for his contribution and his death was a great loss as Fanny had come to rely on him so much. Initially I was of little help but this help increased as I became a more significant member of the council and the only one to give direct support to her and the competition. Absurdly, the council has never appreciated the benefit of this international competition in making Leeds known for its artistic development which has included the new Playhouse, Opera North, the Leeds Dance centre and the Leeds College of Music, which is now the biggest in the country. I became more and more involved in the competition but never becoming a member of the board of trustees as that would have meant declaring an interest both in the LIPC board and council every time an issue involving the competition came up. I became a trustee following my ceasing to be a City Councillor at the behest of Fanny who felt she might need support on the board.

I had many delightful musical occasions at her home, one remaining clearly in my mind. Edward Heath, MP and PM, was a keen musician and Fanny invited him to one of her evening soirees. He was a music lover and a very good pianist. Fanny and he were pressed to play a duet on the two grand pianos in Fanny's sitting room. They agreed and set off in perfect unison, most mellifluous, but the music at some point changed to something which sounded like so-called modern atonal music – awful discords and broken time signatures. He had turned over two pages which had the effect of causing cacophony. Laughter all round. They started again and all went well. I could not stand Heath as a politician but as a musician he had my admiration. I also welcomed the opportunity to join in conversation with him in which he was quite disarming. I have enjoyed a number of such evenings at Fanny's and over the years have been able to help her and her ambitions in many ways. When I was Lord Mayor at the turn of the Century, I was happy to host a big party after the competition in the Civic Hall, a quite splendid bit of architecture, which made a very favourable impression from the many who came from all over the world.

Although as her age advanced from her 70s into her 80s and finally in to her 90s, her energy seems undimmed. She has a remarkable brain for someone approaching 100 years but her resignation as artistic director became inevitable in 2015. She has, however, conjured up a new artistic director who I trust will take the competition on to an even greater success. The farewell messages she received were from all over the world and from some of the most famous pianists in the world. As a tribute to her going, Lang Lang, the most celebrated pianist in the world, which does not necessarily mean the best, agreed to do a fundraising concert to honour her in Leeds Town Hall. It was a sell-out and in a small quiet party in the Civic Hall thereafter, which I arranged, it was a privilege to hear the discussions and praise for this amazing woman.

Connolly

It has been my luck to meet a successful entrepreneur with a social conscience, namely Peter Connelly. Connelly had established a business in Leeds, Yorkshire Design Developments Limited, with its offices and exhibition space in the Calls, a rejuvenated and now highly desirable area after many years of dereliction. The area has an antique air and properties are valued at a premium.

I got to know Peter by casual contacts, when in discussions and chats, we established a warm relationship. As Chairman of West Yorkshire Playhouse I had been involved in buying a broken down former factory for the Playhouse to use as a costume and prop store. The building had a substantial ground floor space and an equally large cellar area. Peter wanted to make the site a centre for jazz music with a long bar. This idea appealed to me enormously as I saw it as an addition to what was being created on the Quarry Hill site for which I had been working for some years. It fitted perfectly in my concept of the creation of an artistic Quarter which could be unique in the country. The bar was to be called the Warehouse and would provide food, drink and be a centre to attract the jazz followers. I additionally was keen on this scheme, for as chairman of the Dance Centre next to and contiguous with the proposed Warehouse, I wanted a good neighbour and one which would add to the artistic variety of the Quarry Hill site. Formal discussions between the Playhouse were interminable largely because my colleagues on the board of the Playhouse were uncertain about him and his ideas. I felt quite frustrated too. On 30th July 1998 Peter wrote in a letter: "This project could begin immediately although this may seem over optimistic in terms of practical matters to be addressed. It should be understood that these proposals are the result of almost three years of discussion between Playhouse and ourselves." It is not a little surprising that it took three years to determine the matters which required settling. There is, of course, a mass of financial and legal details to be considered and incorporated in the agreement which was finally agreed, consisting of 45 pages of small print. One reason was my colleagues on the board of the Playhouse were initially not convinced that Connelly was the visionary he purported to be. On the board we had a number of big hitters in the world of finance and development who wanted every dot and comma to be checked and if possible added. This is just as it ought to be with the caveat I would add: this should be done in a speedy yet comprehensive way and not be the result of antipathies or personal prejudices.

The Wardrobe, a pub by any definition, situated in two floors of the old Playhouse property, has operated successfully since it opened. It has added to the Cultural Quarter a host of individuals with creative interests and done much to preserve the jazz culture for those who follow it. Connolly developed the cellar as a very interesting area, a fairly large space for dancers and surrounding space for seats and bar. The basement opened up in a blaze of publicity and Peter asked me if I would take to the dance floor to baptise it as it were. My style of dancing is straight old fashioned quick quick slow, VIctor Sylvester style or boogie and jive, so I am sure the jazz aficionados who came for the opening of the bar would have thought this was a quaint demonstration of the arcane/absurd, an old geezer (me) dancing with this lovely young lady. I attribute these feelings to pure jealousy at my cavorting with a lovely young lady, though secretly it makes me laugh in retrospect.

Peter was always on the lookout for a good deal for the Playhouse and came up with an absolute whopper. At this time, the board of the Playhouse was considering extending their workshops and Peter came along as a friend with a scheme which entailed letting off part of the site to build a substantial block of flats. This should bring into the Playhouse a substantial sum to fund the development of the new workshops. Acting initially pro bono, he introduced us to a possible developer and discussions took place about height, number of flats, access, etc., and in due course, agreement was reached which meant the Playhouse should receive something in the region of two million pounds. As normal, the agreement with Peter's company (YDD) was enshrined in a massive 40-page document which contained that favourite style of the lawyers, namely long sentences of 150 words or more without any punctuation of any kind. I imagine this is a residual memory of the earlier days of the lawyers who were paid according to the length of the document they were preparing. The ambition of this deal woke the council's interest and they indicated they wanted at least half the spoils. They held the whip hand as we had built the new Playhouse on the Quarry Hill site without having any formal document, leasing or conveying it absolutely. There was on record a decade's old agreement for a lease and nothing more. As it was working well without a lease I had been reluctant over the years to press for a formal lease or conveyance, knowing this would inevitably lead the lawyers to complicate matters. The system was working so why interfere? Now the position had changed as the developer quite naturally would not proceed unless the Playhouse could convey, without restriction, the land on which many millions were to be spent building the large block of flats. This meant we had to agree to cede half the selling price to Leeds if they would give us a conveyance of the land so we could sell or lease the space for the flats. To some of my Playhouse colleagues this seemed unfair. It did not seem unfair to me as the land belonged to the citizens of Leeds via the City Council.

Ultimately all went well. The flats were built, the council received a sum of £1 m pounds and the Playhouse received the same, and a lease for the first time in its existence. The only person who did not do so well out of it was Peter who came up with the idea, found the developer and offered space to the Playhouse for its costumes and scenery in an old property he had just bought near the Royal Armouries. I visited it with Peter and it was in a very poor condition, having been unused for two or more decades. Peter has since "done it up". It looks splendid and is doubtless income-providing. I think my colleagues, despite my protestations, rewarded Peter Connolly very modestly indeed. I felt ashamed. I have always regarded him as a successful entrepreneur with a social conscience and an interest in developing the cultural assets of Leeds. I liked him and greatly respected him and had every reason for so doing. Not every successful business man is devoid of a social conscience or ambitions for the community. They may appear to be few and far between but appearances can be wrong. In Leeds we have been blessed by the generosity of so many who have been so generous. Peter was to assist us again in a major development just off the site – St Patrick's Church and associated buildings and a school building. Against the wishes of some of the board of NBT I bought the church and adjoining Priest's House and the Church of England purchased the school for an outpost of Emmaus under the guidance of Peter. Again I thought his contribution was never properly recognised. The church was developed as a store for scenery which it remains today and the Priests House sold at a profit. In selling to the Playhouse, several lovely altars and other artistic features of the church were legally preserved by order.

Blunkett

David Blunkett was a committed Socialist in Sheffield which gained the name as the Sheffield Socialist Republic because of its Socialistic policies. I held him in the highest regard. Subsequently this opinion changed as he moved up the political ladder, finally becoming Secretary of State for Education. I lost all faith in him as an honest politician when he supported the privatisation of the Education Services in Leeds. His plan was to put our excellent educational services in the hands of an independent private company, Education Leeds, led by a person who later fell from grace in a most public way, Peter Ridsdale. I was totally opposed to this typical Tory proposal and asked David to meet a deputation to argue the rights and wrongs of this proposal. I received a letter dated 10th May 2001 from Estelle Morris saying he was too busy to meet us. It was a complete contrast to his early political stand and to me seemed a total betrayal. In the end he had his way and the private body, Education Leeds, took over the 300 plus schools only to have the process reversed some few years later as satisfaction with Education Leeds declined and its leader became embroiled in other controversial issues like Leeds United. The campaign I led was extremely well supported by some MPs and a large number of bodies like the trades unions which had been instrumental in Blunkett's rising career. I would never trust him again. He was, in my view, a traitor to his own former standards and the Labour Party.

I approached him directly on another smaller matter but one of high principle. Blunkett decided that where facilities were used by both education and other bodies, if the educational use was 50% or more then that facility became the property of Education Leeds or a school or college. In my ward there was a large playing field used by both the adjacent school and the public, being used by football teams from around that area and a pleasant area for walkers and informal games and similar public use. This was a public games area, not quite big enough to called a park. The school wanted to have control of a large area and could prove that one area had been used for years for their football teams. I was quite happy to have them continue this use as an honest and reasonable decision. However, Blunkett decided that though the council had used the whole area since it became a playing area, the school use of the pitch had been more than 50% so that part of the area would become the schools. I wrote challenging his decision and interpretation, even quoting some of his speeches made when he was a socialist, something which had enabled him to rise to a senior post in government. He was determined and refused again to meet a delegation. He was dismissive to the extent that he did not reply to my letters. He had someone else do it for him. I did beat him in another case which involved a building which housed a very heavily-used civic theatre used extensively by local companies and the public. The same building was also used by the College of Music which I strongly supported as part of the education system in Leeds. The college was strongly supported by Blunkett's intention to emasculate local government, the vehicle he had used to gain power, influence and, of course, a substantial wage as Secretary of State. The college claimed the whole building. They could prove that they used just over 50% of the building based on square footage but I could prove we had slightly more based on volume. I made it clear to Blunkett by letter that I was prepared to go to court if this decision was challenged and take it to the most Supreme Court in the land if necessary. I promised him that the case would be against him personally for making the decisions of which I now had copies. I would subpoena him for a start. Fortunately the college decided to build a new and modern music college which I strongly supported and for which I suggested a site, Quarry Hill, in what I hoped would become the artistic enclave it is today. The result of this final decision is that Leeds has now the largest music college in the UK, a splendid asset for the city. I had always supported the College of Music and was delighted to see the new building go up and to note how very splendid it was in its studios and performance areas and the excellent staff it was able to employ. I was very honoured indeed when I was awarded the very first Honorary Fellowship of the Leeds College of Music. I was very nearly the second, not the first, recipient of this great honour as the world famous Courtney Pine was awarded this fellowship at the same ceremony. Alphabetically, as it was explained to me as if at junior school: A for Atha comes before P for Pine and B for Bernard comes before C for Courtney which made me first though in all truth I did not rate in any way against Pine's record as a musician with a worldwide reputation.

Hugh Gaitskell

Gaitskell, in contrast with Blunkett, was a middle-class academician coming from a quite wealthy middle-class family. He was elected MP for Leeds South in 1945 and remained its member until his untimely death. A major issue was assailing the Labour Party. The question was "Do we have nuclear weapons or not?" This very serious debate inevitably caused strong dissension. The retention of a nuclear weapons policy was finally won by a movement led by Hugh, of which I was an active partner. I found him a most agreeable person. He had close friends in his constituency who were men and women of the working class. With Hugh, class was irrelevant: it did not concern him and he quite definitely loved representing the working-class constituency, South Leeds. He was supported strongly by Alice Bacon, the two getting along very well, sharing similar views and adjoining constituencies. I have retained a number of his notes or letters to me as for so long as I have them they are the reminder of a splendid gentleman whom I admired greatly. I remember one moment with some embarrassment. I was a delegate at the Labour Party National Conference. I was called to speak. My theme and proposal was that families which had been council tenants in the same house for three generations should be allowed to buy their own homes, having in effect, paid for them many times over. I had prepared for this event by preparing a number of notes on separate short memos. As I was getting up to the microphone I dropped these notes which flew in many directions. I expressed my feelings involuntarily by a short ejaculation of non-parliamentary language. This was caught by the "mikes" and broadcast and caused much merriment and much handclapping from the delegates. I got an ovation before I had spoken. I had to proceed without notes but, being well prepared, I made my contribution with some panache fortified by a few words of encouragement from Hugh Gaitskell. He was kind enough to send me a note of congratulation on my speech which I greatly appreciated at the time.

Although I liked him personally, I was at odds with him over a number of major political issues of the day. He did not accept that nationalisation was necessary in a socialist society. He proposed prescription charges and opposed many of the policies of the trade unions. I did, however, strongly support his views on personal liberty and the freedom of the individual. I never could become part of what was then known as Gaitskellism. I was much more a supporter of Aneurin Bevan, the parent of the national health scheme which has done so much to make the lives of the poor so much better than it had ever been. I nevertheless was greatly saddened when Hugh died at such an early age. It was a tragedy for the Labour Party. People like me wish to see in their leaders an excellence in anything or everything, something we will never see. People like Bevan, however, do stand out. I remember one very wet Sunday afternoon when Bevan came to speak in Leeds. He attracted a large crowd in the city centre which then followed him in droves to a local park which contained a large lump of concrete called a stump, put there for speakers to stand on when addressing the crowd they attracted. The rain became torrential but the crowd remained to the end, a manifestation of the support he engendered in his followers. I know of no other speaker who could have retained the attention of a large crowd in such torrential rain.

Howell

Denis Howell had a successful period as a councillor in Birmingham and when elected to the Commons, became in turn, Minster for Sport, Local Government, Education and Science and was from time to time given jocularly not merely the title of Minister for Sport for Recreation but for Snow and the Floods when Britain suffered an arctic winter.

I had known him for many years and was one of his greatest admirers. This did not prevent our having a very public argument asto who should follow Walter Winterbottom as Chief Executive of the Sport Council. I wanted to appoint a cleric, The Revd Nicholas Stacey who was also an athlete of the highest quality. He also had the strong support of the Oxford and Cambridge sporting gliteratti. The press was very interested in our exchanges which were often broadcast over the Wireless as it was known then. He won and we could not make the appointment that I and my colleagues wanted after a proper search and interviews. In retrospect his decision was seen as reasonable and led to a successful appointment of which he could approve. Howell was a great lover of sport not merely of the elite but of the whole population. He recognised the many social and health benefits which come from a nation which is keen on sport. He also recognised that the only way to meet the call of Sport for All was to help the local authorities. He saw them as absolutely crucial if Britain was to become successful internationally and the whole of society benefiting from participation at all levels in terms of health and social cohesion. With his local government background he decided that each region would have a regional Sports Council to ensure the sport for all strategy could be achieved. He appointed me as the first Chairman of the Yorkshire and Humberside regional Sports Council which I remained for ten years. Each region was instructed to draw up a ten year plan for sport facilities. We in the Leeds HQ of the new Regional Council, using the incredibly motivated staff, many coming directly from the old CCPR, produced a plan which was extremely ambitious. It was ridiculed by Tory politicians as being totally too ambitious and would come to nought. They were wrong as we in the Yorkshire Region achieved virtually all the developments we had planned for and which had been ridiculed as impossible a few years earlier. This was made possible because Howell had the power to allocate or approve Government resources or permission to borrow to build facilities. He engineered a law which gave to Regions the right to approve schemes for Government grants or approvals. There is talk today about regional government. We need to look no further back to Howell's power and influence to show that if the will is there and regions are allowed to determine whether a scheme is eligible for capital approval without which the scheme could not proceed, is a system which can work and which did work. His delegation of Central Government control to Regional Councils worked extremely well. Sadly Howell's imaginative and extremely brave decision has not been followed by either Tory or Labour Governments. It seems that when one is elected to the Commons one is immediately affected by the belief that "We know best and those in the regions and cities are not capable of making sound decisions." When Howell made the rule that Government approval for the making of capital grants or permissions to borrow be devolved to regions he was breaking brand new ground. It took courage and ability to get this through. The progress stemming from this decision of Howell was an enormous surge in sports development both in terms of facilities and numbers participating in sport. Later as Britain experienced enormous snow falls he was given the role of dealing with the crisis. Later he had a similar tasks in relation to exceedingly damaging floods and was jocularly known in the press as the Minister for Snow and Minister for Floods.

One of his major achievements was the creation of Sports Aid. My colleague Cyril Villiers and I had set up three centres of sporting excellence in Leeds and were setting up a fund to assist the needy to meet the cost of travel to attend the Centres. We called this fund Sports Fund for the Gifted. He was very interested in our activities asked for details asto how we did it and within a period of a year he had set up Sports Aid UK which has served sports people so well up to the present time.

I look back with great pleasure that I knew Howell so well. I admired him enormously and felt a great sense of loss when he died as a member of the House of Lords in 1998. May he rest in peace though I do not doubt that he may still be active in heavenly reorganisations.

Mrs Thatcher

Mrs Thatcher is a person whose politics I hated. I could not however do other than admire her many outstanding qualities. She was very intelligent, a grocer's daughter but with the deportment of the upper class from which she certainly did not come, and a determination to have her own way no matter who stood in her way. She was to me as right wing as any of the old Tories. She was also always well groomed and a good looking woman. On one occasion I was invited to a "do" in 10 Downing Street, It was a hot and humid summer's evening and I was standing near one of the windows overlooking the Street. She floated over to me in a floating dress and asked me to help her open the window which required her to stand on a window bench. I agreed and had the awful thought as I opened the window that just one push would change history. She smiled and thanked me for my assistance and floated off around her guests. I am still ashamed that I had had that thought even though it would never have been followed by the push. To have thought it was a sin. I also remember that occasion for another reason. Standing alone and not part of any group was a good looking chap whom I immediately recognised as Group Captain Leonard Cheshire VC. He was a man I most admired for his outstanding bravery, his enormous skill as a pilot and someone who after the war turned his talents to helping the very poor and those in need. I looked and wondered but had not the courage to go up to him and voice my admiration. I have regretted my social cowardice ever since.

Many years later when her best friends booted her out of Office Mrs Thatcher came to Leeds to address her followers. The Town Hall seats over a thousand people and it was jammed packed with standing room only to hear her speak. They were a very dense crowd of fanatically devoted fans of this woman wishing to worship at her feet even though she was no longer PM. After she had performed and had a long interminable ovation she came into large reception room for refreshment in the company of a small specially invited entourage. I often see an animal in a person. Some men suggest Boxer dogs or poodles. Some suggest an elephant, others a mouse. As she entered the room after this amazing endless round of applause I thought of an old hen pecking her way along looking for food. We engaged in a few pleasantries, she thanking me for making the occasion possible and shortly after she pecked herself off. I felt sorry for her which was quite stupid but for some reason that is how I felt albeit for a very short time.

Murder

Through my horse riding activities I met a host of people who became good friends. It is a strange UK custom that dog walkers often form friendships with complete strangers who are dog walkers too. The same phenomenon applies to members of the horse riding fraternity. It was thus that I met and became friendly with a very interesting chap, Joe H. He was a very good looking athletic individual, very fit and with what I saw as a problem. He was a bookie but felt the necessity to keep showing he was well educated and highly intelligent, unaware of the rule that if you are highly intelligent you do not have to keep proving it. He had a lovely young woman friend who also came from a bookmaker's family. At that time a small group of us horsey folk ran an annual horse show which became, for a time, one of the biggest in the country. On one occasion, the man who was the director of the show became ill and I had to step into his shoes at very short notice. This was a highly specialised job for which I was not prepared but all went well because of the expert advice and help of the members of the organising committee. Joe proved very useful and competent.

An incident occurred which I look back on with sadness and embarrassment. In the company of Joe and his girlfriend, I visited a night club in Leeds as a result of an invitation from the management. It was a very respectable business and was highly regarded by those who frequented night clubs, a declension which did not include me. I did know the proprietors as they were willing givers and supporters of a number of initiatives I was involved in to help the poor and aged in that area. We were warmly welcomed and I listened to a singer who was engaged for that week. The peacefulness was disturbed by an outbreak of sudden violence. Apparently, some man had made an inappropriate observation to Joe's girlfriend, accompanied by inappropriate touching and Joe had immediately attacked the offender who was then supported by a number of his companions. The fight was stopped after a table or two had gone over and we left. It transpired that the group of men who had intervened were off-duty policemen who had joined in to help their mate. This I only found out when I was told that the police were investigating the fight because it had involved members of the force and Joe had complained formally that his girlfriend had been molested. I had not been present when the altercation had taken place and so was not able to provide any information or knowledge of why the fight started. I did, however, rightly or wrongly feel that Joe had been looking for a fight to demonstrate his strength and masculinity. This caused me some embarrassment for I was, at the time, Chairman of the Watch Committee and therefore responsible for the police. The chief constable was an Aberdonian and had been appointed to clean up the police force in Leeds which had developed a bad reputation during the war and the years after. He demanded the highest standards from his men and was shocked at the allegation which made Joe start the fight. This then involved me in the very unpleasant task of attending an identity parade to pick out those who had been present. This involved my walking down a line of more than 25 policemen all dressed the same, all looking forward into the distance so they would not make eye contact. I am sure they did everything possible to look as much like the "offenders" as possible to make identification impossible. I could quite understand and sympathise, knowing that the consequences for some of them could lead to dismissal which they really did not deserve. The evidence of the girlfriend, however, shocked the chief constable and he wanted to be rid of any who did not match his standards. I also recognised, possibly the Irish coming out of me, feeling the hostility and menace of the 25 bobbies. It was almost tangible. I felt like pretending I could not recognise any of the miscreants but did in fact choose one whom I actually saw entering the fight. This was an experience I still remember vividly. In the end, a number of disciplinary hearings took place and I believe one or two were suspended or sacked. I spoke to the chief constable and expressed my concerns that a moment's stupidity could damage a man for life. He, however, was shocked at what he had been told was the comment and touching which caused the ruckus and said that such a person should not be in his police force. I was also advised by another very senior policeman whom I got to know very well, against remaining a friend of Joe. He said Joe was someone who, despite his urbane manner, was a person who would come to a bad end as indeed he did. I accepted the advice and let my relationship die a peaceful death. For a long time I had no contact with him until years later I received a letter asking me to call on him urgently. He said he was being charged with murder and was in Armley Jail. I was shocked. Murder was a crime for which hanging by the neck until dead had only recently been abolished. I could not understand why he was asking me for help. I was tempted to not reply but after a day or two of worrying, I finally decided that I should at least go and see him. I remember my mother's words: "If someone asks for your help, give it." I have often asked the question: What would Mam say when faced with a moral question or dilemma? I visited Armley Jail and Joe told me he had been in a fight, had knocked down his opponent, had immediately left the premises where the fight had occurred and that when he left immediately after he had knocked his opponent out, his adversary showed no signs of death or serious injury. I asked him about his legal advice and was pleased to hear it was an old university friend who was now a well-established solicitor. I assured Joe that the only solicitor better qualified to help him was Jack Levi, a solicitor who was held in the highest regard by the criminal fraternity for getting them off. He was great character and said he would prefer 10 guilty men to go free rather than one innocent be found guilty, a phrase which I had learned in Law School and which I hold to today. I was unable to offer Joe any assistance as he had a good solicitor in Ronnie Teaman who had been a colleague of mine at university, graduating in the same year as myself and by a fairly odd circumstance had briefed a very well established Barrister, Gillie Gray QC, whom I had known well at university too. He had been a mad fellow and tremendous good fun. He now was a very established criminal lawyer. The trial was held at the Leeds Court's Summer Assizes in July 1968 before a well-known judge, Mr Justice Cantley. A jury was sworn in and the trial started and lasted four days. The judge, after all the evidence was heard, outlined to the jury their four possible verdicts: guilty of murder, guilty of manslaughter, guilty of causing grievous bodily harm with intent and lastly, not guilty. His summing up was clear and absolutely fair. The jury were back in under two hours and found Joe guilty of murder and the Judge sentenced him to life imprisonment. Joe had been given the option of pleading guilty to manslaughter initially but this he refused as he believed he was not guilty of murder or manslaughter. Joe went to prison in Liverpool and decided to appeal. In essence, he told a tale of previous animosities, jealousy over illicit relations and his view was that the deceased Reynolds was there on the night in question to beat him up as revenge for something Joe had done previously.

Joe kept contacting me and asked if I would get a private investigator to do some research into the characters involved and what actually had happened on the disastrous night. This was foreign territory to me but having taken advice, I employed, at Harrison's expense, a respected firm. They produced a lot of information which persuaded me that there was the strong likelihood of a miscarriage of justice. For instance, they could produce evidence that the dead man was an enforcer, that before he could recover from being knocked down he had been removed by others, his head banging on each step down as they carried him down to the ground floor. There was evidence that the dead man was there to attack Joe. I fed the information to Harrison through his solicitor and wrote to the Attorney General and others voicing my concerns. All replied courteously. Permission was given for an appeal which was successful, the murder conviction being overturned. I have never met Joe since then and do not know where he went or what he did. Knowing him was an experience. He was a flawed character, a person with two personalities. One was a well-read sophisticated and pleasant companion. The other was a testosterone-fuelled individual who liked to demonstrate his fighting ability. This latter was exemplified by an incident which happened long before the murder trial. Joe, myself and another splendid friend, M, significantly older than Joe, were in Joe's flat having a glass of wine in a most friendly relaxed atmosphere, chatting about horses which both owned. Joe began playfully to arm wrestle M who was very fit. Joe lost one round and he began to horse play jokingly with M. This playfulness deteriorated into serious wrestling on the floor. M was very fit but Joe was much younger and possibly much fitter. To me, the wrestling was getting serious and they refused to answer my instruction to stop. I was concerned for M whom I liked immensely so I got the wine bucket, now full of icy water and ice, and poured it over them. This broke up the wrestling match and, to my relief, both laughed and shook hands as though it had just been a lark but I had seen the dark side of Joe. I often wondered what became of him but never tried to find out. Enough is enough.

Leeds Industrial Cooperative Society

The Leeds Industrial Cooperative Society was a major organisation in the decades following World War One. It offered decent simple food in a large number of shops dotted around the City of Leeds, and a major Central shop which was situated in one of the busiest streets in the centre of town. I imagine that if any octogenerian was asked for his old Coop number he or she would remember it just as an ex-serviceman would remember his "last three" i.e. the last three numbers of his identity disc. Every year the Coop declared a dividend, the divi as it was called. In one year I remember as a child it declared a dividend payable to members of half a crown i.e. two shillings and six pence in the pound. That is for every pound recorded as paid one received a half crown paid out in dividend. A half-crown was one eighth of a pound. Many reserved their spending until they received their divi – a lifeline for many of the families where the father was unemployed and the welfare state did not exist except in the minds of some intent on creating a fairer society. The Coop nationally and locally was seen as a friend of the Labour Party both having similar aims of a society which is fair and which supports the week, poor and unemployed.

I was asked to stand in the election for Directors of the Leeds Coop by the then Chairman of the Board. Eric Brierley was an old fashioned socialist with very strong convictions. He was in addition a successful business man. I stood and was elected to the Board. I had always been a strong cooperator as I remembered how important the "divi" was in my youth. We always looked forward to hearing what the dividend would be and how much we would get. Nearly all our spending was at the local Coop shop a ten minute walk away in Carlton Hill and in the big shop which was situated in the heart of the city on both sides of Albion Street. For many in the working class areas the Coop was a central part of their lives. I remember as a small child going to pick up the groceries from Carlton Hill and being served by a man who from time to time would give me surreptitiously a broken chocolate biscuit, broken because he had just broken it so he could give me it. Biscuits like everything else were rationed but biscuits had to be sold whole as people would not accept broken biscuits as part of their rations. So he broke one so he could give it to me. The memory of this little kindness to a little boy remains warm in my memory. He was a Labour man, later elected to the Council and after many years elected Lord Mayor. His daughter followed in his footsteps, being elected to the Council and ultimately Lord Mayor of Leeds also.

The Board of the Leeds Industrial Cooperative Society when I joined it was riven by incredibly stupid asinine political differences and ambitions. The elections to the Coop were contested on Labour versus Conservatives terms and this led to the election of some incompetents and worse. Often decisions were made on Party lines as the Conservatives regularly managed to elect a handful of directors. Some were downright destructive. One however, a very old fashioned true blue Conservative, was an excellent Board member with the good of the Coop his aim and ambition. On the Labour side there was considerable competence but some odd characters from time to time. One I remember well as on one occasion he spent the large part of the Board meeting lying down on the floor of the Boardroom contributing his views from the floor for most of the meeting. Another I remember was a woman Conservative who joined the Board. While drunk she drove her car causing a deal of damage to property. There were always one or two Coop employees on the Board which was in accord with Coop principles but did not provide any independent voice. They were not of the calibre of earlier staff members who were confident enough to express views which challenged or tested the views of the CEO. I strongly support members of the work force joining a Board of any business. The danger is they can be absorbed by the other Board Members or that they feel it essential to object to developments or that they did not understand fully what was going on or they were aware of the results which might follow if they decide to speak out about sensitive issues. When I joined the Coop, it was a major commercial force in the city. It possessed two large dairies, factories, an enormous number of milk rounds, retail food businesses, a major coal business, barges and a city centre coal stathe, a large number of horses, a fleet of heavy vehicles, a host of small stores throughout the city, a large department store in the heart of the city, a substantial television sale and repair business a number of workshops and a large number of premises spread across the city, then of only half a million people. The Fall of the Roman Empire was a book often in my thoughts as I saw the Leeds Coop gradually bleed to death not through an endemic corruption but quite simply because of crass stupidity, incompetence and ignorance.

Unfortunately Brierley decided he had served long enough and persuaded me to step into his shoes when he retired. I was elected and shared for a short time the benefits of working with the much respected Chief Executive. I was very concerned when he decided to retire as I could see the need for a major restructuring given the changes which were taking place in the retailing world. I knew that major changes would have to be made to meet the competition and for the Leeds Industrial Cooperative Society to remain an independent company. Such a major restructuring needed a man of his quality and it was possibly the magnitude of this task which decided him to go whilst the Coop was turning a sound profit every year. His loss proved to be a major factor in the years of decline to come. The new Chief Executive was a competent member of staff but his promotion from the relatively small business of running a number of successful pharmacies to running a surprisingly large conglomerate proved to be too great. I liked and respected him as a person and understood the pressure he was under to succeed. We were late in the large stores proliferation and the two we opened were most attractive but in the wrong place and both were without the needed car parking.

They were doomed to failure. Bit by bit our assets were sold off. The two stores in Albion Street were sold, prime sites worth a fortune, and the Coal Stathe was sold and the Hilton Hotel built on it. All over Leeds premises which were once Coop stores were sold off and if one drives round the city one can still see innumerable buildings with the stone carved sign Leeds Industrial Cooperative Society.

As someone committed to the Cooperative movement I was intensely worried. Any effort I made to induce a sense of reality failed. When it got to the point where we had a debt of £ 12 m I formally proposed we should join one of the other Cooperatives lock stock and barrel. The CEO seeing his job at risk got to the members of the Board and preyed on their loyalty to the Leeds Coop. I indicated that this was an issue which was fundamental in my view to continued trading. I was defeated by the Board, the Tories joining up with the employees' representatives to defeat even the question of investigating such possibilities which I had suggested as a compromise.

On 4ᵗʰ May 1996 I wrote to the Board Members of LICS a letter of resignation, something which without being in any way dramatic was a soul searching experience. I was lost in a pool of regret and despair. Such reactions come to us all when faced with a major problem we cannot solve as we see a cherished institution flounder. My letter went: "The recent decision of the Board to refuse to commission an outside independent firm to review our recent past commercial activities, the decision not to meet to discuss the future of the Society plus the decision not even to discuss the possibility of exploring the advantages and disadvantages of a possible merger are decisions I cannot support." I pointed out that between 1981 and 1994 the " Society had only twice produced a profit before distributions, had sold each year substantial assets and still had to transfer from reserves seven years out of thirteen years and how total assets less liabilities declined from £ 17.9 m to £ 14.1 m in 1993–94". I went on to say that I thought that I was in effect a trustee of the LICS which was in effect a conglomerate of small businesses some of which are successful others are not which every year for the past 15 have failed "to produce an adequate return on capital and meet the considerable overheads of the Society".

It was rather revealing when some colleagues said we must be alright as the banks seem very keen to lend. I pointed out that was true because we had assets which would cover any debt and that is no way to run a successful business. In the letter I made the following point. "Last year showed a transfer to reserves only because of the multi million pound sale of our coal wharf and a windfall return of tax of £ 332,000 which really should have been returned to the customers. Our assets for sale are running out. The unwillingness of the Board to act in a manner which I consider to be consistent with prudence, good business practice, its unwillingness to consider a variety of options open to it and its determination to proceed on the course of remaining an independent Society without assessing the feasibility of the future effect on our employees leaves me with no alternative but to cede the position of President to another. I am sure you would agree that it would be quite inappropriate for me to be involved in the appointment of a Chief Executive feeling as I do". I felt extremely sad in large part: because I must be fundamentally soft; partly because I hate to be beaten when I am right and am sure of it ; because I would have loved to see the Society grow and serve the public and because for many years each fortnight I had had a meeting of the Board. I felt for the poor dear Coop which was once of such great importance to the working class in Leeds. In the words of the poet "Parting is such sweet sorrow". Some years later the Leeds Industrial Society was absorbed into the main Cooperative movement and to my disgust the Board members all received a considerable pay out for so doing.

A modern form of blood money they should have had no right to claim.

Malaya

I received a letter from Malaysia asking about two young people being sent over to Huddersfield to study. I replied and in due course two delightful young women Fei and Yen Chin arrived. They were the first overseas students the College had which soon became a regular flow. They were so innocent and unwordly compared with the local girls of the same age. They were two very lovely individuals who had been "put in my care" by the father of the two in a letter and so I felt an enhanced personal sense of concern. I met them at the station and took them to where they were going to live whilst here in Huddersfield. It was a Yorkshire style family and I felt confident in leaving them in the hands of the lady of the house. She had assembled her family to greet Fei and Yen and introduced each one in turn. I left feeling quite happy about our first two overseas students. A day later I called on the two and took them by car to the College where they would be studying. Fei asked me if everyone in Yorkshire started their name with "Ar". I was a bit confused when they told me that a Welshman they knew in Malaysia called his sons Ab or Ap. I then realised that the landlady had whilst I was there introduced the family by saying " and this our son our Harry" or "this is our Cis " which came out as Ar Harry Ar Cis. They stayed with the family for some time when the question of the loss of some valuables arose and in consultation with the two girls I arranged for them to take over and rent a small flat which was ideal for them and cheaper though money never seemed to be a problem. They remained essentially unchanged in regard to worldly matters-protected by their ignorance of the world they had come to live in. My colleague Peggy the senior Lady responsible for Female issues was as always totally helpful.

433

In conversation I said I was intending to visit Malaysia and hitch-hike round the peninsula. This greatly excited the two girls and they made me promise that before I went off travelling, I would meet their father. They were going back home for the holiday period. This I was very happy to do. The girls had once seen me at a student party drinking a pint of beer. This really surprised them and confirmed in their minds I was a very serious drinker which is very far from the truth.

On arrival in Kuala Lumpur I was, to my surprise, stopped by two rather intimidating individuals, Malays, who had been sent to pick me up. I got into their very impressive car and was whisked off to the hostel in which I had booked a bed for two nights. They waited whilst I booked in and had a shower and then was taken to the home of the Chins. The father was an interesting man, obviously successful as a business man and very broadminded by comparison with the Malayan society which appeared to be rather stuffy. We met in a lovely garden and I was plied with beer. I did not at this time know that Fei and Yen had told their father I was a prodigious beer drinker and so, as I kept refusing more, I later learned he thought I was being polite. In the course of the evening and drink at the request of Mr Chin I explained my plans to hitchhike round Malaysia for a couple of weeks. I had not worked out an itinerary other than north, then east and then west again before flying home. It is the kind of holiday I have frequently had. Walk for miles, take local buses, get a boat if there is a local river going in your direction and find somewhere to sleep preferably a place with a shower and clean bed or sleep out under the stars. He seemed very interested in my "plan" and he asked me why I was going to hitchhike, which was virtually unknown in Malaysia. I explained I wished to experience Malaysia which one cannot do if you are in a train or taxi or staying in one hotel for the duration of the holiday. Just before I was ready to depart the party in my honour, Mr Chin made me an offer I could not refuse. He asked me if I would take with me on my travels Fei and Yen and a young man, Thannee, another student to become a lifetime friend. The deal was: Mr Chin would provide a car with air conditioning, two Malay drivers and the cost of the trip. He said he used Malay drivers because in the event of an accident, Malay drivers would fare infinitely better than a Chinese driver would in a Malay village or town. They had in some cases been hacked to death. I would determine the route and the holiday. This was an amazing offer coming right out of the blue. I accepted with alacrity, realising that this holiday would be totally different from the one I had expected but it would, on the other hand, be so luxurious, too good to refuse and doubtless just as interesting in a different way.

What did surprise me enormously was the faith the father was putting in me. In this case, a man of some experience, namely myself, was being given the company of two delightful young women without any supervision for a fortnight. I was totally surprised and I must say, flattered. The holiday was delightful. The three young folk, as Thannee was to be in the party, were excellent company and were seeing the country in luxurious comfort and finding every day some wonder or something to make us laugh. One experience remains etched in my memory. Somewhere on our travels we came to a town where a very strange ritual was taking place. A large crowd had gathered to watch men stripped to the waist, performing actions that appeared to be doing horrific damage to their bodies by putting swords through the flesh of their bodies or arms or legs or hooks through the back or chest to pull heavy vehicles and to show no sign of pain or bleeding was wondrous but disturbing. I understand that the men undertaking these remarkable acts of self-harm were in some form of a trance. Where one expected to see blood pour out of the wound, there was no blood. There must be lessons here for the scientists and medics. For me, it was a sight I shall never forget.

I have had very many trips abroad and to some weird places. This holiday is one which has not dimmed or disappeared. Fei and Yen are both alive and well and mothers and maybe grandmothers. I do know that Fei and Yen were two lovely persons and two excellent students. Thannee remained in England, went to the university and finally went home to pursue a very success-

435

ful business career. A true and much-loved friend. God bless Mr Chin, now I presume long gone.

I still get letters out of the blue. For instance, in December 2016 I received a letter from another young woman, Julia, who had been successful in her career. One paragraph illustrates the obligation of teachers to let their students know they have capacities which can surprise them. "You were always my best teacher – you made education fun, you gave me a chance when I flunked my GCEs and most of all that course 1969–1971, you and the lovely individual students on it, made me feel it was ok to be ME! They were 2 of the best years of my life! I loved coming to college every day and I never felt that way about school before or work since – well occasionally!"

I find such letters very flattering and emotionally warming. It is a privilege to be a teacher, no matter at what level, and with it goes the obligation to each and every student no matter what they are like, male, female, young, growing up or pursuing higher education.

A sort of film career

One of the Joseph brothers, who ran the City Varieties Theatre in Leeds and also ran an agency for actors, mentioned my name to a young film director, Ken Loach, as a possible candidate for a film he was making. I agreed to meet him in the Fenton Hotel which was a pub just opposite the BBC HQ at that time. I went in expecting to meet a big man cigar smoker – a mental picture I had of a film magnate, but met a young man, slight in build and of very gentle nature. He explained what he was doing and offered me a job in his new film, *Kes*. I had no idea or inkling of the significance of this offer. The role I was to play was that of a careers officer. My view of careers officers was not complimentary as at one school I knew, Woodend in Shipley, I had seen how careers officers had low expectations of the pupils. If a girl was reasonably bright she would be suggested burling and mending and for the less bright, just a mill worker. Never did I hear them suggest evening classes, technical college or anything more than the lowliest jobs in one of the adjacent mills.

I arrived at a school where filming was to take place, not having received a script. When the time came for my scene, Ken Loach explained to me what he wanted. I was to be exasperated by the lad, played brilliantly by a local boy, who clearly was not interested in what I was telling him as he was worried his brother would kill his pet bird. Fortunately, making the dialogue up as requested, I could draw on my experience of the system and of how badly pupils could be served by the career officers who had to get through a number of interviews in one session and the jargon of further education, GCSE, OND, ONC, A levels, etc., escaped their attention. The scene occurs very near the end of the film and played by just me and the boy who was quite brilliant.

When the film was completed, which is a technical and an artistic exercise, the distributors would not give it a showing. It had been seen, however, by a number of film critics who mounted a campaign to have it shown. Their demands were ultimately answered and listened to and the film got a showing. It proved a great success, touching the nerves of many across the social divisions. It was soon being talked up as a masterpiece and so it is, depicting life in a mining village which was so true to life at that time. There were hosts of excellent films to follow which explored the same territory most successfully.

I, of course, had no idea that *Kes* would survive for decades and is still a most popular film now, reduced to a digital form. The book on which it is based is a set book for study and so the film is now being seen by one new generation after another. I would be wealthy if I had a tenner for each time I have answered the question: Were you in *Kes*? Almost like asking someone: "Have you really been on the moon?"

I was lucky that I got to know Ken Loach as he offered me a number of small parts in succeeding films and in one in which I played a significant role, a medic looking after a woman with a mental breakdown in a film called *Family Life*. I have always been a fan of Ken Loach as all his films deal with social issues and human conflict, problems and divisions from a particular political standpoint which gives his work great immediacy. Just as I admired his work from a political view, I also liked the gentle lunacy of *Last of the Summer Wine*. I appeared, or did not appear, in two different episodes as an extra. It was only much later when I was given the part of a traveller on a bus meeting one of the magic group of odd fellows. It was a Christmas show and so was seen by millions. This was a real pleasure. My morale was boosted when I arrived on set and was given the honour of a seat in the Winnebago (a real seal of acceptance) where the main characters could relax, have a drink or just wait for the call. This was seen as a real privilege and the main characters were very kind and warm in their greetings to a strange face which is not always the case on film sets.

Another very popular show was the long series of vet stories *All Creatures Great and Small*. In one of them I played the trader who provided the canary which was to replace a dead one belonging to an old lady without her knowing. The site for this transaction was in North Yorkshire where there was a professional breeder of all kinds of birds. He was something of a magician in my mind as most of the birds he raised seemed to be allowed to fly freely, always coming back in time to eat and sleep. It was strange to see parrots and other exotic birds flying round in the open air. A more exciting episode had me as a local farmer who kept pigs and had the piglets neutered. This was castration by injection of drugs in the rear of the animal. At one point in the scene I had to hold a large piglet in front of me, holding its back legs so its front feet were lower than my knees but its mouth was right where, if it bit me, I would have been the one castrated. The farmer had an apron which provided him with some protection from the piglets which did not like being hung head down and I feared for my future but the show had to go on. I held the piglets so the vet could insert the syringe which carried the chemical which would spoil the love life of the animal for life. I had to appear to "come all over faint" and collapse on the floor when the needle was injected. This was accomplished without harm to me and no one asked the piglets. The characters were good company and showed me every kindness. We stayed overnight in a small hotel where conversation was aided by a sufficient amount of alcohol. I just loved sitting back and listening to their anecdotes and reflections. A good raconteur is worth at least three brandies if it kicks him or her off. I found Robert Hardy a little pretentious in that he began to give the impression he was really a vet. His two colleagues, Paul Davison and Christopher Timothy, were excellent in their characters and equally pleasant and affable off stage.

I enjoyed a small part in a programme called *Airline* which gave me the chance to fly in a Dakota again after many years. This workhorse twin-engined prop aircraft is one if not the longest operational aircraft ever. It served during the war, flew hundreds of sorties to break the Russian attempt to block off Berlin and decades after that. Whilst flying through China I saw a large number of these reliable old aircraft flying local passenger routes.

I also appeared in a film of *All Creatures Great and Small* (I think that was the title) and was given the role of a policeman. As we were shooting in a busy market town location, we spent most of our time waiting on the street. There was a heated argument going on between two street traders which looked as though it could become physical at any moment. I heard one woman say to another "Why doesn't that copper sort it?" I heard her neighbour say: "He isn't a proper copper. He's too small."

Coronation Street is a phenomenon, running for so long and still attracting major viewing figures. I first appeared in it as an extra, then as a "walk-on" when I met the actors like Violet Carson, Pat Phoenix, Thelma Barlow, who amazingly had captured the imagination of the nation. Later I played a number of small parts over a period of time as there was a rule that if one had played a small part, sufficient time must elapse for people not to recognise the same face in a different role. The last part I played was officiating at the TV wedding of two of the most popular characters. I was given the script and agreed to be bound legally not to reveal it to anyone, such was the public interest. A series in which I had a momentary appearance was an episode of a saga called the Beiderbecke Affair, so called because music by the musician, Bix Beiderbecke, was featured throughout and became an integral part of the success of the series in which I played a returning officer. It was a small part but even so, as the cult following of this series developed, I was frequently asked about my day of fame working with James Bolam and company. The Beiderbecke Fan Club still remains decades after the series was first broadcast, doubtless due to its fixation with the music of Bix Beiderbecke.

During Mrs Thatcher's reign as "Queen Mother II", I received a phone call from the director of a film to be made about a nuclear incident. He asked if I would play a rather seedy reporter who hears of the incident and makes it public despite efforts to cover it up. A coup of a lifetime for him. I was told I would feature in three or four scenes with Francesca Annis, an actress I truly adored. He asked me if I would agree and the fee would be £ 3,000. I was immensely pleased to be asked and the figure offered was quite outside my experience. I said clearly I agreed to his proposal. He said he would be in touch. He did not because out of the blue Mrs Thatcher, as PM, intervened, expressing her total opposition to the making of the film as it so clearly spelled out a truth and a danger which she did not want the public to know existed. There had been a very secret cover up of two serious incidents involving highly reactive material and Mrs T wished this to remain out of the public domain for political reasons. The producers of the film were put under the strongest pressure to cancel the film and the establishment knows exactly how to put this pressure on. Faced with the pressures Mrs Thatcher brought to bear, the decision was made to pull the proposed film. I was horrified by this direct interference by Mrs Thatcher which, in my view, was an example of simple corruption and unlawful, something one can expect in a non-democratic nation, and not the UK which boasts correctly of its freedom of speech. So I never got to work with the woman I so admired but I did receive a cheque for £ 3,000 on the basis that our telephone conversation had made a deal which the producers regarded as a binding contract and therefore had to be honoured. They could so easily have said to me: "Sorry, we cannot make the film and so your services are no longer required", or claim that if there was a contract it had been legally frustrated by the government intervention. What a contrast in moral terms with Mrs T's actions! In the States, a film of identical nature was made despite, or possibly because of, there being a number of serious nuclear incidents as cause for concerns. In the States, a country which is based on Big Business and its modus operandi has stronger laws protecting freedom of speech than we do here in the UK.

If the £ 3,000 I did not expect was the biggest I received, I did well out of another "cock-up".

I was contracted to play a clergyman standing in for the local vicar in an episode of Emmerdale Farm. The story was that a very revered character was being buried in the churchyard and I, as the Reverend Jackson, was standing in for the normal incumbent. The whole cast was standing in the churchyard dressed in uniform black and looking extremely sad at the funeral of a revered friend. I had to bustle up and say: "My name is the Reverend Michael Jenkinson and am standing in for your vicar who is not well," or something on those lines. Sadly, by some idiotic quirk, I bustled up to the waiting crowd of desperately sad mourners and said: "My name is Michael Jackson and I am etc., etc." This caused at first no response but as they tried to bottle their laughter, first one and then the other burst out laughing. I did not know why they were laughing until I was told what I had said. How can anyone be so stupid! I do know why I inadvertently named myself Michael Jackson the super star. I had that morning had a phone call to ask me if the Michael Jackson cortege could bring two extra-large vehicles into the compound at Roundhay Park, reserved for the vehicles. We, that is Leeds City Council Recreation Department, which I chaired, were putting on a live outdoor show starring Michael Jackson to several thousands of people who had bought tickets. I was always being called about some such detail. Thankfully the cameras had been running and captured the whole detail of a crowd in the depths of despair at losing an old friend unable to contain their laughter until they all burst out laughing. This clip was shown at least twice on a BBC programme which was a series of similar incidents which made people laugh. For this I received a miniscule fee, but that was of no concern. However, sometime later I received a call from the USA asking if I would give permission for them to show the clip. They offered me a fee of £ 500 to show this clip across the USA where Michael Jackson was a true star. The show was entitled The World's Biggest Boobs. So I had achieved world status. This was underlined when I had a similar offer to repeat the showing of the clip which was so popular. I agreed with pleasure and awaited another £ 500 pounds and the further confirmation that I was one of the World's Biggest Boobs.

My connection with, and involvement in, the world of TV and film was always exciting and interesting, not least because one got the opportunity often to chat with the directors, each one of whom was a fascinating individual. I enjoyed on two or three occasions chatting to a very promising young man, Michael Apted, who later became a film director in the USA of big budget films. Steven Frears was another with whom I had the opportunity of chatting. He was a public school educated boy who went to Cambridge to study Law. It was when he heard that I had an LLB and had been called to the Bar that he made a point of chatting in the interludes of filming. The film was an oddity as Frears seemed to be making it just for his own amusement and interest. It featured a typical school in a poor area where discipline was strict and education largely dispensed to very large classes by rote. I was asked to play the Victorian-style headteacher who would be filmed giving a lovely small boy punishment by hitting him on the hand for six strokes with a strap. The strap we used was identical in appearance with the real strap but was made of a soft material which inflicted no pain even though it looked ferocious. In the street outside the school gates I called the little boy over and said we should practise the beating so when it was filmed it was properly rehearsed. I took the boy's wrist and then hit him six times with some force on his upturned hand. It looked barbaric but was painless. I did this rehearsal three or four times when a big woman struck me on the shoulders with a grocery bag she was carrying as she thought I was some kind of monster hitting the little boy who was crying as part of the rehearsal. She was restrained, informed what was going on to the amusement of the crew who had been startled when this great lady had descended like an angel of retribution on me. The grocery bag attack created warm memories of my youth when women used their shopping bag occasionally as weapons of offence or punishment.

Another occasion which comes to mind was a scene in which I played the part of a little fellow who was trying to escape the demands of a very formidable Salvation Army woman played, as always, impeccably by one of the most talented female actresses we had seen on our screens, Thora Hird. I think it was called Hallelujah. The scene was shot in the Scarborough Hotel, a pub directly opposite the Leeds Railway Station. In the scene I was sitting quietly in the pub when I saw my nemesis coming in collecting, almost forcibly, coins for her collection box. I was to get up quickly and exit the pub before she could get me but a big bruiser, an admirer of her, was there to stop people escaping. He grabbed me by the front of my jacket and held me almost off my feet for the benefit of a camera which was filming from the high wall of the station just opposite. As I was being held on tip toe by the bruiser, a shifty fellow sidled up and said to my enemy: " Look out, there's a copper coming" and then he slunk away. This, of course, meant the incident had to be filmed again but we did find it amusing that the informant had been warning the bruiser so he could get away rather than giving me the comfort of knowing safety was at hand. It was when we were in the studio and stopping for a 45 minute tea break, I saw Thora Hird at her best. Immediately after the break there was to be a longish scene between her and a young woman clearly new to the business. Hird went through the whole scene bit by bit, encouraging the young woman and assisting her in what was a complex conversation when filmed. This was a great act of kindness as so many other established actors would just turn up and expect the ingenue to perform as required.

A pleasant recollection is of playing the part of a doctor in one of the Sherlock Holmes series. This was very congenial as we were resident in a fine country house for a few days and Brett, arguably the best representor of Sherlock Holmes, was an excellent raconteur and so evenings were most congenial.

I was fortunate to be selected to pay a major role, that of a local Labour councillor in a film which really did challenge Thatcherism by telling the sad story of a woman wanting a home for herself and child. Based on a specific case, it was very true to life, very hard hitting and making a very strong case for a society which enabled all deserving individuals to have a home of his, her or their own. The story followed very closely the tragedy of a young woman committing suicide because of her inability to cope with being homeless. The film was called *The Spongers*. It was very hard-hitting and seen by many as a political diatribe. The maker rightly said they were telling a tale which should be heard.

Appearances in two Bronte stories shot in Haworth did give me a first inkling of the genius of the three sisters although I still do not enjoy reading their work except for some exceptional poetry. I had a small part in a play, Bahn Wham – dialect for Going Home, written by Brian Glover, a remarkable working class man who performed immensely comically in *Kes* as a sports master and went on to write a number of very successful TV plays. I also got a part in a series which was rapidly pulled called The Market which did not catch the popular taste.

I have been extraordinarily lucky in having been able to enter and participate, although at a very modest level, in the life of cinema, television and the theatre. They are different worlds from the world of reality most up of us inhabit. One oddity I do preserve to remind me of my very modest film "career". It is a statement from London Weekend Television telling me that an Alan Bennett play I had appeared in had been sold to Yugoslavia and that my "residual payment" was 78 pence. The statement is dated 11th March 1980 and shows my agent's deduction of 10%.

Sometimes the technology takes over. I was appearing in a film which was to be used promoting something I cannot remember. The person running the production was none other than David Frost with whom I exchanged a few social comments on the production. All very friendly but there was no doubt who was in charge. At one point, when we were acting the scene of the moment, he came over the tannoy being pretty caustic about progress. A little later he burst on to the studio floor and, with the use of much alliterative vocabulary, he indicated that he was not pleased at all. He gave quite a performance and we were given 20 minutes for a cup of tea. We were all individually wired, that is miked, and one of the actors, forgetting this, commented to another in the queue that Frost must be on drugs or he would not behave in this wild manner. Seconds later, Frost roared onto the floor, obviously in high dudgeon, wanting to know who had broadcast that he was high on drugs. This final act made me think that perhaps the unknown broadcaster was right and Frost was on drugs, his behaviour being so extreme. Frost was a remarkable man and his satirical shows must have been a great aggravation to the then Conservative Governments. His shows broke new boundaries and he later produced some excellent serious programmes and became a pillar of the establishment.

I have been lucky to have been able to dabble in the world of film and TV, two remarkable creative worlds which have such an impact on all our lives.

Odd experiences

I was at home reading a book when there was a loud knock on the front door, the kind of knock the police use. I looked at the clock, 11.45 pm – a bit late for visitors. On opening the door I saw a very tall solidly built oldish man in a trilby, something one rarely sees now. He did not look at me. Just stared straight ahead and said "Can you help me?" I asked what help did he want and he said that his wife had gone missing four of five days ago. This did not answer my question but I invited him in, thinking he was possibly someone suffering from mild dementia. When I asked him where he lived I found it was a few doors away from me. I suggested we go to his house to see if she had returned. We walked the short distance and entered his house which was rather cluttered but what struck me very forcibly was the amount of money in notes spread around the room. He repeated his wife was missing so I thought I had better look for her, alive or dead, in the house. A quick look round and under the beds. There was, to my relief, no body but there was a plate on the table containing a half-eaten meal and certainly look-ing to be a day or two old. Having looked through his house, I joined him in his living room and spent a few minutes collecting up a large amount of money in notes. I did not count it but it must have amounted to several hundred pounds. I put it into a used en-velope which was on the floor and put the envelope in his trou-ser pocket. He kept telling me his wife was missing and he did not know where she was. In due course I said I would have to go and that he should go to bed and we would look for her in the morning. I got no response. I then left but found it was not possible to lock the door. The lock was broken. Two minutes later I phoned Social Services knowing that they have staff available through the night and I phoned the police and left a message with the officer in charge.

Being worried about the defenceless man with all that money, I went back to his house with an iron bar which I hoped might give some security to the house by jamming the door. He was still sitting in the same chair and position. I told him I had rung the Social Services and the police and he should go to bed so we could go looking in the morning. I thought that this promise would persuade him to go to bed as I was conscious that he could knock on some else's door to ask for help and that might prove to be a bad move. I jammed the door to the house as best I could and went back to my house at about 1 am. I had a coffee, pipe of tobacco, a whisky in that order and went to bed. I had not been in bed more than five minutes it seemed when there was a loud knock on the door. I thought he had come back to see me so I got up, opened the door and was met by a policeman. I asked him to come in as one does on this kind of occasion and he said he had been told to go to the address I had given to the police and that on the drive to the address he had seen a middle-aged woman walking alone. Given the late hour, he stopped and asked if she was alright and she explained she was going to the very address he was going to. It seemed she had only been "missing" for a day. The policeman told me he had seen her safely in and had secured the door and that Social Services "would attend them early tomorrow" which should have been today.

I was very impressed by the way in which the police had responded. It simply could not have been better. I slightly revised that view when having just got back into bed and snuggled down there was another peremptory blow on my bedroom window. The policeman had left his torch and notebook in my house. I got up, wondering what next could happen. He was very apologetic. I was just amused by the whole odd business.

On another occasion at about 2 am I was awakened by a banging on my bedroom window and a voice shouting for me to get up, not touch any switch and to evacuate my home immediately. He shouted there was a gas leak and our houses were on top of the leaked gas which might explode any moment. I dressed with alacrity in the dark and left the house. A fireman told me that I would not be allowed back in my home until the gas had cleared which he hoped would be in the mid-morning at the earliest. He asked me to move my car in the drive by letting it run backwards down the short drive and be pushed up the street before I could start it.

A kindly neighbour further up the street, one of a fair crowd of residents who were watching the events with interest, offered me overnight accommodation which I declined with sincere thanks and I drove off to a spot just a mile away in the country adjoining the Moors. I kipped down in the car and had only just got to sleep it seemed before I was awakened yet again, this time by a policeman and his buddy who, passing in their car, wondered what my car was doing in this spot at this hour of the night which appeared to have a body in the back. Explanations followed. They suggested I follow them two or three miles to the police station where I could park without problem. I thanked them but said I was quite happy where I was. It was a mistake because it seemed only minutes later, though in fact perhaps three hours later, I had to move the car to let out a herd of cows which were being driven back to the farm for milking. I got little sleep thereafter and returned home by 8 am. I was told by the Gas Board man that it would be all clear by 10 am. I gave up and drove into the city to find a place for breakfast.

In my 57 years on Leeds City Council I have been involved in a large number of odd, funny sometimes tragic occasions. One story always amuses me by its incredibility. My colleague, Cllr Illingworth, received a serious complaint from a large lady, a tenant in a multi-storey block of flats. She complained that whilst sitting on her toilet she was blown off it by an explosion. It seemed that the tenant below her had developed a peculiar habit of putting petrol down his lavatory and igniting it which caused a minor localised explosion, the force of which was transmitted by the large soil pipe to the flat above. The old lady said she hated going to the toilet in case she got caught again in *medias res*, my phrase – not hers. She was very explicit how the force of the explosion lifted her off the toilet seat.

I did not believe the story as told and visited the old boy in the flat below. The evidence of heat on the soil pipe from the minor explosions was there. We never discovered why he had taken this particular method of clearing his toilet. Mr Crapper, of early toilet fame, would have been interested had he lived into this century. The tenant was solemnly warned and, though finding it amusing, it does not remove the very serious concern about people having petrol in their flats. This matter was dealt with seriously but with a secret smile.

Another odd occasion occurred in 2003 when I received a letter from a former student who sent me a photograph of her and asking if I would confirm that the photograph of her was B ... P ... As I had not seen her since she left college some 20 plus years previously, I felt unable to do as she requested. I wrote: "This is a picture of a very glamorous mature young woman but I cannot say on oath that I would have recognised her from that photo." I continued to say I would be happy to say, in a sworn affidavit, that to the best of my knowledge and belief K ... C ... is the person I knew as B ... P ..."

B ...P ... sent me a long document outlining a most bizarre history of sexual exploitation, difficulties in establishing a legal persona affecting her for example by being refused a passport and having trouble at work and in academia over her identity. I gave her as much support and advice as I could, never knowing whether the long and detailed report she sent me was the fruit of a deformed memory or some mental imbalance. However, I felt that if I dismissed her allegations as fiction arising from a disturbed mental state, I was just looking for ways of not getting involved in a saga which would or could have many implications. I felt extremely sorry for this woman and gave her much advice including a suggestion that she write to her MP and seek an interview. She told me she had done this but had not received a reply. I do not know how this case ended as my final letters to her were never acknowledged.

I have always known that there were established sex rings in the UK which used children and young women as sexual toys.

In 2015 these old allegations were beginning to be investigated and perhaps poor dear B ... P's ... claims vindicated. Cases like this arouse in me the same feelings I felt when I was in my Kafka Reading vein many years ago. Those writings created in me a sense of deep despair as the machine of state rolled over the individual.

Among my memory of such cases I have always been amazed at pure coincidence. I attended the Paralympics in Australia and one lovely morning I joined the crowds moving towards the iconic Sydney Opera House. I heard a voice say "Hello. What are you doing here?" The speaker was a local Leeds councillor representing Otley, a small town which is in the Metropolitan City of Leeds. On another occasion whilst sunning in Perth, Australia a young fellow leaned across from his table of four people and said, "We are having an argument. You are a doctor, aren't you? " I said no, I was just on holiday – something of a non-sequitur. He persisted and it seemed that he and his colleagues in their training had been watching a film by Ken Loach in which I had played the role of the doctor involved in the case of a very disturbed woman. The film was being shown to educate its watchers on how not to treat a schizophrenic person. I enjoyed their hospitality, their generous hospitality, so in due course I was not sure whether I was a doctor or just a schizophrenic, slightly inebriated.

Another unlikely meeting occurred when on holiday in Florida. I was on the final Key on the string of Keys, a string of small connected islands that stretch from the mainland and end up in the final Key. This is a very attractive holiday attraction as besides its beauty and its place as the most southern part of the USA was the home of the testosterone writer Hemingway, who loved to play the role of the brave men he depicted in his tales. I have always enjoyed Hemingway's work and was sitting down in the bright sunshine outside his house thinking about his interest in bull fighting when I heard that now familiar question, "What are you doing here?" The speaker was one of the two marvellous Joseph Brothers which kept alive the Leeds City Varieties, a gem of an old music hall theatre. The odds on such a meeting occurring would be so vast that only a Turing could attempt to calculate.

Metropole Russia

On my first visit to the USSR decades ago when it first began to allow in tourists, I was sitting at the bar of the Metropole Hotel in Moscow when I was joined by a very beautiful young woman. She came and sat down beside me and asked how I was enjoying my first visit to Russia, though how she knew it was my first visit caused me to wonder. I looked on her with some suspicion as though, in my wild dreams I look a handsome fellow, I was equally aware that this was not necessarily the views of a beauty like this one. After some general chat over a drink or two and no more she asked me if I could help her to get in touch with an RAF officer whom she had met when he was based in the British Embassy staff during the war. She spoke with some intensity, communicated by her holding my hands. I had told her in our conversation that I had been too young to be involved in the war. She gave me the name of the officer, a Group Captain Jixxxxy Gxxxx Jxxxx who now lived in London. She said she was known to him as Dolly and her name was Vera Gorchakov, c/a Poste Restante in Moscow. She said she would be enormously grateful if I would agree to help and suggested we could have an evening meal together as she enjoyed having the opportunity to speak English with an Englishman. I did wonder that the most reasonable reason for her picking me up was that she was an upmarket prostitute and dinner would lead to something more physical later. I was saved by two New Zealanders whom I had met on the boat which brought us to Russia via the Baltic and Leningrad. They arrived in the bar in their usual lively boisterous state, saw me with this very attractive female and made an immediate bee line for us, effectively changing the dynamics of the occasion. After introductions, she made her excuses and left. I complained to them that they had just broken a romantic alliance and it was their turn to make good this interruption by buying me a beer. They expressed their admiration for what they called my pulling power and we all had a good laugh. I did not tell them of her interest in the RAF group captain but on my return I wrote a short letter outlining the conversation to the Foreign Office for which I received a two-line letter of acknowledgement and nothing more. I could have pursued it further by looking up the name of the group captain in the RAF list but declined to do so, believing in the saying that a small stone thrown into placid water can cause an intensity of unintended ripples.

My two NZ friends were terrific company which led to another amusing result. In the hotel there was a system by which formidable women were responsible for each floor as Floor Manager. That same night we met a group of four English young women who invited us to their rooms for a nightcap. It was an innocent and friendly gesture and nothing more. We agreed to join them but to get to their suite we had to do this without letting the Floor Dragons know. We managed this by, in the words of my NZ friend, skulking, but in the course of the evening our party became a little too noisy and we heard a loud banging on the door and some incomprehensible language. We three lads immediately, for a joke, hid under the table and one of the beds. The Dragons entered, looked round and pulled us out physically one by one, in my case by being grasped by the ankle, pulled out from my mock hiding place and only then allowed to get up. We were issued out in a very peremptory manner, nearly hysterical with laughter. The next day we went to the Mausoleum where the bodies of Stalin and Lenin were on display. I was allowed in. They were not on the ground that they were inappropriately dressed – shorts and shirts and open sandals. Stalin has now been removed leaving Lenin in lonely splendour. I have been back to Moscow a number of times since and have never wanted to join the queue again to see the remains of a man who changed our world. The queues were to be seen every day, rain or shine I was assured.

I have over the years been approached by a variety of organisations and individuals. One of the strangest came with a letter dated 15.01.08 addressed to me at my home address. It was a letter from a Mr Schwab living in Heidelberg. "I am a 25 yrs old Movie fan from Heidelberg and since I saw you for the first time in "Play for Today" I am a big fan of You. I admire you especially for your part as Dr Carthrew in "The Dancing Men" an absolutely amazing performance in the best Sherlock Holmes movie ever!!! So I would be very pleased if you were to be so kind to sign the included picture for me and perhaps add a signed picture of yours. Being a Fan and not a seller it would naturally be a special Honour and Pleasure for me if you were so kind to personalise the picture to me. I wish you all the Best for the Future and hope to see you in German Cinemas again soon. Yours sincerely." I found this letter interesting because it was so unreasonably fulsome. I wondered at the time if this was some way of establishing a persona using my name, address, etc., as the cover for illegal cyber operations. I replied formally just in case this was a perfectly honest individual although to some extent unhinged. No sensible person looking at my incursions into the world of film making could have written so warmly. Nevertheless, if the letter was genuine I would not wish to hurt the feelings of someone who appeared to me slightly unhinged. I responded by thanking him for his kind words, enclosing a signed photograph of me wearing a beard and heavy spectacles from an early production which would have been useless if he was to set up a fraudulent account in my name.

Biog Genee RAD
Branson Health and Safety

I have always had a very soft spot for the Royal Academy of Dance – the RAD – having progressed through their grades to Elementary and Intermediate examinations. I was training to do the Advanced exam and Solo Seal exam when I was conscripted into His Majesty's Armed Services, in my case, the Royal Air Force. So, when Luke Rittner contacted me in 2005 about the Adeline Genee competiti on, I was most sympathetic. As a member of the Arts Council I had known Luke Rittner as a very effective officer – highly competent and ambitious for his favourite art form – the ballet.

The Adeline Genee competition celebrated Genee's memory. She was an iconic ballet figure with a distinguished record as a dancer and was held in the most reverential way by balletomanes. The competition was one of the supreme international competitions run on very similar lines to the major piano competitions held internationally. It had been held most successfully in places like Sydney Opera House, London, Hong Kong and Birmingham.

Rittner contacted me because he knew of my passion for classical ballet and that I was in a position to assist in his plans to have the competition in Leeds and of my ambitions to make Leeds a major city known for its riches in the arts. The Genee competition was a worldwide competition and there would be great spinoffs for Leeds if we were to hold the competition in the city. It would rank in status and international recognition with the Leeds International Piano Competition.

I got the general approval and support from the Regional Development Agency – Yorkshire Forward – and ultimately all the details had been fixed. All that remained to be done was to get the council's final approval. The political situation in Leeds had swung. The Conservatives were now the Party in control and it was a Tory Councillor responsible for the Arts who had to sign off the scheme. Sadly this situation was bit like putting the arts in the hands of Vlad the Impaler. After much planning a scheme was finalised involving all organisations to hold the competition in Leeds in 2007. On 2nd September 2005 I received a message from the officer dealing with this matter that the scheme, as worked out with such care, would go to the councillor to sign on 5th September. This idiot, as some called him in private (some might see that as a complimentary description in his case), now responsible for the Arts refused to sign which meant that the proposal had to be dropped as it could not happen without the council's cooperation as agreed. This abrupt last minute decision I attribute to the "little Hitler syndrome". So sad. So wrong. There was nothing I could do to get the decision changed, though of course I tried. I was disgusted and embarrassed and my appeal to the leader of the Tory Party was a wasted but necessary effort. I felt shame on behalf of the city.

The councillor concerned is a sad case. He is intelligent and can be quite genial. He has, however, when gaining the position of considerable power, used it to damage excellent ideas and projects, even though he could have inflated his ego, if that was possible, to appear a charismatic leader of the arts. He could be quite vindictive and he behaved as a bully. An example of this occurred when I was in charge of Leisure Services and had established a venue in Roundhay Park which could accommodate tens of thousands of fans of such groups as the Rolling Stones and such stars as Madonna and Michael Jackson. I personally found the following for some of these groups bizarre. I thought the noise they made was unmusical and the awful gyrations on the stage childish and pathetic. My personal appreciation was irrelevant. If these acts could attract thousands to their concerts then, in my view, we were catering for a particular taste which was as valid as my own and at no cost to the council. It was part of our grand tapestry of the arts which I hoped would see Leeds recognised as a cultural force and thereby enhance, through its reputation, an economic benefit.

We had done our due diligence in choosing a company to organise these mega pop events but this councillor burst into the office of the Director of Leisure and demanded to see all the correspondence re the appointment. He was rude and demanding but his theatrical behaviour did not phase the Director of Leisure, a woman for whom I had great respect and affection. She was tough and refused to be browbeaten by the obnoxious character. Normally his bullying worked but not with her. He wanted another company to organise these events but refused to tell me of any connection he had with the company he was espousing. This public argument became something of a *cause celebre* because into the foray came Richard Branson who was then flying round the world in a balloon hoping to gain a world record for the journey. It was really a scrap between the three of us but the addition of the famous self-publicist and without doubt serious adventurer, Branson, made this newsworthy across the UK and also the States. The arguments were conducted over the air with Branson and so were open to everyone to know exactly what we were discussing. It had also the great value of making sure that there was an enormous amount of publicity for the shows to come. Nearly a week elapsed before the others capitulated and our choice proved to be a very successful one. I did notice, however, that I was flattered to be addressed by Branson as Bernard and my addressing him as Richard.

During one concert in Roundhay the crowd had reached its maximum and we were extremely careful not to overstep any rule or restriction which had to be obeyed. A fairly large group of youths decided to force their way in. They pulled down the boards which surrounded the site only to find they were breaking into the police compound and the police waiting with open arms and handcuffs. The bewilderment of the invaders was comical to see. The courts in Leeds were busy for some days hearing charges against the interlopers.

The putting on of these shows in Roundhay Park was strongly opposed by a local environmental group which later formed themselves into a formidable force. Initially there was a great deal of snobbery involved. I feel that if we had been having the London Philharmonic playing Mozart, Schubert and Beethoven, there would have been little opposition but here we were bringing the music of the cultural *untermensch* onto this beautiful park. This protest group has subsequently proved to be a most valuable asset in retaining Roundhay Park as the park to beat all others.

An accident occurred at one of the open air concerts we organised. It was a lovely day and the site was covered with mainly young folk enjoying the music and the sun. Out of the blue and for no apparent reason, one of the large pylons which carried the heavy broadcasting equipment collapsed. By a miracle the heavy equipment, which would have killed any one hit in the fall, hurt no one other than a very nice girl who made no song and dance about the injuries which were slight and had been caused by a piece of equipment flying off on contact with the ground hitting her on the leg.

The Health and Safety warriors descended on us like a cloud of avenging angels. I strongly supported their participation as I and the whole team wanted to know what had caused the collapse. The Health and Safety team came in their glory and after the most exhaustive investigation could find no reason for the collapse. We ourselves had experimented with identical pylons trying to cause a collapse and we failed as had the National Safety Body. This did not stop the senior officer in the National Health and Safety Organisation sending me a serious letter drawing attention to the liability of the council and myself for safety and demanding that we take every precaution to ensure this collapse did not recur. I was pretty vexed by this instruction and so I wrote back asking for their clear instructions which matched their highest standards as to how I might do this. What steps should we take specifically which we had not done before? Perhaps if they could tell me their reason for the fall it would be helpful. I did not receive a reply so I repeated my letter, and this time received an acknowledgement but no substantive answer. Despite this singular experience I strongly support the work of the Health and Safety Executive. It has, to my knowledge, dramatically reduced the number of deaths and injuries in the workplace and just how much this was needed was exemplified by the number of accidents which occurred before the new organisation and after. It helps to save us all.

Sports Council

In August 1974 I was appointed to the Sports Council along with the likes of John Disley, Mary Peters and Bill Slater, all worldwide respected stars in their own firmament. The chair was held by another word famous athlete, Dr Roger Bannister. I found Bannister a fascinating figure. He had won worldwide acclaim for his record time for a mile. He also was a distinguished medic and was, in addition, a very nice chap as he was described to me. I had great respect and liking for him despite his unassuming but patrician-like aura. He invited me to meet him for a chat which I found helpful. He was particularly interested in how local authorities like my own, Leeds City Council, could help to achieve the aims of the Sports Council. I had great respect for him as an honest and committed individual and was pleased to retain contact by Christmas cards for a few years after he left to pursue his medical career. Sir Robin Brook and John Disley were appointed vice-chairmen of the council, Robin to become acting chairman almost immediately as Bannister decided after three years at the helm to resign and pursue his career in medicine. I came to like Robin just as I had liked Bannister. Sir Robin was highly intelligent and sensible, as one expects and is so often disappointed. He was a good leader never ostentatious or ego centric and the Sports Council made excellent progress despite many difficulties during his leadership. I was almost immediately made joint vice chairman with John Disley and chairman of the Facilities Committee and member of the Finance Committee.

By 1979 Dick Jeeps of rugby union had become chairman with Disley and me as vice chairmen. The council consisted of 32 members in all and included Jack Charlton (famous footballer), Sir Harry Llewellyn (who won an equestrian Olympic Gold medal, the only one if I remember aright), Laddie Lucas, DSO DFC, Lord Rupert Nevill, CVO DL JP, Alan Pascoe, a distinguished athlete, Bill Slater (international footballer), Sir James Wilson, KBE MC BA, and the super female athlete, Mary Peters It is worthwhile noticing that Sir James was a representative of the Tobacco Advisory Council. There were also six observers attending representing the other Home Countries. Attendance was very high and so meetings were attended by 45 to 50 people, excluding the secretary and staff. This, according to so-called experts today, is far too large to be effective. The truth was that it was effective and the large number attending brought a range of expertise and connections which were invaluable. I have always been a lover of, and participant in, sporting as well as artistic activities and hold them in the same regard. Who is the greater – Cassius Clay/Mohammed Ali or Gigli? Or Robeson or Callas? Meaningless questions I feel. There are so many greats in each sport or art form as to make comparisons of no real value. Occasionally one has to recognise someone who breaks all barriers, like that lovely girl Olga Korbut who, decades ago, amazed the world not merely by her incredible physical moves but the inherent beauty and artistry in her work on the mat or on the bars. I still gain much enjoyment and stimulus in meeting the stars of the sporting or artistic world.

The Sports Council gave me many opportunities to indulge this pleasure. The chief executive was a chap called Walter Winterbottom. Totally forgotten now but once a football player whose name was familiar to all. He became chief executive in which role he performed extremely well though he was very conservative in attitude to new or interesting experiments or the introduction of something new. John Disley was a world-class athlete with a fine medal total who later went on to manage a most splendid trust, doling out large sums of money to sporting ventures from a big fund which comes from the London Marathon. Sadly, he died in 2016.

Jack Charlton attended the board meetings very regularly. He never said much but when he did it was clear and incisive. I did not know him well though I had come across him when he was a star of the Leeds United team and the England squad. He once said to me that he wondered why he was on the board. My response was that he brought with him the respect of the sporting world and this was enough to help validate our decisions. Wherever he went he attracted immediate recognition and respect which reflected favourably on the rest of us.

Another member of the board for whom I developed a great respect was Laddie Lucas. He had had a distinguished career in the war as a most successful fighter pilot and he had been awarded successively the DFC, DSO and Bar and the CBE later in life. He flew Hurricanes and Spitfires in the defence of Malta when hopelessly outnumbered by the Germans and flew on operational sorties throughout the war right up to its final days. He had been a journalist in Civvy Street and he returned to that trade effortlessly being so well connected. He was elected as a Tory MP and was in addition a brilliant sportsman. He never played the war card as many did, the war being still part of everyone's experience. We got on extremely well as I was an enormous admirer of his war record. He was Biggles times three. The fact that I was a passionate member of the Labour Party and he a Conservative MP was almost a bond rather than the reverse. His contributions were always concise knowledgeable and insightful. He knew sport well. He had a successful business career as well as his journalism. It was a pleasure to serve on the board with a person of his quality and to enjoy his friendship. Lt-General Sir James Wilson and I became quite friendly although in opposite camps when it came to smoking. This did not prevent his writing in an article for the *Times* One mans' week: "Early up and then car to London for Facilities Committee under excellent chairmanship of Bernard Atha, a man who does his homework and expects others to do the same."

The list of members of the Sports Council at this time showed a total number of only two women. One was Mary Glen Haig and the other the splendid Mary Peters, a gold medallist. It is true that there was another woman present at meetings but she just took the minutes. That would be misleading as Sheila Hughes was expert in showing how to get things done and was always most helpful to me. In some respects she was more knowledgeable than anyone other than her boss Winterbottom. Mary Peters was a splendid woman and gold medallist in that order. She came from Northern Ireland, a small area, but one riven by the most awful and often despicable murders. She refused to acknowledge the divide between so-called Catholic and Protestants and was more than once menaced in words and physical attitude that she could be in trouble. In Northern Ireland at that time such threats were serious threats. She continued as before and brought energy and light to any committee on which she served. She was a joy, bursting with energy and good will. The other woman, Mary Glen Haigh, a fencer, was redoubtable. She almost could have had a sign saying "Don't mix it with me." She was rather upper class but not snobbish, short with incompetents or the lazy, and a person I admired and liked. We certainly got on well over the years and I was sad when she had to resign from the Sport Aid Board in London where she and I were the oldies with a past record in sport. Sadly she died in 2015 and I felt an unexpected sense of loss which indicated to me the respect I had had for her.

The Sport Council was fortunate to take on, at its inauguration, staff of the CCPR. This was a great organisation having a small number of highly committed individuals, male and female, who were most positive in developing sporting activities across the sporting scenario. They were sport addicts. In Yorkshire I admired their tireless approach to sport development. They were not merely committed to developing sport; they had the ability to achieve this goal. When the Sports Council was formed, a large number of highly-skilled and energetic sport leaders became Sports Council staff. This is a factor which would be critical in developing the Sports Council over the years. The Sports Council also owned and managed a number of national centres. These included Bisham Abbey, Crystal Palace, National Training Centre, Cowes, Holme Pierrepoint Water Sports Centre, Lilleshall National Centre and Plas y Brenin Centre for Mountain

Activities. These were a financial drain on the Sports Council but did do an excellent job. I shared the chairmanship of Holme Pierrepoint with the local authority from 1978 to 1984 and that is worth a saga on its own. When it was opened by the then Prime Minister, it was one of the best facilities of its kind in the world. It was run by a very astute competent manager employed by the Sports Council. He and I became good working friends. The meetings I chaired consisted of myself, the manager and a number of local authority members both town and county. Our meetings occurred on a regular basis and the manager, a man whom I admired, provided a handsome meal and lavish liquor. This led to a certain degree of insobriety and the warmth of feeling that each one of us had for the others. On one occasion, for instance, one of the councillors of very considerable proportions fell off his chair and it took three of us to restore him to his seat. In reality, I regret to say this was the worst collection of local representatives I have known.

The centre was very successful due to the acumen of the director, a man I greatly respected. He was always looking at ways in which expenditure could be reduced and income enhanced. One of the most spectacular and lucrative activities he introduced was powerboat racing on the course and pursuing methods by which athletes competing in white water sports could practise. The centre also included an adjacent water area which was used for water skiing and jumping. On my first visit, the chap in charge of this facility asked me if would like to try water skiing. He expected me to decline but I was keen to sample for the first time this particular sport. I was provided with a wet suit and sat on the end of the small pier from which I was whisked away by the boat but being completely new to the sport, I travelled for the first few seconds underwater. When I finally settled down I was able to stay up but would have got no marks for elegance. It was a splendid feeling when I did properly gain my balance. After going round a few times I felt master of it all, a feeling I lost when "coming in to land" as it were, I miscalculated and let go too soon, finishing my experience underwater yet again.

It was two years later when I had the sad duty to prepare a report to the Sports Council on the death of two water skiers. As the chairman it was my duty to investigate and report to the Sports Council, a process quite independent of the police and coroner. This was not a new challenge for me and I went assiduously into each of the unrelated deaths. Both skiers had hit obstructions – that is, structures used in training and competition and both deceased were skilled skiers. My report was undertaken as part of my role as chairman and therefore, ultimately legally responsible. It was discussed extensively by the Sports Council and all at the centre. After the most detailed discussions with experts it was agreed that both deaths were accidental. In my confidential report I did query the remote possibility of foul play in one of the incidents as my investigation had seemed to reveal some personal hostility in one case by another involving marital issues. There was little to go on but I did mention this to the police as an unlikely but possible consideration.

I did have one contact with Plas Y Brenin which I shall remember. John Disley had, on two consecutive occasions, attended the annual meeting of Plas Y Brenin. There he had been given a rough ride from the members to such an extent that when he received an invitation to the annual meeting again, he flatly refused to go. As the other vice chair, I was put under severe pressure to stand in for him and this I was really happy to do as I wanted to visit the centre. I arrived, was greeted courteously by the committee and offered a strong drink "as you will need it". I took the drink but not the reason and later got up on the stage to give my prepared speech. Immediately there was a heckler who was easily disposed of as, in my early days, all political meetings were heated, often full of personal abuse and the occasional resort to fists. This atmosphere was a lot like going home. As I dealt with one or two of the hecklers, the crowd started to get on my side. It is strange how one can feel this change. That came when I said that I had given up all hope of delivering my prepared speech and would just listen and comment when necessary. This all went down well and the hospitality became even

465

more pressing. I watched some amateur filming of climbers and climbs which made my hair stand on end. I had done enough climbing with friends who were very competent and advanced climbers and I had, therefore, an understanding of the amazing things these climbers can do. I was fascinated by a film of an Italian group who climbed bare footed. I cannot say my visit to Plas Y Brenin was successful. It was, however, fun and it took at least a good twelve hours before I decided I was fit to drive back to Leeds. I did get another invitation to join the centre which was kind but declined.

I have many recollections of the Sports Council, some which still make me smile. For instance: I would normally drive down to London and when I had arrived I would change from informal slacks into a suit. I normally did this exchange of dress in the car, parked in a suitably quiet bit of road adjoining Hyde Park. I was, on one occasion, in the stage of changing trousers when I heard a tapping on my side window. When I looked up I could see a female face upside down and her finger indicating I should roll down the window. This I did and found that the upside down face belonged to a police woman riding a horse, hence when she bent down to tap the window she appeared upside down to me. I explained what I was doing. She seemed to accept my story and suggested a much better site nearby where I could do my dress change in future. Satisfied I was not some dangerous pervert, she laughed, told me to put on my trousers and not to be caught again without them and trotted off. The memory of the upside down head still makes me smile, mentally.

Another incident also resonates. We were having a meeting in the Sports Council offices which were then close to Harvey Nichols. Our discussions were stopped abruptly as we heard the sound of a distant very loud explosion. We surmised what it would be. Could it be someone breaking the sound barrier or an explosion of a gas works? It transpired to be a bomb which blew up a member of Parliament in the Parliament site. Just another example of the bloody campaign for Northern Ireland independence from the "English Yoke". What madness. All over the world people of different religions, faith and politics live together without these horrors but daily today elsewhere, those awful excesses are being experienced by civilians who have no means of saving their lives other than fleeing and joining the waves of refugees who are a daily indictment of man's inhumanity to man.

Sport
My perspective

Sport is good per se no matter at what level it is pursued. My main interest, however, lay more in the effect of sport on the mental, social and physical health of a community and the individual. Sport should be enjoyed for itself but its wider benefits are more important. My contention is that sport should be pursued per se by the individual but the wider effects should concern the policy makers. Sport can play a crucial role, for instance, in the fight against obesity, combatting social deviation, providing the means of social contact essential to the mental health of many, the integration of different races and social cohesion. The Paralympic Games in London were spectacularly successful in educating the public re the ability of the "disabled athletes" and their value as role models.

In 1980, as vice chairman of the GB Sports Council, I had the task of running a Year of the Disabled campaign. I was horrified to discover the discrimination suffered by people with a range of disabilities and on society's concentration on disability rather than the often amazing ability of the "disabled athletes". I asked the London Marathon organisers to allow wheelchair athletes to compete and was refused, twice, by the Mayor, Ken Livingstone and his buddy.

Of all the disabilities, the one which suffers the worst treatment was that labelled mentally handicapped. Inspired and guided by a member of the Sports Council staff, Liz Dendy, I set up a new organisation, the UK Sports Association for People with Mental Handicap, now Learning Disability. This organisation has fought now for more than two decades to achieve parity with other sports bodies. It has yet to succeed despite outstanding progress. I was later horrified years later when financial support from the Sports Council was stopped, forcing the organisation to be reduced almost to extinction.

The US organisers of the Atlanta Paralympic Games refused to include the "mentally handicapped" despite a campaign lead by the UKSA in the UK and by sister bodies elsewhere. We finally forced them to admit these athletes by the threat of a legal action under the US Discrimination Legislation. The British team did well as a result of the gold, silver and bronze medals won by the athletes with a learning disability. A most welcome change in the UK team in Atlanta was the change in the attitude of the wheelchair athletes to the learning disability athletes as they came to recognise their skill and training. Animosity burgeoned into strong support and kindness. I was more than once told by those who professed to know that the hostility emanating from the leaders of Special Olympics arose because they saw the inclusion of mentally handicapped athletes as a threat to the Special Olympic Games. The antagonism of the British athletes and that of other countries to the mentally handicapped athletes was replaced by warmth and support. Sadly this change did not affect the hostility of the US organisers which was manifested in a number of disgraceful ways. Even more sadly was the exclusion of LD athletes for two subsequent Paralympic games caused by the disgraceful dishonesty of the President of INAS, Fernando Vicente, the international body of Learning Disability Sport. He was also chairman of the Spanish Association. He fraudulently included a number of non-disabled athletes in the Spanish Paralympic team in order to win medals. The fight to get the restoration of LD (i.e. Learning difficulty or disability) athletes has been hard, enervating and only achieved in a token manner in the London and Rio Paralympics. However, there are welcome signs that the campaign for full inclusion of LD athletes is progressing.

The social benefits of sport can be exemplified by this example. Two parents sought me out at the Atlanta Paralympics to thank me for what I had "done for their daughter". She was mentally handicapped (the term then in use). As she matured into womanhood she had become a most severe and complex problem. They were distraught. She, by chance, took up swimming in a club for the mentally handicapped, became, over time, a very good swimmer, accepted the advice and direction of the women swimming instructors and this changed her whole personality. Her parents said with conviction that swimming had possibly saved their marriage, the problems of their daughter being so severe. I pointed out that the wonderful people who ran the voluntary club at their own expense were the ones to be thanked. In the UK, the social benefit of sport is being threatened by the monstrous cuts being made in central finance to local authorities, many of whom have had to reduce drastically their support for sport development and facilities. Sports centres are being closed. Sports departments are being effectively closed. Swimming pools closed. Sport development officers sacked. In time the volunteers, the backbone of sport in the UK, facing cuts in grant and facilities will find it impossible to continue and dire social consequences will follow. "Sport for All" was a splendid war cry. It should be resurrected and made the rallying cry again before it is too late.

UK Sports Association

As Vice Chairman of the Sports Council and guided by Liz Dendy of the Sports Council, I had established a UK Sports Association for People with a Mental Handicap (UKSA_PMH) following my running the Sports Council's Year of the Disabled Campaign. The UKSA-PMH Board was a large and highly regarded body with representatives from bodies like the Directors of Social Care Organisations and the Sports Council. I felt that we were making sound if slow progress – often meeting with enthusiastic words but little action.

One Social Services director was particularly interested in the formation of an international body to represent the sporting interests of the people with a mental handicap. I felt he and his similarly interested colleagues were more interested in the foreign travel than in any other thing. Despite my lack of enthusiasm, this small group went ahead with discussions which would later lead to the formation of the international organisation INAS FMH – the International Sports Body for People with a Mental Handicap, later changed to Learning Disability or Intellectual Impairment. I was wrong to assume their motives to be more selfish than idealistic and now look back with admiration for their enthusiasm and commitment.

There were just 14 nations represented at the first meeting of INAS in January 1986 but the new organisation soon received recognition from the international organisation of that time which ran the Paralympic Games, namely the International Coordinating Committee (ICC). This was a remarkable achievement in a very short time though none of us at that time could conceive of an organisation which now has more than 70 national members, 15 annual events worldwide and 3,500 registered athletes.

I became part of the UK delegation and over a very short period of time came to know a host of individuals from all over the globe. Some of them were the most committed members one could desire The general concept of the UKSA was based on a theory of a distinguished and highly individualistic academic from the prestigious University of Uppsala, Bengt Nirje. In condensed form he preached "Normalisation", a theory that people with a mental handicap should be treated as normally as possible, enjoying the passage of each day week and year exactly as other people of the same age and gender. My view is very similar, namely that a person with a mental handicap should be entitled to enjoy all the opportunities that everyone else has. In short, no discrimination no matter how well intentioned.

A small town in Sweden called Harnosand offered to meet the central costs of the UKSA and this included providing the salary of the General Secretary of the organisation. This was an exceptional example of generosity and enabled us to employ a very competent young man Mats Hamberg who served the organisation splendidly for a number of years.

In 1980 the First World Games for athletes with a mental handicap were held in Harnosand which was a major first step to have our athletes competing exactly as everyone else competes, i.e. normalisation. Had Harnosand not been so generous it is doubtful if the organisation would have survived. Meetings in Harnosand however required expensive air travel which was outside the competence of some countries to meet and therefore attend. INAS had started off as a very open and democratic body but it changed when Fernando Vicente from Spain became President. He seemed to have limitless resources to spend and he was more of a General Franco by disposition than a Saint Francis. His term of office lasted four years and he was standing for re-election. The AGM was held in Harnosand and Fernando arrived with a sizeable entourage. He was very unpopular with many of the countries represented who found him bombastic and dictatorial. He was seen by so many as a dictator and not a democrat. As there was no one prepared to stand against him I was put under great pressure to stand for President, something I was keen not to do given my already full calendar of responsibilities one of which was earning a living and meeting the very considerable expenses of travel though the Sports Council did pay some of these expenses as it did for other organisations.

After receiving great pressure to stand I finally agreed but counselled all the conspirators not to reveal my challenge before it happened in the Meeting. Strict secrecy was enforced and we all felt a bit like kids enjoying a game. Game however it was not. When the chairman called for nominations Fernando expected to be unopposed and he was completely taken aback when after the Spanish delegate nominated Fernando someone nominated me and that was quickly seconded by a number of delegates in chorus it seemed. Fernando was furious and even more furious when I won with a great majority. He got up, waved theatrically to his entourage to follow him and made an exit, a flounce of which Bette Davis in her prime would have been jealous. Fernando left Harnosand without paying his hotel bills and other bills he had accumulated which fell on the Town to meet. Quite despicable but in keeping with Fernando's way of working.

Fernando was an enigma. I was told that he had started off as a social worker with little or no fortune. At his height before his fall members of INAS were invited to visit his home/farm. They were amazed by the opulence and wealth displayed. It reeked of wealth – great wealth. The question immediately raised in one's mind is, how did he do it. We were to find out later.

He was a man of ambition. He told me he wanted to stand for the EU Parliament and thought that as chairman of a major Charity like INAS that would help. He sent over to London two of his henchmen who explained Fernando's ambition and promised me substantial financial benefits if I were not to seek re-election as President of INAS. I naturally refused but was impressed that Fernando could set such store upon becoming President of INAS once again. He was very well connected. He seemed to be able to call on two Spanish Princesses to attend competitions and even meetings and I ended up on first name terms with them.

They were very genuine people with a real interest in people with a disability and it was always a pleasure to meet them.

The first Paralympic Games for people with a mental handicap took place in Madrid. A large number of nations competed, the majority coming from Europe. The Games without qualification were successful. They had shown that our athletes with proper training could compete at a high level and that it was only the mental handicap which prevented them from vying for a place in the Olympics. Fernando had of course been crucial in organising this event and quite rightly bathed in a warm glow of real success. He was particularly keen to meet Prince Edward who very kindly came over to Madrid and made a great impression on our athletes which he met for prolonged periods on a number of occasions in a four day visit.

Fernando was quite determined to become President of INAS once again. On Monday 17th February 1997 I met the brother-in-law of Fernando who came to London just to put a proposition to me. He offered me a deal on behalf of Fernando. The plan was that I should not stand for the Presidency but allow Fernando to be elected un-opposed. Fernando would then set up an office in Madrid and send me on a long trip to canvas nations in the third world with Fernando meeting all the costs. Fernando would pay for delegates to come to the General Assembly if they promised to vote for him. If Fernando was not successful he would set up another international organisation in competition with INAS something he had tried to do three years earlier and failed. I responded by pointing out the illegal nature of the proposition. I also pointed out that for four years Fernando had not played any part in INAS and indeed had been two years behind in paying the annual subscription.

The next General Assembly met in Germany and the vote for me was 18 and Fernando 19. Fernando had bought tickets for a number of individuals who had promised to vote for him and he had been lavish in providing entertainments for all. He was jubilant but being the great performer he could not have been more generous in his praise of my Presidency. Most of those who voted for him came from countries which had no significant schemes and in some cases no schemes of any kind to develop mentally handicapped athletes and who had never sent athletes to an INAS event. As someone who has all his life been involved in politics, local, national and international I am a bit case hardened but I did feel by letting this happen we were going to put back our cause significantly and that made me sad. I however accepted defeat despite the dirty tricks and promised to remain fully involved in the future. Two women delegates from West Africa came to see me and apologised for voting as they did. They said that a number of the delegates including themselves had come because Fernando had agreed to meet all travel expenses without which they could not get home. I re-assured them that I understood. They were two very nice individuals coming from countries which have very few public services and extremely poor standards of living. That they were able to do anything to help the mentally handicapped was in itself very impressive.

I was however disgusted when Bob Steadward, the Chairman of the IPC – International Paralympic Committee paying a courtesy visit to the General Assembly virtually directed the delegates to elect Fernando. This was not so explicit as it appears in these words but it was exactly that. This surprised me because I had been much involved in the early days of the IPC and indeed had helped to get him elected as Chairman of the new International Paralympic Committee. I learned later that Fernando had promised a large sum to an organisation in Canada which Steadward would lead.

In due course Fernando got his "come uppance." He was determined that Spain would do well in the Paralympics in Sydney so he picked as part of the Spanish team a total of fifteen athletes who had no mental deficiency and who had not been examined for eligibility at all. This could happen because Fernando had taken registration of athletes into his control. Only registered athletes could compete. The Spanish Team indeed did do well but the problem for Fernando was that he had picked as one of the illegal team of athletes a man who was a journalist who had been researching Fernando's Life and Life style. He broke the news and this was a tremendous body blow to INAS because it was their President who had engineered this quite atrocious subterfuge. He could do this because by his bribery which took many forms, he controlled the registration of athletes' eligibility, paid the expenses of some of the countries which could not afford to send athletes abroad and controlled every aspect of the work of INAS FMH.

When the story broke Fernando suddenly and wisely felt compelled to visit his second wife's country, Columbia in South America most urgently. A detailed police investigation of his business in Spain revealed a very profitable if not always a legal business.

Two years later he appeared before a Spanish Court to answer criminal charges. On 7th October 2013 the Spanish Court fined Fernando 5,400 Euros for his role in the scandal and he was ordered to return 142,355 Euros. It was confirmed that at least fifteen members of the Spanish team were not mentally impaired in any way and had not been given any test which was an essential part of the establishment of the impairment. The journalist provided all the evidence to justify criminal charges against Fernando quite apart from those involved in the Paralympic scandal. Fernando had put back the movement for inclusion of the athletes with a learning disability and which led to INAS athletes being barred from Paralympic and World Championships for ten years. This may not sound too awful but it meant that many countries ceased to support their mentally handicapped athletes and their organisations and so for nearly a decade athletes with a learning disability/mental handicap had all financial government support withdrawn. All the athletes who could have competed on the world stage at Paralympics and International events were denied this opportunity.

Fernando did enormous damage to our cause for athletes with a learning disability. It provided all the arguments needed by those who did not want "these people" in the Paralympics. Their opposition was based on the need to maintain the sanctity and purity of the Paralympics something I strongly support. I do not approve in any way however if it is used as a tool to exclude INAS athletes. I have no doubt in my judgement that this disgraceful episode was used over the years as a weapon to exclude Learning disability athletes from any IPC event.

The antipathy this attitude shows is attributable to any number of causes. For instance, if the Learning Disability athletes are admitted to the Paralympic Games and given a full calendar of events they will be taking up space in the programme and in the physical resources that their athletes, Cerebral Palsy, amputees, wheel-chair etc could fill. The resource to finance the elite competitors is relatively small and if the LD athletes are admitted every one else would get less. Others still have the "Does he take sugar?" syndrome. That is, if you are in a wheel chair with your helper or friend who is engaged in conversation you are left excluded and diminished or even worse talked down to as though mentally deficient. I concede without reservation that this was a widely held view and that it was a real hardship for many people in wheel chairs. Thank God the position is now quite changed in the UK thanks to the great success of the Paralympic Games in London and Rio.

It was with some pride when for the first time since the Fernando tragedy INAS athletes were permitted to compete in the London Paralympics. The events were very few, almost insultingly so but they set the precedent for INAS athletes to participate in the world of the IPC. One must not forget that in Atlanta it was the medals won by the Learning Disability competitors which put GB near the top of the medal table and indeed there was one exceptional track athlete, Kenny Colaine, a black mentally handicapped sprinter trained by Lynford Christie who was awarded an MBE. He clocked 11.33 sec for 100 m and 22.90 sec for 200 m better than some of the non disabled Olympic runners of that time.

The LD athletes all over the globe were denied their right to compete through the dishonesty of those who were elected to be their champions. History tells us of the danger of allowing power to fall into the hands of a few powerful people. We allowed this to happen in Germany, Italy, Russia and many other countries and the effects are always dramatically horrible.

Fernando is a good example of the stereotype "baddy" who is at the same time endearing. Fernando could be a most generous host, liked a laugh and high spirits and could be as convivial as anyone. Half of me liked him enormously. The other half would have wanted his head for the damage done to our movement. Prior to the scandal breaking he invited all the delegates attending a meeting in Madrid to an evening at a bull ring which is used to train bull fighters. The conviviality was extreme and so when it was suggested that we could try out our skills in the ring with a small bullock without horns the chance was too good to miss. The animal I was provided with was the size of a donkey and did not appear to be aggressive, more puzzled I thought. I knew that one held out the red cape to one's side so the bull would charge that and not you. My problem that at that moment I was bedevilled by the fact that having quaffed immoderately I could see two bulls and chose the wrong one to excite. Little the little bull might be, it charged me, sent me completely apex over base, performing a backward somersault and landing more or less on my feet having executed 360 degrees involuntarily. I received great applause not for my athletic skill but because I was still pipe in mouth smoking. The next day I had a knee the size of a football. The price one pays when Bacchus replaces Sobriety.

The UK has been very well represented at the international level by the UK Sports Association for People with a Learning Disability. In the early days of UKSA we were fortunate to employ Roger Biggs one of the most effective CEOs I have known. He was extremely sharp and intelligent but he had one of the most persuasive talents and techniques I have known. He really put the UKSA on the map and was widely respected even by the "enemy" whoever they might be at any time. I was profoundly sorry when Roger decided to take a job in the Far East but the loss was lessened by having left someone to fill his place, a highly intelligent woman who during her time with us obtained an LLB and was called to the Bar. We could not have found a better replacement for Roger than in the current CEO Tracey McCillen. I have been equally blessed by the good friends I have made across the Globe through our international relations. Outstanding among these is Jos Mulder, a Dutchman of incredible honesty and integrity, totally reliable, highly intelligent and committed. I was delighted to have him nominated and elected as Chairman in Acapulco to replace Fernando as what INAS needed most was someone who was honest fair and incorruptible. INAS is now a very effective international organisation. It offers a wide range of events world wide but it lacks in the UK the support other similar sports organisations receives.

Special Olympics

There has been another problem from the very beginning of the formation of INAS FID. Special Olympics International (SOI) is a world wide organisation with HQ in the US and is most generously funded by the Kennedy Clan. It is a very worthwhile organisation and commands my respect and support. The Americans however saw INAS as a competitor and were very obstructive so when I was elected President of INAS I felt my first task was to make some accommodation with Special Olympics. I asked for a meeting and was given a date and time in Washington. I booked a return flight arriving in Washington in time for the meeting which lasted under an hour. I spent the rest of the day sightseeing and flew back the day after. As I was paying my own fair and expenses I told myself this was a holiday and to my surprise I believed it for a moment.

The chairman was a Mr Shriver of the Shriver Family, a family of great wealth, influence commitment and close ties with the Kennedy Family. Our meeting started rather oddly. I had been made comfortable by a secretary in his HQ and was waiting the arrival of Shriver when I heard him as he approached say in a loud voice: "Who is this guy?" It made me smile as I was immediately able to put him on the defensive by saying to him as he entered the room: "I am this guy who has just flown over to the USA to meet you. I am the President of INAS. You may, if you so wish, address me by my name or title." From this falsely pretentious rocky start, we went on to establish a more congenial attitude to one another. My message to him was that Special Olympics had nothing to fear from INAS, that we operated quite differently, and that a clear understanding of this relationship should be made apparent to all. We should not be seen as competing. I saw no objection to Special Olympic athletes competing in INAS events if they met the required standard as in able bodied sport. He was clearly concerned about SOI athletes competing in INAS events, seeing this as competition with his company, Special Olympics being a company with a worldwide spread. It is run like a business and some countries so objected to the way SOI operates they refuse to recognise Special Olympics. I said I would, as President of INAS, seek to get this embargo lifted.

After the first rather prickly start, which secretly I had rather enjoyed seeing this egotistical character pushed on to his back foot and not knowing whether to apologise or be aggressive, the atmosphere became less charged but I left after some time feeling that I had not achieved my objective of establishing mutual aims and methods of operation. To me, Shriver seemed analogous to a chief executive of a company with a monopoly being faced with a competitor which threatened that monopoly.

Special Olympics operated on the principle of letting every one participate. Thus at an athletic event there could be several 100 metre races each one with a first second and third winner. The aim, most creditably, was participation. Thus at one major championship there could be a small handful of winners of the 100 meters or other events and several in second place and also the third place. It also operated on the basis of rewarding runners with a hug at the end of each race. The Special Olympics in Great Britain has changed significantly since those early days. I had a fairly explosive meeting with a Tory MP, Eldon Griffiths, who headed up the Special Olympics in the UK during a lunch organised by Lord Rix to bring the two organisations together – namely SOI England and UKSA. All was formal English discussion which gradually developed into a fierce argument between Griffiths and me. I hated his sense of superiority as he was an MP, an ego which I enjoyed puncturing. Rix just sat back, very surprised but no doubt amused that his peace meeting had so quickly become a war of words. Rix later told me he had quite enjoyed the unexpected battle of words between myself and an arrogant and obnoxious (my words) Eldon Griffiths. Rix was the former absolute star of stage farces, a brilliant comic actor turned committed supporter of Mencap and its president. I had loved seeing his Whitehall farces which seemed to run for decades and found it difficult to reconcile my two extremely diverse visions of him.

Antipathy has disappeared now, thank God, and been replaced in the UK by mutual support and friendship, the members of Special Olympics making sure the US HQ does not micro-manage the affairs of GB SOI (Special Olympic International). It is sad that some small countries still do not allow Special Olympics to operate in their countries to the grave adverse effect on the poorest individual. Until 2016, UKSA received a grant to support its activities. The withdrawal of the annual grant was disastrous for UKSA as it was for a number of other sports bodies. The idea of Sport for All has gone. UKSA is now operating on a miniscule scale, largely because its chief officer, and only one now, is maintaining its existence virtually out of the goodness of her heart.

Sports Aid National

Sports Aid was established in 1976 on the prompting of Dennis Howell, then the Sports Minister, just one of his major contributions to sport in the UK. Most of the nationally famous athletes came from the wealthier classes as they were the only ones who had the resources to train: many aspiring athletes could not afford the costs of training, costs as mundane as cost of travel to train and the dearth of clubs which could produce the best in Britain. It was an inspired concept of Howell and has led to the UK competing internationally most successfully worldwide in a vast number of sports.

In 1974 I met Howell and in discussion about a number of things I explained how in Leeds we had established four Centres of Excellence at the internationally recognised centre of excellence, Carnegie College. We, that is Cyril Villiers, Chief Executive of the Yorkshire Sports Counci and I had become worried that many young people could simply not afford the costs of getting to and from the centres three or four times per week and we were starting the process of setting up a separate charity to help the needy athletes to attend the centres. Our concern had been triggered when we saw a very talented West Indian girl being withdrawn from the centre because the mother could not afford the fares to take her child there three times a week, the minimum attendance for the advanced class. He was intensely interested and we discussed our plans at length. I promised to send him a paper outlining what we were doing.

Howell took up the initiative and set up the International Sports Aid Foundation. Our Sports Fund for the Gifted then became a regional arm of the national body. Many of the athletes who have received help became world recognised sporting idols. They include such as Steve Redgrave, Tessa Sanderson, Daley Thomson, Sharon Davies, Jonathan Edwards, Tanni Grey-Thompson and Linford Christie. Known then as the Sports Aid Foundation, its main function was to raise money to aid athletes with their cost of training throughout Britain. Initially the new body was welcomed in a very wholehearted manner and the great and the good were quickly enrolled. For instance, the annual report for 1988–89 listed 101 individual statutory members, 36 members on the Board of Governors which included such names as Sir Robin Brook CMG OBE, David Coleman – distinguished commentator, Sir Arthur Gold – a world recognised figure in athletics, Major-General Ian Grahame CB, Anita Lonsbrough – a world class swimmer, Sir Ian MacLaurin who ran TESCO, Sir Leslie Porter who owned TECSO, Bill Slater – an international football player, Dennis Thatcher MBE, Adrian Metcalfe – a world class athlete and Paul Zetter, owner of Zetter Pools to mention just a few.

The executive committee was more of a manageable size, namely 16. In addition to myself, the committee consisted of *inter alia* Sir Robin Brook CMG OBE, Sebastian Coe MBE, Mary Glen Haigh CBE – a former Olympic fencer, my favourite Major-General Graeme CB OBE, Adrian Metcalf, Sir Leslie Porter, Bill Slater, Paul Zetter and Denis Thatcher.

Sitting in meetings with Denis, as he asked to be called, was for, me quite an experience. I abominated Margaret Thatcher for her philosophy, for selling off national assets and municipal undertakings, closing down the mines, and her whole apparent philosophy which was money, money and survival of the richest. My hostility was palpable, but to my surprise, I found Denis of very sound judgement as one would expect of a successful businessman and balanced in his view. He was very forceful in expression and I remember him clearly arguing most strongly that we should not give grants to golf players as the golfing world was rich enough to look after its own without any problem at all. The money should go where the need is. However, whenever I looked at him or heard him speak, a picture would spring involuntarily into my mind of the two well-known comedians who had put on TV a series of sketches lampooning Thatcher and his buddy so well that this image began to overpower the reality. They were hilarious, not too unkind and Denis said he found them fun.

My favourite major-general was someone I came to admire enormously for his incredible memory, his commitment and his honesty, namely Ian Graeme. I more than once had cause to call on him in his West End home. It was a fine four-storey house on what is now a Millionaire Row. His office looked chaotic but he knew where every item was. He wrote very clearly in a minute script which made his notes difficult to read. He gave an enormous amount of time researching times, distances, etc., and recommending who should receive grant support and who should not. A sterling character. If Ian was my favourite Major–general, shades of Gilbert and Sullivan, my favourite brigadier was Noel Nagle. Noel was the Director of Sports Aid Foundation i.e. Chief Officer of all the Sports Aid organisations and committees. He was excellent in the job in a most friendly and persuasive manner. We were extremely lucky to have such an individual in charge of the organisation. I was particularly impressed when he produced a very well prepared document which suggested that an organisation should be set up to help athletes at the end of their athletic career to prepare for the transition from sports man/woman to life in business. It was costed properly and worked out methodically as one would expect of a person of his rank when in the army. This was a far seeing idea as today athletes have to become full time athletes to achieve success and their position when their elite competition ends can be devastating. Another late recruit was Cecil Parkinson who had enjoyed a sexual relationship for an alleged twelve years with his secretary. She ultimately bore his child which was handicapped. The story roused immense interest and Parkinson was forced to resign from his ministerial post in the Conservative Government. The matter was all laid out in the press and television and his reputation was greatly damaged. I felt that he joined Sports Aid as a means of rehabilitation, restoring his reputation in some way. The Establishment looks after its own. I personally thought he had behaved abominably to his daughter. He contributed very little, if anything, to Sports Aid. I was, however, impressed by his hands which were well manicured and delicate. He did not remain long, unlike another who experienced the blaze of bad publicity. David Mellor had also been involved in a relationship with a lady who was something of a well-known celebrity by merely being a celebrity. The papers, or some of them, mocked him for making love to her in a shirt of some football club he supported. Chelsea I suppose. I doubt whether this was true and if it was, it was of little concern. However he joined Sports Aid as Parkinson did as a way of restoring his public image. He later became chairman and in that capacity was, in my view, effective, though there was a feeling among my colleagues that he came in, did the meeting and then left but that his contribution was nevertheless satisfactory. Originally I met him with a strong feeling of dislike. This changed as it often does when one gets to know someone. He was a Tory and protected by his Tory colleagues though he is now best known not for his politics but for his genuine interest in and knowledge of classical music.

In March 1987 the Executive Committees of the SAF and Sports Aid Trust (SAT) set up a review group consisting of myself as chairman, Seb Coe MBE, Colin Moynihan MP and Adrian Metcalfe from the Sports Aid Trust (SAT) and Norman Sarsfield OBE MC, best known for his work on the Commonwealth Games. The terms of reference were very broad including whether to apply a means test, what practical help including education other than financial assistance should be given, should athletes in return reciprocate in some way in the future development of Sports Aid and how best the Foundation and Trust could best work together.

A list of specific questions to be addressed by the group was compiled, the West London Institute of Higher Education kindly undertook to engage in its own research programme and a questionnaire was sent to governing bodies. The specific questions, 41 in number, included issues relating to sporting qualifications, means testing, grants to teams rather than one in the team, loan or grant, reciprocity, i.e. grantees help Sports Aid in return for grant, relationship between Sports Aid and Sports Council, attitudes of BOA, concentration on top athletes only or wider than that, the role of governing bodies, et al. One set of questions reflects the attitudes of the time: should Sports Aid support people with a mental handicap, the unemployed or the disadvantaged? It is significant to think that in our more enlightened days, the question of whether to assist the mentally handicapped (sic) had to be asked. Quite quickly it became apparent that my colleagues would find it very difficult to meet the requirements in terms of time as each was heavily committed in many different ways. It was therefore agreed that I would do the review myself. After much consultation with a diverse number of athletes and officials, I produced a report printed in book form by a young man that ran the printing department in my college costing me nothing more than the cost of paper and a small gift.

The majority of my recommendations were agreed and adopted. There was one which I included not as a polemic, but merely as a statement of the obvious. By the 1950s one could see how some countries, particularly in Eastern Europe, were producing world class athletes by a process which seemed, in the case of East Germany, to be similar to the way in which the Nazis had brainwashed a nation. It was absolutely clear to me that the true amateur would never be able to compete with these professionally-trained full-time athletes. The old rather mythical idea of the amateur athlete such as we saw before the war and immediately after it, would never achieve success against these trained professionals. I, therefore, argued strongly for us to reject the old idea of amateur and professional and have just sportsmen and women. The future, whether it was liked or not, would be one in which only the athlete working full time as an athlete would have a chance of success. Thirty years ago this was a view hotly contested by those who believed in a world which had ceased to exist. We must remember also that at one time, to compete in the Olympics, a person had to fund himself/herself which ruled out more than 90% of athletes. I remember speaking to an old man who had been a miner and was a first class weight lifter. He told me he worked a shift down the mine, went off immediately at his own expense to compete in the Olympic Games, won a medal, returning immediately and going back down the pit the day he got back. He had to meet all his expenses which he did by borrowing and paying back later. I wish I had made a note of his name and the year he attended the Olympics.

We have gone a long way since then but there is still some way to go. Forty-one percent of the medal winners at the London Olympic Games went to privately educated individuals; the best public schools have very good sports facilities and coaches. Another statistic is relevant. Four private schools and one sixth form college in Cambridge sent as many students to Oxbridge as 2,000 state schools combined.

Sports Aid

Sports Aid since then has had a varied history from the heady days of substantial grants from the Foundation for Sport and the Arts and similar resources to periods of decline involving bad management, stupid decisions such as moving into expensive office accommodation, changes in personnel until today when it has an excellent new CEO, a very reduced board and ambitious plans for the future.

I have been privileged in many ways, one of which has been the involvement in an organisation from its inception which has seen our athletes achieving worldwide success in Olympic, Paralympic, World and Commonwealth Games. The athletes owe those men and women who over nearly 40 years have given them the opportunity and satisfaction of achieving or failing to achieve outstanding success in their sport, acknowledging that those who do not win a medal have achieved heights of performance that 99% of us will never achieve and can only wonder at. One also remembers the statement: there are no winners without losers. Today, Sports Aid supports around 1,500 athletes per year, distributing over £ 1 m in awards to talented athletes. Sports Aid is delighted to have a new Royal Patron, HRH Duchess of Cambridge who showed her support immediately by attending three major events in as many months. Happily, Sports Aid continues its work as its need remains apparent, securing an additional £ 500,000 for athlete awards, £ 6 m for Tass Awards (a fund to support athletes and their costs in universities, colleges and full time study), and assurances of Sport England funding up to 2017.

One drawback arises from the success of an athlete, particularly a bonny-looking female athlete who achieves worldwide or even just national public recognition. He or she is offered contracts to advertise their products or services and have a clause in the contract restricting any public appearance and support of causes without their permission. One cannot blame these fortunate athletes who have worked so hard to achieve success. It does mean, however, that Sports Aid cannot use them in its money-raising efforts which was not so before. I am constantly reassured of the sense in supporting elite athletes on the basis of their example, inspiring others to undertake physical effort in a variety of sports. Olga Korbut, that magical wisp of a young girl, electrified the world by her gymnastic prowess decades ago. What an example leading to a surge in young girls taking up gymnastics and thereby gaining all the social and health benefits which sport endows. In 2015, bringing the Tour de France to the UK has seen a tremendous boost to the number of cyclists in the UK.

Sport Aid has the capacity to inspire greater activity and participation in sport with its extremely significant positive effect on health and social cohesion. I believe elite sport is an essential, fundamental tool in developing a healthy and active population and providing a means by which natural talent can be discovered and nourished.

Visit South Africa

During the 1970s there were two strongly held views re South Africa and international sport. One view was that there should be no sporting contacts with that oppressive regime. The other was that sport is above party politics and so sporting relationships should be encouraged. Rugby in the UK strongly favoured the second view and urged the government to approve a rugby tour of GB by the South African all white team. This rapidly became a highly contentious matter. The Sports Council, on 1ˢᵗ October 1979, agreed to send a fact-finding mission to South Africa "To appraise the current situation on the organisation of and participation in sport in South Africa with particular reference to major sports and to produce a report." This was only one of a number of visits by sportsmen and women from different countries. Many believed that such a visit was likely to be either biased or misleading. The *Muslim News* dated 25ᵗʰ January 1980 carried a report which was pretty typical.

"There is no doubt that Dickie Jeeps leans towards the breaking of the rugby isolation but his leanings could, to a certain extent, be countered by the vice president of the British Sports Council. Mr Atha, who emerged in my opinion as the most lucid thinker on the mission and the one seemingly the most capable of making an objective, impersonal assessment of the facts."

I respected and liked Dickie Jeeps, the chairman, but I felt that his coming from the rugby union world in which he had gained a great reputation and as a member of the upper middle class, his view of apartheid which I had experienced in a previous visit would be as biased for inclusion as I was against it. I also felt that Arthur Gold, Chairman of the Commonwealth Games Council and a former elite sportsman, was favourably disposed to

GB sending or receiving teams from South Africa. I felt, rightly or wrongly, that Dick and Arthur would be seduced by the South Africans and come to a recommendation which I thought wrong. I made clear that I went or there would be a public debate on impartiality. The one person I really welcomed was Olive Newson, a senior executive officer in the Sports Council, a woman of great integrity who would record dispassionately and honestly.

The members of the delegation were Dick Jeeps, Chairman of the Sports Council, Bernard Atha, Vice Chairman of the Sports Council, Arthur Gold, Basil D'Oliviera and Olive Newson. D'Oliviera was an outstanding cricketer who had to escape from South Africa to play in top class matches and he, of course, came to play with great distinction for England. Basil was a charming, honest and modest individual, impossible not to like, with a cricket history which was quite outstanding. Around this time there was a series of issues involving sport and politics and international relations. These included a hotly-debated tour of South Africa by a white rugby team and participation in the Olympic Games to be held in Russia. My previous experience of South Africa had been as a tourist when I was horrified by the apartheid system and the way non-whites were treated.

Dr Verwoerd, a former Prime Minister whom we met twice, said apartheid was based on the separate development of the various racial and ethnic groups, namely White, Black, Coloured and Asian. Each black African ethnic group is to be identified with its own homeland and Africans in towns are to be regarded as migrant workers. "The four colour streams are separate and must remain so." There was legislation of mammoth proportions governing the separation of White, Black, Coloured and Asians and one of the harshest police forces to enforce it.

The laws today seem to be unbelievable: mixed marriages were illegal, sexual relations between Whites and non-Whites were illegal and the Population Registration Act required every individual to be registered as belonging to one of the racial groups. This is just as Hitler organised his brief Third Reich as a precursor to the extermination of the Jews, Socialists, gypsies, the mentally handicapped, et al. Legislation also required each racial group to live in demarcated areas to which entry by a member of a different racial group had to have a police issued pass. The Reservation of Separate Amenities Act provided that every public vehicle, premise, building or amenity could be reserved for one racial group. Thus all the best sporting facilities were reserved for Whites only. One provision enabled it to accord a person "honorary White Status" which then permitted the individual to enter White-only property. Thus, when we stayed, as we did, in the best hotels, Basil became an honorary White so the act's prohibitions did not apply to him at that moment.

Government policy did change but the rule remained that each coloured person had to belong to his or her own clubs, i.e. Asians to Asian clubs and compete in their own leagues. However, where mutually agreed, a council or committee may, in consultation with the minister, arrange leagues or matches enabling different racial groups to compete. This was a definite concession in theory but as such occasions were extremely rare. this was window dressing.

My attitude to the trip was basically that I wanted to seek the truth as to the current situation, to praise whenever justified, and to be as honest in my criticism as I could. I knew, however, how such visits could be organised to show the very best picture possible. I decided to contact "subversive South African" groups in the UK. I called them subversive as that is how the police, under direction from some unknown authority, treated them: as subversive. My approaches were treated with great suspicion in London as I was, of course, a possible stooge working for the Secret Service. Sounds silly now but then it was a real fear. The reality was, as we have found out a decade or more later, that the police did create files on many senior politicians, one of whom became Minister of Justice later, as well as many others. I was, however, delighted to meet a number of individuals who were totally opposed to apartheid and desperately attached to sport. A person who impressed me greatly was Mr Sam Ramsamy, overseas representative of the South African Council on Sport and the South African Non-Racial Council Olympic Committee. He exchanged letters with Jeeps, Jeeps stating he was only interested in sport and not politics and Ramsamy saying it was not possible in South Africa to separate the two.

Ramsamy was initially reluctant to see me, presuming I was of a similar mind to Jeeps. However, through the mediation of a colleague, Paul Stephenson, we met. He told me in person and Jeeps by letter that he thought "your council's decision to send a delegation to South Africa extremely absurd and highly irregular." Clearly he and his colleagues felt the result of the visit would be a whitewash of the South African regime, something I was determined would not happen though I think I did not persuade Sam Ramsamy of this at the time.

In South Africa, which we toured most extensively, we were treated "right royally" wherever we went. We were shown facilities which were splendid. The big question was: who could use them? The answer was Whites only. We were taken to a very plush golf course where the only person on the first green was a black man. He was shown to us like a fat calf is shown at an auction in the Otley cattle market, as living proof that the facility was open to all. It transpired he was a millionaire and the only black member of the club. What was startlingly obvious as we undertook a most extensive tour of that lovely big country, was that the facilities for the Whites were splendid and those for the other groups poor to abominable and in some areas, non-existent. We met some of the most eminent ministers in the government and met Mr Botha twice. He was an impressive politician and in a guarded way seemed to acknowledge the case against apartheid. The fact that we met so many high ranking politicians and white sports people made us all realise how our visit was more affected by the politics of the matter and not its original purpose.

Dannie Craven, in White South Africa, was the nearest thing to a god in the eyes of the White Establishment. He represented rugby and was the ultimate figure to be revered in South Africa by the Whites. I had always rated him as a deeply entrenched supporter of apartheid. To my surprise, we got on splendidly. He was quite frank in saying that apartheid was doomed to go and that there would have to be radical changes. He deplored that some excellent talent was being denied development because of the system. To hear Dannie Craven speaking in this vein was as real a surprise to me as would have been my surprise if Mrs Thatcher had spoken out as a supporter of the trade unions. On leaving, we were presented with six wine glasses embossed with the arms of his university, Stellenbosch. I still have them and put them to good use, each time being reminded of our meeting and of one of the most revered individuals by the White South African community who had been courageous enough to change his mind.

I also met very brave white men who suffered drastically because they opposed apartheid generally and in sport in particular. The Watson brothers, for instance, in Eastern Province were the sons of a man who had been a soldier in Tobruk and Benghazi, had been captured and escaped from three Italian war camps, who seemed to have inherited their father's spirit. They were both excellent rugby players who seemed to play fast and loose with the apartheid rules. They went into the townships and were amazed at the undeveloped talent they encountered. They organised a rugby cup competition and final game on the Kwarus ground in New Brighton, a black area. The rugby clubs played on a piece of unclaimed ground, i.e. a ground not reserved by law for one colour group, on which the brothers built a site with rudimentary facilities like changing rooms and toilets and showers, all without legal permission. The authorities craftily then designated the site as Black which made the brothers illegal users and liable to prosecution. Undeterred by this anticipated action, they continued by organising a competition and the final between the two most successful teams. After the final, the two competing sides went to the home of the brothers for a meal, staying after 10.00hours which meant that the brothers had openly broken several apartheid laws, each punishable by jail sentence. I felt honoured to have had the good fortune to meet two men of such courage, a courage I doubt I would have had had I been in their company. Our group travelled extensively across South Africa, meeting countless bodies representing the different sports, Olive Newson taking copious notes. On returning to the UK, Olive and Jeeps prepared a final report. This was detailed and comprehensive. Abundantly clear was that the apartheid system meant that in sport as in other walks of life. to be White was good and for the other groups very poor. It seemed that in sport there was a scale with the Black at the bottom, the Coloured next then the Asians and finally the Whites, all the direct result of totally obnoxious and unfair apartheid laws.

The initial report was prepared by Jeeps without any consultation and having read it, I prepared another independent report which was much more savage in outlining the injustice and disparities in South Africa. I had to do this in a couple of days and sent it to Basil to see if he would sign it. Unfortunately he did not, perhaps because he did not have time or I think more likely, that he did not wish to be involved in any further dispute. At the press conference I made my views clear which I summarised in a letter I sent to Sam Ramsamy with whom I was now on friendly terms. My letter said apartheid was a detestable regime, denying rights taken for granted elsewhere in the world. It is bolstered by a mass of legislation and a police force which resembled and behaved like the police in Hitler's heyday and not one of a civilised society. I believed, however, that changes had been taking place despite the apartheid laws and that there were many in the white community who genuinely wanted to see the major changes necessary and not merely in sport. I felt, however, that sport could be a catalyst to effect these changes and once started could rapidly gain momentum. I favoured continuing dialogue to achieve this change which must be such as to receive the support of Sanroc and other Black and Coloured organisations.

I concluded by saying I thought South Africa could be a paradise but the present system was running head on into a situation where there would be an uprising leading to a blood bath which would have made the immediate past atrocities of white police on black people seem modest. Sport could be a way of releasing the pressure, not by an explosion but by speedy and rational change.

I regretted that my personal report was not published as it was not possible to get Basil's approval given the short length of time available. The press reaction to the official report varied with the right wing press saying it offered hope and welcomed it. Others were less impressed, especially as some of the right wing press said this offered some hope to the South African Government. The Sports Council finally adopted a resolution proposed by John Disley, my fellow vice chairman, which recognised the progress which had been made in South Africa but regretted any action by a governing body which contravened the spirit of Gleneagles and Lusaka, effectively banning segregated teams.

The political temperature was raised because a rugby union club, The Barbarians, had invited a South African rugby team to play a number of matches in the UK. The issues were a matter of wide general discussion involving the Sports Minister, Hector Munro, who was known for his love of rugby union. The *Daily Mirror* challenged Mrs Thatcher in an article headed "Chicken! Mrs T opts out". She had said that the government would not interfere and left it to Hector to take all the flak. Finally the hot air bubble was pierced when the South African visit was cancelled. Hector Munro sent me a personal letter thanking me for my open support of his need to stop the tour organised by the Barbarians.

Certain wisps of recollections of the trip persist. For instance, in Cape Town I went with Basil to visit his family. It was a nice night and we ate and drank in the open air. Most civilised. Basil said to me: "Do you realise you are breaking the law by being here at this time in a coloured area without a pass for which you could be arrested by the two plainclothes men nearby watching us?" I was certainly watched but not arrested. Another recollection which was more warming was that many hard-line Boers and supporters of the regime so often came up to Basil to shake his hand and to express their admiration for his cricket success. This seemed to me strange but illustrated how sport can break artificial boundaries. On another occasion, returning from a short stroll, I spoke to a small group of white ladies wearing the sash which denoted their opposition to apartheid laws. I expressed my utmost admiration for their courage in so openly demon-strating their views. They explained they had chosen to stand outside our hotel for as long as we stayed there, to indicate their opposition to segregation. We conversed for about ten minutes and then I said goodbye and entered the hotel. Two plainclothes men came in and spoke to the person at the reception desk. They were obviously asking about me as they deliberately made a show of talking about me by pointing at me. When they left I went to the reception desk and asked who the men were. The atten-dant said they were members of BOSS, the secret police. I can-not feel other than moved by the courage of those white women demonstrating in this way.

One evening I was leaving the hotel for a short walk as was my wont and I stopped to talk to the very large black man in uniform who stood outside the hotel entrance. We chatted and I made clear my stance. He said with complete openness that we, the party, would never be shown the dark side of the system. I said I would like to see this black side and he suggested some-one I could contact. I was just a little concerned that this could be a set up as they used to say in gangster films. However, I got the address and directions from him and the next day arrived at a house in the black area, quite close to the hotel. I was warm-ly welcomed and taken out by car to look, talk and listen. The group of three accompanying me, took me to a "black" drinking place where I was treated "right royally" although I was illegally there, a white man in a black drinking den and was introduced to the Deputy Mayor of Soweto, T J Makhaya, who agreed to show me Soweto in its many aspects. The next day I was picked up by limousine and driven round Soweto. I was amazed at its size, by the appalling conditions which existed in large areas but also by some very fine grand housing which I was told belonged to wealthy black entrepreneurs. I was pleased on my return to the UK to send the vice chairman my thanks and best wishes.

I visited South Africa on a number of occasions in the apart-heid times and felt that there was going to be one terrible out-break of violence which would be a bloodbath on the lines we had seen on the Indian sub-continent at the time of partition. No one could foresee the release of Mandela and his guidance which changed the history of that great nation. I had asked to see Mandela as part of our tour of the country but this was flatly denied, he still being categorised by the State as a murderous revolutionary not fit to be released ever. How wrong we and they were, thank God. Again, by one of those oddities of history, I was able to meet Mandela many years later when, as Lord Mayor, I welcomed him to the City of Leeds.

Sports Lottery

I was appointed a member of the Sports Lottery Panel from its very beginning. I pointed out to my colleagues that many clubs in the poor areas could not access Lottery Funding because they could not find the necessary initial sum. In short, the greater the need, the less likely was a grant to be made. Moreover, many such clubs did not have the membership with the appropriate skills and competencies necessary to prepare an application. In contrast, many golf clubs, bowling clubs, sailing clubs, cricket clubs, etc., had members who were accountants, developers, builders and lawyers. In short, where there was the greatest need there were very few applications. Where there was reasonable affluence, there were many. A few applicants were wise enough to show how physically accessible their development would be but little evidence emerged to show that the Lottery Funded Scheme significantly increased use by "disabled people". Providing a "disabled toilet" was the ultimate concession of many applications. I continued my litany about the poorest failing to share in the sudden grant resource.

A boxing club in Mrs Thatcher's constituency applied for a grant and was rejected as it was a very poor application. I was appalled and visited the club to see for myself. It was a good club but in desperate need of a successful application. They did get a grant in the end but only after considerable debate and effort. I was constantly suggesting that our grants, though totally worthwhile, did not include bids from the poorest areas in the country. In the more deprived areas there often is no one with the abilities to prepare a good application and as the old saying goes, the rich get richer and the poor get poorer. I was a bit boring raising this view at almost every meeting we had and my colleagues, who were a splendid bunch, ultimately agreed to look at this situation. Led by a splendid officer, David Carpenter, the officers whom I held in the highest regard produced a major scheme better than I could have hoped for. It was called the Priority Areas Initiative and was based on two considerations: the measurement of deprivation and an analysis of applications received. An initial 70 areas were identified and each member received the extensive details of all the local authorities showing the depth of poverty, etc. Ironically, one of the country's most deprived pockets in the UK was in the ward I represented on the City Council in Leeds. I received a healthy bit of leg pulling over this. This new Initiative worked extremely well and we began to see applications coming in from the poorest areas in the country. The normal grant would not exceed 65% funding though most were well below that figure. Under the new Priority Area Initiative, to get above this figure the applicants had to show how their scheme would help to get rid of recreational deprivation, or they failed to raise the money required and it fitted within local plans. The Initiative was a great success in my view. I felt pleased that my constant wail about the poorest in the country and the unfairness of it all had led to a change of quite splendid proportions.

Travel

France-bed Tour of US, Little Rock, Jamaica, Haiti, Voodoo, Tunis to Cairo

I enjoy travelling by myself as the little "adventures" occur when they would not if travelling in company. Travelling alone is certainly more exciting but not necessarily more congenial and pleasant. I have been blessed by having friends, both male and female, over the decades who have proved to be excellent travelling companions. Ann and Joan are both lifelong friends of mine who have joined with me on some of my most memorable trips. Had either been with me on one occasion, I would not have experienced an act of great generosity from a stranger. Travelling alone hitchhiking in France two or three years after the war ended, it was late, the night was dark and I was alone on a lonely road with no habitation nearby, no convenient barn to creep into. I came across a small café whose lights spilled on the highway. I decided to go in for a hot drink before finding myself a place to kip. It was a smoke-filled room with just a handful of locals to judge by their apparel. I became engaged in conversation in French with the barman who asked what I was doing. I explained I was hitchhiking and would be looking for a decent place to sleep. An ugly looking customer, dressed in very worn and dilapidated workmen's clothes, overheard this conversation and suggested he could put me up for the night. I was extremely grateful and when I finished my coffee we set off into the darkness. We turned off the road to a track and I began to wonder if this chap was genuine or after robbing me. I pretended to trip in the absolute dark of the night and picked up a rock the size of a cricket ball as a possible weapon if needed, quite unseen in the pitch dark. We arrived at his home which was a farm house and he shouted up to his wife in bed something I did not understand. After a few minutes conversation he ushered me upstairs and pointed to a large double, bid me good night and left. I walked over to the big double bed and it was warm as though it had just been vacated. I realised then that the shout upstairs to his wife had been to tell her to get out of bed and out of the room. I was mortified that I had caused this act of generosity but nevertheless had a good night's sleep in a bed which seemed to envelop me completely. The next morning I was offered coffee, not in a cup but in a bowl, and after that and some bread. I bid them *adieu* with the most sincere thanks for their kindness. They rejected my offer to pay. So soon after the war had ended, the great feelings of gratitude to former allies was extremely strong, something quite forgotten today. This inconsequential, miniscule event has remained burned into my subconscious mind.

I have been to the USA a number of times, often staying with friends in New York but have always wanted to visit the Wild West of my cowboy fixation or the equally absorbing world of the gangsters or the life of the coloured depressed millions in the south. I decided I would take a few weeks off to do a grand tour alone, as I expected it to be physically demanding if I were to see what I hoped to see within a modest budget. My first port of a call was a couple of days with dear friend, Carol, and then on to stay with an uncle I had not previously met as he had emigrated many years earlier when he was a young man. He lived in Buffalo and he invited me to speak at a large annual meeting of an organisation of which he was chairman for the year. I agreed and was surprised to see an audience of several hundred in this rather palatial building. There were a number of jocular remarks about the British by my uncle in his invitation to me to speak, including a statement that American whiskey was better than Scotch whisky. It was all good fun and friendly. I felt it necessary to speak up about our national beverage – tea. I said there was nothing better to make you keep your pecker up all day if necessary than tea. What I did not realise was that the word pecker is a name given to a specific part of the male anatomy. When I said this quite innocently there was a ripple of laughter which developed into a laugh and then loud applause. I was a wit without knowing it.

My uncle's son was a scientist working at the site of the nuclear tests in the desert and I promised I would see him on my trip. I had decided to use the Greyhound Bus system in which, on long runs, one is expected to sleep. This had two advantages. I would be able to sleep overnight on the warm bus on a long journey and that would save hotel bills. I set off through Iowa to Salt Lake City which was truly outstanding in its architecture and then on to Reno. What a contrast – it seemed to be a home for every gambling joint there was and one could get a divorce on demand cheaper than in Las Vegs, so notices proclaimed. My next step was to San Francisco which was as beautiful as I had imagined and in parts as bad as I had imagined. I enjoyed eating at a restaurant on Fisherman's Walk, something I had read about in American Literature and in my favourite Steinbeck's writing. I was not disappointed. Los Angeles was much the same but I seemed to know it more than I knew San Francisco, doubtless because so many films were situated in LA. Las Vegas was no disappointment. I was fascinated by the enormous hotels and clubs which were just places to bet before or after seeing some of the world's best entertainments. I had a flutter on one of the machines, but it was not my day as I lost two dollars. Watching the play at the table was also interesting but one was gently moved on if one spent too long looking and not betting. I stayed overnight at Flagstaff because I felt I was entering cowboy country and wished to get the experience of it. Next day on to Tucson via the Grand Canyon. Words do not do justice to this remarkable spot on earth. It is epic, beautiful, awe-inspiring, etc etc., and each is an understatement. Having pondered the meaning of life, I moved back into more familiar territory, Tucson, the heart of my cowboy fantasy world. This, however, was the precursor for

the big one, Tombstone, where in the OK Corral wooden figures represented the goodies and baddies. I hired a car in one of
these two towns to get out into the country. There were big notices on leaving the town asking drivers to check that they had
the full water bags you might need. A strong warning was repeated by posters so clearly this was a dangerous place to be lost
in and without water. The irony of all this was that I and others
encountered a massive rainstorm and a number of cars, including
mine, drove to a spot on the road which was significantly higher
than the rest of it and there we remained for nearly three hours,
surrounded by water before some stalwarts decided go. I waited
until I was almost the last, amazed at the force of the storm and
how so quickly floods could start and then disappear in a desert.
My next destination, via El Paso, was New Orleans. I was quite
amazed at this marvellous city. One could see coloured boys,
as they were called, tap dancing so well they were doing steps
which only the experts try. Nudity, female only, was open to all.
I had to laugh at a naked woman in a swing swinging from inside the bar or hotel and flying out of a large window space into
a major street. It was here where I confused an oldish black man
who obviously had been an athlete in his youth. He was sitting
alone at the bar. I knew it was the Brown Bomber, possibly the
most successful heavyweight boxer ever. I said a few flattering
words about how honoured I was to speak to him and offered
him a drink. He looked at me and made a kind of affirmative
sound. I retreated to where I had left my beer and the bar man
asked: "How do you know him?" I said that everyone knew Joe
Louis, the Brown Bomber, the best heavyweight ever. The barman then told me I was mistaken. The man had been a bouncer
but was now retired. He was not Joe Louis. I wonder what the
man thought of my approach. I enjoyed enormously my visit to
this vibrant city, particularly the jazz that was heard throughout the centre of town. It was Dixieland jazz to be heard in almost every bar or in the street. The effect on me was always the
same, namely a desire to get up and dance. Surely it is time this
art form should be restored. I next travelled to New York via the

Kennedy Space Centre to stay for a couple of days with Carol and her flat mates, also hostesses (sic) on the same airline. They were a lovely trio and such good friends who went wild when so much later they heard that Carol was dead by her own hand. They deluged me with anger that I had allowed this to happen.

Little Rock

On another occasion I was travelling again in the USA and visited Little Rock which had become known all over the world for an attempt to remove the colour bar in the school system. A decision of the Supreme Court had ruled that segregation of black and white was illegal and the attempts to integrate had led to very serious pubic disorder. I was keen to see this small town which was on the world stage. This was a time, of course, when the Ku Klux Klan and their adherents were murdering men for the colour of their skin. As I walked up a road in the centre of the town, three black young men made some unpleasant remarks about me who was wearing shorts, open-necked shirt and carrying a ruck sack on my back. I walked over to them and told them I was English, I opposed segregation and I would like them to tell me their story. Their hostility disappeared and we agreed to find a place to have a drink and have a chat. I saw a nice looking café and suggested we go in there to which they replied, as they were black, the café would not serve them. We found a street cafe in an area populated by black people and I was the only white in sight. We had a fascinating time talking. They were intelligent, very coherent and very pessimistic about change. As time passed, their doubts were shown to be true. I gave them my UK address at their request but I never did hear from them. They were right about the position in Little Rock. It would make a good film about courage, persistence and the rottenness of the people in charge of Little Rock at that time. Years later I was walking down the docks in Jamaica when a group of black young men shouted obscenities to me. I was amazed at what they promised me for six-pence. I did not think it wise to engage them in conversation. They were definitely dangerous. White visitors to Jamaica were strongly advised not to visit the dock area unless accompanied by people who could keep them safe. I was staying in a large hotel in lovely grounds surrounded by a strong fence. I was told that many who came to the hotel never left its protection and there-fore never saw the real Jamaica.

On my visit to Jamaica I was accompanied by a great friend, Caroline, whom I had known for a long time. We agreed we would cross the island as Jamaica was more than beach and sand. We crossed this island using local transport and found the locals very welcoming. People were interested in us as few foreign vis-itors ventured inland. We moved on and decided to stay a few days in a small hotel in a small town on the sea front. This was a lovely place to relax and relax I did one day. I relaxed in the shade, fell into deep sleep not thinking that the sun moved and I was subject to its strong rays which I only noticed when I awoke. I had received a very substantial sunburn and I developed over the next day, an enormous burn the size of a large dinner plate on my stomach. This produced an enormous blister which was of such magnitude that the locals with whom we had become so friendly said it was something they never had seen before. I at-tracted a lot of attention, being asked from time to time if they could touch it. I became a talking point of much good humour as the size of this new phenomenon was unique in every one's experience. After two or three days of being a local attraction, I punctured the blister in front of a small crowd of new friends and I felt sure nearly half a pint of liquid was released to a small cheer. So for a few days I had become a celebrity. The long-term effect was strange as I became much more resilient to the strong sun and was for the rest of my life able to walk and sit in the sun without having to spend my time looking for the shade. Finally we left this paradise and took ship for the home of the notorious and evil ruler, Papa Doc, Haiti.

This quite small island of very poor people was ruled by a monstrous dictator known as Papa Doc, a ruthless tyrant of whom Vlad the Impaler might have approved. It was a visit I shall always remember for a number of reasons. The man who owned the small hotel in which we stayed was very friendly towards us and an obvious admirer of Caroline. On our second day a young attractive woman travelling alone arrived and immediately received the attention of the owner. She was a bit of a flirt and her light approach to the other sex quite captivated him. One late evening I was in bed, naked, sweltering in the humid heat. No air conditioning of any kind. I was awakened by loud screams coming from the woman's room just down a short corridor. It sounded like screams of real terror and a shout of my name "Bernard, Bernard." I immediately jumped out of bed, shot down the short corridor, stepped on a small mat at the door in question and shot straight under the bed on which something of a struggle was going on. My scream and sudden disappearance stopped the struggle as I imagine both were looking to see who had screamed and then disappeared. There was a silent pause as we all tried to rationalise this sudden appearance and disappearance. I now felt at some disadvantage. I was naked with the only thing available to preserve my modesty a small mat on which I had trod with such success. Should I get up from under the bed and hold the mat in front of my lower person or get up and use it to hide my behind, though that would have meant any conversation I would have with them would have to be undertaken over my shoulder. One thing was certain, I had stopped the battle for supremacy on the bed. I got out from under the bed, stood erect as though I was used to lecturing stark naked but for the small mat. The manager got up and disappeared to his room and the Vestal Virgin adjusted her dress and thanked me for my intervention. I told her she should not lead him on and did a very effective about turn, the rug, I trust, covering adequately my rear in one aesthetic sweep. It is so difficult to appear severe when one is at such a disadvantage. The next day the owner acted as if the previous night's adventures had not occurred, gave us a good breakfast and was the epitome of a good host. He invited me to see some of the activities which were normally not seen by outsiders. One evening he took me to a strange voodoo event. I am a sceptic but was interested in seeing something of the sort. Caroline did not fancy this idea and stayed in the hotel. Late that night my friend took me some distance on foot to a fairly large hall in the jungle which was full of the local population. The night was hot and sticky and I felt a sense of energy in the congregation, individuals beginning to look ever more wild and erratic. I was the only white person present but this did not seem to matter. This was their place and I was a visitor. As the evening progressed things became ever more confused and exciting. Quite early on, a priest they seemed to call a Houngan or something like that, went to the centre of the hall and after some speech and weird goings-on, bit off the head of a live cockerel, which I was told started the evenings worship. The normal way of killing the chicken was by beheading by knife, or hatchet. Biting was special.

According to academics, when the black slaves were brought to Haiti they were christened Catholic but secretly they persisted in their own religion in their own sub-culture. However, because the two existed side by side I found fascinating little similarities with the Roman Catholic tradition. The evening was extremely hot and humid, a condition alleviated by considerable consumption of beer and unusual liquids. My pipe smoking was looked on with approval. I think they thought I was smoking weed when in fact it was Erinmore Mixture. As the evening progressed I felt the growing, almost palpable, tension in the crowded hall, a space which may or not have been a temple of some sort. One could almost feel the electricity. As time passed more and more individuals, mainly women, would start screaming, behaving wildly until ending up in a catatonic state on the floor. A woman shoulder to shoulder with me suddenly changed from a perfectly normal woman with whom I had previously conversed into a wild thing. She let out a most piercing cry right in my left ear. I think for a moment I took off. She took off, facing up to men and women, face to face with theirs in a way which I thought would start a fight. These very high energy bursts seemed to lead to the individual ending up as rigid as a corpse. Others went round singing or screaming. It seemed anything could go and in a way I found this just a bit frightening as the whole hall was a mass of energy, physical, mental and sound. It was a night I shall never forget. A hot steamy night, isolated spot in a remote tropical forest and people exhibiting every sign of madness and returning to what for them, normality the next day. I am not able to dismiss this experience as an example of the backwardness and simplicity of the dark-skinned residents of Haiti. It is quite possible that voodoo was a factor in preserving the lives of many who would otherwise just have died in slavery as so many did. Certainly I felt privileged to have been given this chance to see a regular real voodoo religious meeting and know I have been given the chance to see, not some stage performance which most possibly never pays its dues to the real thing, but to see the real voodoo as practised in the interior and at which visitors like me are not normally seen.

This experience contrasted with my later trips.

I have always been interested in Egypt and its history. Three incidents remain in my memory. One was on a solo trip. I took a train out of Cairo and ended up in a desolate looking place, El Alamein. The site was pretty desolate when I was there many years ago but one had only to look around and one's imagination wonders what it was like to be stationed here holding off the juggernaut of the German army. One cannot but despair at the thought of so many men, German as well as British troops, who came to El Alamein and died there. What a shocking indictment of our political leaders down the decades. I found the experience very moving. The place was pretty deserted and broken down which suited my mind at that time.

On a jollier note was a hilarious accidental experience. Near the pyramids I decided to take a trip on a camel. I approached one person and was put on a splendid looking camel. I had no sooner got on its back when, enjoying the freedom when its tether was released, it suddenly took off at full speed across the desert. The camel owner tried to catch the tether, missed it and cried to me to stop it. He chased us for a few moments, crying out to the camel in some language I did not recognise. I had no idea how to control the animal and I was given the splendid pleasure of a hair-raising dash on an animal over which I had no control. No brakes, no reins with a curb chain. The Arab raced back to his camel, got on it and set off in pursuit. My camel was faster than his and it took some time before it reduced its pace to a gentle canter and then to a walk. Finally, after at least a mile and a half, the camel man caught up with us and grabbed what I called the reins, but was just a strong rope and he led us back to the starting point to a loud applause, ironic in nature from the other camel drivers offering rides. He explained to me that he had just bought this splendid animal from a dealer who lived some miles away and that the camel had decided to go home. We spent some time arguing how much I should pay for my ride which had taken several times longer than I had paid for. I had enjoyed the ride so much that I was prepared to go half way on payment. The other experience was seeing, in the middle of the desert, a ship steaming across the desert. It was an out of normal experience. I had wanted to see the Suez Canal and had hired a car to get there, well away from the city. Approaching from a distance, what I saw was a ship apparently on the desert, sailing south. It was a strange picture, a bizarre fiction. As one got nearer one could see the canal and the ship in it proceeding at very modest speed. I had seen mirages in Northern Africa which had seemed quite real. This was the reverse as what appeared to be a mirage was, in fact, real.

South Africa
Ann Safari in tent Jamesons

I have always been entranced by stories of derring-do in Africa from Tarzan of the Apes when a child and when an adult, the true account of the man-eating lions in the Tsavo areas when the railway was being by built. It was a stirring story but just one of the many which had stirred my interest in Africa. I was bent on a substantial trip, seeing and meeting some friends who were out there. Anne was a splendid travelling companion, quite undeterred by any disaster. She was very intelligent but was not well versed in politics. This was evidenced by a little vignette when we were crossing the border from South Africa to Southern Rhodesia which had declared its independence. This resulted in harsh embargoes, one of which was to limit trade with the former colony. This meant that petrol was rationed and I needed to get Rhodesian vouchers to buy petrol. Going through customs into Rhodesia, the officer dealing with us made the comment when I asked about coupons: "This is what you are doing to us." Anne asked what did he mean, being unaware of the crisis between this former colony and the UK, something which had been the subject of endless broadcasts and discussion for months.

Before we left South Africa Ann wished to visit some old friends of her father, a family called Watson. We phoned them and they invited us over for a meal. They lived in a very comfortable home and their black house-servant lived in a one room cottage immediately adjacent. I believe she was well treated by those standards and at times appeared almost a part of the family. Mr Watson was obviously keen on sport, particularly football and cricket of which he seemed to know a great detail. I was fascinated by some of his anecdotes until it struck me like a lightning flash that he was the most distinguished Walter or Willie

Watson who had uniquely played regularly for England as a footballer and also for England as a Test Cricketer. He was something of a legend and I was amazed after we left the Watsons, that I had not realised this initially. My only excuse is that one does not expect to meet a sporting star so far away from home nor one so normal and honest. Typical Yorkshireman.

Our first port of call in South Africa was the Kruger National Park, an enormous area populated by most animals in the bush. I was very keen to get some good photos and so I suggested that Ann should drive slowly and as quietly as possible and I would stand on my seat and look through the open roof of the car. Ann was a good driver and took things very slowly when, out of the dense foliage of one side of the track, emerged a large family of large elephants. Their sudden appearance put the fear of God into Ann who shot off so precipitously that I fell back in the car, taking a superb involuntary photo of the sky. What I remember most about this little experience was how so many animals of such huge proportions could emerge so quietly. It was quite magical.

Kruger was a most fascinating animal sanctuary though poaching, we were told, did take place. We saw all the big beasts: elephants, lions, cheetahs and on one super occasion, the sight of a leopard in a distant tree, getting up, stretching, running down the tree and disappearing totally from view. Leopards, we were told, are the most difficult big cats to see. Just as imposing were the very large crocodiles which lived in the area and the hippos which did on one occasion frighten us. We were with a small group of tourists near a large pool where there were some quite enormous hippos. A guide with the group we had just met told us that the hippos were very dangerous and could move very quickly. Looking at them, this was hard to believe. However, as we approached the pool to get some photos of the hippos basking in the sun, one got up and suddenly charged towards our group, each individual of which seemed able to run at Olympic level. I do not believe we had been in danger but we certainly would have been had the beast allowed us to get nearer. Its speed over the ground was surprising for such a heavyweight animal.

It was when driving north in Rhodesia to meet some old friends of mine, we had an experience which I shall always remember. We called at a large hotel and sat outside in the sun to order lunch. We, however, had left it late and we were told very politely by the waiter that lunch was over. He pointed to a large notice which said just that. We were too late. Up came a white man and aggressively berated the poor black waiter with the words I shall always remember: "The white man is always right." This mantra he delivered three times, most offensively. He told the waiter to apologise to us but I stood up and told him I would not eat at such a racist establishment. I could have said a helluva lot more, I was so incensed but knew that the only result would be greater castigation of the innocent waiter.

Similar discrimination existed everywhere in the former British Colonies. In the centre of the capital of what is now known as Zimbabwe, there is a bar well known because of its frequent mention in testosterone travellers' tales, including the inevitable Hemingway. I wanted to see this well-known watering hole which was called Jameson's. I walked into the bar at a very quiet part of the day. There was a long bar, at one end of which was a line on the floor and the word "coloured". Thus the bar was divided so that all of it was open to white drinkers and there was a small area for non-white drinkers – coloured black. I asked for a beer and the barman continued to talk to me as he was interested in why I had come to Rhodesia and what I thought of it. A smart looking black man had entered the bar in the segregated area and waited. I asked the barman to serve him and then we could talk. He said the blackie could wait. I then decided to use my freedom to invite the black man to have a drink with me. I joined him in the coloured area but the barman would not serve me when I was in there. I got my second drink when in the white area and then joined the black man in the segregated area. It was all so silly and I am not sure the black man was happy to be a player in this pantomime.

I have always been entranced by my vision of Africa and its wildlife and history, and have been on a number of safaris, the best one of which was several days in the bush and sleeping in a tent. I was travelling alone in Kenya where I had come for a meeting of the International National Sports Association for People with a Learning Disability and decided to stay on a few days to visit the bush. I joined a small group of people including a family of two white parents, very middle class but very agreeable people and their two delightful daughters, one about 18 and one about 15. They became very friendly with me because the older sister had seen the film Kes, in which I had played a small part. She asked me if I was he and on getting the answer, she and her sister remained my close friends. We all slept in tents. My fortune was to share it with a splendid chap who could out snore anybody I had come across. Two men remained on guard overnight armed with rifles in case of predators. On the second morning of our camping safari the guide in charge showed me some lion pug marks a few yards from our tents. He wanted to show me how near they had come. I am no expert at all but did wonder if this was just a device to make us feel like adventurers. It also threw some doubt as to the efficacy of the two overnight guards.

This was one of the most congenial and pleasant safaris I had ever undertaken. This interest is, I suppose, like drug addiction. I feel that I could willingly go on such a safari until I am a hundred. The more one goes on safari, the more the appetite is sharpened. Also, the money spent on safaris does have a significant economic benefit for quite small communities. It was on this safari that I witnessed a lion charging its prey. We came upon a large herd of wildebeest and a lioness and her cub. Our guide was concerned for he said that this lioness who had with her one cub, would certainly lose the cub, and as lions hunt in groups, as a sole lioness she would have to leave her cub unattended and, therefore, vulnerable. The wildebeest seemed unconcerned but kept a close eye on the lioness some distance away. The lioness suddenly took off towards her prey. I cannot image any energy more frightening or fearsome than what I saw in that charge. Sadly for her, the herd split up and out paced her. They stopped and turned to watch her again. She went back to her cub which had remained where she had been left and the two moved off towards the herd and the longer grass. I shall never forget the concentrated energy of the lioness in her abortive charge. Our guide said he did not think the cub would survive much longer and that the only hope for the lioness would be to join another pride but this very rarely happened.

On another walking safari with a small group of Europeans, we met the quite amazing local Masai tribesmen. All of them seemed tall and thin and carried spears. I was told they often did kill lions using their spears only. Apparently, the lions attempted to get in the thorn bomas in which the cattle were kept overnight and, if successful, would do a lot of damage. Facing a lion with only a spear seemed to me quite mad. This, however, was a rite of passage for young warriors. My attitude to lions was probably the result of my reading years earlier a book called *The Man-eaters of Tsavo*, a factually accurate report of the damage lions can cause. It is a chilling down-to-earth memoir of an engineer building a rail road and how man-eating lions were killing and then eating the native workers so routinely, the building of the rail road had to stop.

Sadly, as the decades have passed, the natural fauna are being displaced and killed off in what I see as a horrible crime against us all, past, present and future who want to see nature in the raw and not destroy it.

South America

One extended journey to South America I remember well because of its remarkable history and variety. I decided to join a formal holiday group as the best way to see some of the places I wished to visit. So in 1984 I embarked on the first lap to Bogota with an interesting group of individuals, including a lovely young woman and her lovely new husband. They were great fun and we immediately gelled. Bogota did not impress particularly. It did claim to be the murder capital of the world due to its development of the narcotics trade and we were warned on more than one occasion of the danger in walking the streets. I went for an extended, but uneventful, evening walk using always larger routes and nothing off the main highways, roads and streets. Our next stop was Lima and then flying to Iquitos where we went on a several hours' boat trip on the Amazon to a settlement of Yagua Indians, which had just become aware of the value of visitors like ourselves. The facilities were very rudimentary and my night was disturbed for as I got into bed I saw an enormous spider looking at me a few feet away. I hate spiders. This was a nightmare spider. I told myself that we would not be here if this kind of spider was a danger but those words did not comfort me. Eventually I went off to sleep and awoke, pleased that the spider had disappeared and then immediately I wondered where it had got to. I remembered an old axiom: always turn your shoes upside down and shake them in case a spider has invaded the shoe. I did this but realised that was daft as the spider I had seen was big enough to eat the shoe not try to get inside it. Thank God it was nowhere to be seen. That morning the Indians showed us their prowess in shooting poisoned darts by blowing down a long tube. We were all offered the chance to try this. The aiming point was a post about twelve paces from the mark. A number of us tried without success until I had a go and managed to hit the post three times out of three. The Indians made quite a fuss of this and I felt inordinately proud of my success which doubtless was due to pure luck and well-developed lungs, the benefit of past hard physical exercise. We were also taken for a long walk in the jungle which was fascinating. I was quite sure that if after just fifteen minutes walking we were left to our own devices, we would never find our way back to the camp. Our guides were excellent in pointing out animal tracks and explaining what the animals were. I asked about spiders and was told of the type of which there seemed many which were poisonous and which were deadly. Later that day we went on a short boat journey to look at the alligators, some of which were very large though none as large as the crocs one could see in Africa. The next day we returned to Iquitos which was an awful place. It looked like a South American slum. The people were very friendly as only recently these trips had been established and so we were objects of great curiosity. The next day we flew to Cuzco, another fascinating historical place. The city still contains enormous ancient structures and one is forced to wonder at the civilisation which created these structures when we in England were illiterate barbarians. Our next stop was a place, now famous, but then newly found and opened up. Machu Picchu. When we visited, the rule was that the number of people staying overnight was limited to just 22 in number and so we had the tremendous pleasure of seeing the night descend on this wondrous site. It was quite magical, even to someone like myself who likes to feel blase in these matters. The following day we walked up and climbed the two little peaks nearby. I shall always remember as though I have a photograph in my head, the picture of this wonderful site. The descent from Machu Picchu was precipitous in the extreme. Young children would see us, make smiling contact and as we moved off, they would do likewise, shinning down the hill at enormous speed and getting to the bottom before we did, to clamour for money when we arrived. They deserved all that they were given for such a display of courage and skill and the children had established a source of income. We all enjoyed our next treat which was a ride in a hydrofoil across Lake Titicaca and then on by bus to La Paz, a city still showing the signs of the Spanish conquest. La Paz is recorded as the highest capital city in the world and some found the rarefied air a problem. From La Paz we flew to Sao Paulo and then onto Iguacu Falls. As a natural wonder, it far outstrips the Victoria Falls which is saying something. It is a vast falls and I was lucky to get the opportunity to fly in a tiny four-person helicopter over the Falls and the immediate vicinity. This was a great experience. I sat next to the pilot in the front of the machine with total unrestricted views. I was so obviously enjoying the joyride that the pilot winked at me and did a few sudden changes of direction and height, a form of showing off minor aerobatics. I enjoyed it but the other two passengers did not. They thought we were having mechanical problems and were delighted to land unscathed. I tipped the pilot and thanked him for a ride I shall never forget.

Our next stop was something I looked forward to seeing, Brasilia. This city was conceived, designed and erected in a few years after the plans were devised in the mid 50s. Most cities which have become capital cities became such during the course of time. This city was designed, built and created as the capital of Brazil, a position formerly held by the city of Rio de Janeiro. Brasilia was designed on the basis of a series of discrete sections, such as the Hotel Section, the Embassy Section, Shopping Section, etc. I found the visit fascinating as here we were in a city artificially created on a blank sheet of paper in the 1950s. I thought it lacked any warmth of feeling as ancient capitals do. This feeling, very subjective as it is, remained with me and was reinforced by two subsequent visits in relation to the subject of sport for the disabled. By comparison, Rio is always in a frenetic state of excitement over issues which appear and then are replaced by the next excitement. This was our last visit before returning home and I spent nearly all of the time walking round the city, never thinking

I would be visiting it many years later to discuss the Paralympic Games there. We were told not to venture into the vast slum areas but a taxi driver told me that there was not a problem if we had a guide. I asked if he could recommend one and he answered that he was such a guide and guardian angel. He was as good as his word and he took us, myself and the young married couple who had become great friends, through such a densely populated area high on the hillside that as someone interested in politics wondered how such an appalling standard could be tolerated and not changed.

As the journey neared its end I came to reflect on some of the aspects which will remain forever in my memory. One such involves two train journeys. The first involved the train mounting a long hill journey which required it to charge full stop up a slope and then to charge in the opposite direction, going a little higher each time. If I remember correctly there were six zig zag climbs before we continued on the normal railway line to loud applause from all on the train. The second memory is also of a most remarkable train journey. We joined an immensely long train pulled by two very big and powerful-looking steam engines. We had a reserved compartment to keep us from the locals for the 10-hour-plus journey. As we were crossing the Andes, the train slowed down until it was moving at a slow walking pace. To my amazement, people got off the slow-moving train in large numbers and walked alongside, stretching their legs. Some children played some kind of tag game. The train continued at the slow pace for some time but as the gradient gradually lessened, it gradually increased speed to a gentle walking pace then to a faster walk and then a fast walk. The train issued a number of warning blasts which I presume was to inform anyone not on the train to be careful they got back onboard in time. I got on post haste, as did two or three of my colleagues but was amazed how many did not heed the warning. Quite suddenly one could feel the acceleration and looking out on the top of this vast space, one could see men and women running for the train. It was difficult to see whether we had left anyone behind but as one local said, it did not matter much as they could catch the next train. They only had to wait 24 hours or so. Another abiding recollection is that of a hydrofoil crossing of Lake Titicaca. There are some moments when one sees something so beautiful it is almost painful. This was such a moment. Only a poet like Keats or Shelley could capture the emotion which such beauty creates. Sadly, this trip came down to earth at Gatwick with goodbyes said with some emotion. I have retained a connection with the "newlyweds" over the decades which consists now of an annual Christmas card. It was a privilege to know them when they were so animated and so human. Just a simple Christmas card can revive those happy memories.

St Petersburg
Ivanova Hermitage

I was rather flattered to receive an invitation to speak at a very prestigious conference organised by the Moscow School of Political Studies supported by the Council of Europe and the Open Society Institute. The conference was to be held from January 25–27, 2001 in Leningrad. I have always been especially interested in what was St Petersburg, then Leningrad, and St Petersburg in turn. Getting a visa was relatively painless on this occasion and I flew to Moscow and then on to Leningrad.

As a young lad I had followed the war from a comfortable home in Leeds which had not been blitzed, hearing of the siege of Leningrad, of the famine, death and heroics. I had also been interested in Petersburg as my grandfather, a very ordinary working man, became a very serious reader in his old age. He would send me down to the Central Library to get books on Hitler, Peter the Great and the Revolution of 1917. I contracted from him my love of history but was far too young to appreciate the implications of what I was reading, consuming them more like an adventure story. I had visited Leningrad a couple of times before and was delighted at the prospect of another visit, even though it was to be in the middle of winter which in Leningrad means really cold.

The Moscow School of Political Studies was only established in 1992, that glorious period of freedom which appeared and sadly has disappeared. I was billed as the Lord Mayor of Leeds, the second biggest city after Birmingham, to speak on Law and Politics. The Russians were fascinated by the fact that then the Lord Mayor was a figurehead and without any real power, all the power resting with the elected members of council, subject of course to the whim of the Central Government. There were more than 160 participants and 24 "experts", of which I was one.

The discussion developed very well and I was surprised by the freedom of expression the participants seemed to enjoy. The freedom of views expressed was in such a sharp contrast to the experience I had on previous visits to the USSR. It is sad to think that the short burst of freedom of expression lasted so briefly. Some issues created fierce discussion. Can an ombudsman survive in a non-democratic state? Do socially advanced countries need an ombudsman? Exactly what do we mean by the phrase 'freedom of speech'? What benefits do members of the business community bring to society as a whole? Can big companies be controlled? Should they be controlled?

Excellent discussion followed the statement by a Russian speaker that Russia was going to lag behind the Western economies. The collapse of the Warsaw Treaty Organisation, the Comecon and the Russian Government had created a host of small independent countries all of which wanted to be linked strongly to the West.

It was a heart-warming experience for me, now tinged with sadness that the bright candle of hopes and commitment to a strong independent local government structure and freedom of speech is more likely to flicker than to grow strong. It is always a pleasure to meet with others sharing the same aspirations and making the same pilgrimage through life. That pleasure was real and genuine. I returned to the UK, optimistic and so pleased. I could not foresee the changes which came with Putin, the Oligarchs and others.

The icy cold weather in Leningrad then was in complete contrast to the weather I enjoyed in my first visit to Leningrad as I always think of it. I was travelling alone and visited the famous Hermitage Museum, where I was "picked up" by a very beautiful young woman who was a guide and lecturer there. I felt she was interested in me for purely selfish reasons, namely to exercise her English in conversation with an Englishman. She later told me she could not do this with Americans as they all spoke differently. She was a splendid guide and we got on famously. She, as a special treat, agreed to show me the reserve collection in the bowels of the building which was never seen by the public.

The store rooms under the Hermitage are vast and temperature controlled. My guide told me that plans were already agreed to maintain proper levels of humidity, etc. I could not believe that so many paintings by world famous artists could be preserved but unseen by the public. I could not believe the extent of some of the collections – French, Italian German, Spanish, etc., etc., but my new friend pointed out that if these masterpieces were put on display, the artists' work currently on display would have to be moved to storage so what had been achieved? I asked about the provenance of these remarkable collections. The Nazis had collected, stolen and appropriated an enormous amount of the finest artistic work in Europe. The Russians in turn had conquered them and had thereby amassed a fantastic hoard of works of art many of which had come from wealthy Jewish family homes and galleries. I was told that all those I had seen with her were not subject to challenge but elsewhere there were collections which might be challenged. I enjoyed having a dinner date with this lovely female whose English was very good but not particularly idiomatic. This little episode illustrates my penchant for travelling alone This little experience would not have been experienced had I been in a group.

I had another engagement in Russia some few years later. As President of INAS, the world organisation of sport for people with a mental handicap – the term in use at that time – I was invited to attend the INAS world basketball championship in Ivanovo in October 2005. Again I flew Leeds Amsterdam Moscow and was then picked up by car and driven to a hutted camp site far from any apparent civilisation, the town of Ivanovo being one of the most depressing towns I had ever visited. The hospitality accorded me was excellent. Vodka helped. The organisers started the morning with a shot of vodka, had another shot half way through the morning, again during and after lunch and then at the close of play. The vodka was served in small shot glasses but full to the brim and the custom appeared to be to to drink it in one go. I decided it was only right that I should follow local custom but by the end of the first day I decided I just could not match the consumption of my Russian colleagues. The accommodation I was offered was basic but clean and warm which was possibly its most important feature. The Games were well ordered but the food for the athletes was not up to standard. A good menu for some is anathema to others. A satisfactory food supply is difficult to achieve as the athletes come from widely different countries, each of which has its own idea of what food should be like. I, however, was doubly privileged because the president of the Russian branch of INAS, my host, had the best chalet on the site and enjoyed a lavish table which I was asked to join rather than join the athletes in the refectory. The president's food was excellent, something suitable for all our different taste buds. The president was a person I did not like and was subsequently involved in a pretty ferocious argument with him. His organisation did not refuse to pay their annual subscription: they simply did not pay it. Finally, when I was the International President, I had to propose the motion to remove Russia from our list of members.

Gulbenkian Arts Council
Redcliffe-Maud Nadine Senior Tanni

In early 1975 Lord Redcliffe-Maud and representatives of the Gulbenkian Foundation came to Leeds to meet me and my colleagues, including our distinguished Director of Museums and Art Galleries, Robert Rowe, to discuss housing the arts and making it more accessible to those who had little or no connection with the arts. Our discussions were wide ranging and radical, my suggesting that access to the arts could be a form of social therapy but were denied to those who could not afford to gain access to it. Our guests were impressed by the way we were tackling the eternal problem. I pointed out that very considerable funds were spent on the arts but only a small proportion of the population actually were exposed or taking advantage of the arts available.

Later that year I was invited to a meeting by the Gulbenkian Foundation. This is an organisation which has expended large sums of money in supporting the arts for which it has gained enormous world-wide respect. It held the keys to large sums of money. The letter referred to "the very useful conversation that I had had with Lord Redcliffe-Maud and went on to suggest "a meeting of a small number of people (twelve in all) involved in various aspects of the problem". I felt, to my shame, proud that I had been invited to this meeting of the great and good or alternatively to be viewed as one of the folk who decides where resources go. I had the greatest regard for Redcliffe-Maud whom I had met on a number of occasions. I must confess in all humility that I impressed my colleagues at the meeting as I had been thoroughly briefed by my colleague, the estimable director of the Leeds Museums. The topics covered in our discussions were extensive: who will be our clients; how can the vetting system be improved; where will the money come from; should there be a housing for the arts fund; are our new buildings too expensive; will we need the Crucible Theatre in fifty years' time; is there adequate research into new buildings; who will be the future "clients"; and what is the role of the local authority? They were very interested in some statistics I provided which showed that 50% of the users of arts institutions in Leeds came from outside the local authority of Leeds and so Leeds was supporting at its costs those who are not its ratepayers. Interestingly, current figures would show an identical proportion. I remained in contact with Redcliffe-Maude for some time and assisted him in some aspects of his major and most significant report published by Penguin: Support for the Arts in England and Wales, supported by the Gulbenkian Foundation.

The Gulbenkian Foundation has been a blessing to this country. It does not, however, aspire to being or is an alternative to, the Arts Council. In 1939 the Council for the Encouragement of Music and the Arts (CEMA) was established which continued its life as The Arts Council. In 1967 the Council was granted a new charter to "develop and improve the knowledge and understanding and practice of the arts to the public throughout Great Britain and to advise and co-operate with departments of Governments, local authorities and other bodies on any matters concerned whether directly or indirectly with the foregoing objects." This, as a young man full of hopeful ideals, I saw as a splendid example of the Labour Government's intention to change for the better the lives of us all. I was then taking advanced ballet classes, visiting the theatres in Leeds and was an avid radio listener to opera and classical music when the opportunities presented themselves.

I was told by a journalist in a TV interview that I am the only person who has served on the Arts Council and the Sports Council which makes me a pukka hybrid. Both the Arts Council and the Sports Council started life as "of Great Britain". I was appointed to the Arts Council, joining it in 1978. It was regarded by many as a collection of toffs who did not know how the other half lived. I think this was entirely misguided. I was impressed by the group I was joining. One particular individual I enjoyed meeting was Richard Hoggart. We had a connection as he was born in Leeds and grew up in Hunslet, an area of back-to-back slums and workshops belching out black smoke. Our relationship such as it was, was established when, on hearing that I came from Leeds, he asked about some of the places he remembered from his youth. He was delighted to hear that the library he used to study in was still intact and heavily used. I was honoured to chat on equal terms with this remarkable chap who published *inter alia The Uses of Literacy* – a book which made and has made a profound contribution to modern thought and education.

Lord Hutchinson QC was Vice Chairman of the Council. He was very bright, friendly and incisive in discussion and someone with whom I corresponded after leaving the Arts Council. I liked him for his clarity of expression, the weighty meaning of his words, his desire for much greater openness and his impartiality.

Marghanita Laski was a splendid contributor to discussion. She was, in those days, one of the people that the broadcasters called on for an opinion on no matter what subject. She was very bright, rather conscious at times of herself, but I thought always made a sensible and forceful contribution. She mentioned at a board meeting that she had been in Leeds recently and had visited a junior school in a very deprived part of the city with a large black community. She said with great admiration she had visited this school and had seen a woman teacher changing children's attitude to discipline and understanding by introducing them to dance. This so intrigued me that I went to the school and saw this lovely young white woman, Nadine Senior, training black children to perform under discipline and restraint. She, in due course, started a professional dance company called Phoenix Dance. She started classes for those who had left school but wished to continue their training. In due course, this became an established school of dance which ultimately became a nationally recognised National School of Contemporary Dance with Nadine becoming basically its chief executive and artistic director. It is based in a converted Jewish synagogue which reflects the local history – an influx of wretchedly-poor Jewish refugees and a synagogue in the heart of some of the worst slums in the country. Increased affluence saw the Jewish community move further out of the centre and its slums and the new synagogue was built. That synagogue became the home of the current college as the Jewish community, becoming even more affluent, moved into the leafy suburbs and very substantial homes and a new synagogue. It is worth remembering that it was due to George Mudie, then leader of the council, that the deserted synagogue was preserved and handed over to Nadine and her new College of Dance. George was a bit of a philistine. I doubt if he ever had visited an opera or ballet or any dance performance. He had, however, a vision for the city in which all had access to resources, irrespective of his/her personal preferences. Whenever I go to see the students perform in their current home which has been splendidly converted, my mind inevitably goes back to those occasions when I had attended Hebrew services there decades earlier, heard the most beautiful singing and felt shocked that the women were penned separately from the men.

Tanni

I met Tanni may years ago when I was a member of the Board of the International Paralympic Committee. She was an outstanding wheelchair athlete and a constant winner in her class. I had the pleasure of giving her a gold medal on one of her regular successes. In those early days when some of us were fighting to have the people with a learning disability included in international sport, there was extremely strong opposition for a variety of reasons from the other disability groups. Rightly or wrongly she was seen originally as an opponent to their inclusion. Her joining the House of Lords has seen a very fully-developed sports politician. She is a dynamic force as almost everyone has come to know her recognises.

Over the years we have met occasionally and I hope her feeling toward me is as a warm as my respect and admiration is for her. Our relationship, such as it is and was, is and was based on current issues. For instance, Tanni e mailed me: "Dear Bernard, Can I pick your brains please? There is a debate on Thursday (in the Lords) on the impact of Lottery funding and I wanted to mention the early Sport England days and how at the end of the first year we found out that a lot of the successful applicants were from bowls clubs, etc. I wanted to mention the work on the Priority Areas Initiative which I know that you worked on. Was there anyone else that I should name check in terms of developing this important piece of work (way before we really talked about Diversity and Inclusion)," I was most happy to reply in full. I later felt I had to send her words of support and acclaim as she has espoused in the Lords the cause of those affected by poverty, ill health and disability. I envy her the means by which she can inform, challenge and recommend. Long may she continue – a lovely forceful advocate.

The Arts Council

The Chairman of the Arts Council, when I was appointed, was the Right Honourable Kenneth Robinson, a former Labour MP and former Minister of Health. He was a "steady as you go" type. I could not think he would be an inspirational leader bringing arts to the masses. Someone who did carry that flair was Melvyn Bragg. I rated him highly. He had a view on every topic, a reflection of his wide interest in, and knowledge of, the arts. He was and is a broadcaster of repute and many of his recorded programmes will be of archive standard. He has since then been appointed Chancellor of Leeds University. Good choice.

The council, composed of 20 members, was served by a relatively small cadre of officers whereas The Annual Report of 1978/79 listed more than 60 panels, committees and sub-committees and several hundred individual members of these panels and committees in a well-intended attempt to ensure the council was well informed in making its decisions. I wonder now what those so-called management gurus would say to such a proliferation. Others taking a different view believe that successive reductions in numbers has been at the price of democratic decision making and that officers have been reduced in number only at the cost of a loss of real democracy and sound judgement. There was also the fear that Arts Council officers could become little dictators in their field and have an overriding influence inside their cadre. This is a real danger. Some call them "Little Hitlers".

I have experienced such Arts Council officers wielding, or attempting to wield, quite excessive powers. I saw a lovely woman who ran very successfully the Yorkshire Dance Centre being forced out by a regional officer who had a knowledge and experience which did not compare with that of the person being hounded. She, thank God, got another position of very much greater importance and I was delighted to give her resounding support when asked for a reference.

Two of the most effective chief officers I have ever appointed were made despite the threats of the Arts Council officers. One was in in the Northern Ballet Theatre Company and one in The Leeds Playhouse. The threats by the officers were serious, namely withdrawal of grant. This device did not work for them in these cases but it was used to get rid of me decades later. The government grant jumped from £ 41.7 m in 1978 to £ 51.8 m in 1979 £ 14.4 m went to the Royal Opera House, English National Opera, Royal Ballet, National Theatre and Royal Shakespeare Companies. More than one third gone, leaving the pickings for the rest. The council's operating costs in England were £ 1.7 m. A quick review of the grants given to a very wide group of recipients very rarely exceeded £ 200,000 and when they did, they were often in London. Nevertheless, the number of grants awarded, big and small, mounted to several hundred. I was interested to note that Red Ladder received a grant of £ 43,457. I was then unaware that I would soon become its chairman primarily to protect that grant which could have been otherwise lost. It was a lovely lady officer who worked in the drama department who gave me and the company a warning, knowing that if a grant is once withdrawn it can be doubly difficult to have it restored. She then went on to ask William Weston and me to take over control of the company which we did, so saving an Arts Council grant for the next decade until funding was finally withdrawn in 2013 to be restored some years later. I am assured no politics were involved in this decision which could have led to the apparently inevitable demise of this socialist body. Happily it is continuing its work with infinite difficulty but also great success.

One of the things which I felt and said should be changed at the Arts Council was the secrecy which covered the deliberations of the council. At times it was extreme. This is "Smiley" country and not that of a public body spending very large sums of public money. One report consisted of a document each with a given number to ensure each was returned. In 1980, Robert Hutchinson QC published a long article calling for greater transparency and his was a voice commanding response. He demanded much greater openness. I supported his suggestion that part of the meetings should be open and when confidential matters were to be discussed, the meetings should continue in private. This was and is a system often used in local government when dealing with Social Services matters or issues concerning individuals in adoption matters, etc.

On this matter of openness I was not alone – quite. Robin Guthrie was a director of the Joseph Rowntree Memorial Trust, an independent trust and an organisation deserving of great respect. Its studies of social affairs from its objective position have been invaluable and have been responsible for pursuing much-needed research into the social conditions of the time. Although a great respecter of the Trust, I had on one occasion charged them with supporting the Liberal Party politically. Guthrie and I were both very keen to ensure that the D'Oyly Carte Opera Company survived difficult times. This support was not to be offered to this venerable company which was preserving a very special operatic art form. I had canvassed support from some members of the council and hoped that if there was even a small number of supporters, a rethink could be possible. I failed. Writing to Robin Guthrie: "My attempt to obtain a change of mind by the Arts Council was frustrated by what appeared to be a well-orchestrated response, prepared in advance to deter possible supporters. This apparently was successful as a ploy because at least three people who, prior to the meeting, had said they were in favour of reversing the original decision, failed to voice that view." It is easy to be critical of others as I was in this case but I remain a strong supporter of the Arts Council and its work without which we would be culturally impoverished. I am also aware that whichever government is in power, the representatives of that government can become destabilising. A very similar position arose out of the proposal to assist financially the infant English Opera North – ENON – later to be called simply Opera North. It is one of the great artistic triumphs of the Arts Council but its birth and infancy did generate some times more heat than light. I received a letter from the chairman which read:

Dear Bernard,

I was rather disturbed to learn that at the a recent ENON meeting you developed an attack on the Arts Council on the alleged grounds of secrecy. It seems to me highly inappropriate that a member of the Council, who naturally has collective responsibility for its decisions and style of working, should embark on such criticisms at a meeting of one of our principal clients. Quite apart from the point of principle involved the ACGB assessor to the ENON Board was highly embarrassed by your intervention. I hope you do not think that I am unduly sensitive about this matter and that you will ensure in the future that your criticisms of the Council are ventilated in the Council itself. I dislike having to write this letter but felt I must do so.

Yours sincerely,

Kenneth Chairman

I responded: "Dear Kenneth, I was inclined on receiving your letter to reply in extremely terse terms to say: a. I did not mount an attack on the Arts Council, b. that the principle of hearing both sides (audi alterem partem) is a sound one and one which you have failed to observe in this case, c. that if the report to you is an indication of the accuracy and objectivity of the assessor then it can only raise the severest doubts as to that person's suitability for the job. Certainly, if she was " highly embarrassed" she must be the most tender plant imaginable and quite possibly unsuited for the difficult times ahead. However, on more mature reflection, I feel I must accord you the courtesy of a fuller reply as I recognise that your letter to which I took considerable exception was written in good faith by you in pursuit of your obligations as chairman as you understand them. Far from attacking the Arts Council, I referred to the initiative in setting up ENON as one of the most adventurous and creative undertakings for a long time and that I would hate to see this bold initiative endangered by ENON's inability to meet its financial commitments. This was said in the light of the North Yorkshire Council and the West Yorkshire County Council withdrawing the support originally promised. My comments, wrongly interpreted as an attack, arose out of the fact that I was unable to report on the discussion that took place at the Arts Council meeting which clearly indicated to me that a number of members of the Arts Council were concerned about the very considerable cost of providing opera in the regions through ENON. I find this kind of secrecy quite inappropriate when one is dealing with large sums of public money but, nevertheless, I observed the confidentiality of those discussions, merely interpreting what I thought to be the current position. In particular I referred to you as an invaluable ally of ENON without whose strong support ENON might be under much more serious review. I have given in some detail what occurred and I have checked my recollections with two members present at that meeting, neither of whom of course know the reasons for my discussing the matter with them. I feel no need to justify my actions to you as chairman but I do feel the necessity to explain as one member of the Arts Council to another. I believe that there is a very real tendency on the part of the Arts Council to feel unduly sensitive about criticism which it wrongly interprets as an attack. Whilst vehemently defending the record of the Arts Council, I nevertheless believe that sycophantic acceptance of all it does ultimately serves the body ill. I, for instance, am critical of the secrecy in which the council itself operates, of the concentration of power in the assessment procedure of clients under the new system, of the arm's length principle being carried too far when millions of pounds of subsidy are given to one client, the confused attitude towards the support of the non-professional activities and of the non-involvement of the Arts Council in what can be seen as educating a much wider base in an appreciation of the arts. I certainly do not feel that I am only able to ventilate these views in the council itself. Such a censorship of views or muzzling of members I would reject outright. Nevertheless, I would not be privy to any attack in general on the Arts Council, on what it has done or what it is trying to do, with which I am honoured to be associated."

This produced a conciliatory letter from the chairman and peace was restored. Robinson was a good man and a creature of that period of time. Freedom of information was a wild exotic dream in Never Never Land. How quickly the scenario changed!

I cannot help reflecting on the differences between the Arts Council and the Sports Council. The former had a budget significantly bigger and was so significant that its funding was absolutely essential to the arts in this country. Had the council been abolished or its Government Grant withdrawn, almost all the theatres and theatrical companies in the country would close, as would all the ballet companies. The performing arts would be destroyed. If, on the other hand, the Sports Council had abolished grants to football, cricket, swimming, rugby, gymnastics, et al, the sports would have continued. Both councils had distinguished members, mainly men, who had distinguished themselves in the arts or sports. One felt that the Arts Council members were much more aware of how distinguished they were but would never dream of asserting anything of that nature. I found the Arts Council members more precious in their attitudes than their counterparts in the Sports Council but in their level of commitment I would think they were the same. The Arts Council members, mainly situated in London, had much closer allies in the Establishment than did the members of the Sports Council. I felt that the members of the Arts Council were relatively distanced from the bodies or art forms they supported whilst the Sports Council members would have been, or were, outstanding athletes or coaches or major donors. I was the obvious exception.

536

Leeds Castle

A meeting of the Arts Council was held in Leeds Castle. This is a fairy tale venue. Beautiful castle, beautiful moat surrounded by beautiful grass land. It must be one of the most beautiful venues and somewhere I would never have been able to visit. We were welcomed by a man very formally dressed whom I thought rather unctuous. We were asked to sign the visitors' book which the butler, if that was his title, leafed through the pages very carefully to show all the world famous individuals who had preceded ourselves. One page carried one signature only—Queen Elizabeth. I gave the butler an almost killing shock by making as though I was going to sign above Queen Elizabeth's signature. It worked. He let out a genuine scream to stop me. He was horrified that I was going to commit this act of *lese majeste*. I, of course, was going to do no such thing. I just wanted, at that moment, to act as a teenager might who wanted to prick the balloon of someone's ego. Pathetic in retrospect. Still makes me giggle.

Our accommodation was of a kind I shall not personally experience again but, illogically, I am so glad that such magnificent places exist and that their history is recounted. A few nights in such a historical site was to me a great privilege. I always feel that history tells a much more fascinating story than the best fiction and places like Leeds Castle exude history, power and politics.

By early evening all those expected had arrived with one exception, a Mr McAlpine, a major donor to the Conservative Party and later its treasurer. He arrived for dinner in a helicopter, one of his own. He was a solid-looking chap who could be most affable and did not contribute much to the debate though when he did, his views were not just what one would have expected.

Our two full days of discussion were quite intense. In a discussion Hoggart summarised current thinking. They included: "the fact that the council could not escape the problem of assessing standards and making judgments. No precise checklist of standards was possible but neither was a total relativism intellectually credible. Assessments must be in written form but would be acceptable only in the context of face-to-face continuing relationships with clients. There was every argument for explaining in writing why a grant was given as well as why it had been withdrawn. Greater use must be made of external advisers. Clients must see that the process of making decisions is fair, well-motivated and much more open than hitherto."

The council reached the unanimous conclusion that a greater degree of openness was desirable in the conduct of its work, that it was not in favour of open council meetings on the ground that discussion might be inhibited, but that from time to time papers reflecting aspects of their discussions will be published.

I was throughout impressed by the commitment and strong aspirations of the council members and though only partially successful in the determination to achieve greater openness, I had to acknowledge that there was a strong intention to be as open as possible about decisions.

The short stay at the Leeds Castle was a memorable experience and confirmed in my mind that the members were committed fully to its various briefs, and that although my pleas for a more equitable share of our resources, though accepted in words, still left the four London clients receiving, in my view, a disproportionate share of the council's annual grant, i.e. about one third of the total grants. I enjoyed my three years on the council but when Margaret Thatcher was elected the question: Is he/she one of us? was the ground on which appointments were made. I was not appointed for a second period which up to then had been the custom, not the exception.

I am a great supporter of the Arts Council. It did do and still does excellent work and I hate to think of what the situation would have been had it not been created by a Labour Government at a time when the nation was facing some of its most bleak post-war years. Apart from my three years on the council I have been in three different iterations of the Regional Arts Council in Yorkshire over the years and have been the colleague of a wide variety of folk, nearly all of whom have been totally committed to their particular art form. We are all the better off for their contributions.

I find ancient places like Leeds Castle of consummate interest. My first of such an experience occurred in 1983. I received, out of the blue, an invitation to spend a few days in Windsor Castle, discussing with others the way forward for our nation. The invitation came in a most courteous letter from General Sir Hugh Beach, Warden of St George's House, Windsor Castle. He explained that there had been a series of meetings/consultations which had been very successful. It was now proposed to have similar "consultation" on such matters as: "What kind of society do we want to see and what should be done to make it that way?" I was initially intrigued and rather sceptical as so many meetings of this kind proved to be highly reactionary in my view as a Socialist. However, Sir Hugh's letter was so warmly written, I was happy to agree to join the four-day consultation in Windsor Castle. I need not have had this concern, for the list of participants, 20 in number, was a very mixed bag which included an MP, soldier, banking executive, editor of the *New Statesman*, trade union official, solicitor, inspector of taxes et al.

Our discussions were stimulating and taxing as the level of debate and discussion was of a high and demanding standard. One reason I had been asked to join was because at that time I was chairman of the second biggest urban education system in the Country. There was one – HM Principal Inspector of Nuclear Installations – which I found fascinating when discussing nuclear issues. I found three days of hard debate quite fascinating too. The discussions were far-reaching and I never noticed one example of a person making a point merely for making a point. The three days discussions were recorded and a summary prepared for endorsement on the fourth day. The evenings were taken up by dinner and continued discussion. We were also very generously shown round the inner working of Windsor Castle. Just as I had never thought I would stay in Leeds Castle, I knew I would never be invited to stay in Windsor Castle. I believe my Irish ancestry has left me with sensitivities which made the walls, rooms, doors, and furniture seem almost to speak to me. Sounds daft I suppose, because it is. However how that may be, I simply loved to absorb the atmosphere of the ancient buildings. All those historical figures which I had read about in history lessons and books had walked the same corridors, turned the same nobs, sat on the same chairs, etc.

Neil MacGregor

I received an invitation from Neil MacGregor, Director of the National Gallery and Trustee of the Pilgrim Trust, to speak at a conference on 15th June 1994 to discuss the future of museums in the country. I was very flattered to be asked and I accepted his invitation to speak and lead a discussion. I was a great admirer of Neil. He was a person of outstanding intellect and retained a kind and respectful attitude to his fellow members; evinced none of those indications of self-satisfaction and intellectual arrogance which others in what is called the Establishment, display.

Attendance at the conference was by invitation only and a very considerable number of people with expertise in or experience of museums was assembled. The conference was opened by Neil in a very business-like manner. It took about five minutes and the first contribution was a joint effort by a director from Bristol and from Norfolk. Next was Simon Jenkins, former editor of the *Times*, a genuine pillar of the establishment, then me and the final morning contribution was by the Director of the National Heritage Memorial Fund. The afternoon session was very similar but despite their eminence in terms of their profession, the discussion was sensible and based on facts and real possibilities. There were frequent references to Leeds having bid for and got the Royal Armouries against some forceful opposition from other authorities and the burgeoning of the arrangement with the Henry Moore Foundation in Leeds. Both these developments were ones in which I had been heavily involved and which had acquired massive interest in the museum and arts world.

I retained contact with Neil and in October of 1995 he agreed to assist me and my colleagues in selecting a person for a new post in Leeds. For years we had had a Director of Galleries and a Director of Museums. My aim was to appoint some considerable figure to make an amalgamation work. I knew Neil's presence on the interviewing panel would have a very significant effect on attracting applicants. He was very generous with his time, showed a real sense of humour and knowledge and we made a very good appointment, Evelyn Silber. I have been lucky to rub shoulders with some very fine folk and Neil is firmly in place in that mental pantheon. I retain one or two of his hand-written notes to me. Bit daft, bit sentimental. But so what!

In the world of the Arts things were moving slowly in a similar direction of mutual recognition and assistance. In 1975 I was asked to chair The Arts Council/Sports Council Symposium. This, I am sure, would not have been possible a decade earlier. We met in the Young Vic, an appropriate venue. The contributors were all of good standard but I felt the general feeling though warm, was that artificial bands or organisations were inappropriate and the future was best left as it is or was thought to be. The occasion was successful in that the different parties became aware of their individual disparate challenges and agreed a desire to offer support when and if necessary.

Subsequently I was invited to make a submission to Parliament's Culture and Media Committee which as far as I could see had had no impact over the years except to ensure a London-centricity with consequent cash benefits. I was known as someone who felt the enormous disparity between the help the northern cities get compared with that of London on a per capita basis, was something which needed remedying. I hoped for a meeting when I could argue the case in person, knowing that the membership of the committee was made up of MPs from widely separated constituencies who might wish to tackle this inequity. My report was greeted with thanks but no invitation to appear before the committee. In those days, television was not permitted in the committee hearings. My only previous appearance before such a committee was with my fellow Vice Chairman of the Sports Council. On that occasion we were delighted by the support the members seemed to offer. More recently, I wrote to the Select

Committee pointing out to the members that the largest group of "disabled people" are those with a cognitive impairment, the mentally handicap in the old expressive vernacular. I emailed them individually to point out that the only organisation which represented their interests was going to wind up because all grant was being stopped. The blind have British Blind Sport, the deaf the British Deaf Sport Council, people with cerebral palsy have CP Sport, the physically handicapped have a whole variety of organisations serving their members. The only organisation existing for the mental handicapped, to use an old-fashioned term, was the UKSAPLD, the United Kingdom Association of People with a Learning Disability, formerly called people with a mental handicap. I received not one response to my e mail from the individuals on the Select Committee. No grant aid to the UKSAPLD in 2016 meant it would have to close. Some argue that the individual sport, be it swimming or athletics or table tennis, etc., is responsible and not a body like UKSAPLD. Sound words, but the problem is that the individual sports are not interested in the mentally handicapped and that as primarily volunteers, they have the right to adopt such an approach. The UKSA remains active only because the chief executive officer McCillen is supporting it enough to preserve its identity and functions. This is a commitment as great as any I have seen. In the UK we have gone backwards. A decade or so years previously, two young learning disability athletes, who were competing in the sprints events, winning at every competition and achieving times which would have entitled them to a place in the Olympic Team, received national honours being awarded the MBE. Now the programmes of the last two Olympic Games and Paralympic Games show the number of events for the learning disability athletes are minimal, although their medals contributed to the success of the UK in Rio as in London.

The fight for equality and fairness will go on, though there are few prepared to lead the charge and those not wishing to see the change necessary seem well entrenched. I am genuinely touched by the tale as told to me of a promising black athlete with a mental handicap who attended training sessions in London with Linford Christie. He had been shown how to go to a particular bus stop and take any bus as all buses on that route passed the training ground. This worked well until the bus company changed the stopping points and route. No one told the athlete who waited at the original bus stop three times every week and of course the bus never came. His position was only discovered when some kind soul from the training team looked him up to see why he had not turned up for training. Thank God for such people.

Leeds International Piano Competition

The Leeds International Competition was the brainchild of Fanny Waterman and her husband, Dr De Keyser. She had a great reputation as a teacher. She herself was a brilliant pianist. She was supported by a small group which included Marion Stein then the Countess of Harewood. I was also added to her supporters, seen as a vital contact with the Leeds City Council. Initially, it appeared to many that it was an ambitious dream and unlikely ever to achieve the prominence it ultimately achieved. I confess in those early years I had my serious doubts but still gave the proposals my strong public support on the basis that if you do not try you will never do anything worthwhile. My support was important as the councillors who saw this as an elitist initiative found it difficult to oppose it publicly.

The LIPC, founded in 1961, is held every three years, although on one occasion there was a four-year gap as the Town Hall was being renovated to make it what it is now, an iconic venue. The first competition was a great success and by good fortune the winner was a brilliant young man from Leeds, something of a child prodigy who went on to have an international career.

The orchestras which have served the competition include the CBSO under Simon Rattle, the BBC Philharmonic under Charles Groves and the Halle under Mark Elder, all of whom showed an enormous ability to accompany the youthful contestants.

I was for a period of some years Chairman of the Cultural Services of the City Council and was able to involve our own distinguished music department in this singular venture, a support which has been consistent throughout the life of the competition. They were a small group of highly-talented young people who always answered the question: "Can we?" with the answer:

"Why not?" I refused to become a member of the LIPC Board as I knew I could offer more support to Fanny as an independent councillor. My connection with the competition has remained throughout the years and I only agreed to join the board when I had formally ceased to be a member of the council. I did so because Fanny asked me to as she was getting concerned there was a move to replace her or at least change her role. This was not the case as I came to see it but I did feel that the way she conducted meetings lead to uncertainties and the lack of some of the controls necessary to such an organisation. The calls on me by Fanny were numerous and it was always a real pleasure to support her in her great ambitions for the LIPC. Being a member of the Jewish fraternity which has made so many contributions to the city, she obtained considerable support typified by the great generosity at one point of need by a most generous gift by the Lyons family. The financial situation was always a matter of concern. At each competition the next competition was announced. In financial terms this meant a proposal and commitment amounting to £ 1,000,000, an intimidating obligation and carrying substantial obligations on the trustees. Fanny, as always, was quite unconcerned about this, feeling totally confident that the money would be there when needed. The trustees who would have to face the legal and financial consequences were not always so sanguine. I have always felt that the LIPC was never quite recognised by the council as a factor in gaining the reputation Leeds deserved as the third largest city in the UK after London and Birmingham. I frequently pointed out to colleagues that, internationally, Leeds was known as the home of Yorkshire Cricket, Leeds United and the LIPC. Sadly, that fame no longer applies to Leeds United. I finally decided to not stand for re-election to the board as any contribution I could now make was minimal. I was very happy as the board agreed to a new artistic director, an international pianist and a new management under an equally talented individual. I feel the competition is in very safe hands.

Adios

I have been greatly blessed in the opportunities which have been open to me, the fine people I have met, the "bad uns" who deserved to be held to account and the fun and energy and pleasure of leading a full life. As I embrace my ninetieth year, I feel I could do a "few more rounds" before I settle down even though I have reached the stage of asking where the devil did I put that pen only to find it safely stored behind my ear, or why did I come in here? I have been blessed by being born into a family in which goodness and happiness were the essential bases of life and which offered to me the opportunities to pursue a full and active life. I find poetry a most brilliant way to capture a thought, memory, belief, argument or telling a tale. For instance, the story of the *Ancient Mariner* cannot be beaten in firing the imagination and creating a feeling of dread; the *Erlkonig of Goethe*, the bursting power of youth and energy in the words: "Bliss was it that dawn to be alive but to be young was very heaven". The 'Odes' of Keats, Hood's compassion which drenches his poems: *The Song of the Shirt*: "It isn't linen you are wearing out but other people's lives" or "Alas for the rarity of Christian charity under the sun. Near a whole city full, Home she had none." Some of the finest poetry is in the plays of Shakespeare. The dying words of Romeo are one long poem in their beauty and erudition: "Seal ... a dateless bargain to engrossing death". Oddly, I do not find Shakespeare's sonnets nearly so appealing as do most who treat them so deferentially. Poetry can be very hip, to use a very outdated phrase. I got a group of lads and lassies about to leave school to jive to a recitation of the poem by Vachel Lindsay.

"Darius the Mede was a king and a wonder. His eye was proud, and his voice was thunder. He kept bad lions in a monstrous den. He fed up the lions on Christian men. Daniel was the chief hired man in the land…" They liked this poem and kept on repeating it so everyone who wanted could use the poem as music. As almost immediately as one finished I was asked by another: "Can I have a go, sir?"

Palgrave's Golden Treasury is just that – a treasure – as is the Oxford Dictionary of Quotations. They are mind traps. You start looking for some specific reference or item and half an hour later you are still browsing.

Now as I grow into the sear and yellow leaf period of my life, I feel again the resonance of Omar Khayyam: "The moving finger writes; and, having writ, moves on: nor all thy piety nor wit shall lure it back to cancel half a line, nor all thy tears wash out a word of it."

One poem I find moving is Christina Rosetti's Poem:

REMEMBER ME

"Remember me when I am gone away,
Gone far away into the silent land;
When you can no more hold me by the hand,
Nor I half turn to go yet turning stay.

…

Only remember me; you understand
It will be late to counsel then or pray.
Yet if you should forget me for a while
And afterward remember, do not grieve:
For if the darkness and corruption leave
A vestige of the thoughts that once I had,
Better by far you should forget and smile
Than that you should remember and be sad."

I have had a full life and seen many friends depart this life but as she says:

better you should forget and smile
than you should remember and be sad.

My View:

remember and enjoy the memories
and be glad.

The author

Born in Leeds in 1928 to a working-class couple, Bernard was the third of five children and had a happy and loving family life. Evacuated during the war, he then attended Leeds Modern Grammar School followed by Leeds University, graduating with LLB Hons and being called to the Bar. He did his National Service as an officer in the RAF after which he began a short career on the variety stage. When his parents became ill he returned home and took up teaching as a source of income, a career he found extremely rewarding. He also enjoyed working as an actor in TV and film for some years. Always interested in sport, he was appointed vice chairman of the Sports Council of GB and helped set up the organisation of Sport for the Mentally Handicapped. His many accomplishments include chairing the Leeds Playhouse Board, being one of the first directors of Opera North and being instrumental in the creation of a magnificent home for Northern Ballet He was the Founder Chairman of the British Paralympic Committee, served on the Leeds City Council for more than fifty years and was awarded the OBE and the CBE for his contribution to disabled sport and local government.

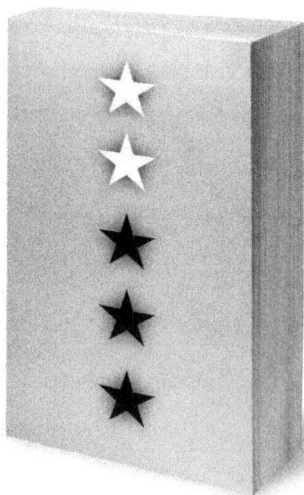